Oh My Goddess!

ああっ女神さまっ TERRIBLE MASTER URD

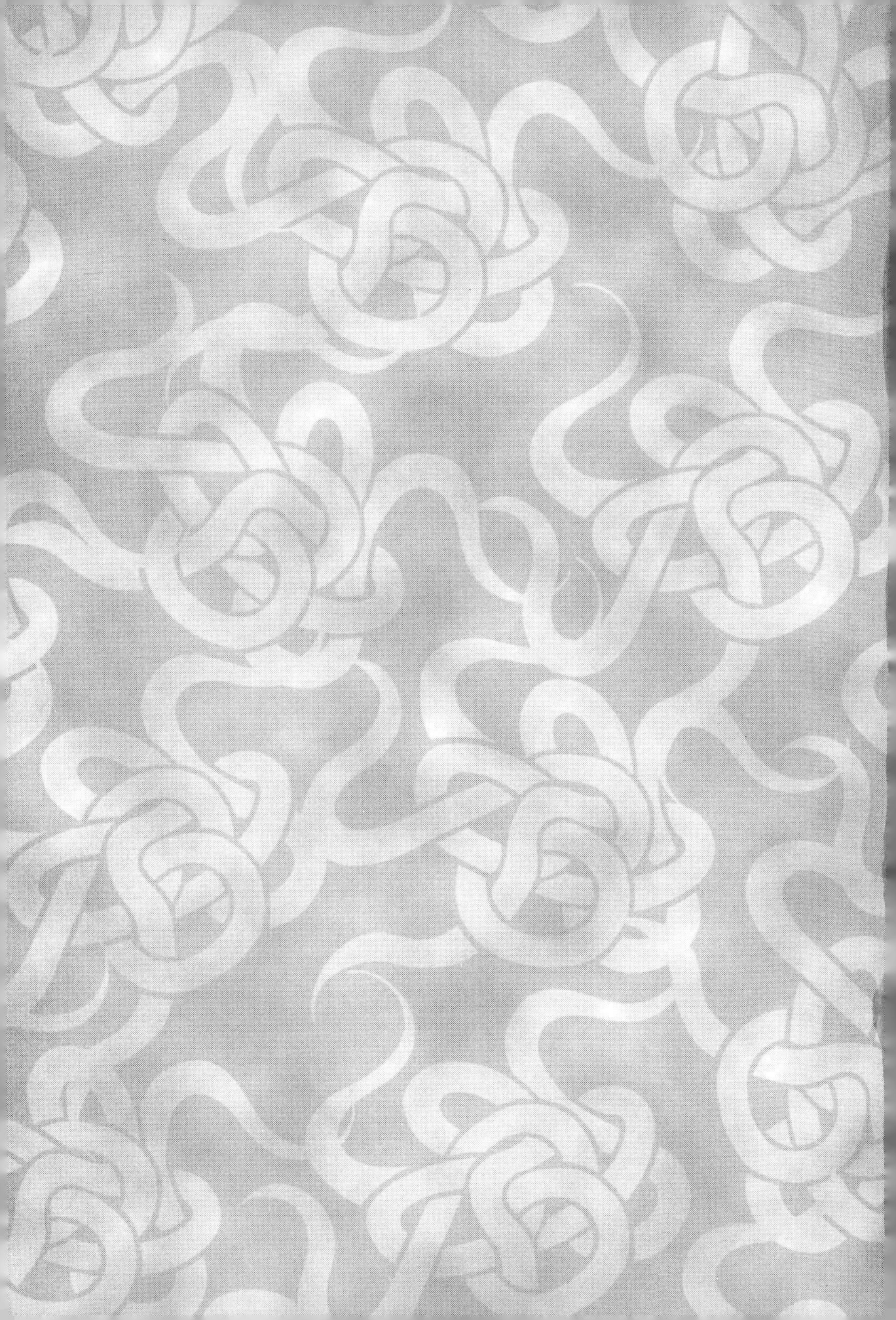

Oh My Goddess!

ああっ女神さま　TERRIBLE MASTER URD

STORY AND ART BY

Kosuke Fujishima

TRANSLATION BY

Alan Gleason, Toren Smith, & Dana Lewis

LETTERING AND TOUCH-UP BY

Susie Lee & PC Orz

DARK HORSE COMICS®

PUBLISHER
Mike Richardson

SERIES EDITOR
Dave Chipps

COLLECTION EDITOR
Chris Warner

COLLECTION DESIGNERS
Julie Eggers Gassaway & Amy Arendts

ART DIRECTOR
Mark Cox

English-language version produced by Studio Proteus
for Dark Horse Comics, Inc.

OH MY GODDESS! Vol. VI: Terrible Master Urd

This volume collects issues six through eleven of the Dark Horse comic-book series *Oh My Goddess!* Part III.

Published by
Dark Horse Comics, Inc.
10956 SE Main Street
Milwaukie, OR 97222

www.darkhorse.com

To find a comics shop in your area, call the Comic Shop
Locator Service toll-free at 1-888-266-4226

First edition: April 1999
ISBN: 1-56971-369-3

5 7 9 10 8 6
Printed in Canada

Urd Goes Berserk

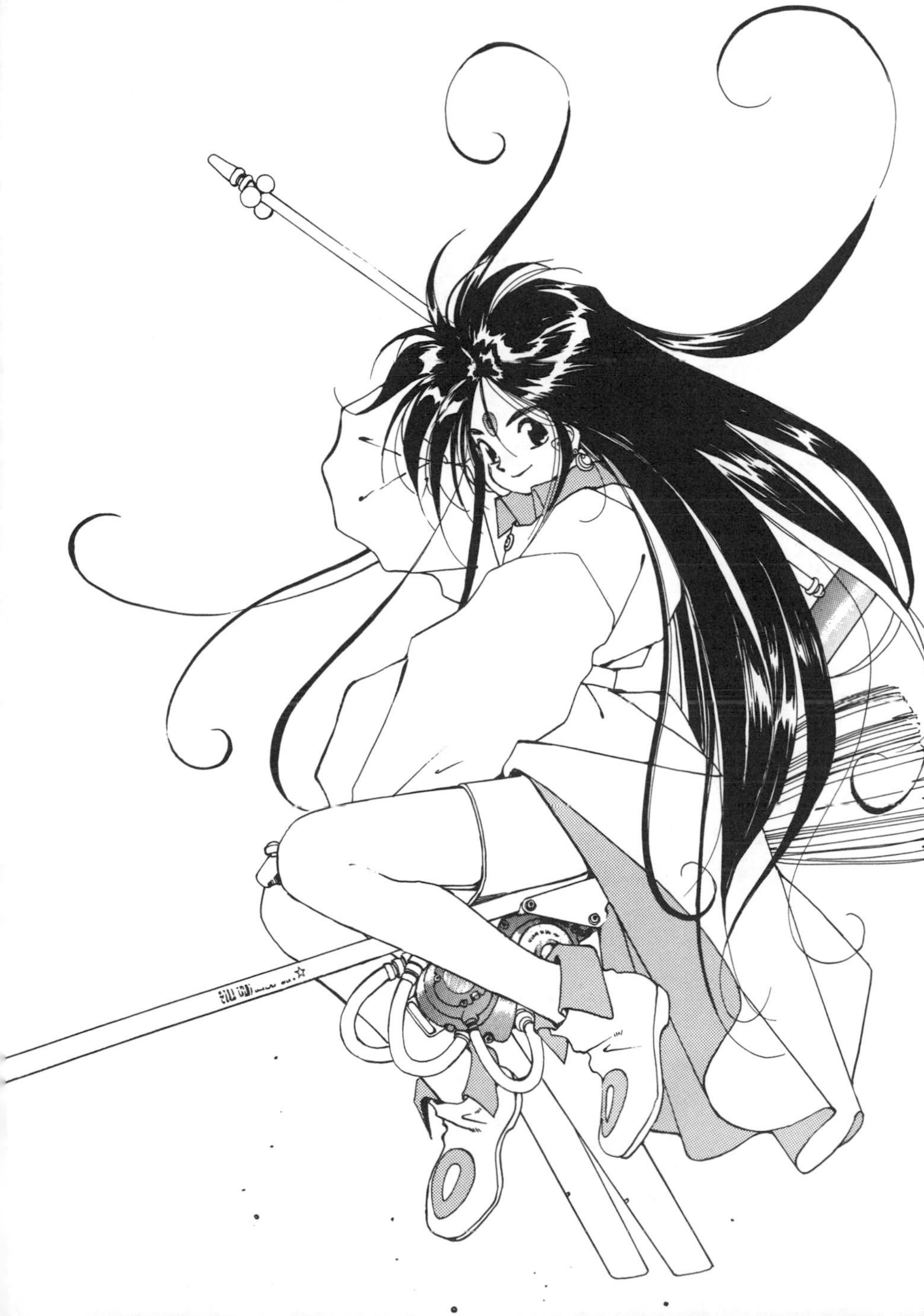

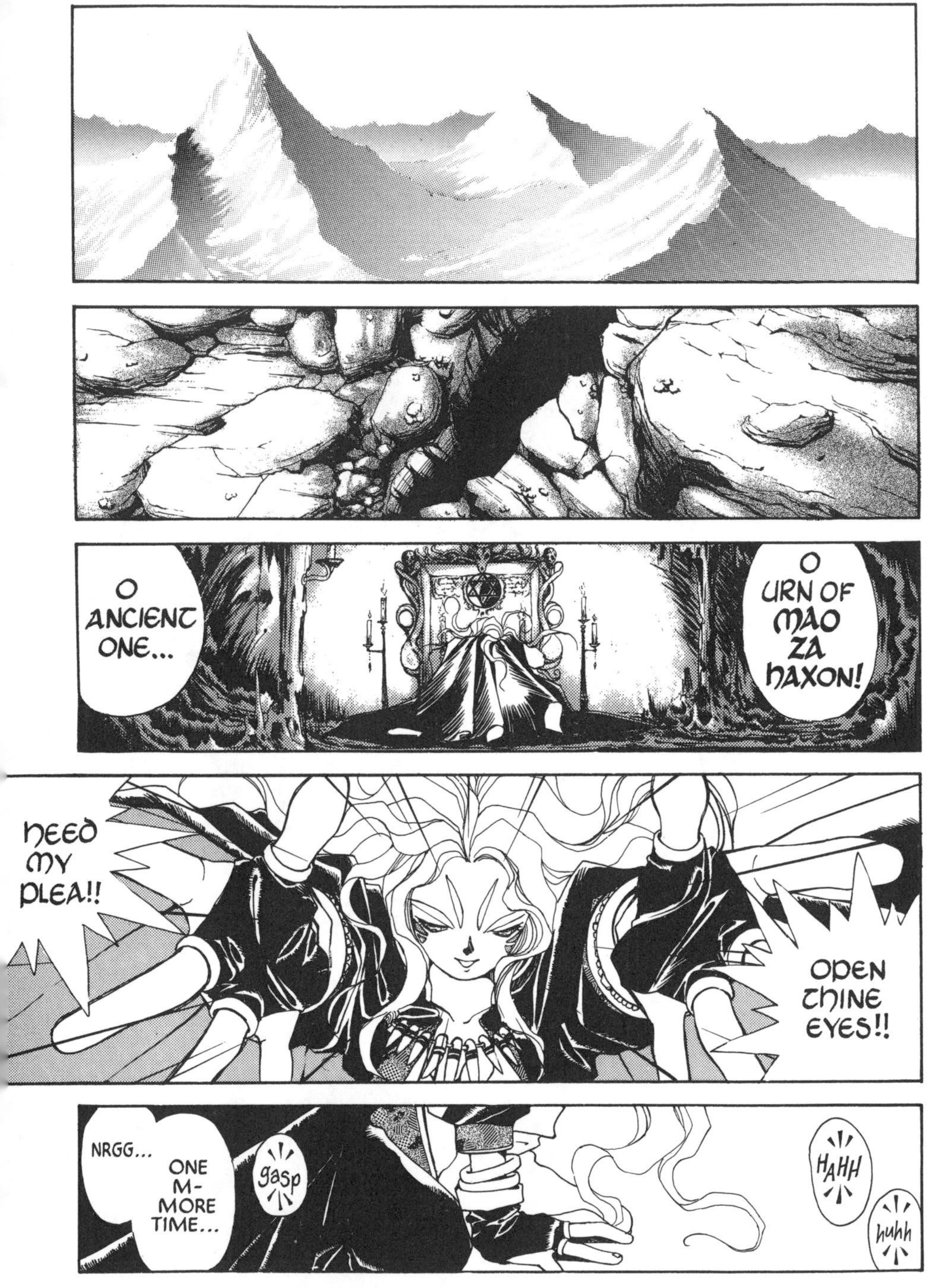
O ANCIENT ONE...
O URN OF MAO ZA HAXON!
HEED MY PLEA!!
OPEN THINE EYES!!
NRGG...
ONE M-MORE TIME...
gasp
HAHH
huhh

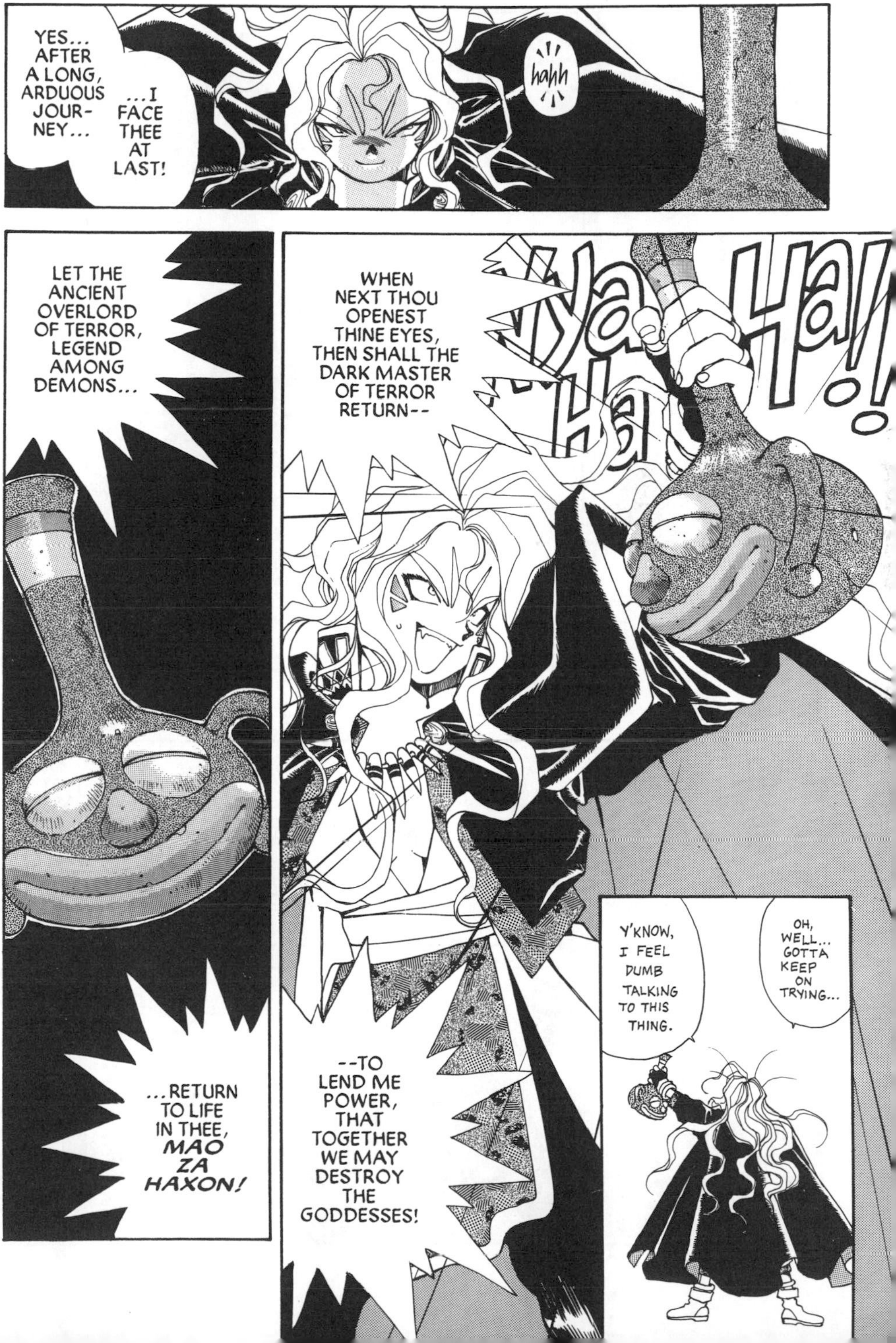
YES... AFTER A LONG, ARDUOUS JOURNEY...
...I FACE THEE AT LAST!
hahh
LET THE ANCIENT OVERLORD OF TERROR, LEGEND AMONG DEMONS...
...RETURN TO LIFE IN THEE, MAO ZA HAXON!
WHEN NEXT THOU OPENEST THINE EYES, THEN SHALL THE DARK MASTER OF TERROR RETURN--
NYA HA! HA!!
--TO LEND ME POWER, THAT TOGETHER WE MAY DESTROY THE GODDESSES!
Y'KNOW, I FEEL DUMB TALKING TO THIS THING.
OH, WELL... GOTTA KEEP ON TRYING...

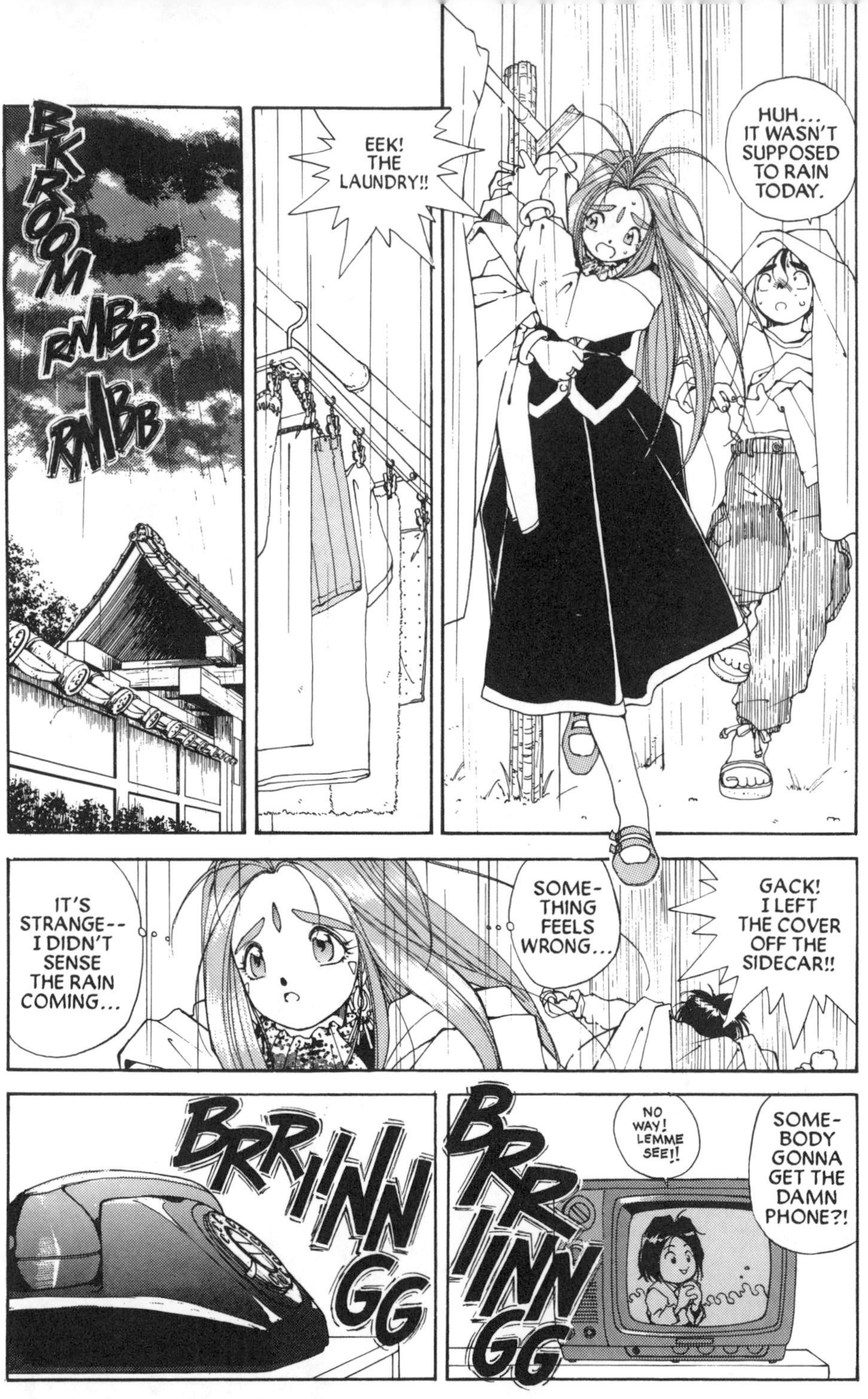
BKROOM RMBB RMBB
EEK! THE LAUNDRY!!
HUH... IT WASN'T SUPPOSED TO RAIN TODAY.
IT'S STRANGE-- I DIDN'T SENSE THE RAIN COMING...
SOME-THING FEELS WRONG...
GACK! I LEFT THE COVER OFF THE SIDECAR!!
BRRINNGG
BRRIINNGG
NO WAY! LEMME SEE!!
SOME-BODY GONNA GET THE DAMN PHONE?!

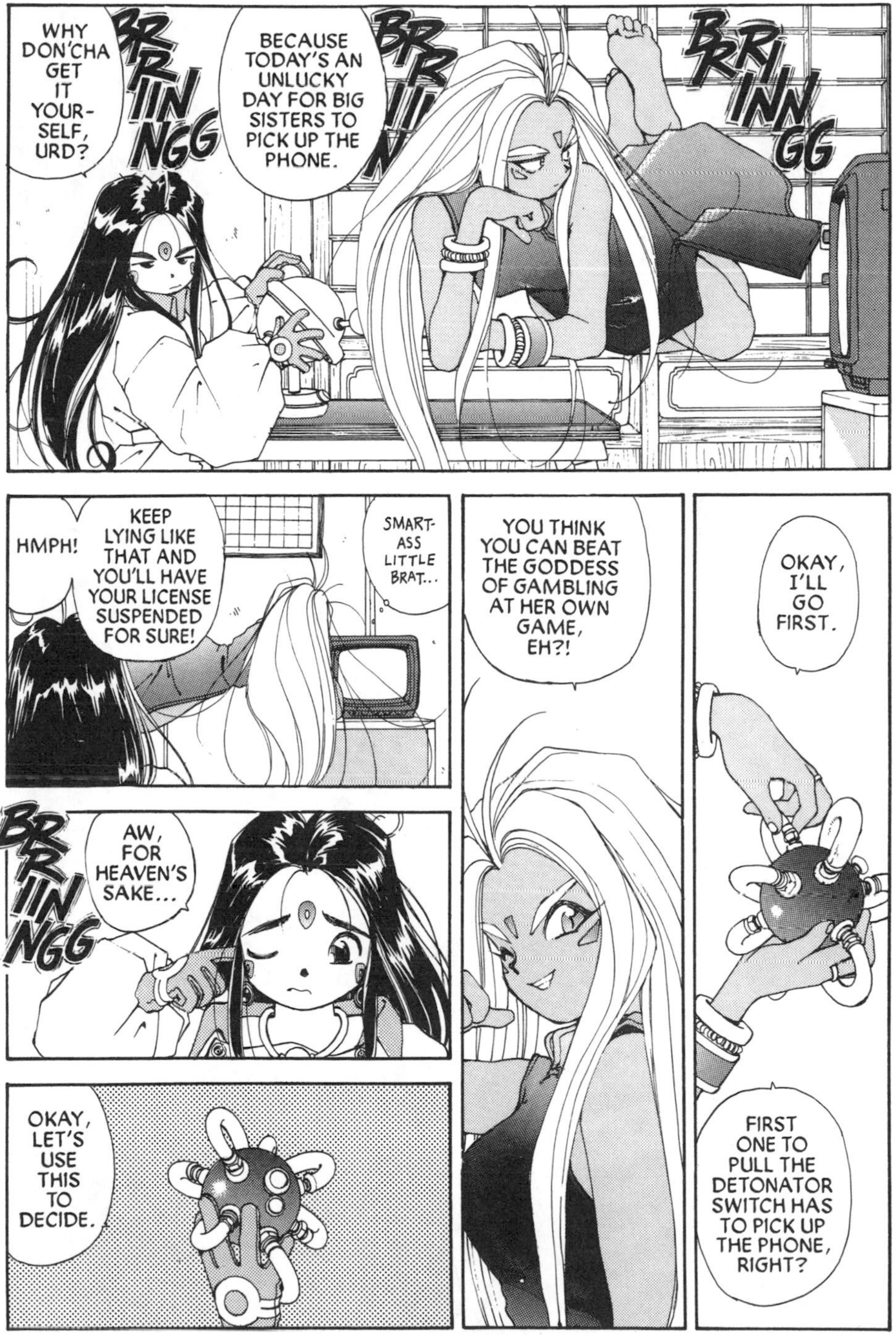
WHY DON'CHA GET IT YOURSELF, URD?
BRRIINNGG
BECAUSE TODAY'S AN UNLUCKY DAY FOR BIG SISTERS TO PICK UP THE PHONE.
BRRIIN
BRRIINNGG
HMPH!
KEEP LYING LIKE THAT AND YOU'LL HAVE YOUR LICENSE SUSPENDED FOR SURE!
SMART-ASS LITTLE BRAT...
BRRIINNGG
AW, FOR HEAVEN'S SAKE...
OKAY, LET'S USE THIS TO DECIDE.
YOU THINK YOU CAN BEAT THE GODDESS OF GAMBLING AT HER OWN GAME, EH?!
OKAY, I'LL GO FIRST.
FIRST ONE TO PULL THE DETONATOR SWITCH HAS TO PICK UP THE PHONE, RIGHT?

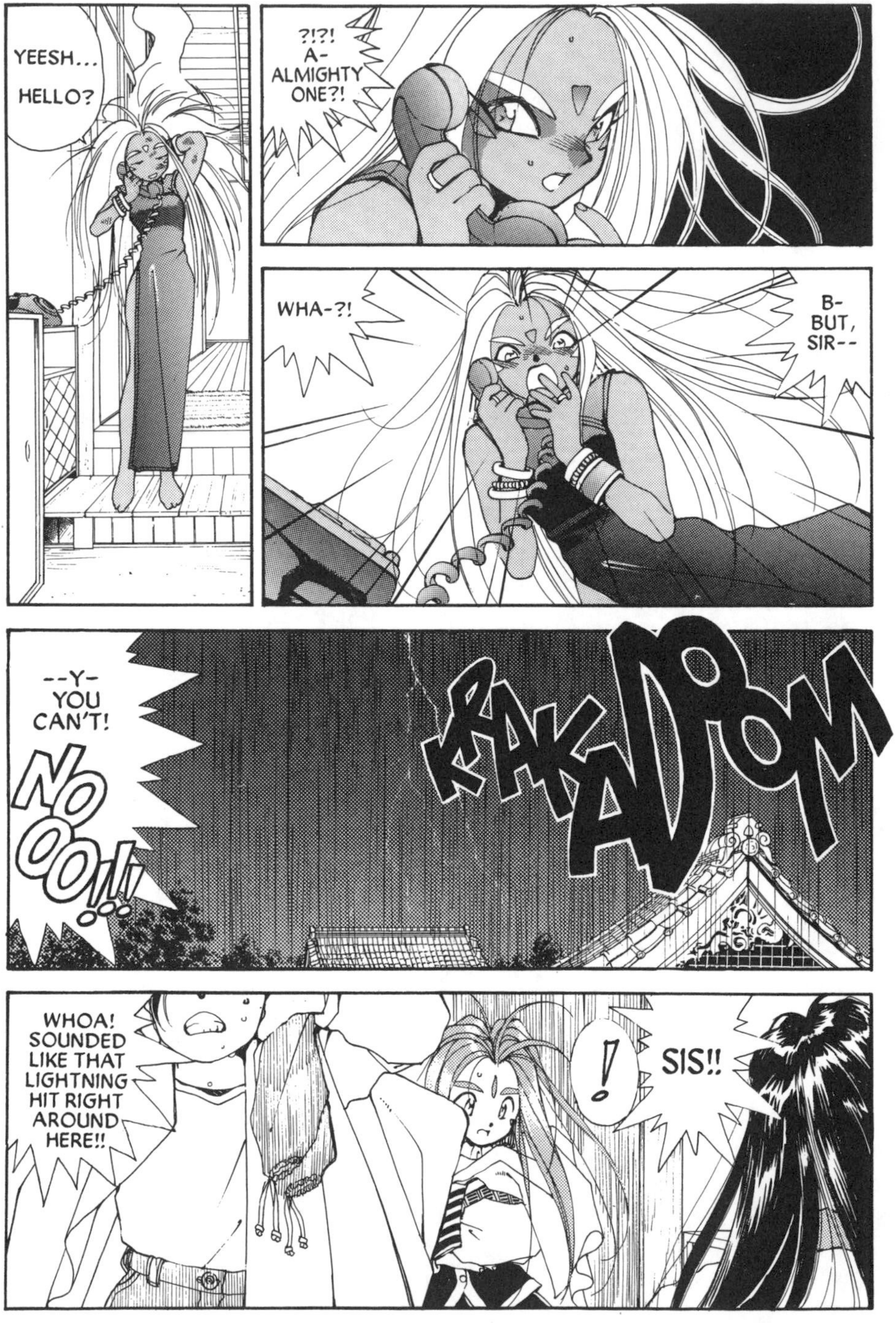
YEESH... HELLO?
?!?! A- ALMIGHTY ONE?!
WHA-?!
B- BUT, SIR--
--Y- YOU CAN'T!
NOOO!!!
KRAKADOOM
WHOA! SOUNDED LIKE THAT LIGHTNING HIT RIGHT AROUND HERE!!
!
SIS!!

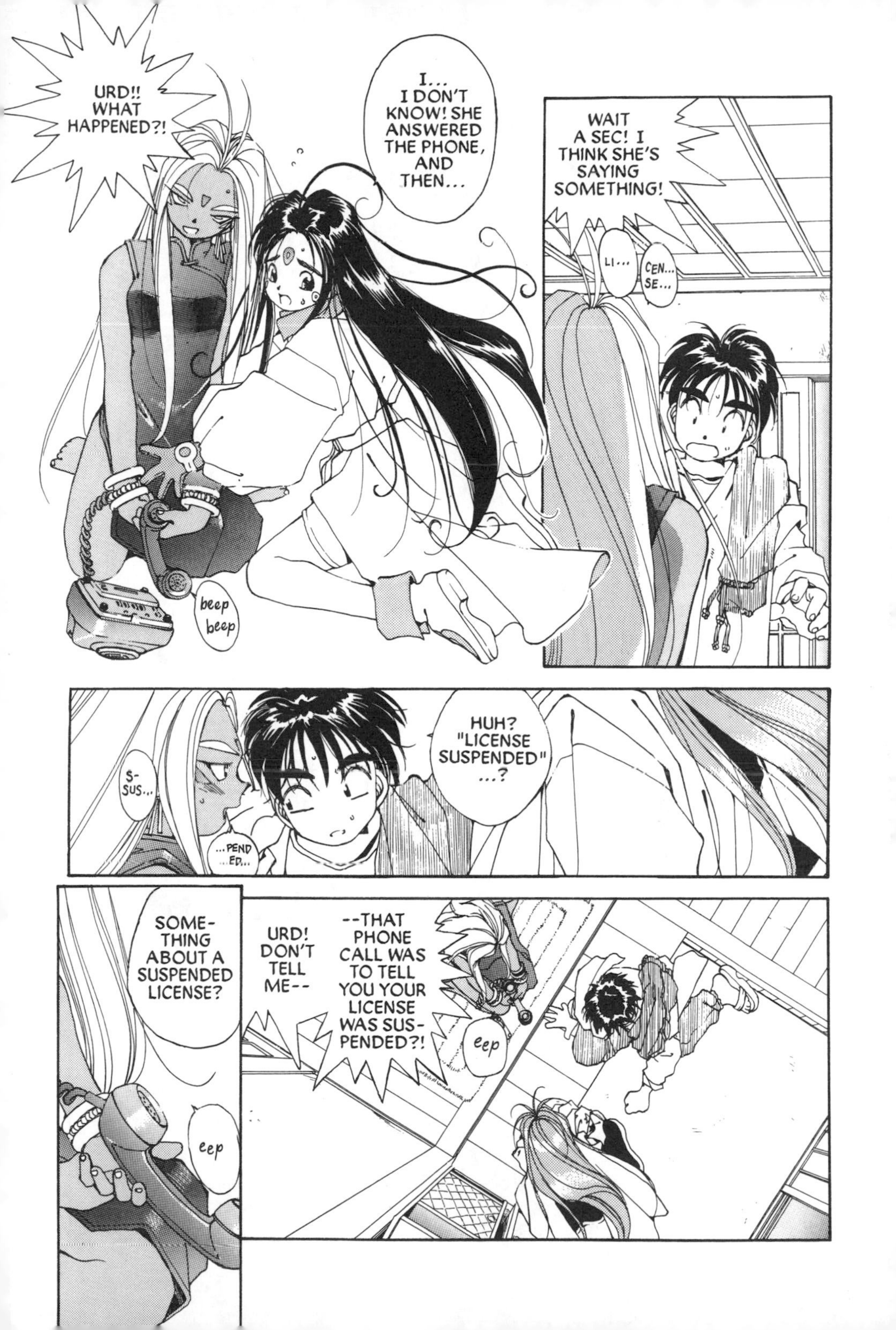
URD!! WHAT HAPPENED?!
I... I DON'T KNOW! SHE ANSWERED THE PHONE, AND THEN...
beep beep
WAIT A SEC! I THINK SHE'S SAYING SOMETHING!
LI...
CEN... SE...
S-SUS...
...PEND ...ED...
HUH? "LICENSE SUSPENDED" ...?
SOME-THING ABOUT A SUSPENDED LICENSE?
eep
URD! DON'T TELL ME--
--THAT PHONE CALL WAS TO TELL YOU YOUR LICENSE WAS SUS-PENDED?!
eep

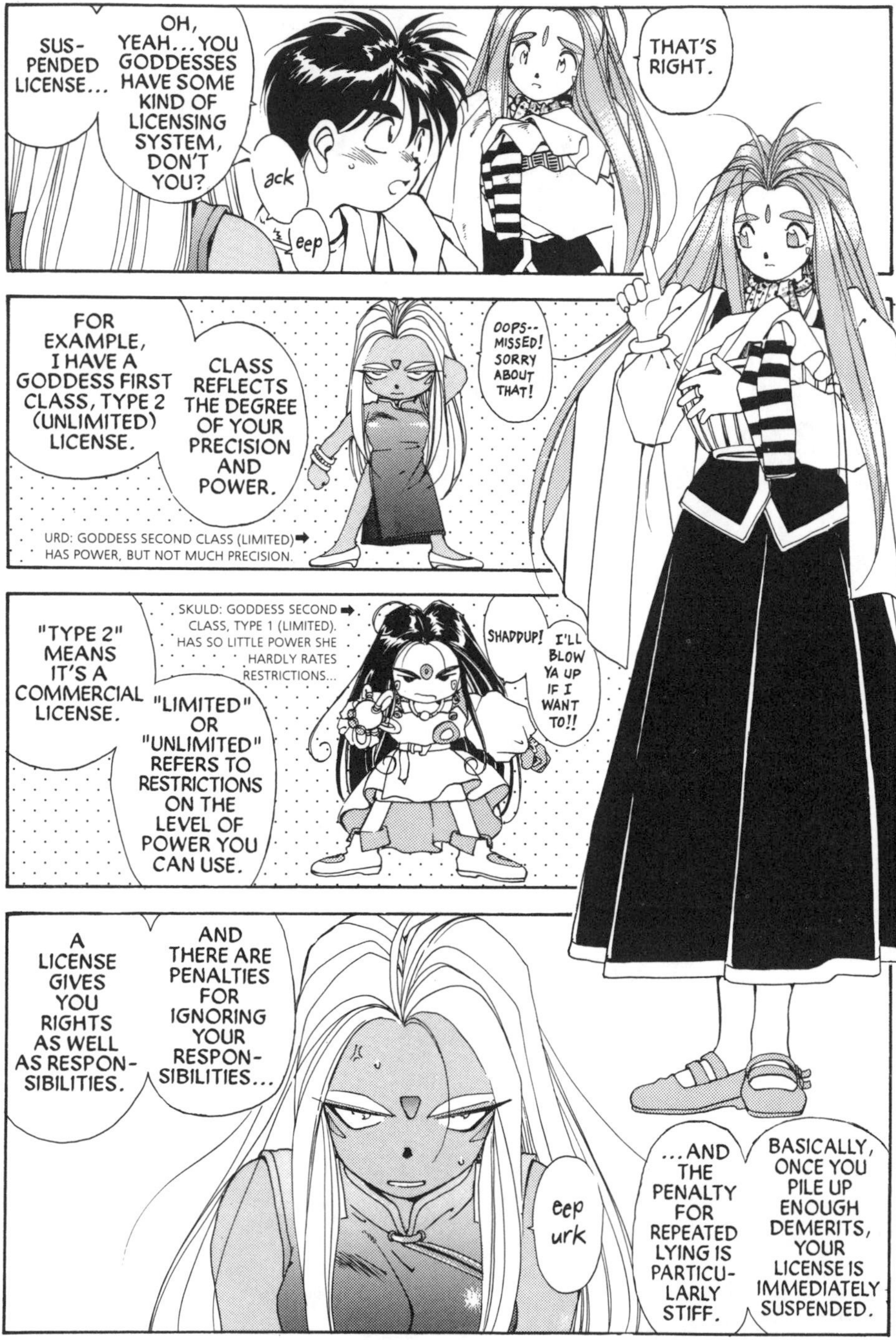
SUS-PENDED LICENSE...
OH, YEAH... YOU GODDESSES HAVE SOME KIND OF LICENSING SYSTEM, DON'T YOU?
ack
eep
THAT'S RIGHT.
FOR EXAMPLE, I HAVE A GODDESS FIRST CLASS, TYPE 2 (UNLIMITED) LICENSE.
CLASS REFLECTS THE DEGREE OF YOUR PRECISION AND POWER.
OOPS-- MISSED! SORRY ABOUT THAT!
URD: GODDESS SECOND CLASS (LIMITED) HAS POWER, BUT NOT MUCH PRECISION.
"TYPE 2" MEANS IT'S A COMMERCIAL LICENSE.
SKULD: GODDESS SECOND CLASS, TYPE 1 (LIMITED). HAS SO LITTLE POWER SHE HARDLY RATES RESTRICTIONS...
"LIMITED" OR "UNLIMITED" REFERS TO RESTRICTIONS ON THE LEVEL OF POWER YOU CAN USE.
SHADDUP!
I'LL BLOW YA UP IF I WANT TO!!
A LICENSE GIVES YOU RIGHTS AS WELL AS RESPON-SIBILITIES.
AND THERE ARE PENALTIES FOR IGNORING YOUR RESPON-SIBILITIES...
eep urk
BASICALLY, ONCE YOU PILE UP ENOUGH DEMERITS, YOUR LICENSE IS IMMEDIATELY SUSPENDED.
...AND THE PENALTY FOR REPEATED LYING IS PARTICU-LARLY STIFF.

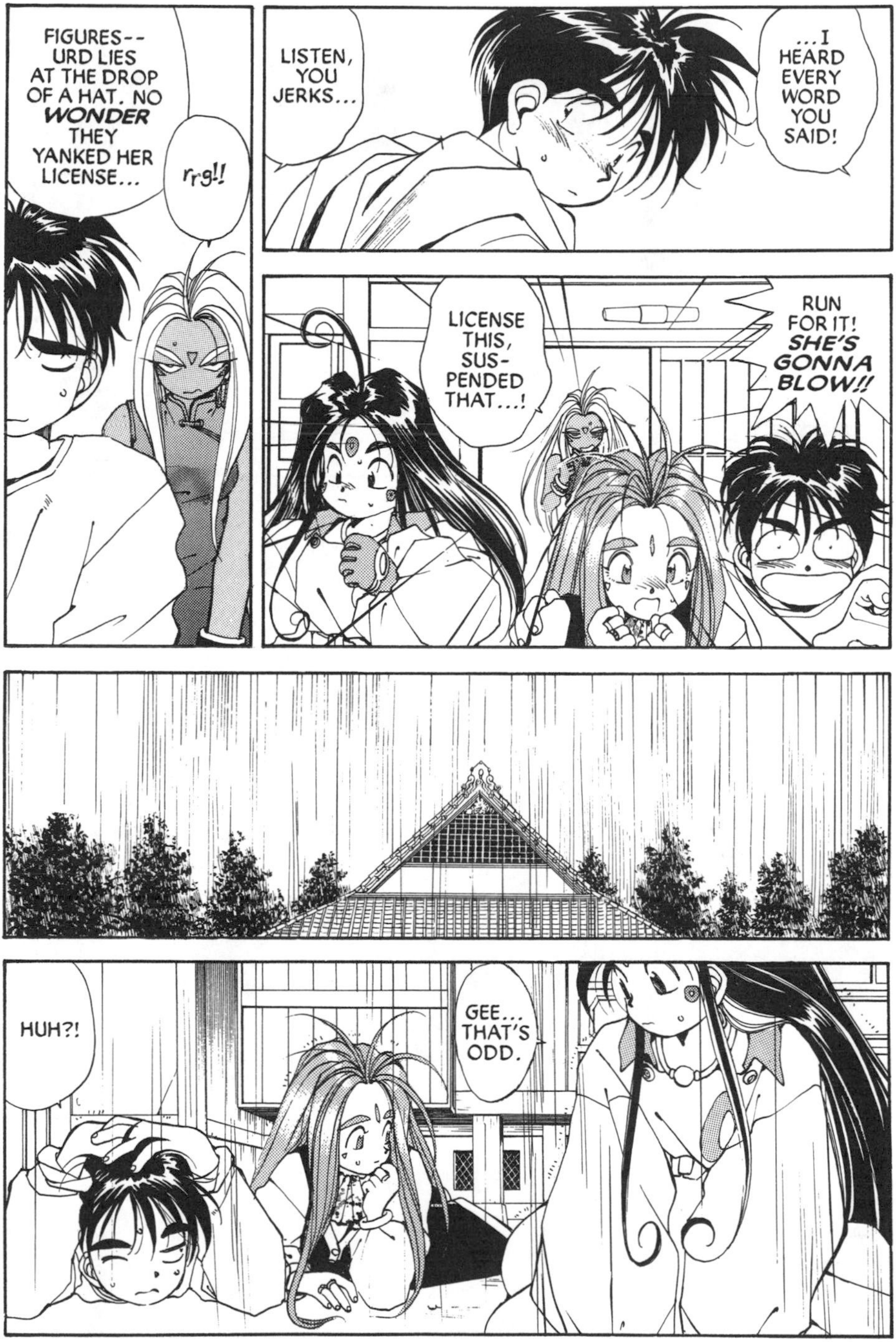

FIGURES-- URD LIES AT THE DROP OF A HAT. NO WONDER THEY YANKED HER LICENSE...
rrg!!
LISTEN, YOU JERKS...
...I HEARD EVERY WORD YOU SAID!
LICENSE THIS, SUS-PENDED THAT...!
RUN FOR IT! SHE'S GONNA BLOW!!
HUH?!
GEE... THAT'S ODD.

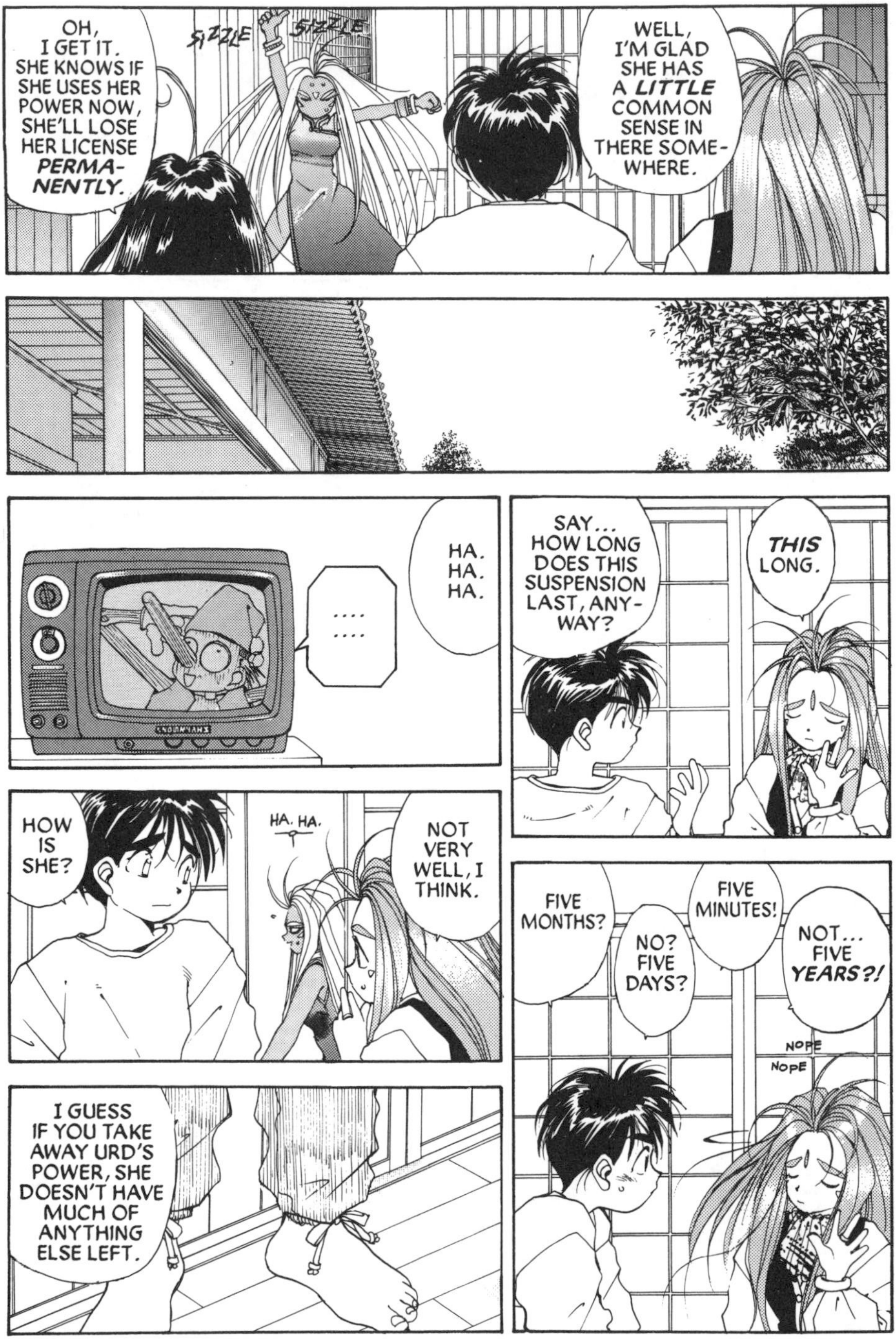
OH, I GET IT. SHE KNOWS IF SHE USES HER POWER NOW, SHE'LL LOSE HER LICENSE ***PERMA-NENTLY.***
SIZZLE
SIZZLE
WELL, I'M GLAD SHE HAS A ***LITTLE*** COMMON SENSE IN THERE SOME-WHERE.
....
HA. HA. HA.
HOW IS SHE?
HA. HA.
NOT VERY WELL, I THINK.
I GUESS IF YOU TAKE AWAY URD'S POWER, SHE DOESN'T HAVE MUCH OF ANYTHING ELSE LEFT.
SAY... HOW LONG DOES THIS SUSPENSION LAST, ANY-WAY?
THIS LONG.
FIVE MONTHS?
NO? FIVE DAYS?
FIVE MINUTES!
NOT... FIVE ***YEARS?!***
NOPE
NOPE

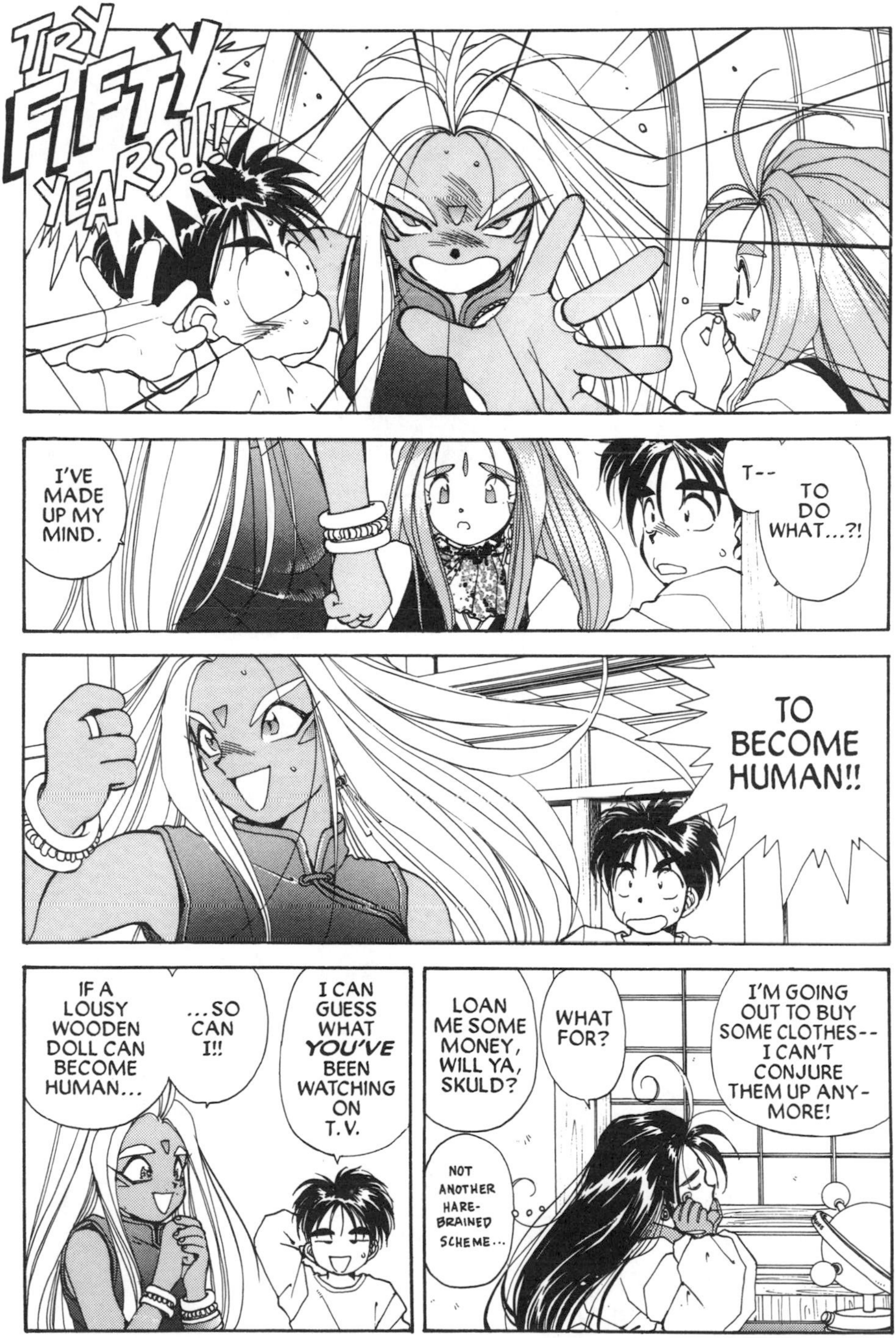
TRY FIFTY YEARS!!!
I'VE MADE UP MY MIND.
T-- TO DO WHAT...?!
TO BECOME HUMAN!!
IF A LOUSY WOODEN DOLL CAN BECOME HUMAN...
...SO CAN I!!
I CAN GUESS WHAT *YOU'VE* BEEN WATCHING ON T.V.
LOAN ME SOME MONEY, WILL YA, SKULD?
WHAT FOR?
I'M GOING OUT TO BUY SOME CLOTHES-- I CAN'T CONJURE THEM UP ANY-MORE!
NOT ANOTHER HARE-BRAINED SCHEME...

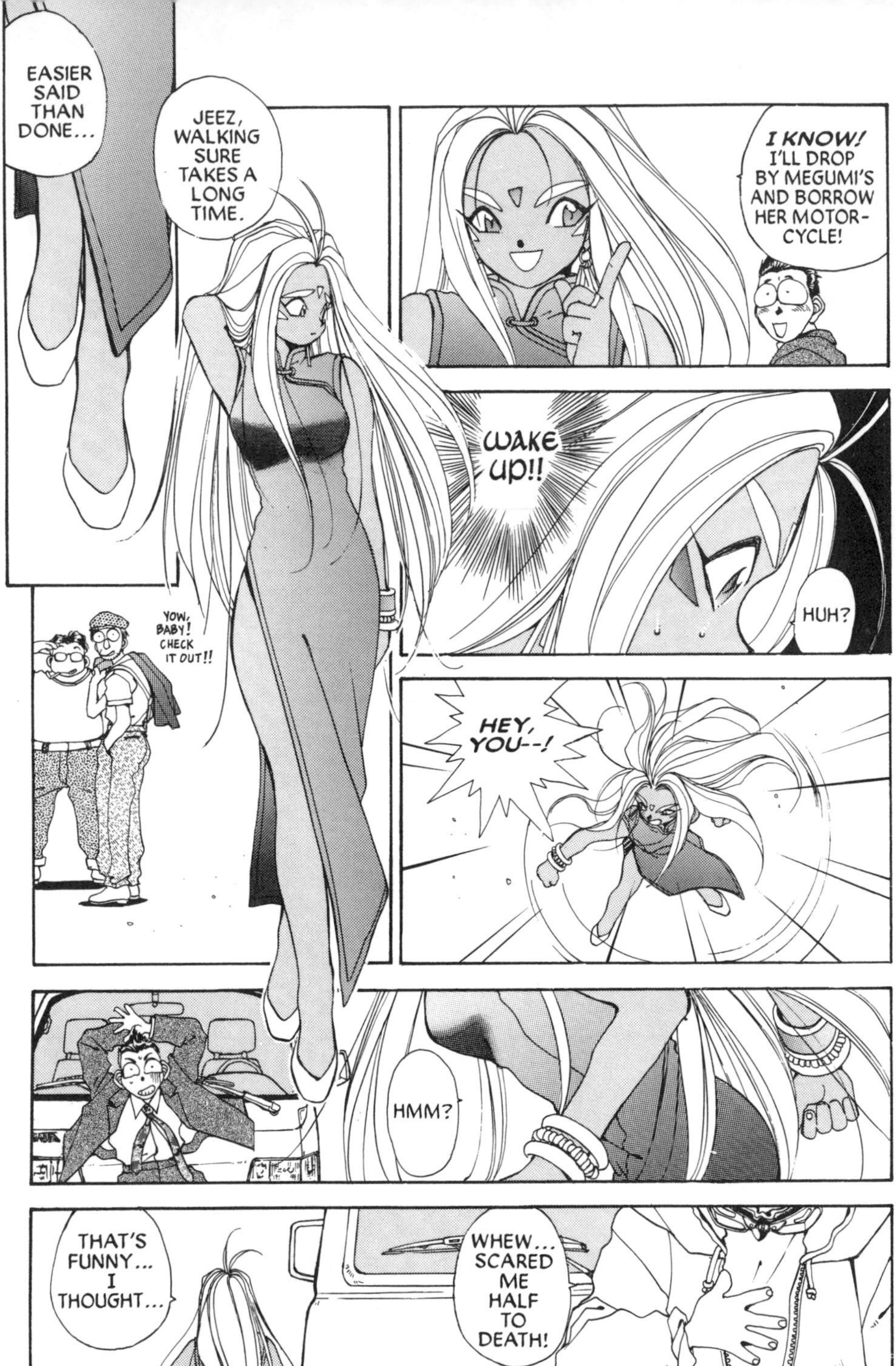

EASIER SAID THAN DONE...
JEEZ, WALKING SURE TAKES A LONG TIME.
I KNOW! I'LL DROP BY MEGUMI'S AND BORROW HER MOTOR-CYCLE!
WAKE UP!!
HUH?
YOW, BABY! CHECK IT OUT!!
HEY, YOU--!
HMM?
THAT'S FUNNY... I THOUGHT...
WHEW... SCARED ME HALF TO DEATH!

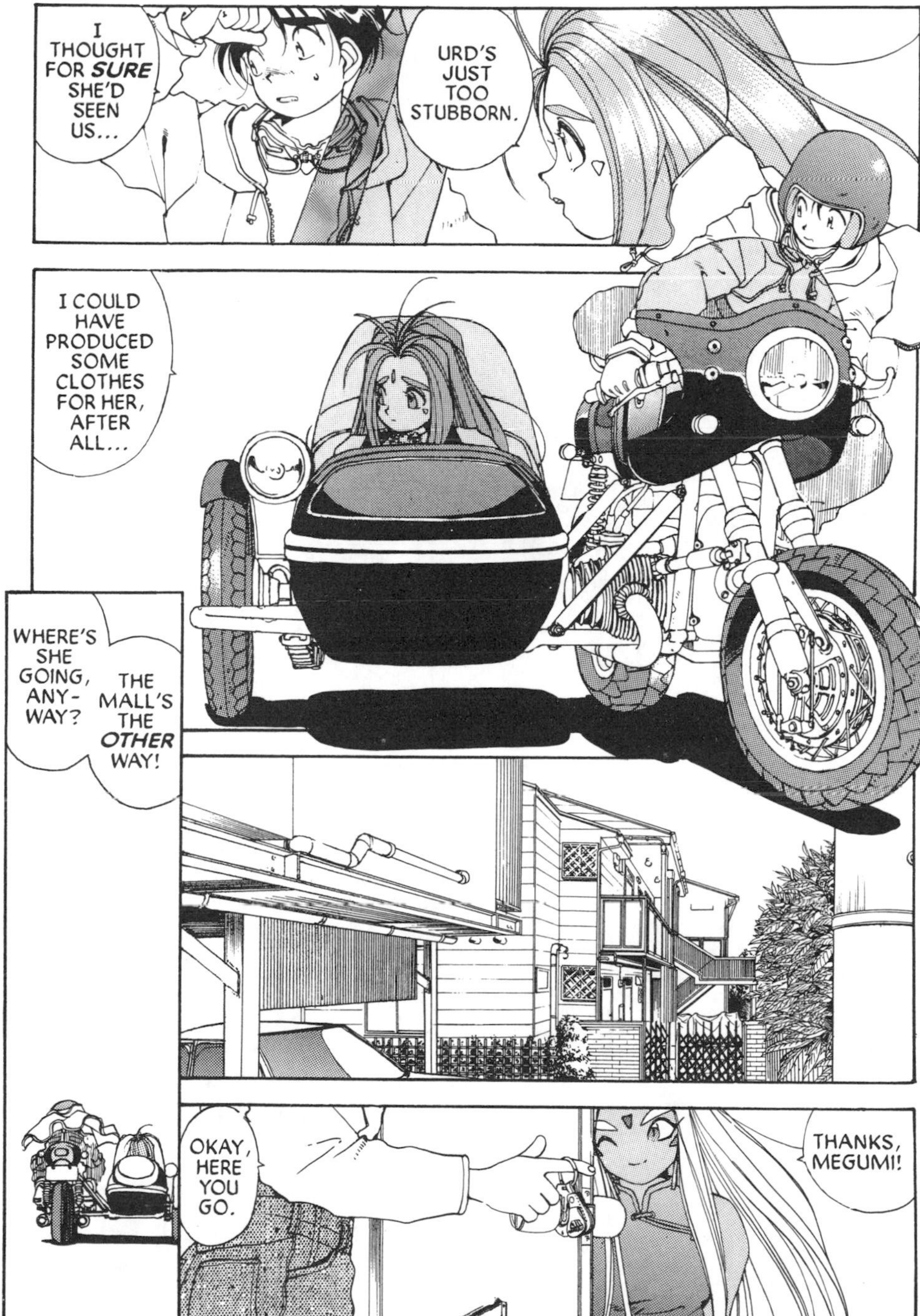
I THOUGHT FOR SURE SHE'D SEEN US...
URD'S JUST TOO STUBBORN.
I COULD HAVE PRODUCED SOME CLOTHES FOR HER, AFTER ALL...
WHERE'S SHE GOING, ANY-WAY?
THE MALL'S THE OTHER WAY!
OKAY, HERE YOU GO.
THANKS, MEGUMI!

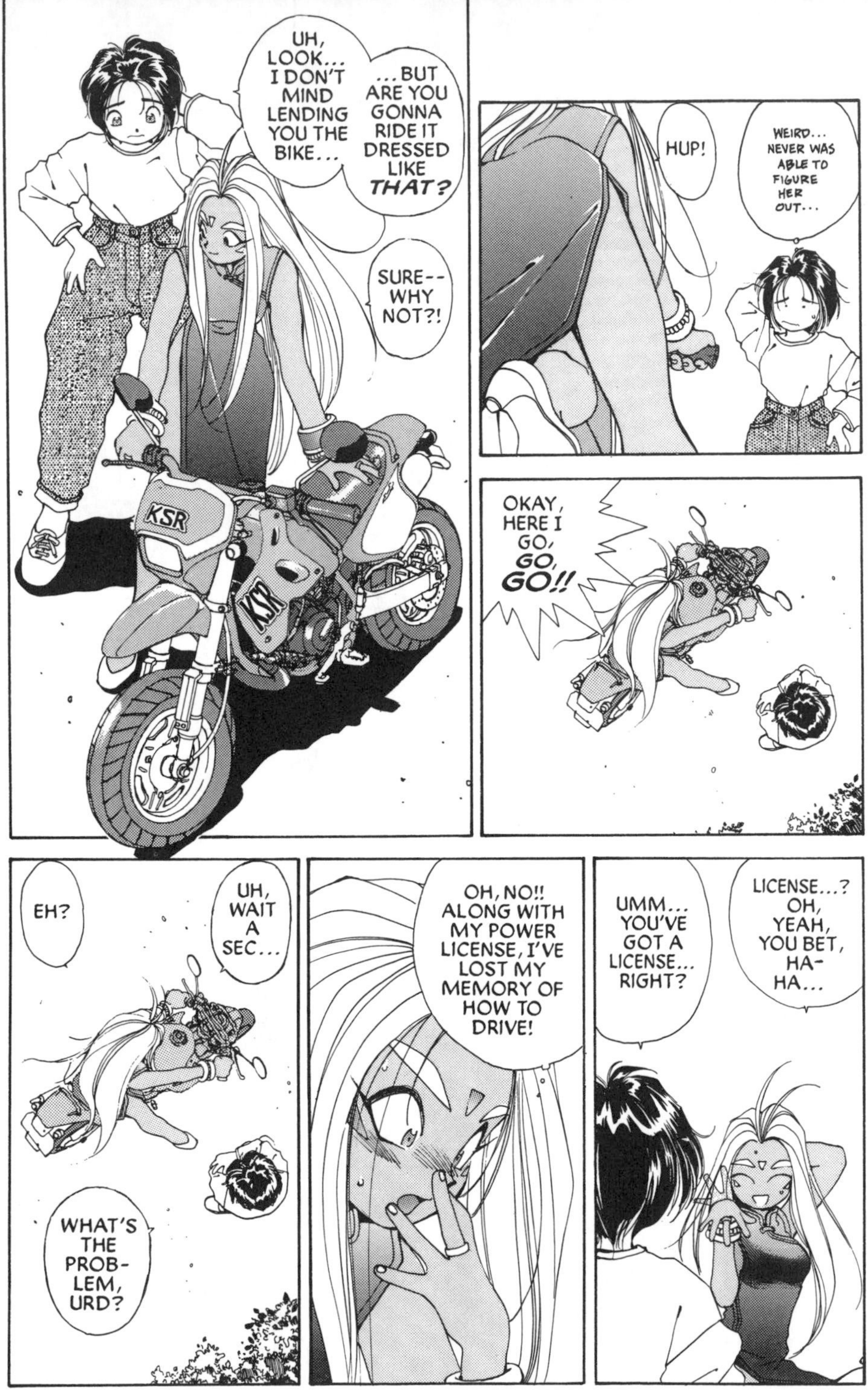
UH, LOOK... I DON'T MIND LENDING YOU THE BIKE...
...BUT ARE YOU GONNA RIDE IT DRESSED LIKE THAT?
SURE--WHY NOT?!
KSR
KSR
HUP!
WEIRD... NEVER WAS ABLE TO FIGURE HER OUT...
OKAY, HERE I GO, GO, GO!!
EH?
UH, WAIT A SEC...
WHAT'S THE PROB-LEM, URD?
OH, NO!! ALONG WITH MY POWER LICENSE, I'VE LOST MY MEMORY OF HOW TO DRIVE!
UMM... YOU'VE GOT A LICENSE... RIGHT?
LICENSE...? OH, YEAH, YOU BET, HA-HA...

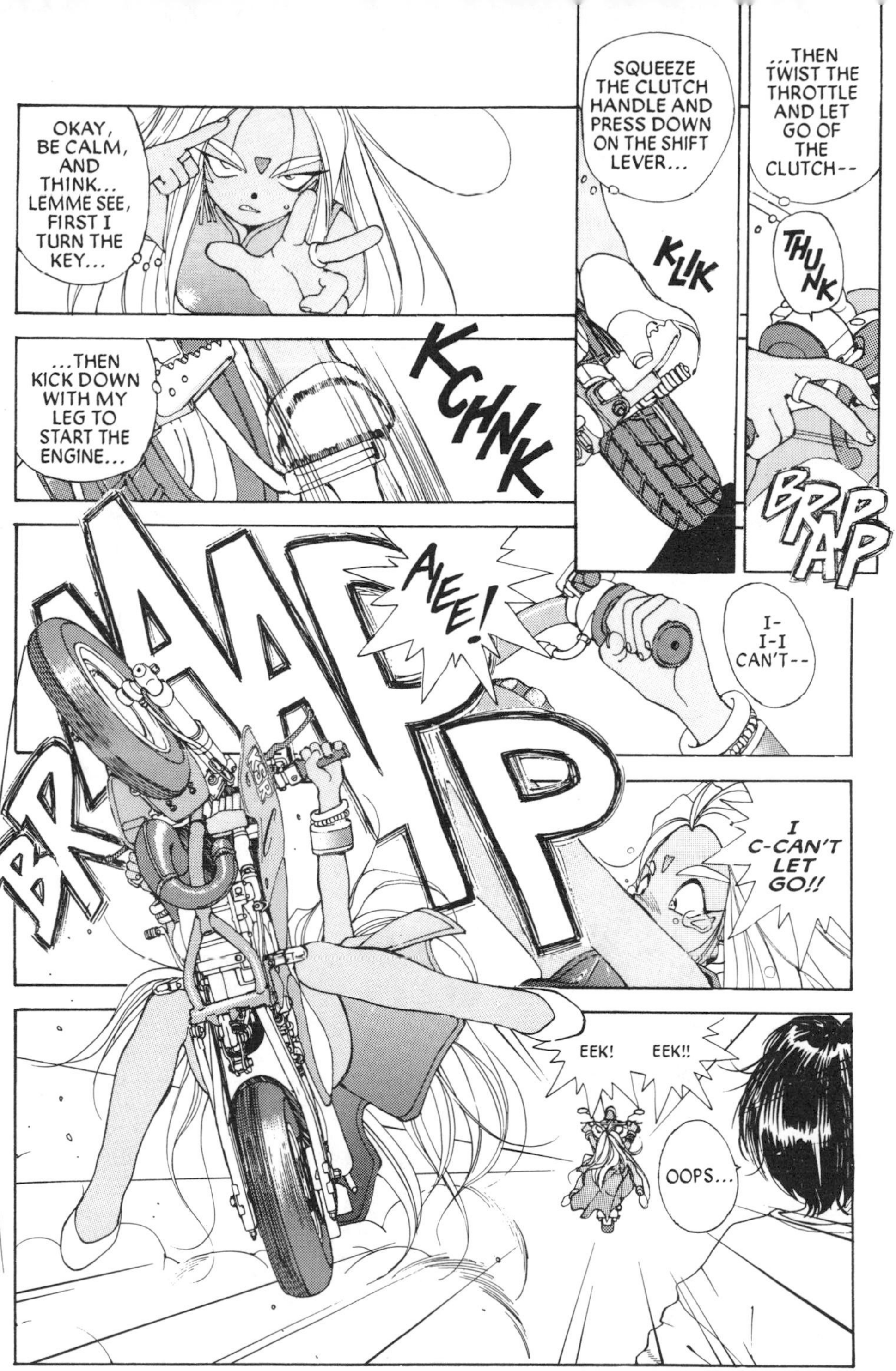
OKAY, BE CALM, AND THINK... LEMME SEE, FIRST I TURN THE KEY...
...THEN KICK DOWN WITH MY LEG TO START THE ENGINE...
KCHNK
SQUEEZE THE CLUTCH HANDLE AND PRESS DOWN ON THE SHIFT LEVER...
KLIK
...THEN TWIST THE THROTTLE AND LET GO OF THE CLUTCH--
THUNK
BRRAP
BRAAAP
AIEEE!
I- I-I CAN'T--
I C-CAN'T LET GO!!
EEK! EEK!!
OOPS...

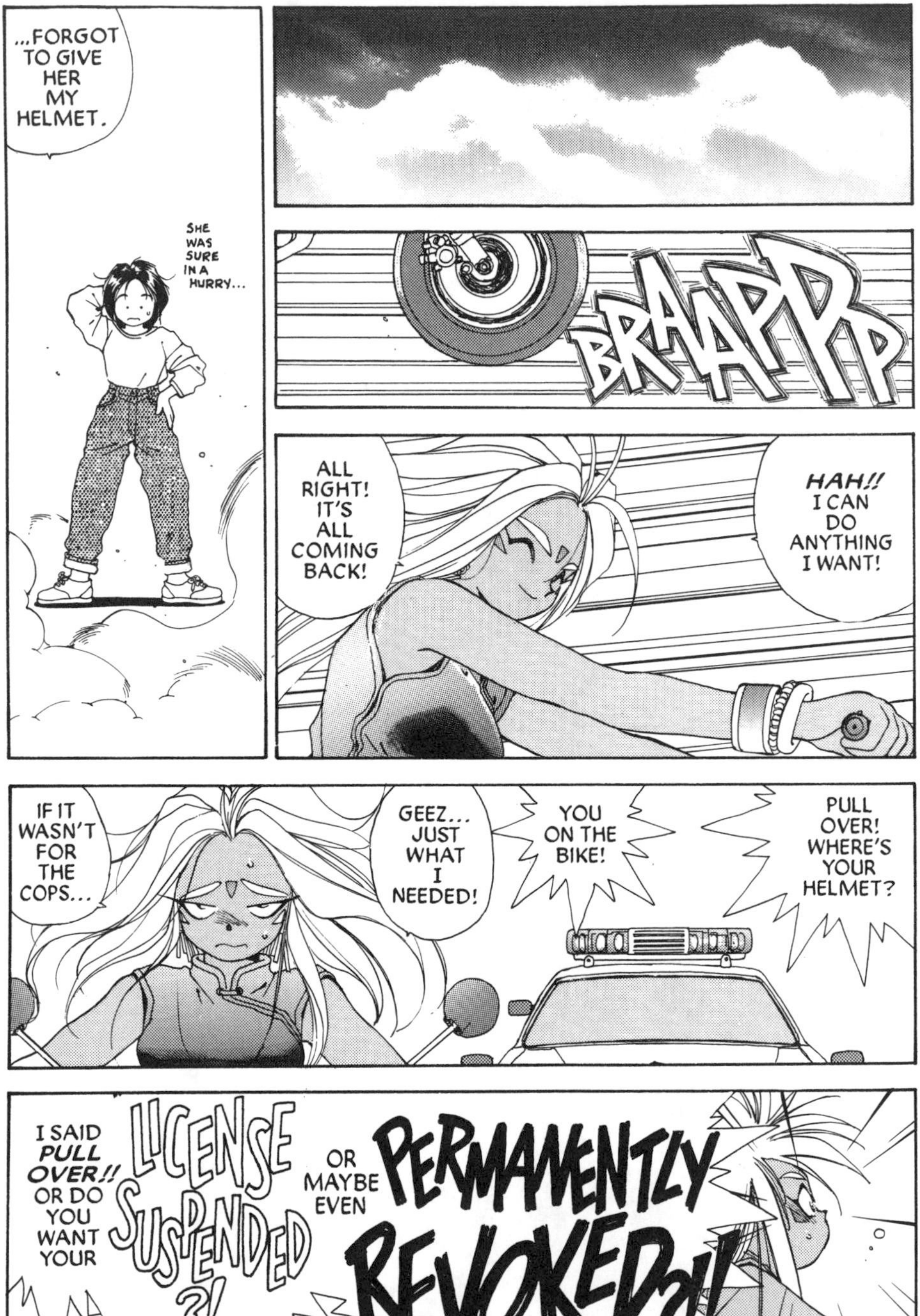
...FORGOT TO GIVE HER MY HELMET.
SHE WAS SURE IN A HURRY...
BRAAPPP
ALL RIGHT! IT'S ALL COMING BACK!
HAH!! I CAN DO ANYTHING I WANT!
IF IT WASN'T FOR THE COPS...
GEEZ... JUST WHAT I NEEDED!
YOU ON THE BIKE!
PULL OVER! WHERE'S YOUR HELMET?
I SAID PULL OVER!! OR DO YOU WANT YOUR
LICENSE SUSPENDED ?!
OR MAYBE EVEN
PERMANENTLY REVOKED?!!

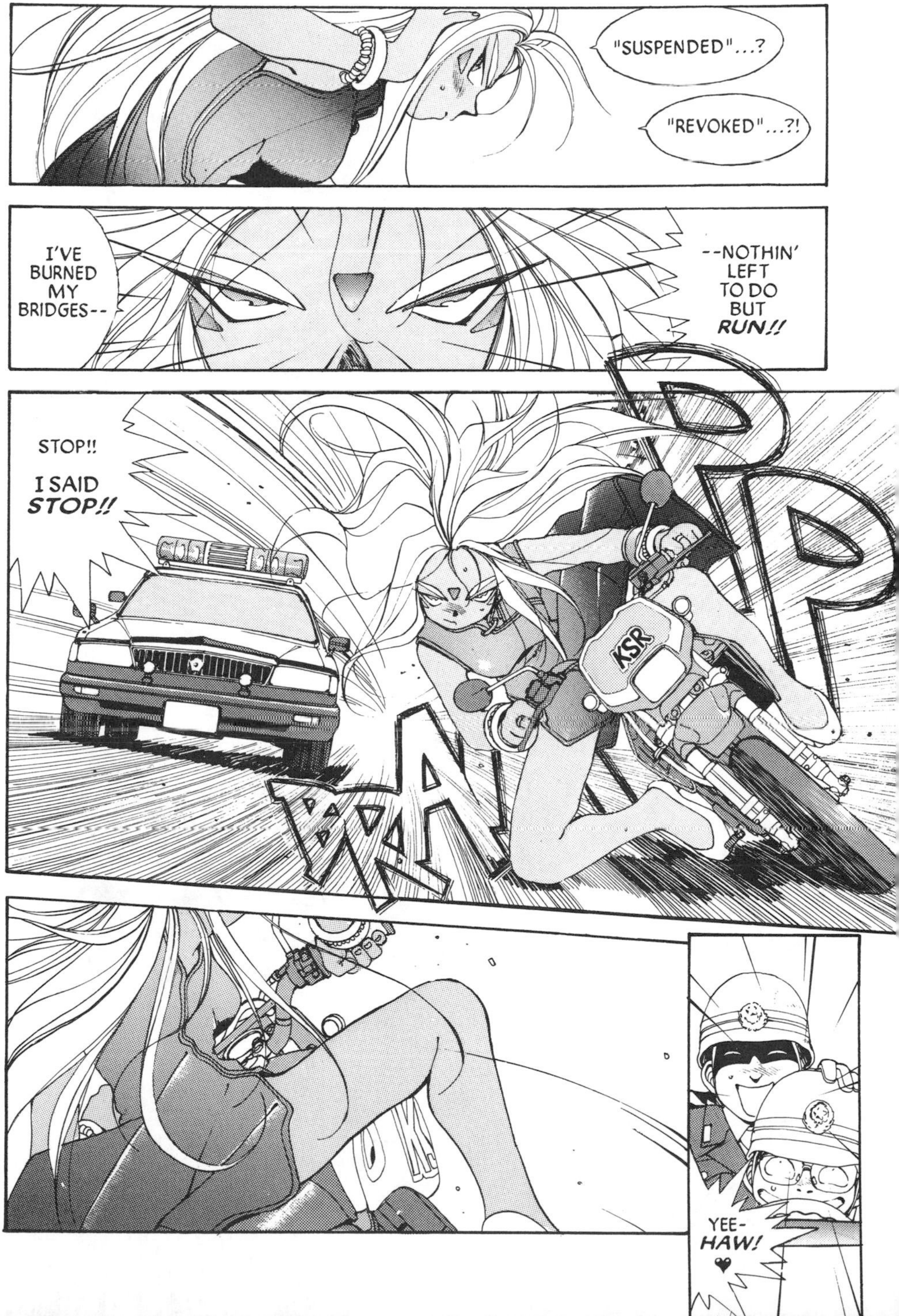
"SUSPENDED"...?
"REVOKED"...?!
I'VE BURNED MY BRIDGES--
--NOTHIN' LEFT TO DO BUT ***RUN!!***
STOP!!
I SAID ***STOP!!***
KSR
YEE-***HAW!*** ♥

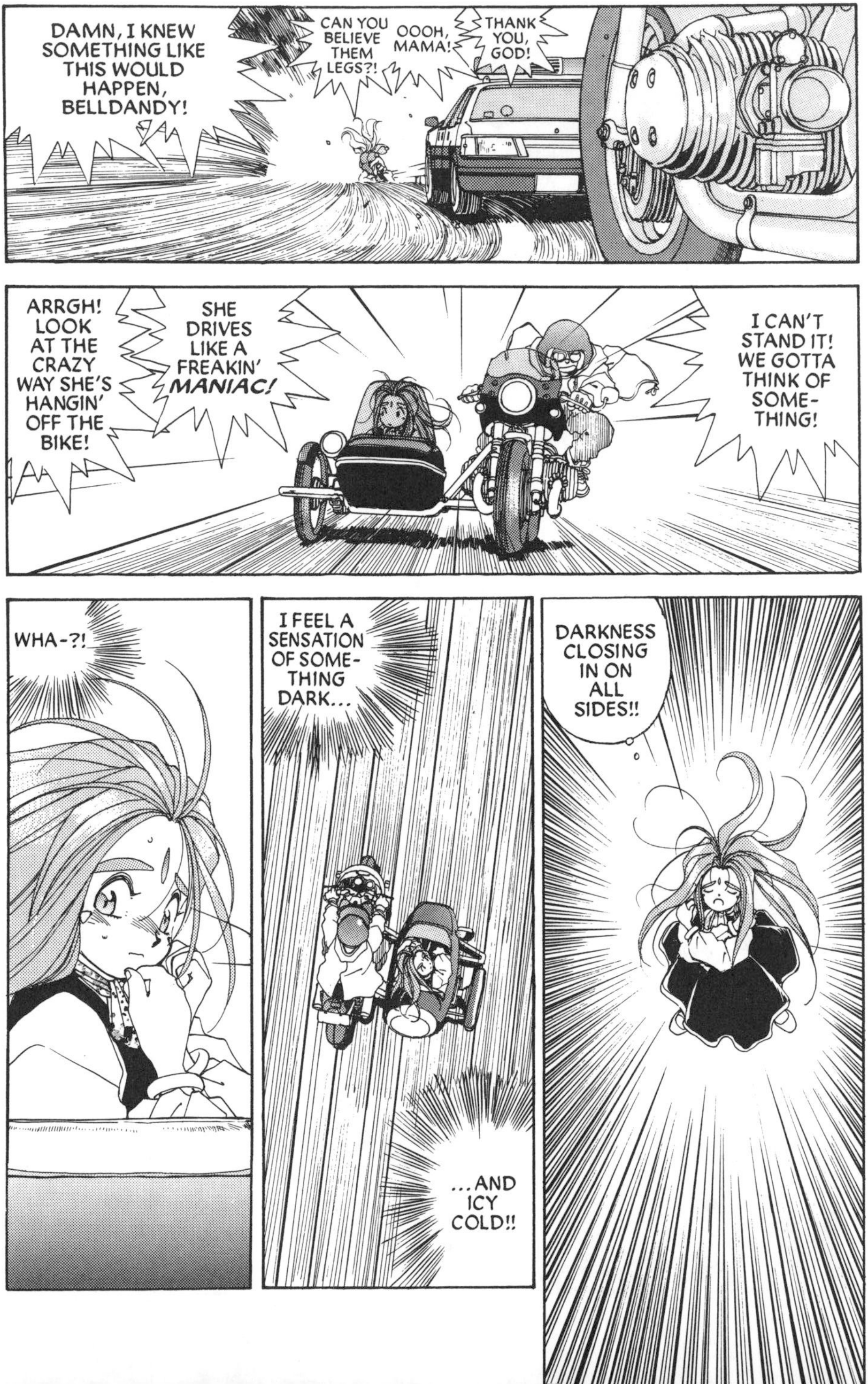
DAMN, I KNEW SOMETHING LIKE THIS WOULD HAPPEN, BELLDANDY!
CAN YOU BELIEVE THEM LEGS?!
OOOH, MAMA!
THANK YOU, GOD!
ARRGH! LOOK AT THE CRAZY WAY SHE'S HANGIN' OFF THE BIKE!
SHE DRIVES LIKE A FREAKIN' *MANIAC!*
I CAN'T STAND IT! WE GOTTA THINK OF SOME-THING!
WHA-?!
I FEEL A SENSATION OF SOME-THING DARK...
...AND ICY COLD!!
DARKNESS CLOSING IN ON ALL SIDES!!

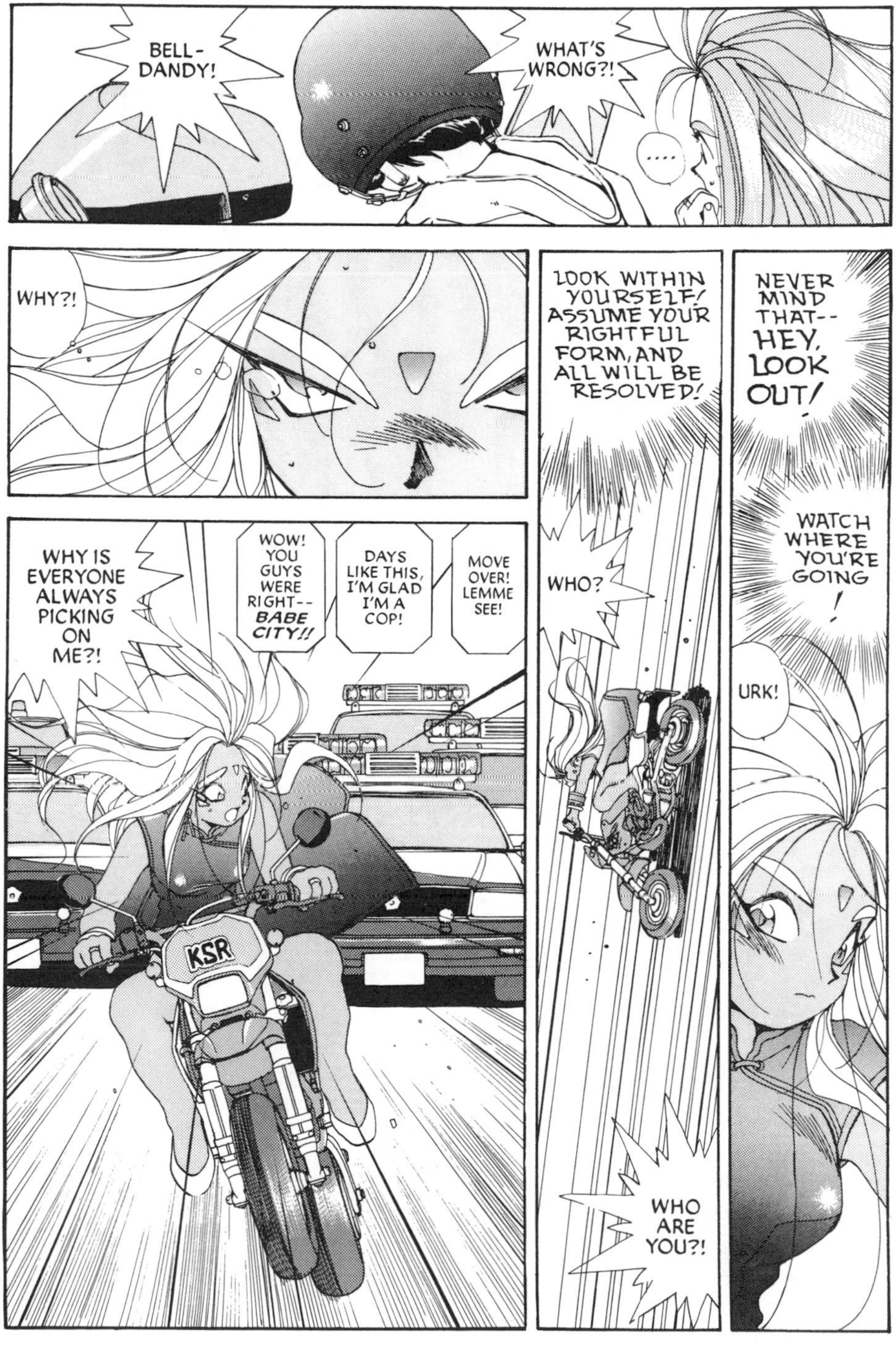
BELL-DANDY!
WHAT'S WRONG?!
....
WHY?!
WHY IS EVERYONE ALWAYS PICKING ON ME?!
WOW! YOU GUYS WERE RIGHT-- BABE CITY!!
DAYS LIKE THIS, I'M GLAD I'M A COP!
MOVE OVER! LEMME SEE!
LOOK WITHIN YOURSELF! ASSUME YOUR RIGHTFUL FORM, AND ALL WILL BE RESOLVED!
WHO?
WHO ARE YOU?!
NEVER MIND THAT-- HEY, LOOK OUT!
WATCH WHERE YOU'RE GOING!
URK!

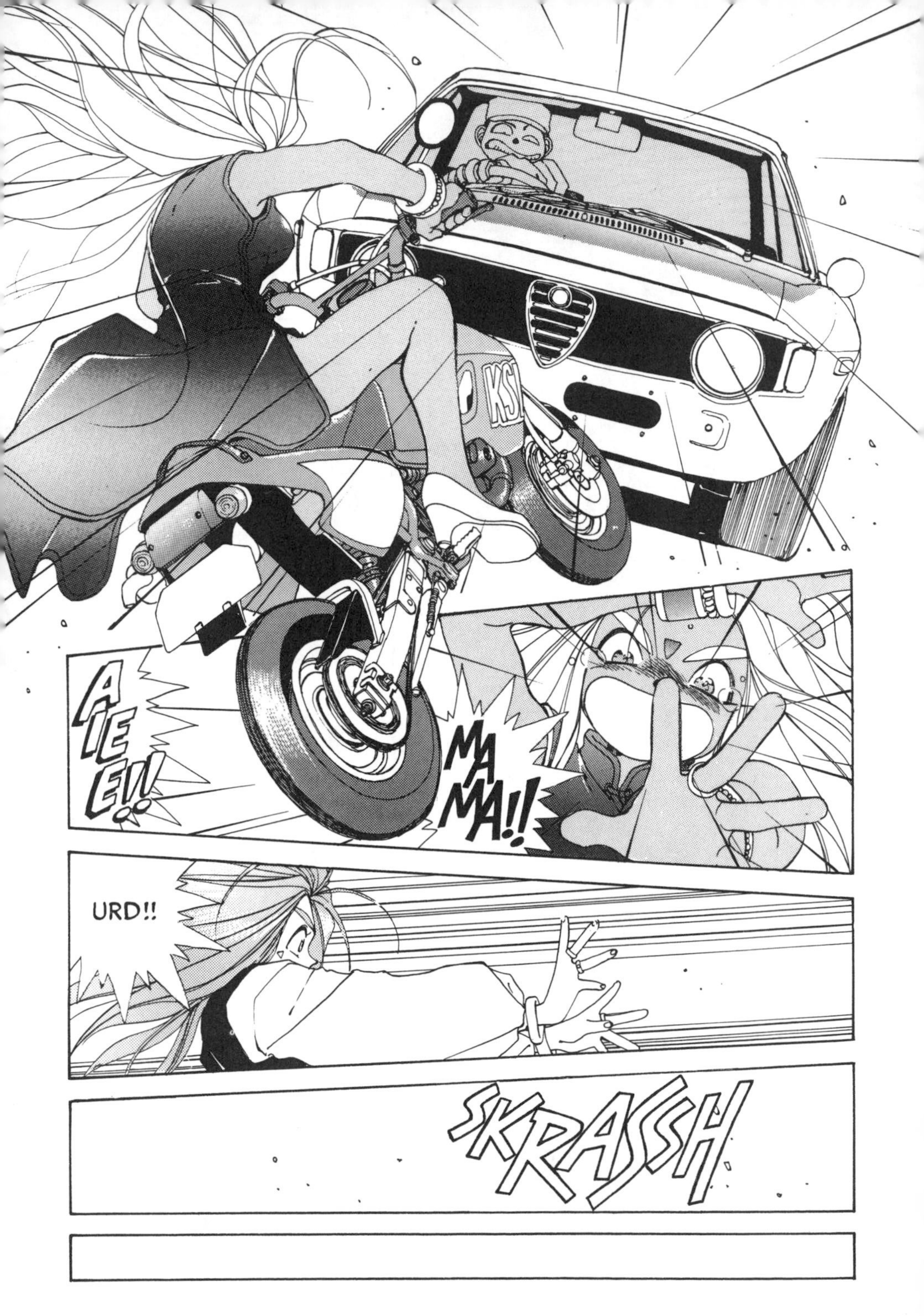
AIEEE!!
MAMA!!
URD!!
SKRASH

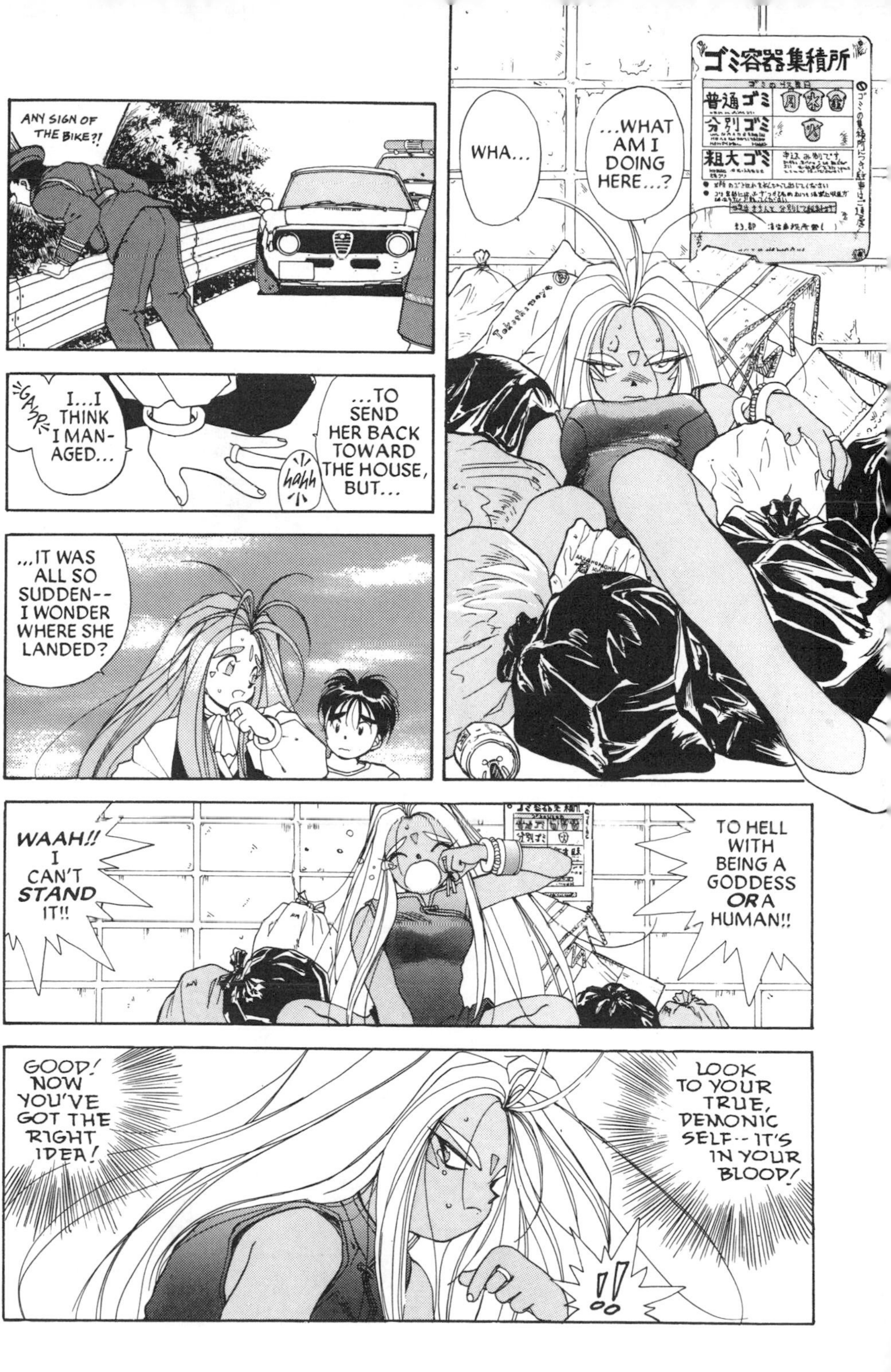
ANY SIGN OF THE BIKE?!
GASP
I...I THINK I MANAGED...
hahh
...TO SEND HER BACK TOWARD THE HOUSE, BUT...
...IT WAS ALL SO SUDDEN--I WONDER WHERE SHE LANDED?
ゴミ容器集積所
普通ゴミ
分別ゴミ
粗大ゴミ
WHA...
...WHAT AM I DOING HERE...?
WAAH!! I CAN'T STAND IT!!
TO HELL WITH BEING A GODDESS OR A HUMAN!!
GOOD! NOW YOU'VE GOT THE RIGHT IDEA!
LOOK TO YOUR TRUE, DEMONIC SELF--IT'S IN YOUR BLOOD!
!!

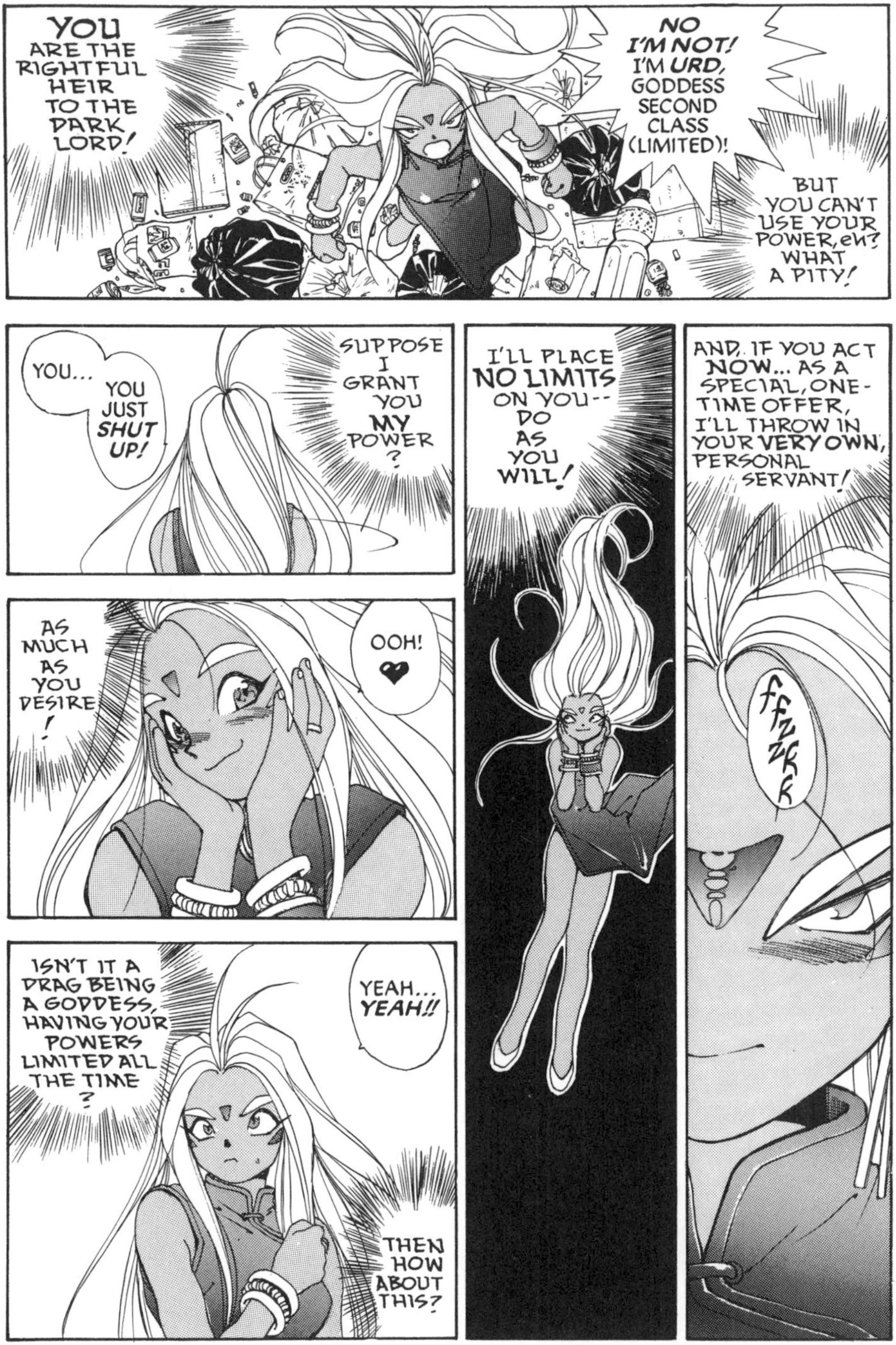
YOU ARE THE RIGHTFUL HEIR TO THE DARK LORD!
NO I'M NOT! I'M URD, GODDESS SECOND CLASS (LIMITED)!
BUT YOU CAN'T USE YOUR POWER, eh? WHAT A PITY!
YOU... YOU JUST SHUT UP!
SUPPOSE I GRANT YOU MY POWER?
AS MUCH AS YOU DESIRE!
OOH!
ISN'T IT A DRAG BEING A GODDESS, HAVING YOUR POWERS LIMITED ALL THE TIME?
YEAH... YEAH!!
THEN HOW ABOUT THIS?
I'LL PLACE NO LIMITS ON YOU-- DO AS YOU WILL!
AND, IF YOU ACT NOW... AS A SPECIAL, ONE-TIME OFFER, I'LL THROW IN YOUR VERY OWN, PERSONAL SERVANT!
FFZZKK

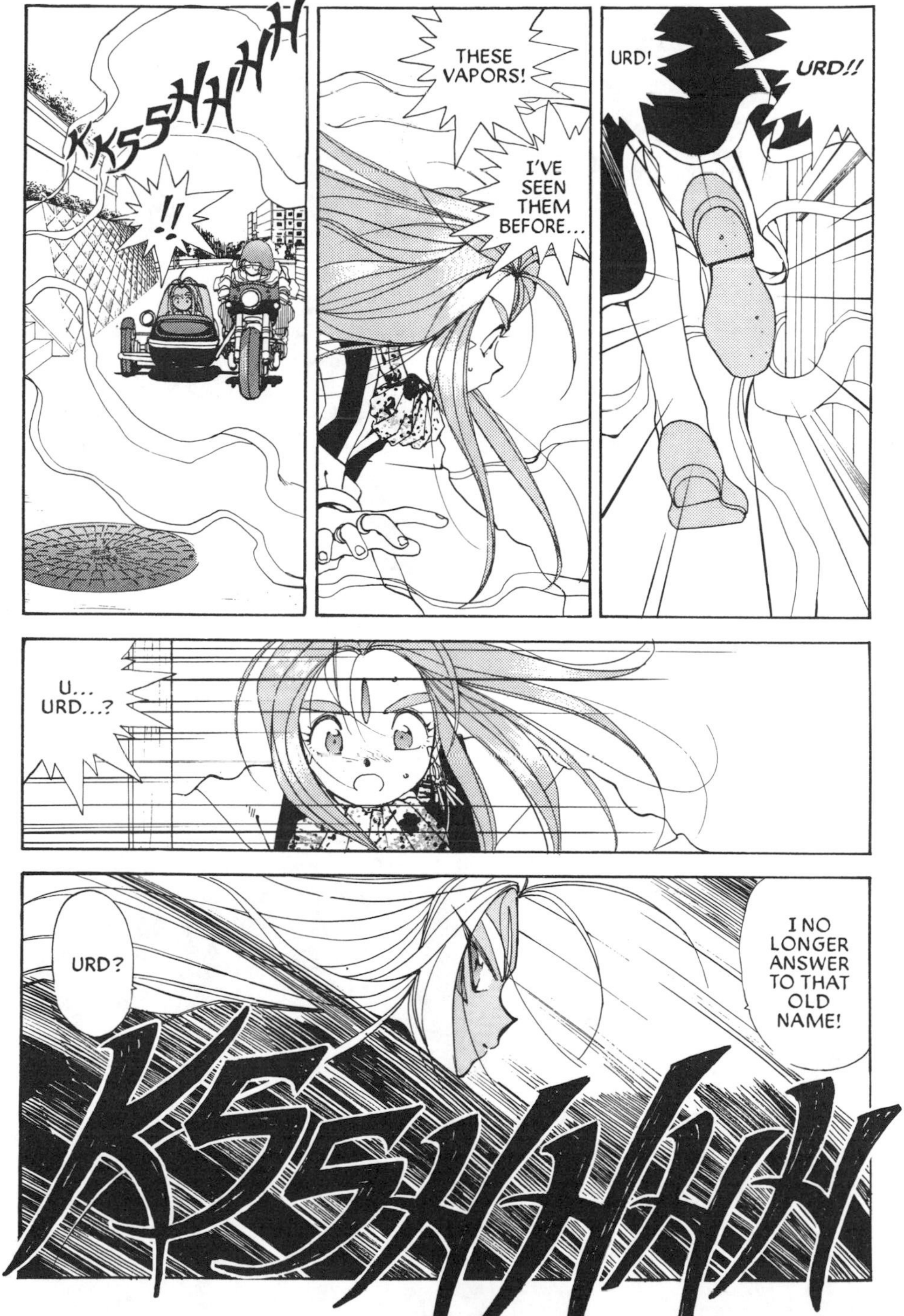
KSSHHHHH
!!
THESE VAPORS!
I'VE SEEN THEM BEFORE...
URD!
URD!!
U... URD...?
URD?
I NO LONGER ANSWER TO THAT OLD NAME!
KSSHHHHH

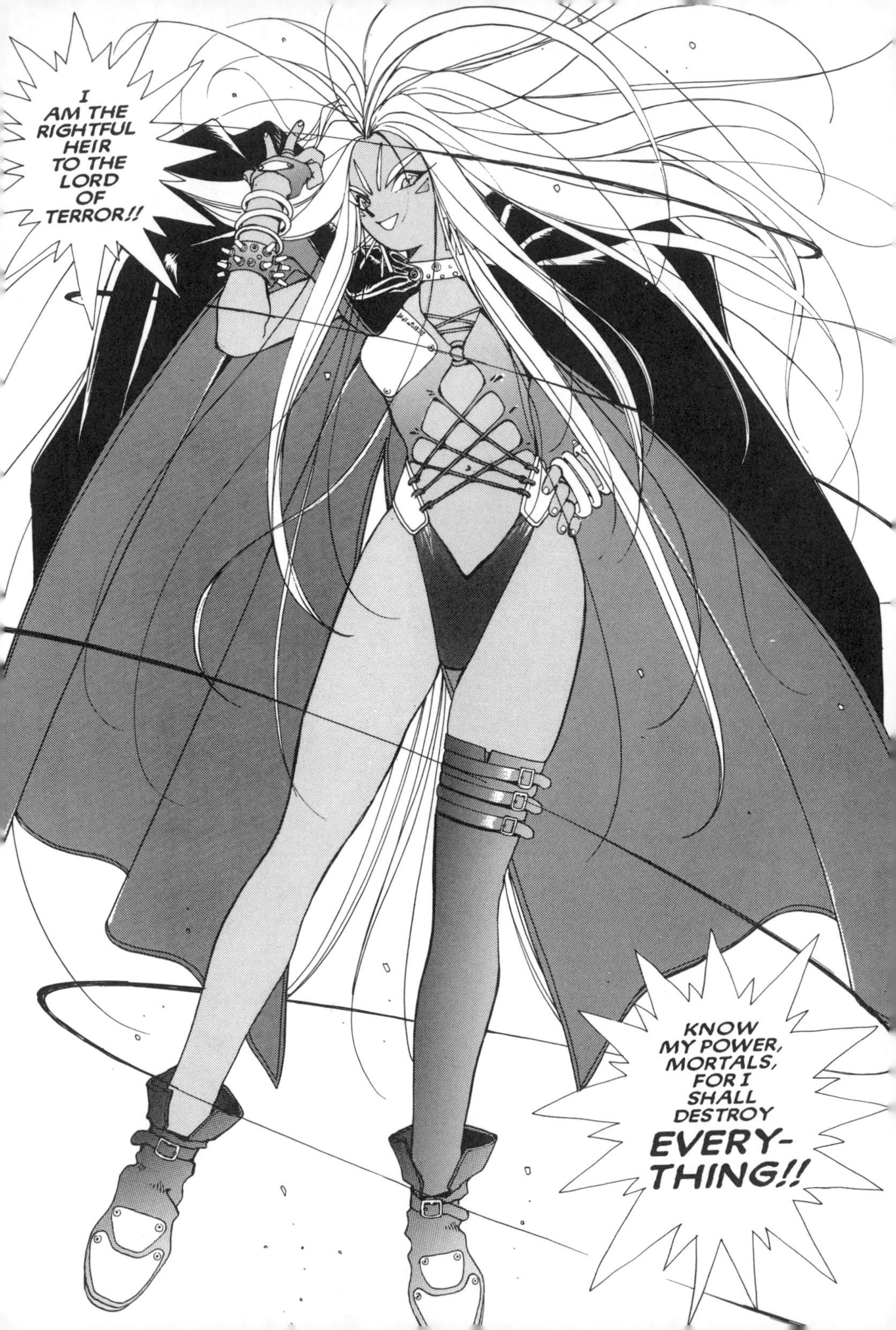
I AM THE RIGHTFUL HEIR TO THE LORD OF TERROR!!
KNOW MY POWER, MORTALS, FOR I SHALL DESTROY EVERY-THING!!

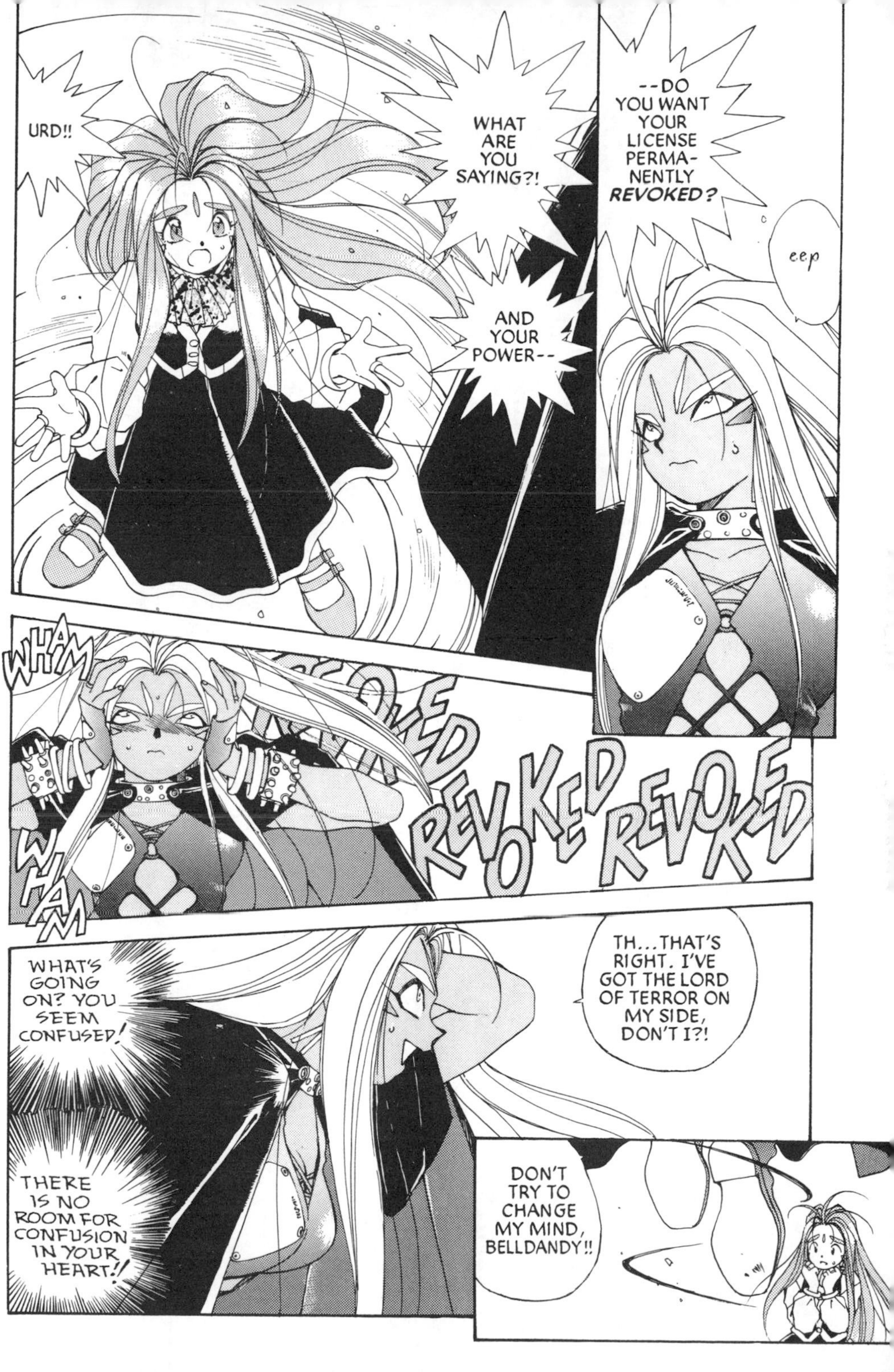
URD!!
WHAT ARE YOU SAYING?!
AND YOUR POWER--
--DO YOU WANT YOUR LICENSE PERMANENTLY *REVOKED?*
eep
WHAM
WHAM
REVOKED
REVOKED
REVOKED
WHAT'S GOING ON? YOU SEEM CONFUSED!
THERE IS NO ROOM FOR CONFUSION IN YOUR HEART!!
TH...THAT'S RIGHT. I'VE GOT THE LORD OF TERROR ON MY SIDE, DON'T I?!
DON'T TRY TO CHANGE MY MIND, BELLDANDY!!

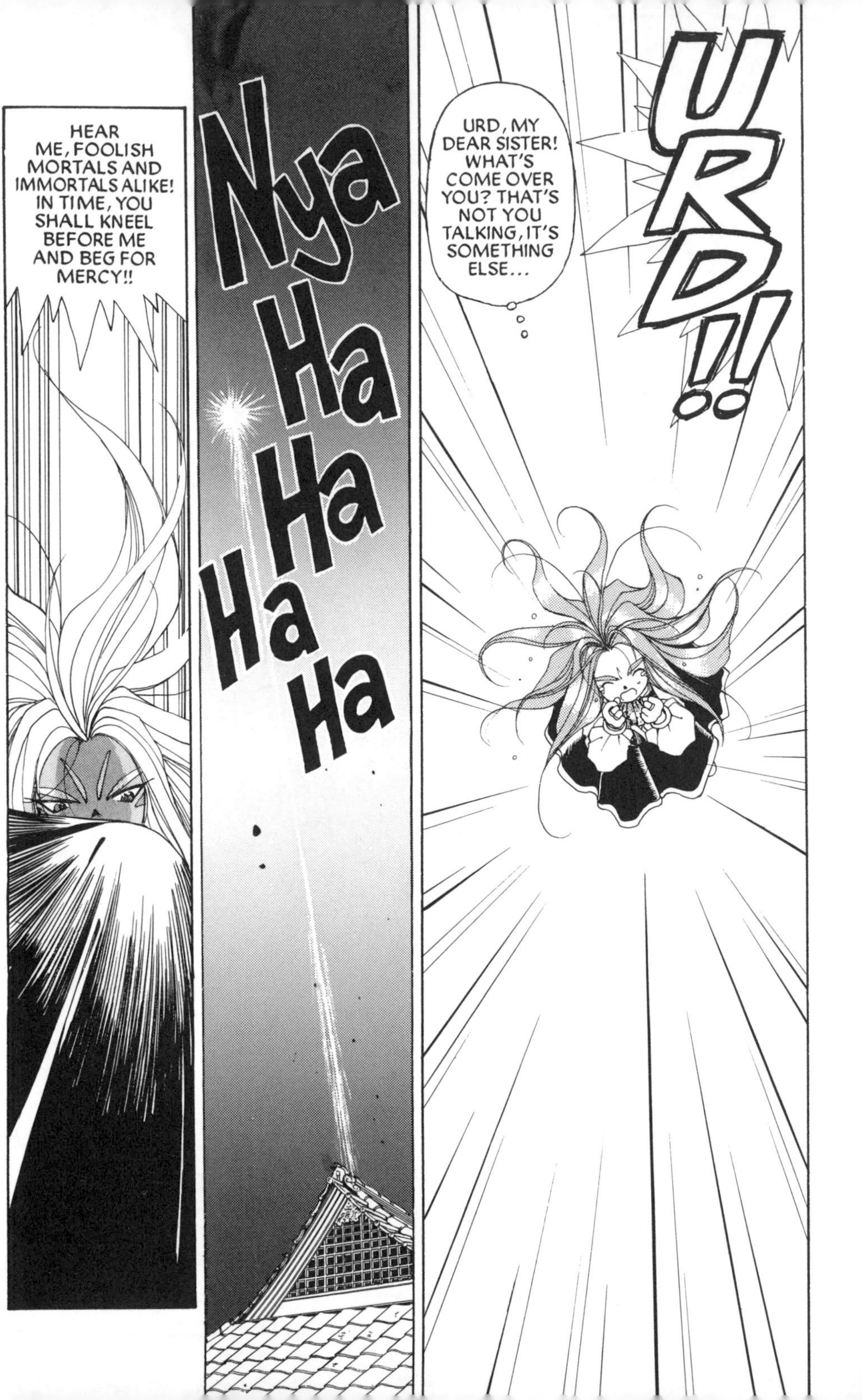
HEAR ME, FOOLISH MORTALS AND IMMORTALS ALIKE! IN TIME, YOU SHALL KNEEL BEFORE ME AND BEG FOR MERCY!!
Nya Ha Ha Ha Ha Ha
URD, MY DEAR SISTER! WHAT'S COME OVER YOU? THAT'S NOT YOU TALKING, IT'S SOMETHING ELSE...
URD!!

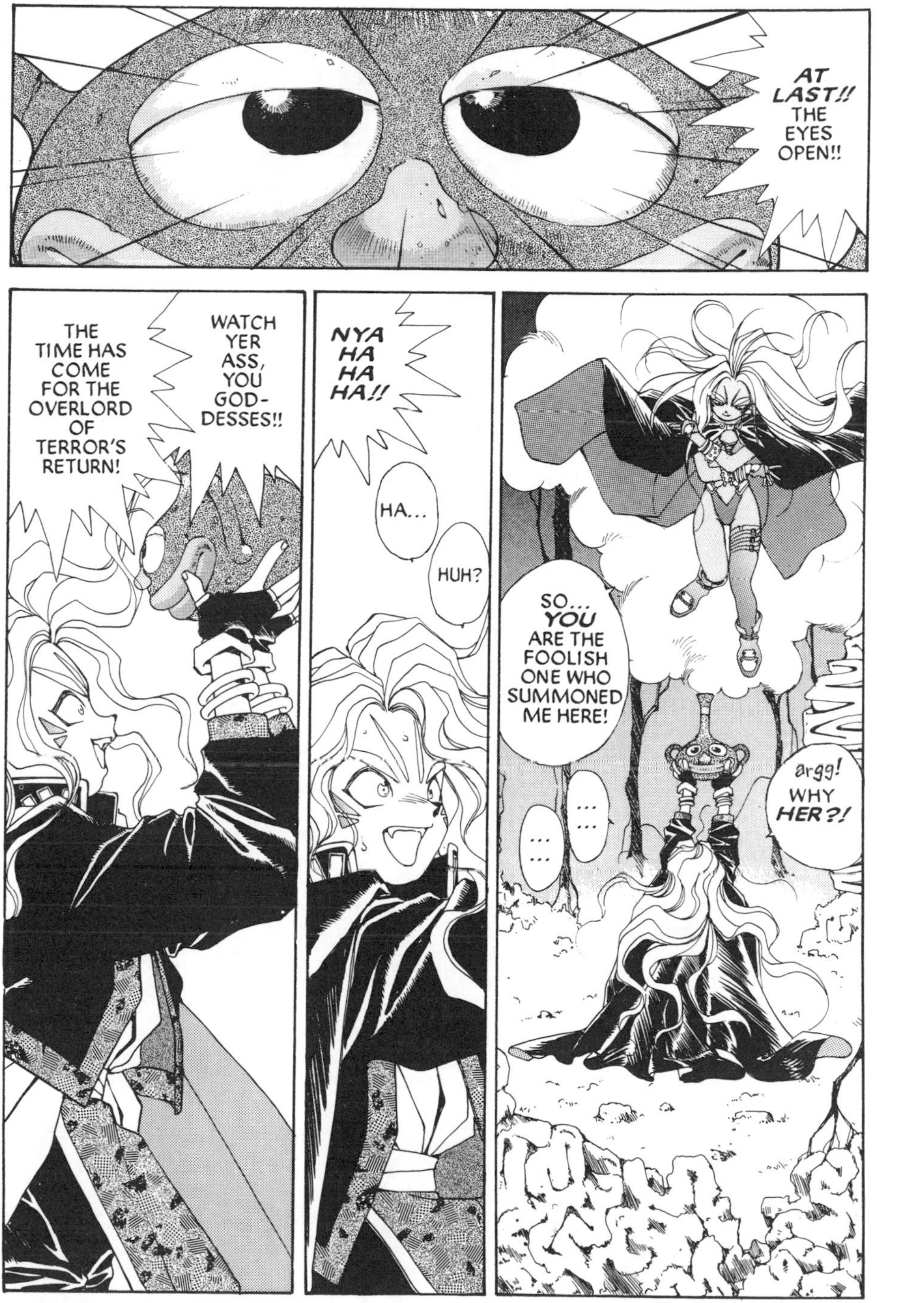
AT LAST!! THE EYES OPEN!!
THE TIME HAS COME FOR THE OVERLORD OF TERROR'S RETURN!
WATCH YER ASS, YOU GOD-DESSES!!
NYA HA HA HA!!
HA...
HUH?
SO... YOU ARE THE FOOLISH ONE WHO SUMMONED ME HERE!
... ...
... ...
argg! WHY HER?!

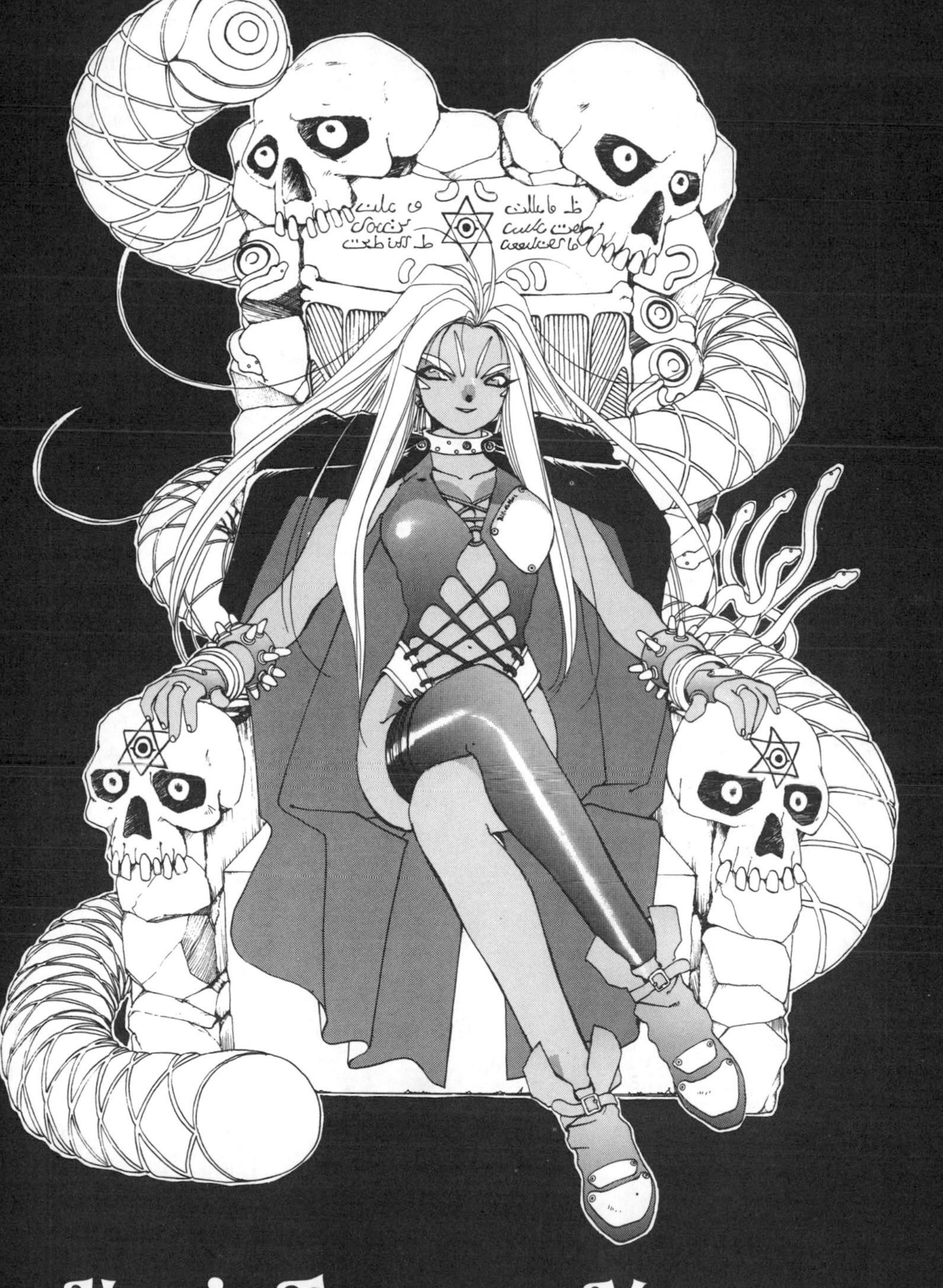

Urd's Terrible Master

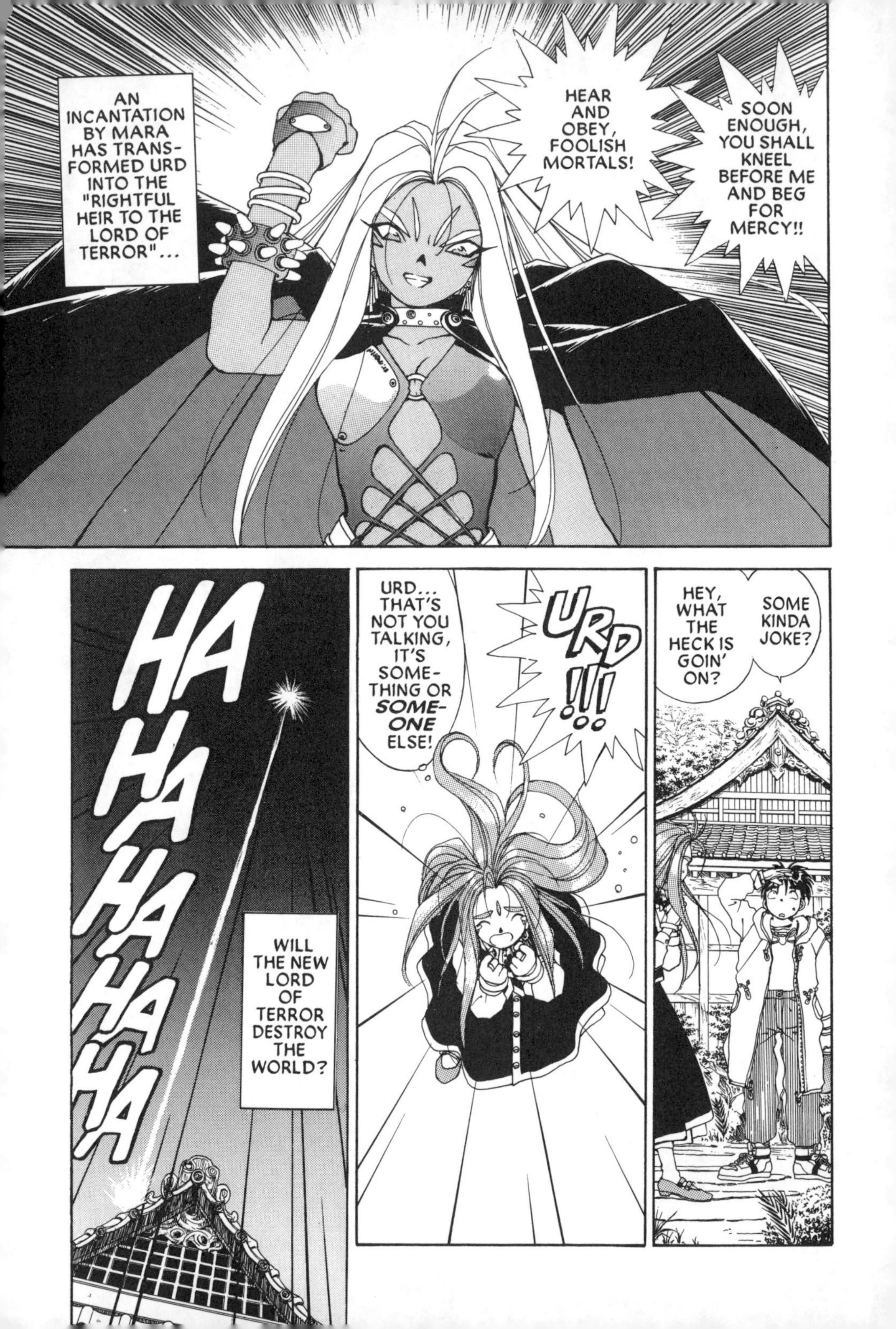
AN INCANTATION BY MARA HAS TRANS-FORMED URD INTO THE "RIGHTFUL HEIR TO THE LORD OF TERROR"...
HEAR AND OBEY, FOOLISH MORTALS!
SOON ENOUGH, YOU SHALL KNEEL BEFORE ME AND BEG FOR MERCY!!
HA HA HA HA HA HA HA HA HA
WILL THE NEW LORD OF TERROR DESTROY THE WORLD?
URD... THAT'S NOT YOU TALKING, IT'S SOME-THING OR *SOME-ONE* ELSE!
URD!!!
HEY, WHAT THE HECK IS GOIN' ON?
SOME KINDA JOKE?

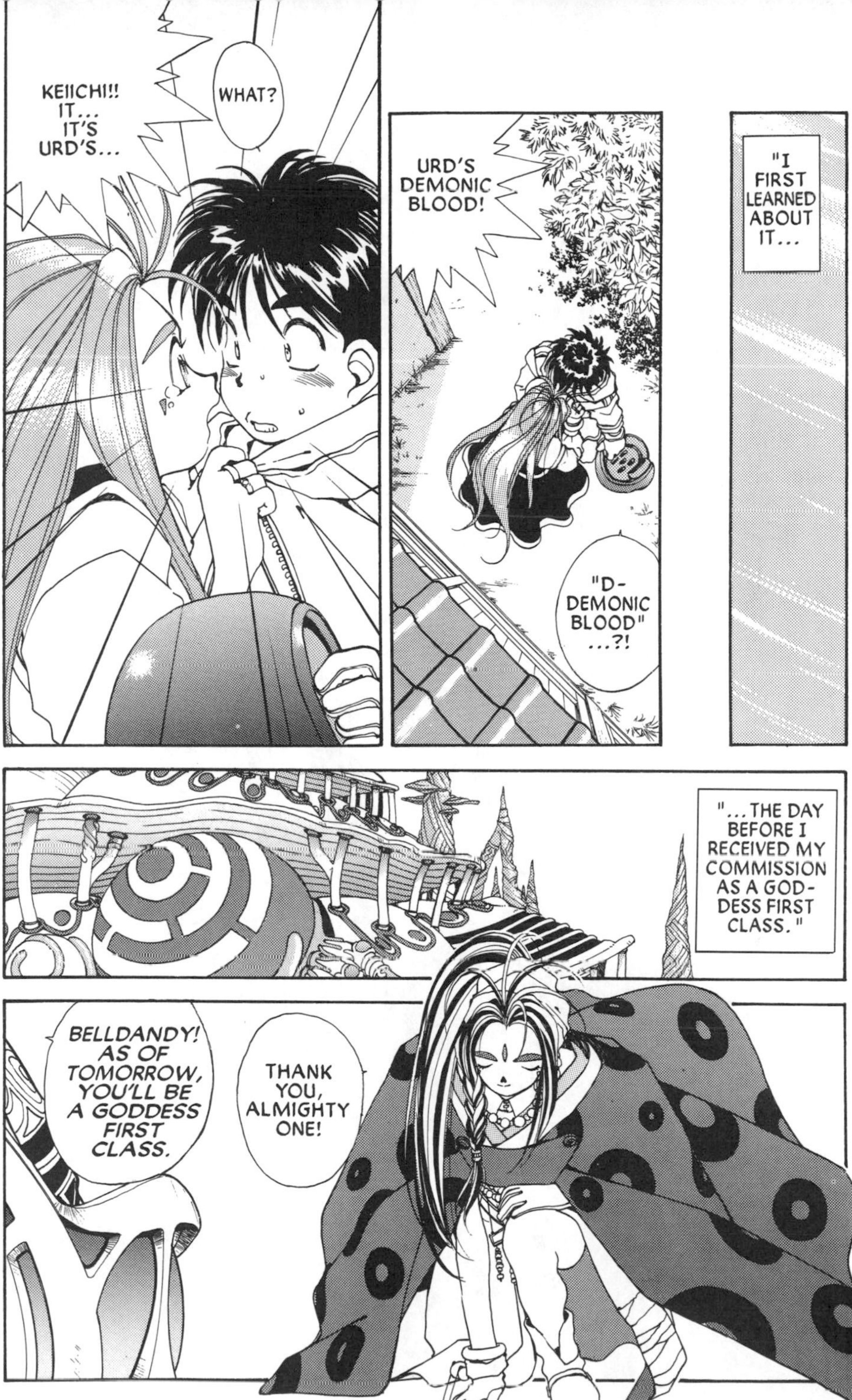
KEIICHI!! IT... IT'S URD'S...
WHAT?
URD'S DEMONIC BLOOD!
"D-DEMONIC BLOOD" ...?!
"I FIRST LEARNED ABOUT IT...
"... THE DAY BEFORE I RECEIVED MY COMMISSION AS A GOD-DESS FIRST CLASS."
BELLDANDY! AS OF TOMORROW, YOU'LL BE A GODDESS FIRST CLASS.
THANK YOU, ALMIGHTY ONE!

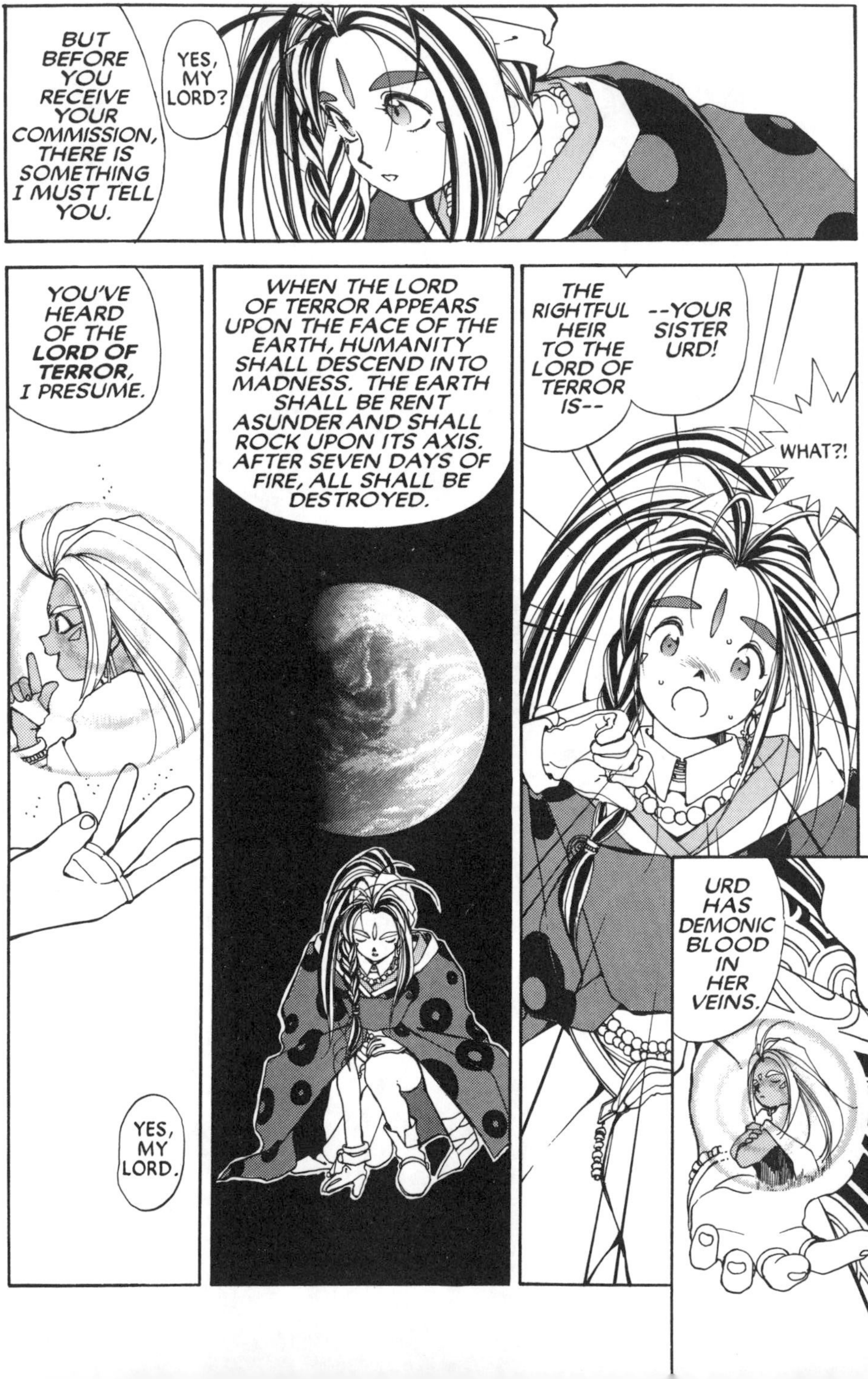
BUT BEFORE YOU RECEIVE YOUR COMMISSION, THERE IS SOMETHING I MUST TELL YOU.
YES, MY LORD?
YOU'VE HEARD OF THE **LORD OF TERROR**, I PRESUME.
YES, MY LORD.
WHEN THE LORD OF TERROR APPEARS UPON THE FACE OF THE EARTH, HUMANITY SHALL DESCEND INTO MADNESS. THE EARTH SHALL BE RENT ASUNDER AND SHALL ROCK UPON ITS AXIS. AFTER SEVEN DAYS OF FIRE, ALL SHALL BE DESTROYED.
THE RIGHTFUL HEIR TO THE LORD OF TERROR IS--
--YOUR SISTER URD!
WHAT?!
URD HAS DEMONIC BLOOD IN HER VEINS.

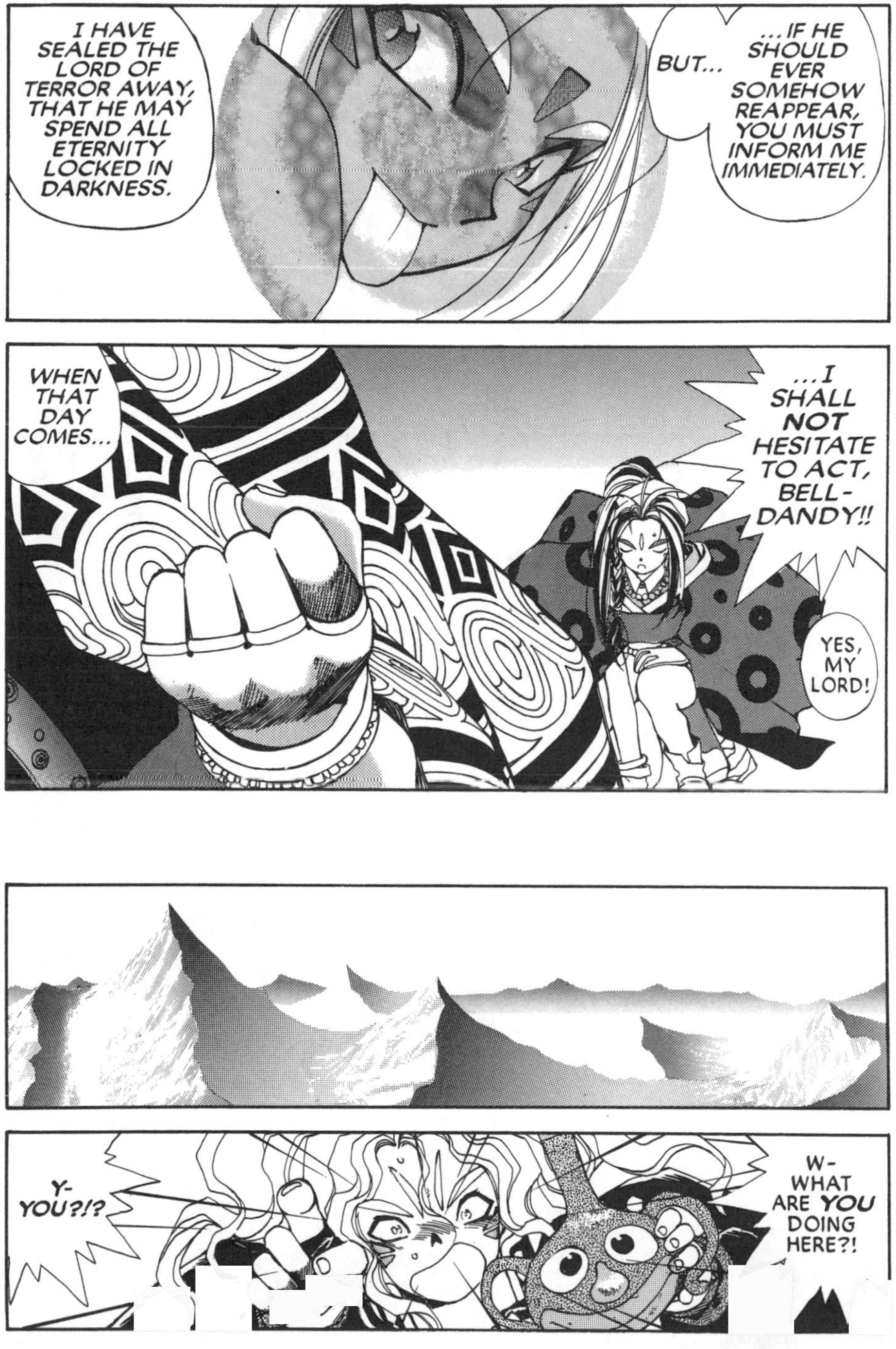
I HAVE SEALED THE LORD OF TERROR AWAY, THAT HE MAY SPEND ALL ETERNITY LOCKED IN DARKNESS.
BUT...
...IF HE SHOULD EVER SOMEHOW REAPPEAR, YOU MUST INFORM ME IMMEDIATELY.
WHEN THAT DAY COMES...
...I SHALL **NOT** HESITATE TO ACT, BELL-DANDY!!
YES, MY LORD!
Y-YOU?!?
W-WHAT ARE **YOU** DOING HERE?!

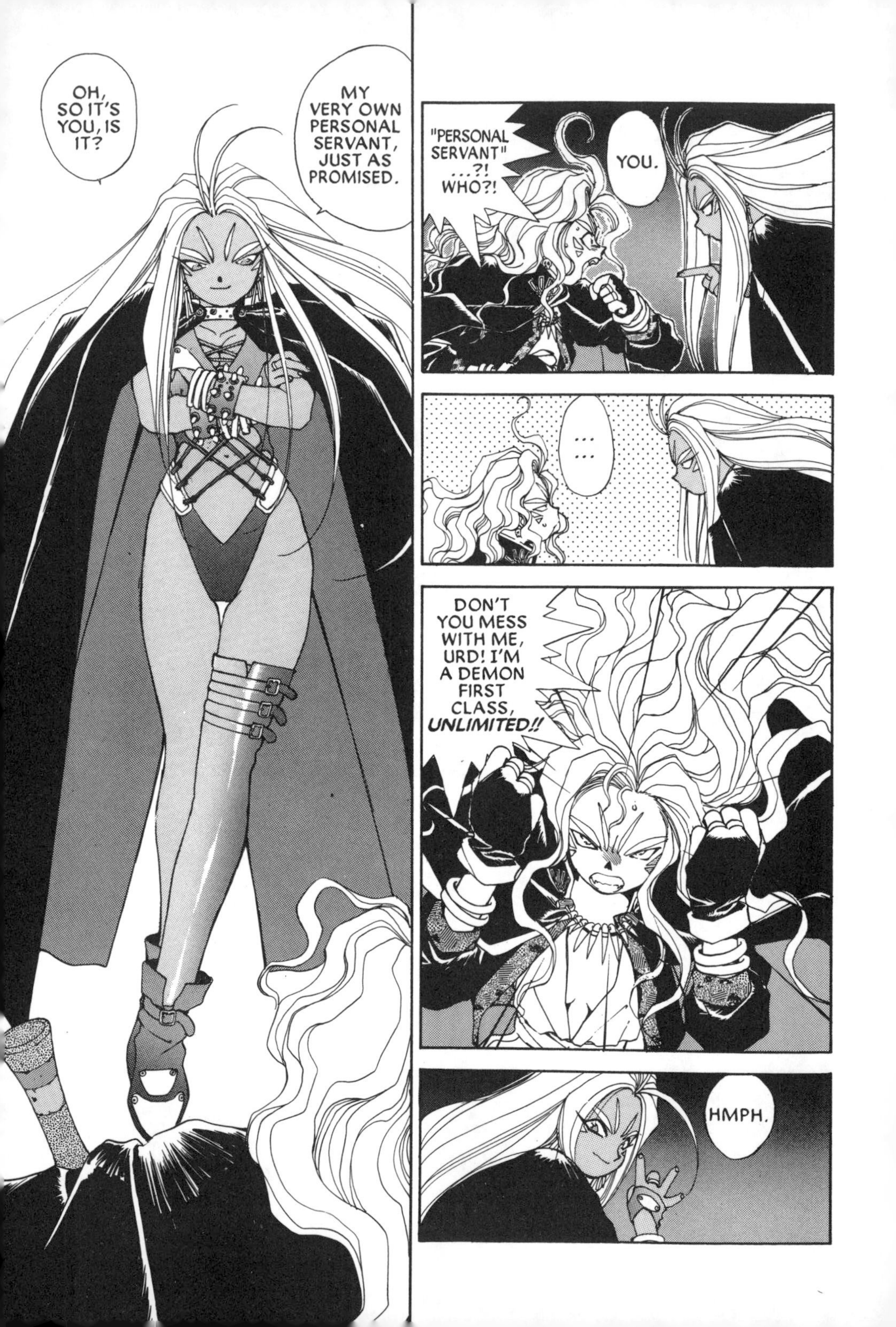
OH, SO IT'S YOU, IS IT?
MY VERY OWN PERSONAL SERVANT, JUST AS PROMISED.
"PERSONAL SERVANT" ...?! WHO?!
YOU.
... ...
DON'T YOU MESS WITH ME, URD! I'M A DEMON FIRST CLASS, *UNLIMITED!!*
HMPH.

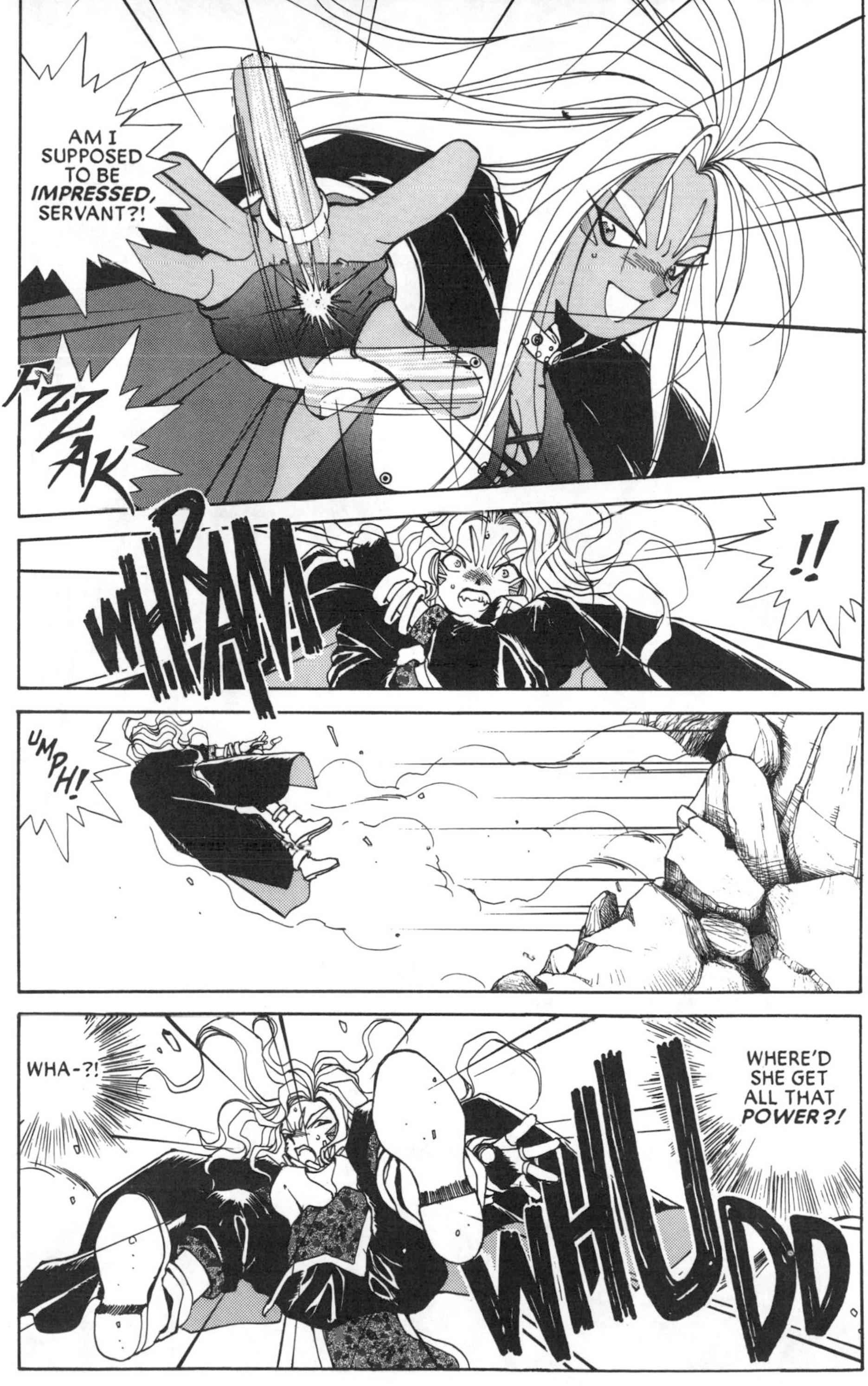
AM I SUPPOSED TO BE *IMPRESSED,* SERVANT?!
FZZZAK
WHRAM
!!
UMPH!
WHA-?!
WHERE'D SHE GET ALL THAT *POWER?!*
WHUDD

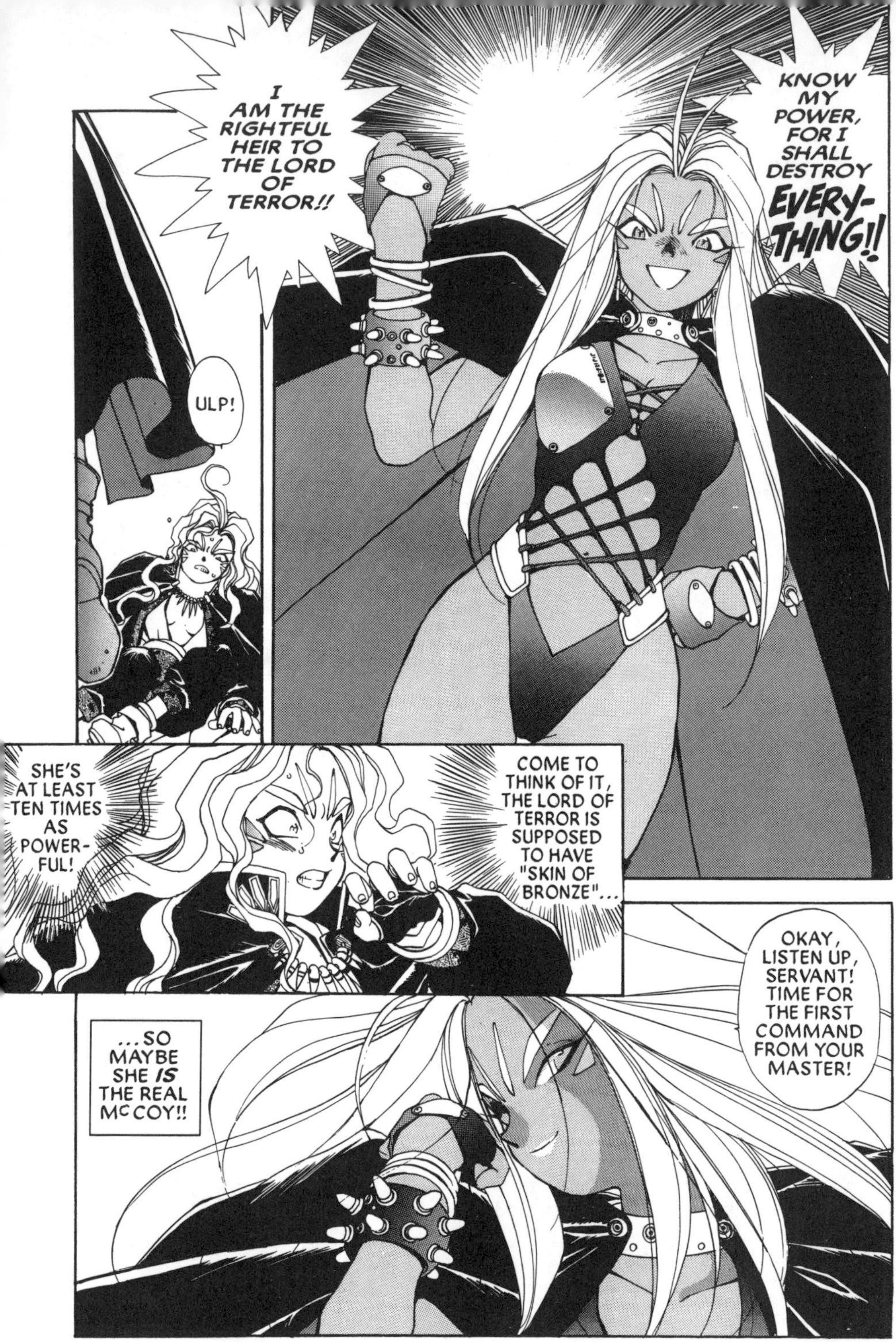
I AM THE RIGHTFUL HEIR TO THE LORD OF TERROR!!
KNOW MY POWER, FOR I SHALL DESTROY EVERY-THING!!
ULP!
SHE'S AT LEAST TEN TIMES AS POWER-FUL!
COME TO THINK OF IT, THE LORD OF TERROR IS SUPPOSED TO HAVE "SKIN OF BRONZE"...
...SO MAYBE SHE *IS* THE REAL McCOY!!
OKAY, LISTEN UP, SERVANT! TIME FOR THE FIRST COMMAND FROM YOUR MASTER!

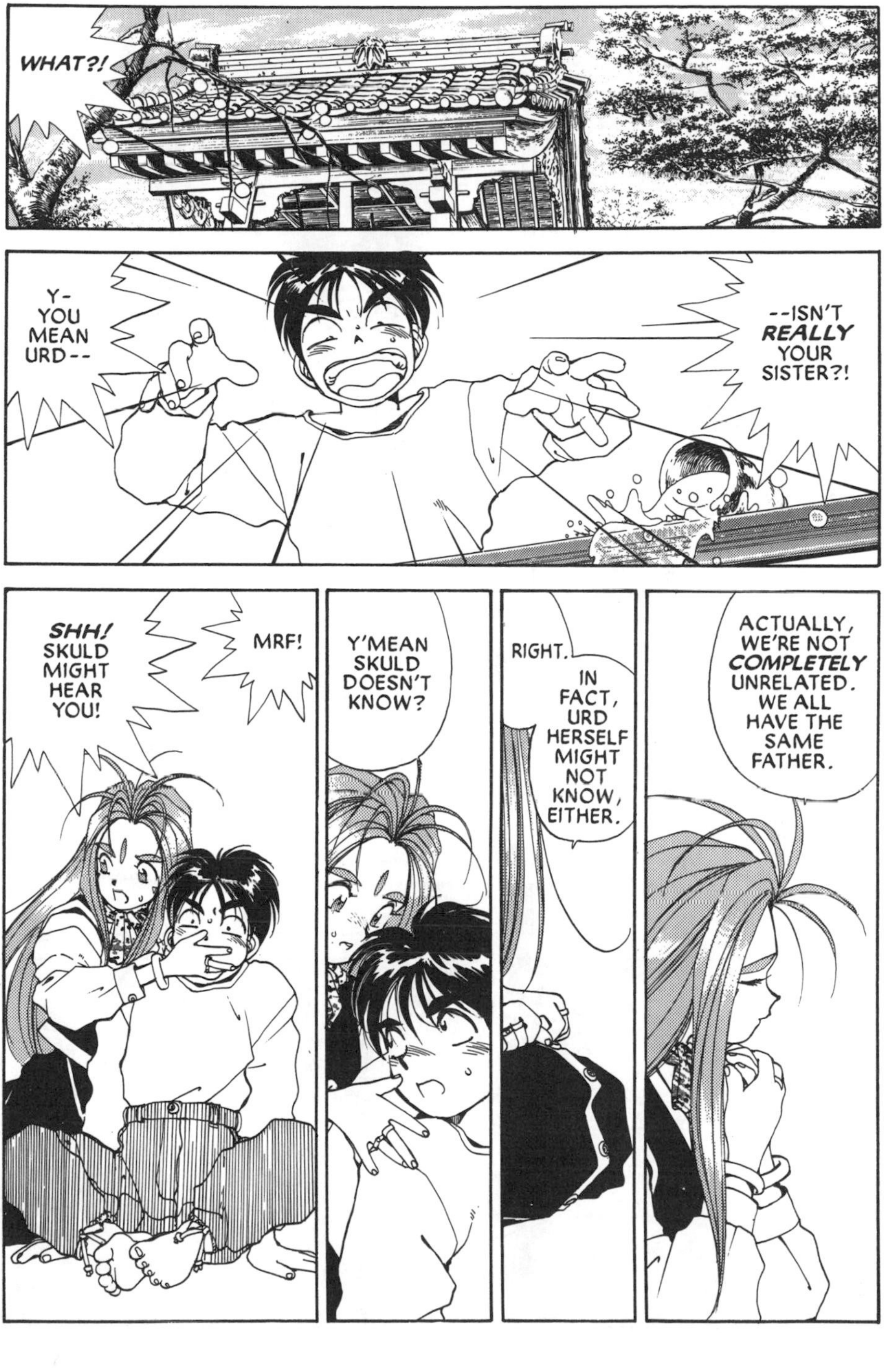
WHAT?!
Y- YOU MEAN URD--
--ISN'T REALLY YOUR SISTER?!
SHH! SKULD MIGHT HEAR YOU!
MRF!
Y'MEAN SKULD DOESN'T KNOW?
RIGHT.
IN FACT, URD HERSELF MIGHT NOT KNOW, EITHER.
ACTUALLY, WE'RE NOT COMPLETELY UNRELATED. WE ALL HAVE THE SAME FATHER.

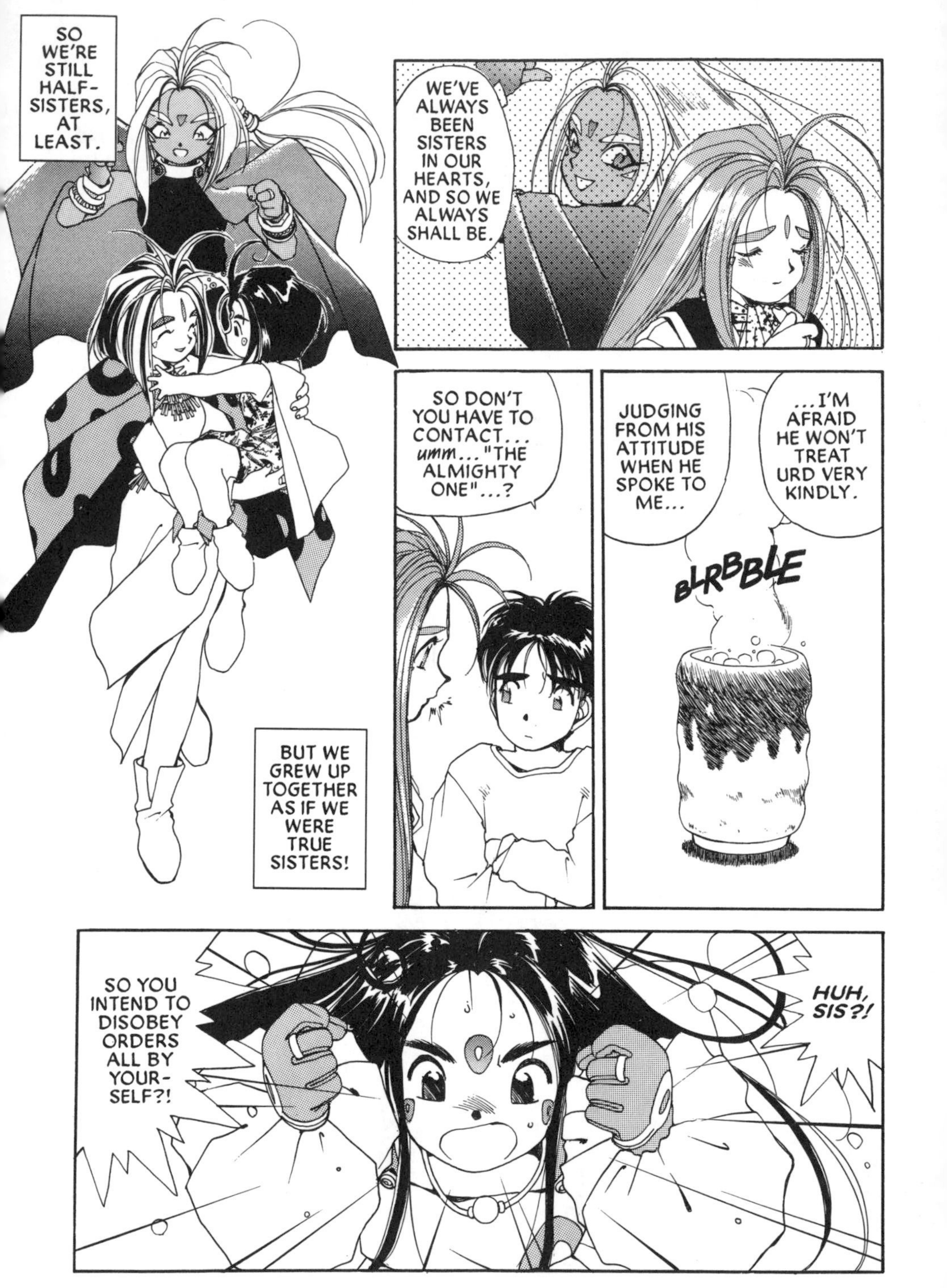
SO WE'RE STILL HALF-SISTERS, AT LEAST.
BUT WE GREW UP TOGETHER AS IF WE WERE TRUE SISTERS!
WE'VE ALWAYS BEEN SISTERS IN OUR HEARTS, AND SO WE ALWAYS SHALL BE.
SO DON'T YOU HAVE TO CONTACT... *umm*..."THE ALMIGHTY ONE"...?
...I'M AFRAID HE WON'T TREAT URD VERY KINDLY.
JUDGING FROM HIS ATTITUDE WHEN HE SPOKE TO ME...
BLRBBLE
SO YOU INTEND TO DISOBEY ORDERS ALL BY YOUR-SELF?!
HUH, SIS?!

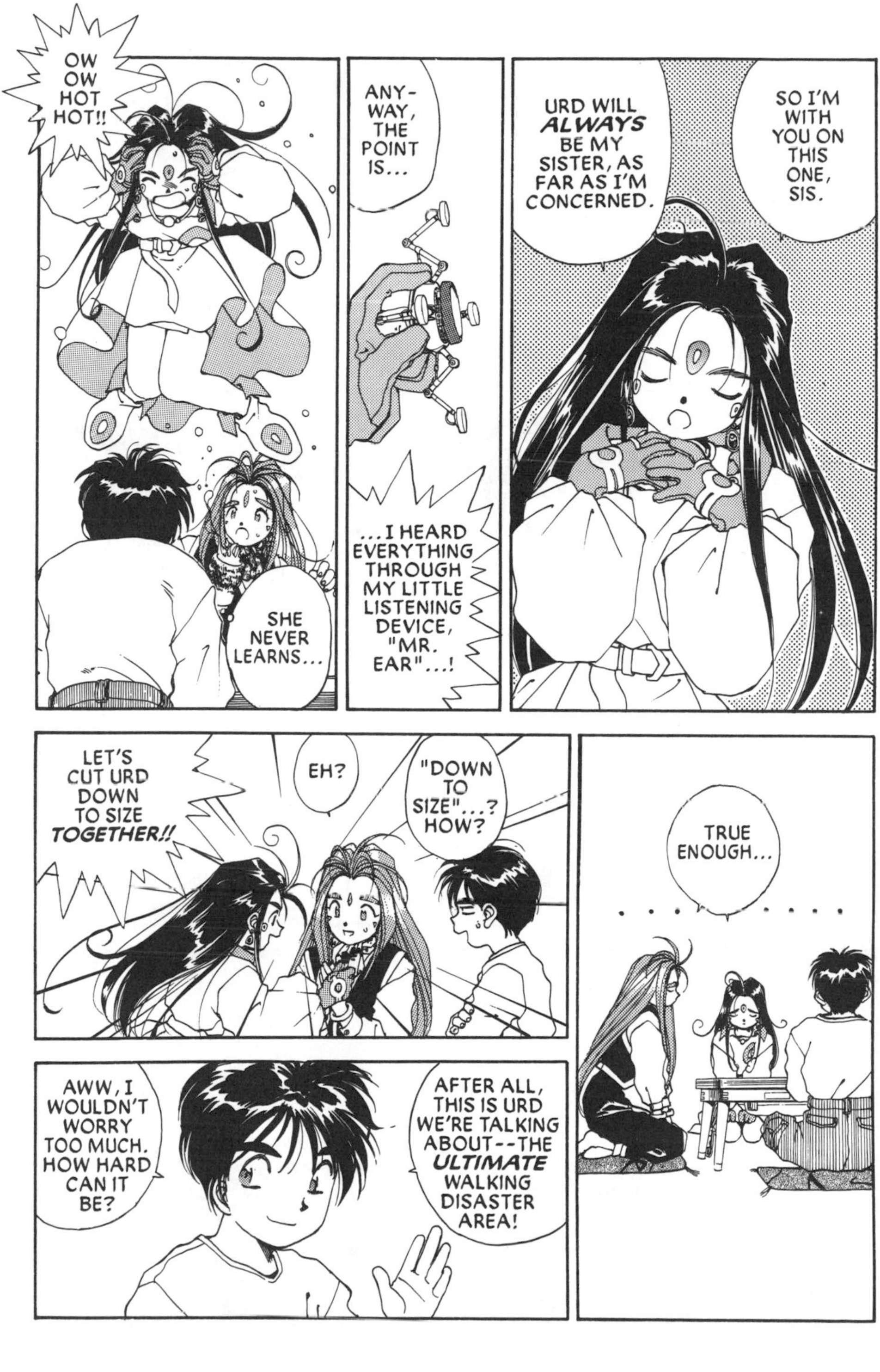
OW OW HOT HOT!!
SHE NEVER LEARNS...
ANY-WAY, THE POINT IS...
...I HEARD EVERYTHING THROUGH MY LITTLE LISTENING DEVICE, "MR. EAR"...!
URD WILL ALWAYS BE MY SISTER, AS FAR AS I'M CONCERNED.
SO I'M WITH YOU ON THIS ONE, SIS.
LET'S CUT URD DOWN TO SIZE TOGETHER!!
EH?
"DOWN TO SIZE"...? HOW?
AWW, I WOULDN'T WORRY TOO MUCH. HOW HARD CAN IT BE?
AFTER ALL, THIS IS URD WE'RE TALKING ABOUT--THE ULTIMATE WALKING DISASTER AREA!
TRUE ENOUGH...
. . . .

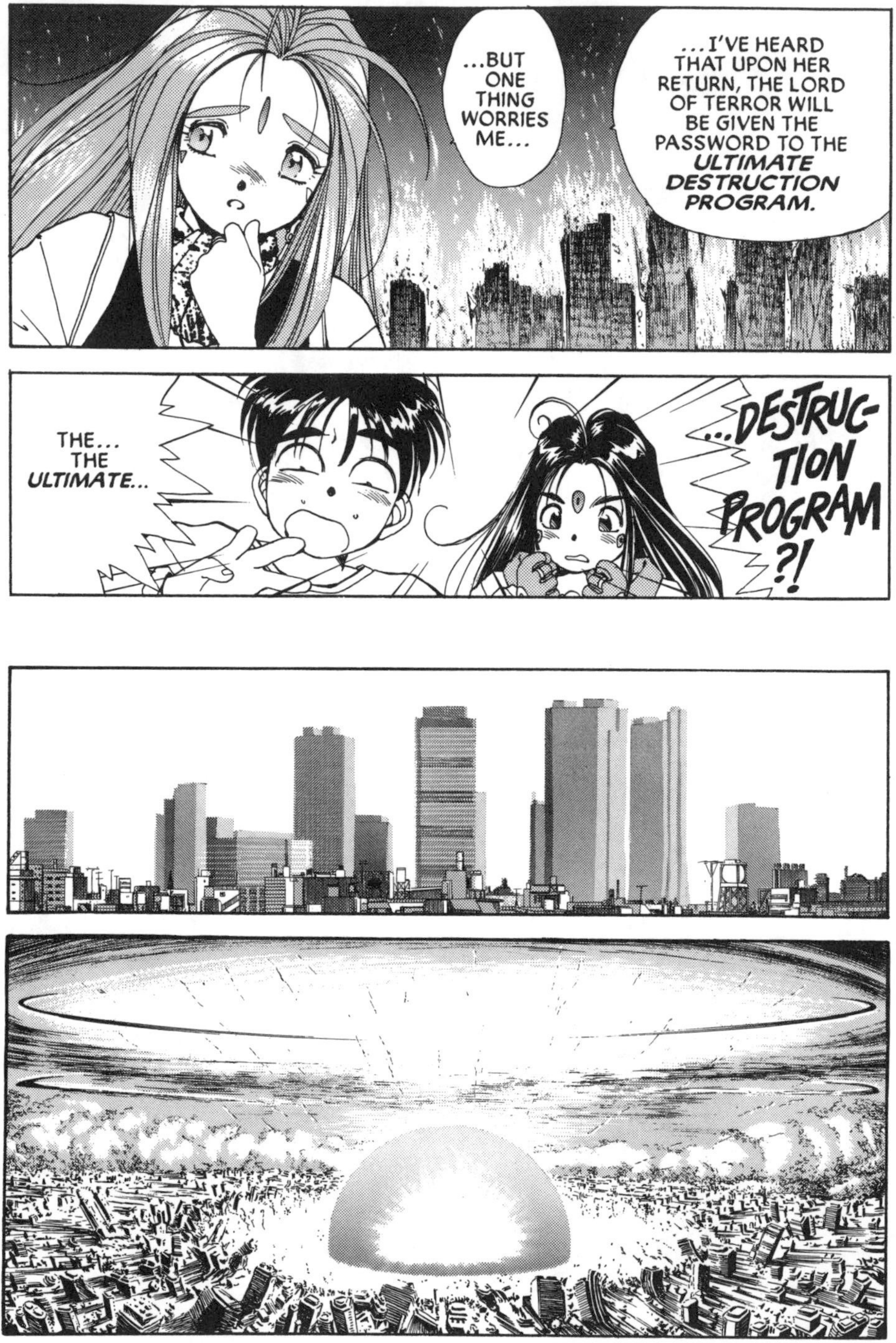
...BUT ONE THING WORRIES ME...
...I'VE HEARD THAT UPON HER RETURN, THE LORD OF TERROR WILL BE GIVEN THE PASSWORD TO THE *ULTIMATE DESTRUCTION PROGRAM.*
THE... THE *ULTIMATE...*
...DESTRUCTION PROGRAM?!

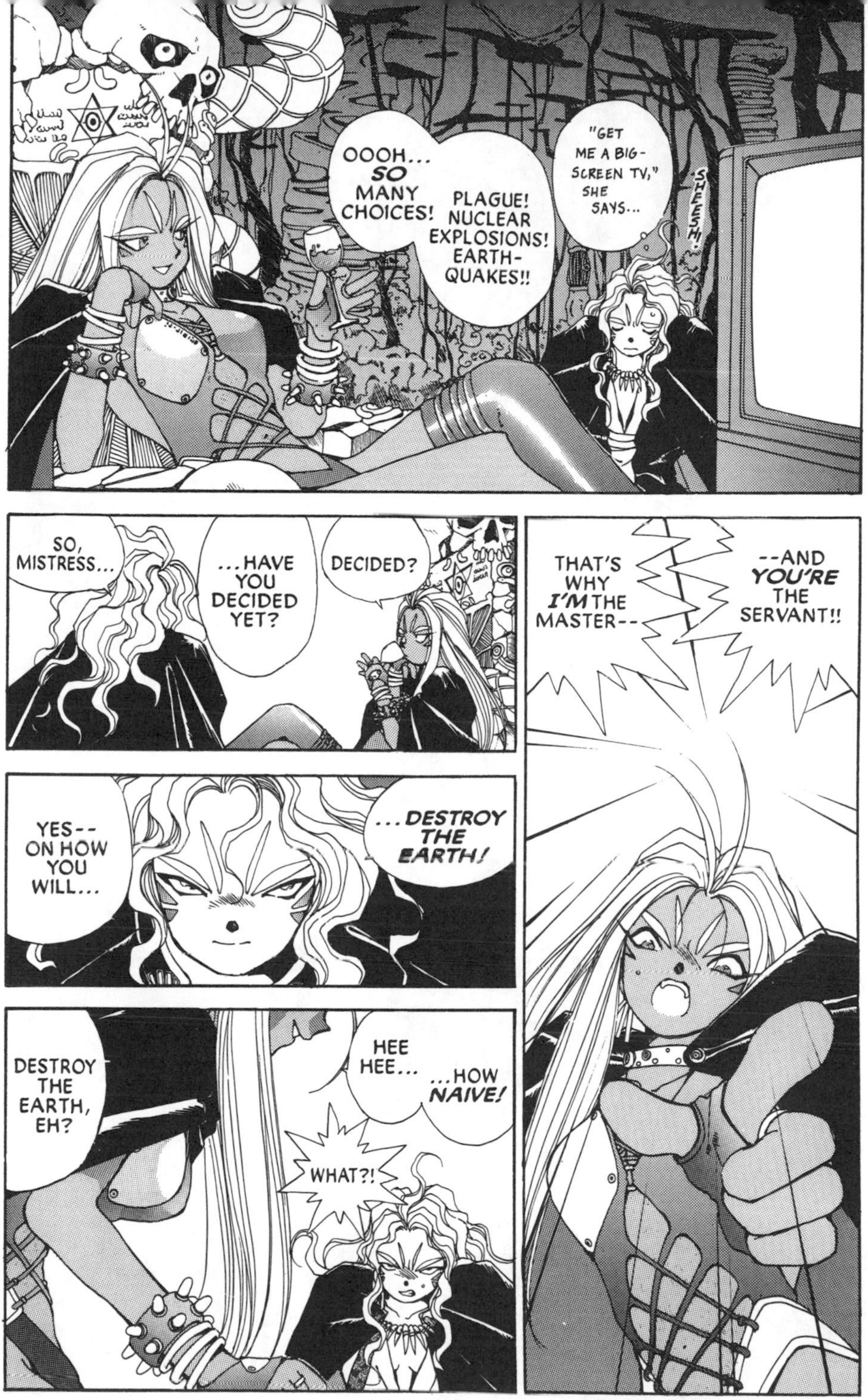
OOOH... SO MANY CHOICES!
PLAGUE! NUCLEAR EXPLOSIONS! EARTH-QUAKES!!
"GET ME A BIG-SCREEN TV," SHE SAYS...
SHEESH!
SO, MISTRESS...
...HAVE YOU DECIDED YET?
DECIDED?
YES-- ON HOW YOU WILL...
...DESTROY THE EARTH!
DESTROY THE EARTH, EH?
HEE HEE...
...HOW NAIVE!
WHAT?!
THAT'S WHY I'M THE MASTER--
--AND YOU'RE THE SERVANT!!

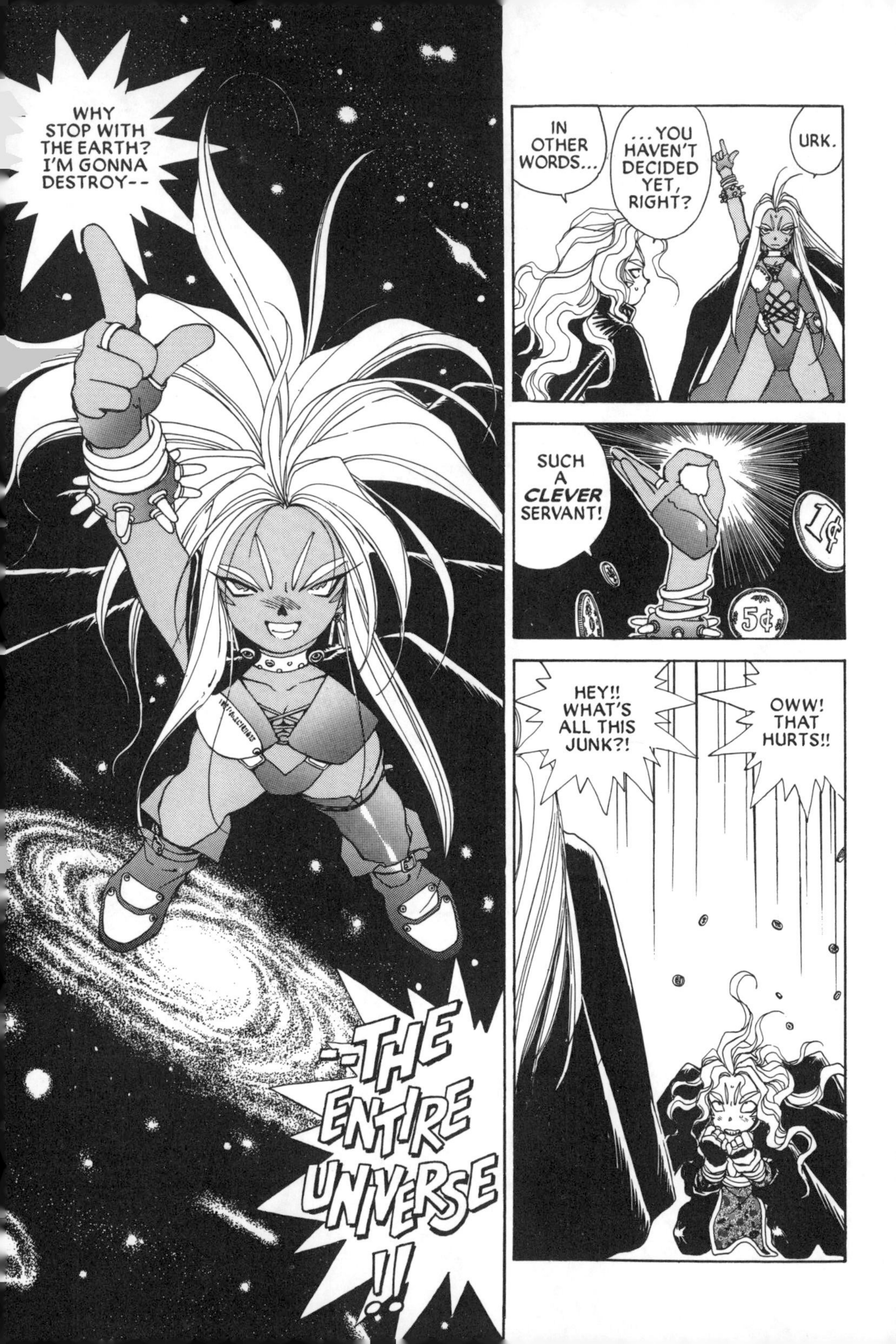
WHY STOP WITH THE EARTH? I'M GONNA DESTROY--
--THE ENTIRE UNIVERSE !!
IN OTHER WORDS...
...YOU HAVEN'T DECIDED YET, RIGHT?
URK.
SUCH A *CLEVER* SERVANT!
1¢
5¢
HEY!! WHAT'S ALL THIS JUNK?!
OWW! THAT HURTS!!

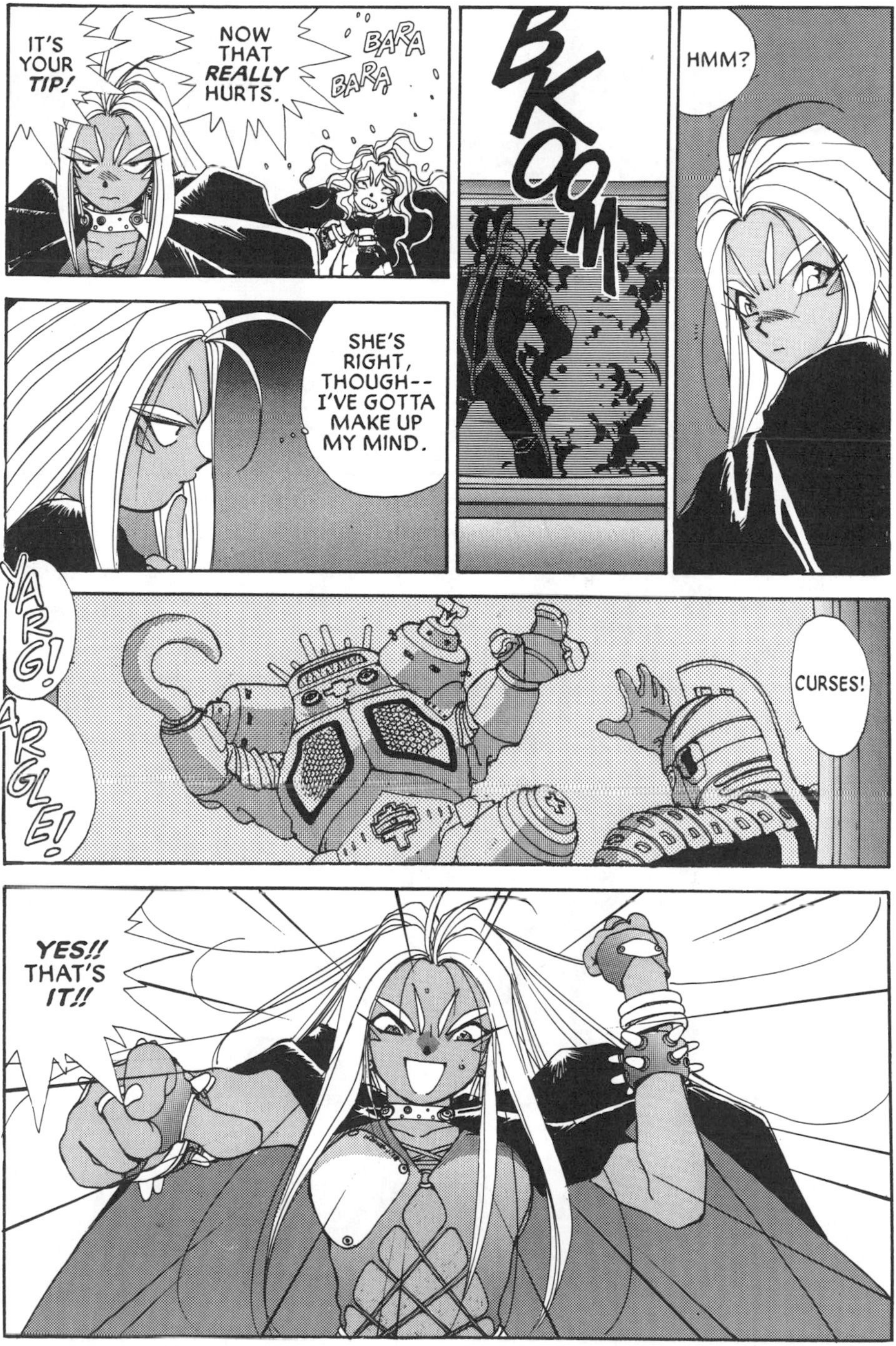
IT'S YOUR *TIP!*
NOW THAT *REALLY* HURTS.
BARA BARA
BKOOM
HMM?
SHE'S RIGHT, THOUGH-- I'VE GOTTA MAKE UP MY MIND.
YARG! ARGLE!
CURSES!
YES!! THAT'S IT!!

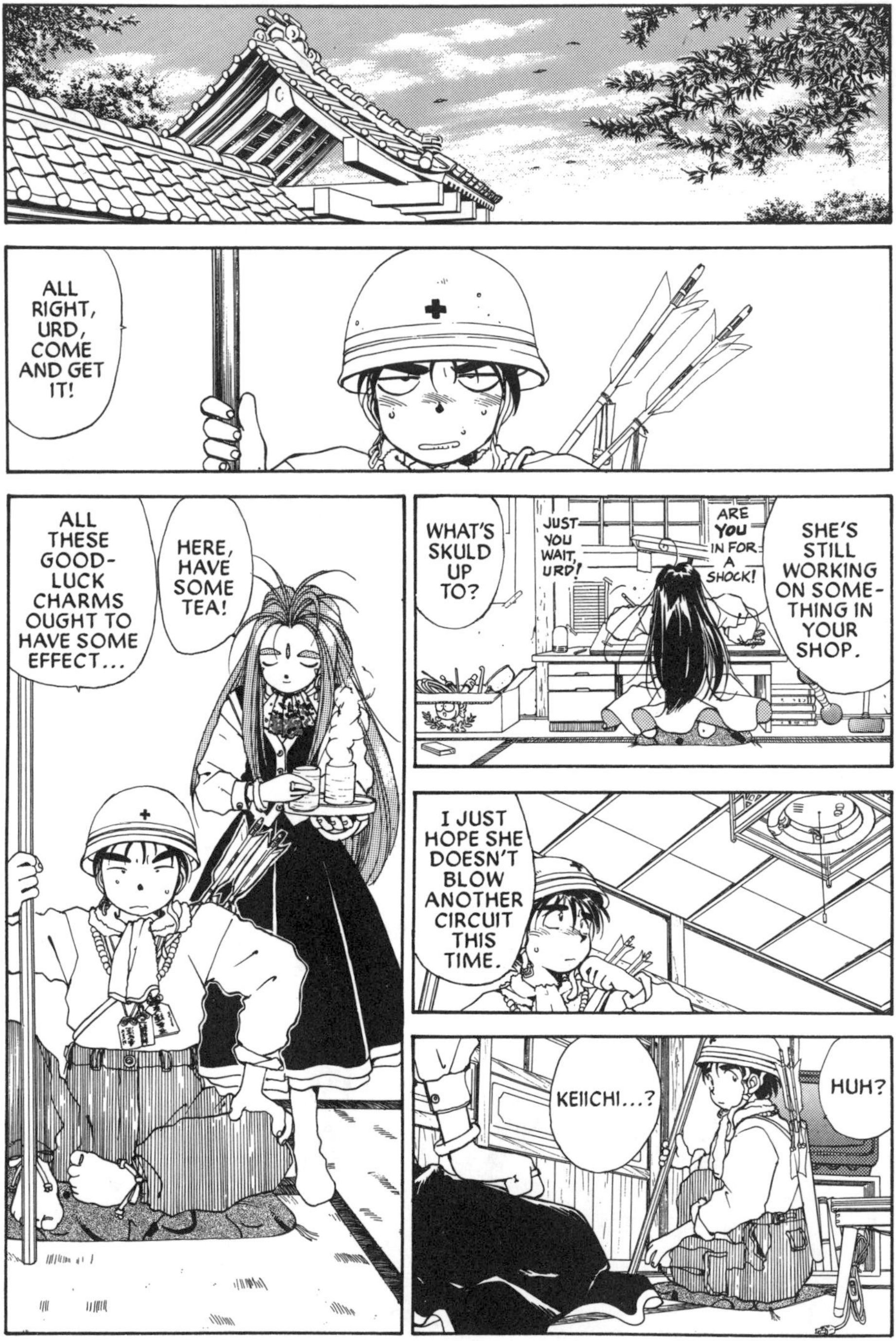
ALL RIGHT, URD, COME AND GET IT!
ALL THESE GOOD-LUCK CHARMS OUGHT TO HAVE SOME EFFECT...
HERE, HAVE SOME TEA!
WHAT'S SKULD UP TO?
JUST YOU WAIT, URD!
ARE YOU IN FOR A SHOCK!
SHE'S STILL WORKING ON SOMETHING IN YOUR SHOP.
I JUST HOPE SHE DOESN'T BLOW ANOTHER CIRCUIT THIS TIME.
KEIICHI...?
HUH?

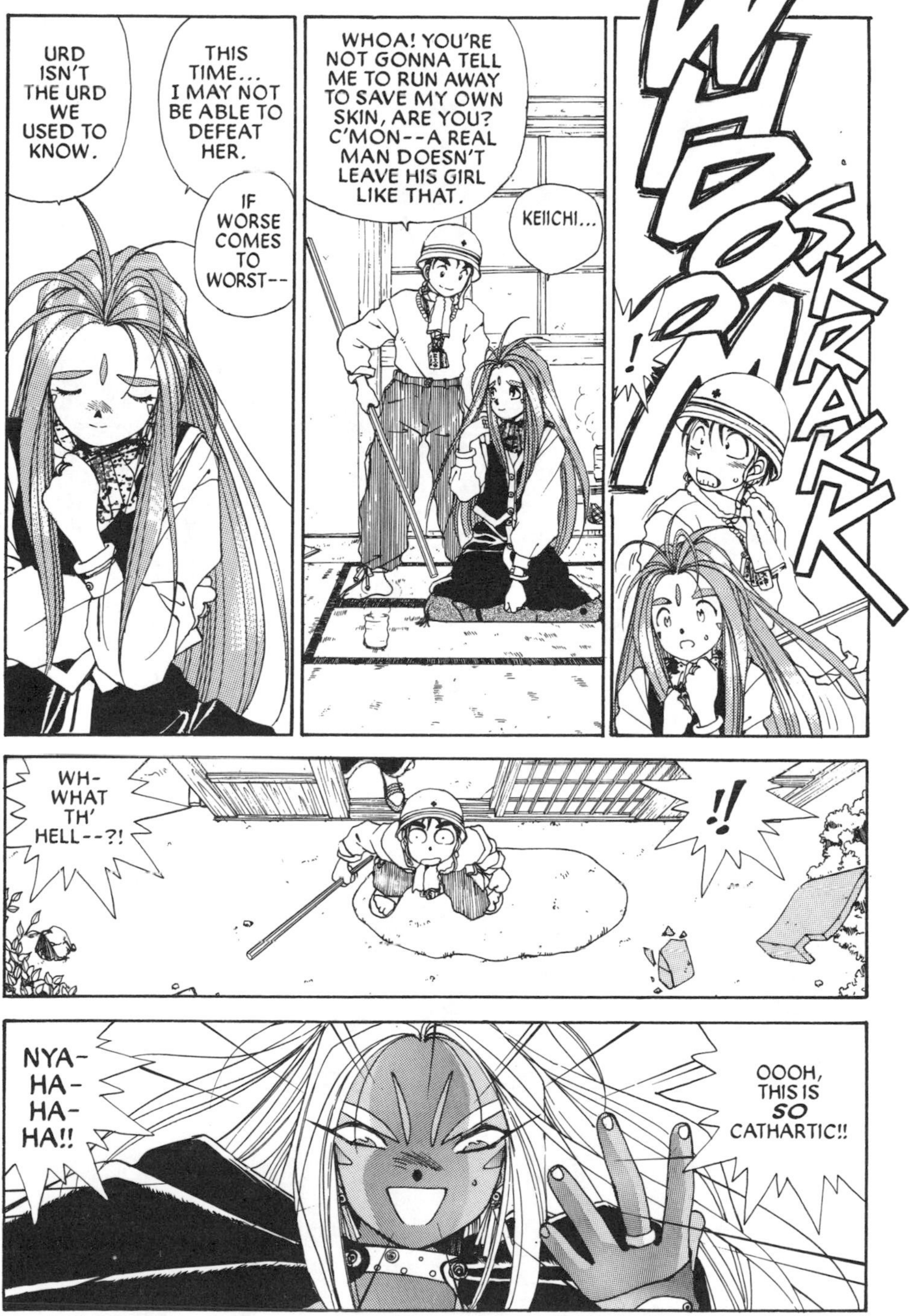
URD ISN'T THE URD WE USED TO KNOW.
THIS TIME... I MAY NOT BE ABLE TO DEFEAT HER.
IF WORSE COMES TO WORST--
WHOA! YOU'RE NOT GONNA TELL ME TO RUN AWAY TO SAVE MY OWN SKIN, ARE YOU? C'MON--A REAL MAN DOESN'T LEAVE HIS GIRL LIKE THAT.
KEIICHI...
WHOOM
SKRAKK
!
WH- WHAT TH' HELL--?!
!!
NYA- HA- HA- HA!!
OOOH, THIS IS *SO* CATHARTIC!!

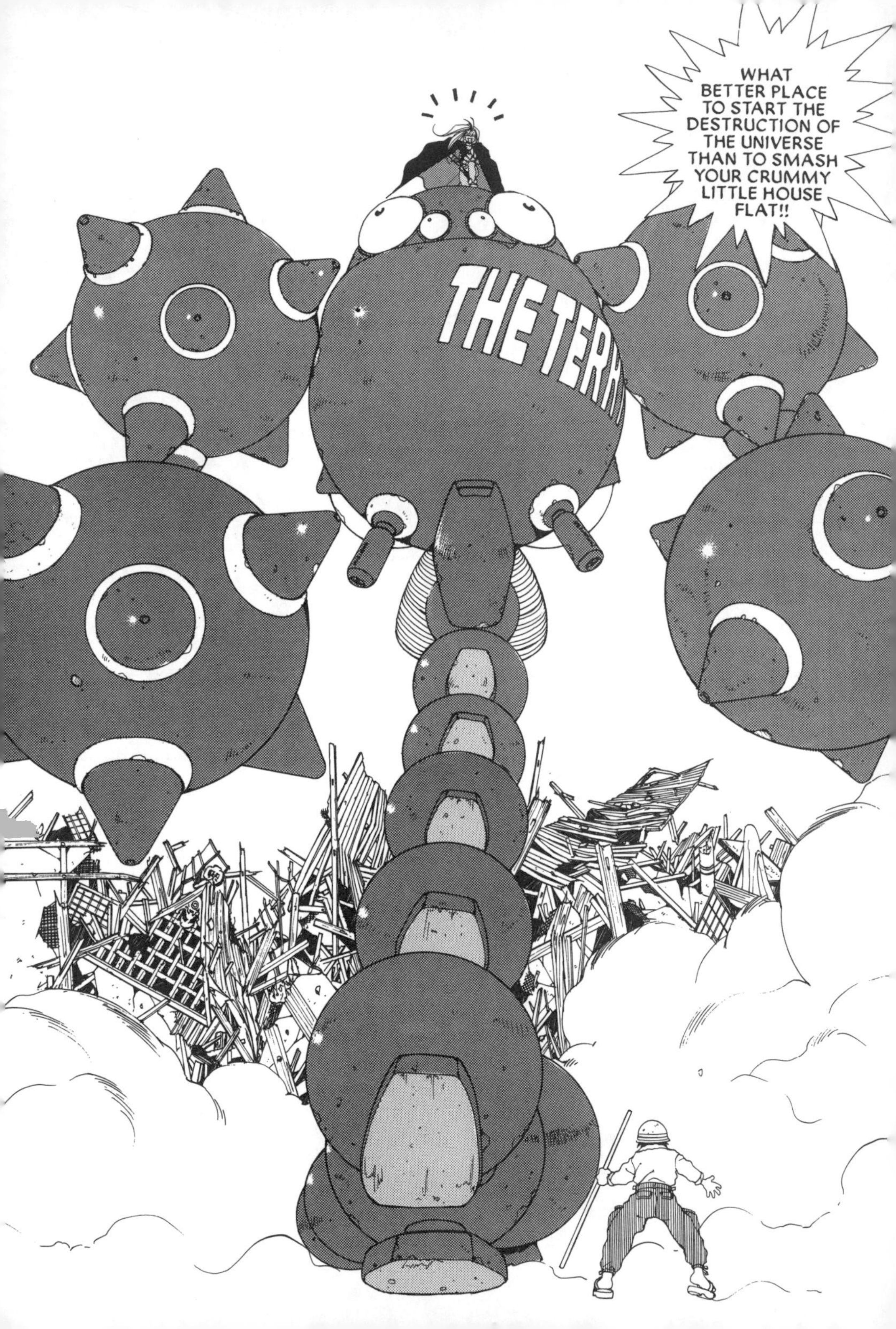
WHAT BETTER PLACE TO START THE DESTRUCTION OF THE UNIVERSE THAN TO SMASH YOUR CRUMMY LITTLE HOUSE FLAT!!
THE TERR

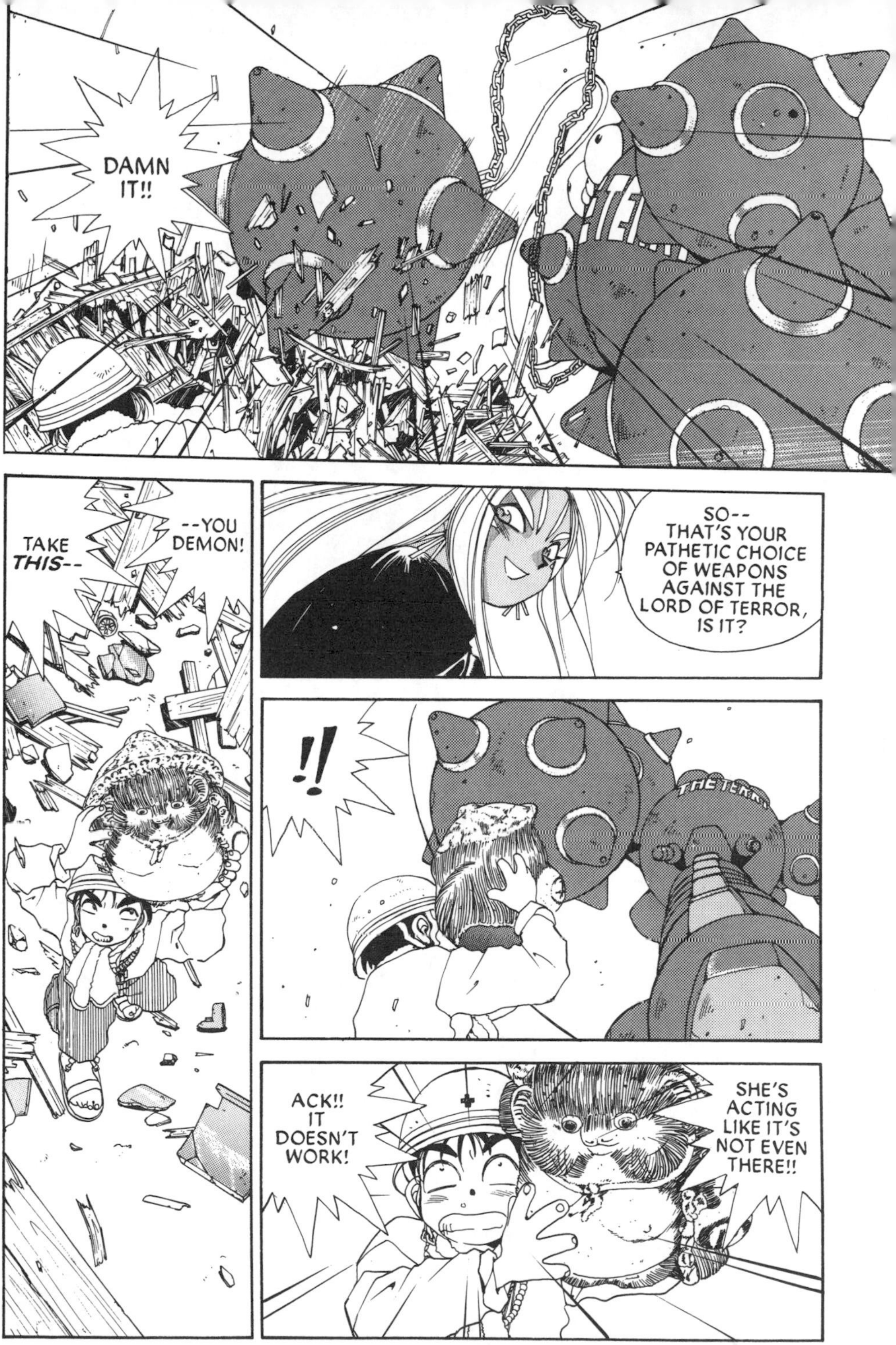
DAMN IT!!
TAKE THIS--
--YOU DEMON!
SO-- THAT'S YOUR PATHETIC CHOICE OF WEAPONS AGAINST THE LORD OF TERROR, IS IT?
!!
ACK!! IT DOESN'T WORK!
SHE'S ACTING LIKE IT'S NOT EVEN THERE!!

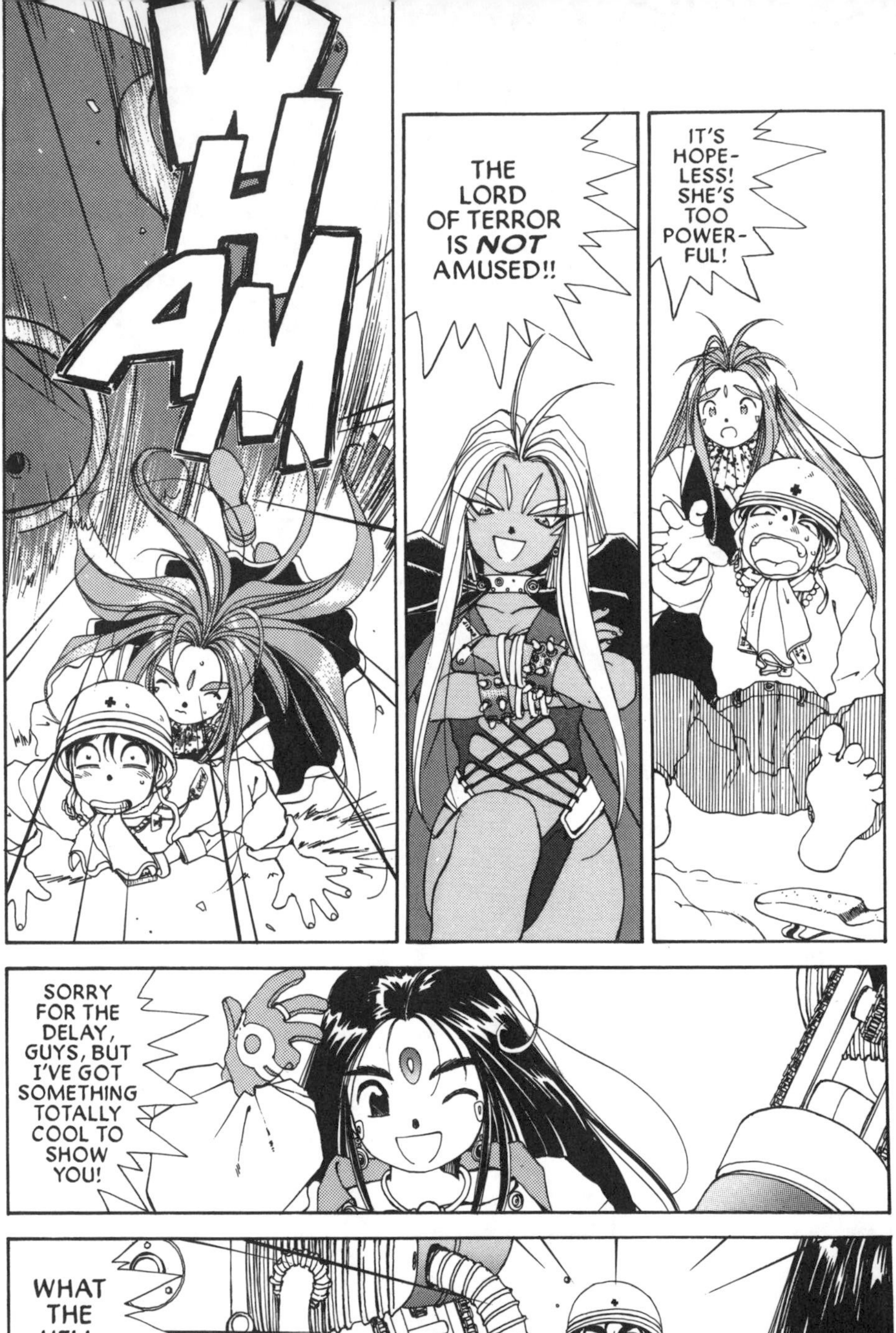
WHAM
THE LORD OF TERROR IS NOT AMUSED!!
IT'S HOPE-LESS! SHE'S TOO POWER-FUL!
SORRY FOR THE DELAY, GUYS, BUT I'VE GOT SOMETHING TOTALLY COOL TO SHOW YOU!
WHAT THE HELL IS THAT?!

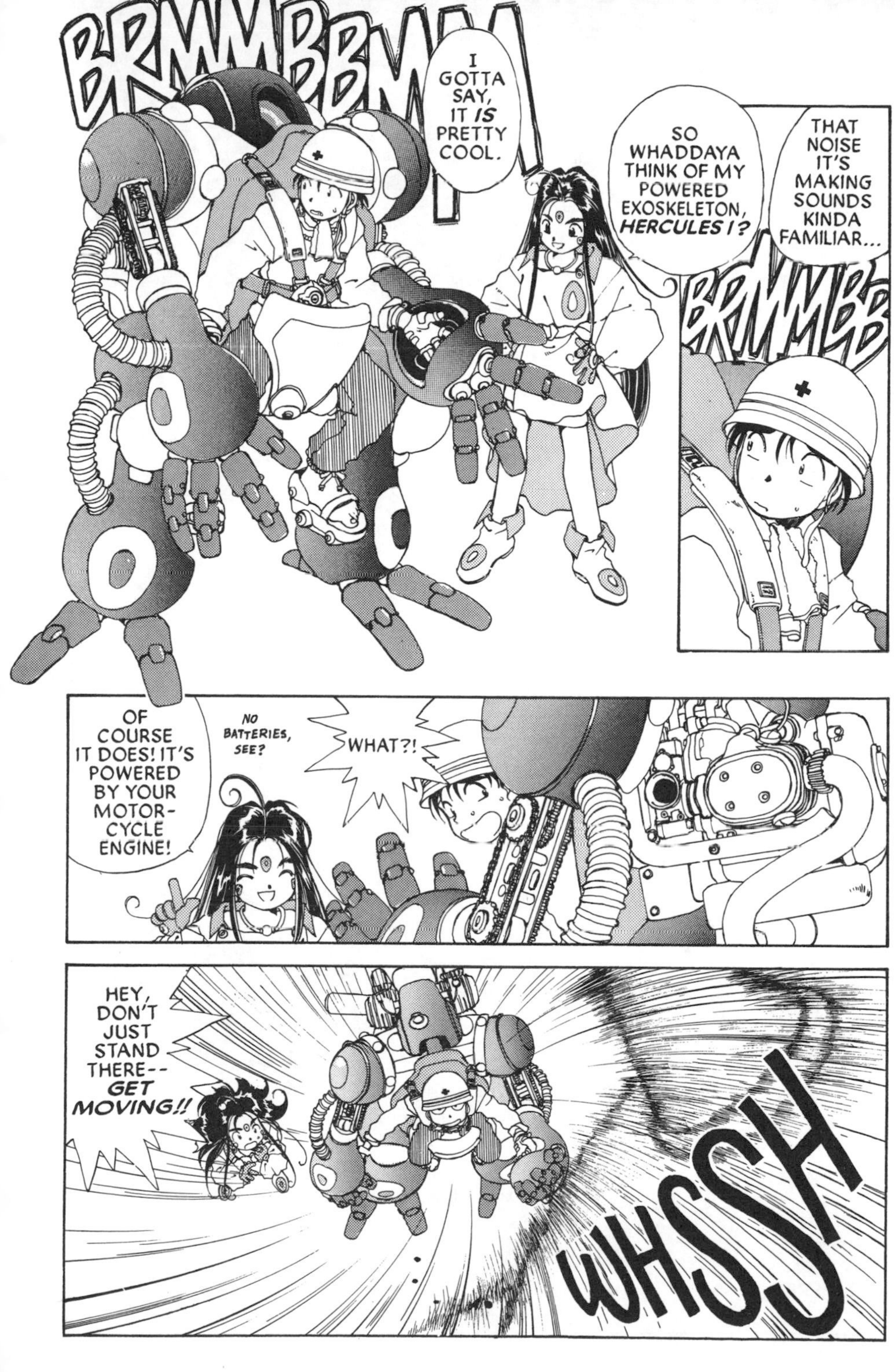
BRMMBBMM
I GOTTA SAY, IT *IS* PRETTY COOL.
SO WHADDAYA THINK OF MY POWERED EXOSKELETON, ***HERCULES!?***
THAT NOISE IT'S MAKING SOUNDS KINDA FAMILIAR...
BRMMBB
OF COURSE IT DOES! IT'S POWERED BY YOUR MOTOR-CYCLE ENGINE!
NO BATTERIES, SEE?
WHAT?!
HEY, DON'T JUST STAND THERE-- ***GET MOVING!!***
WHSSH

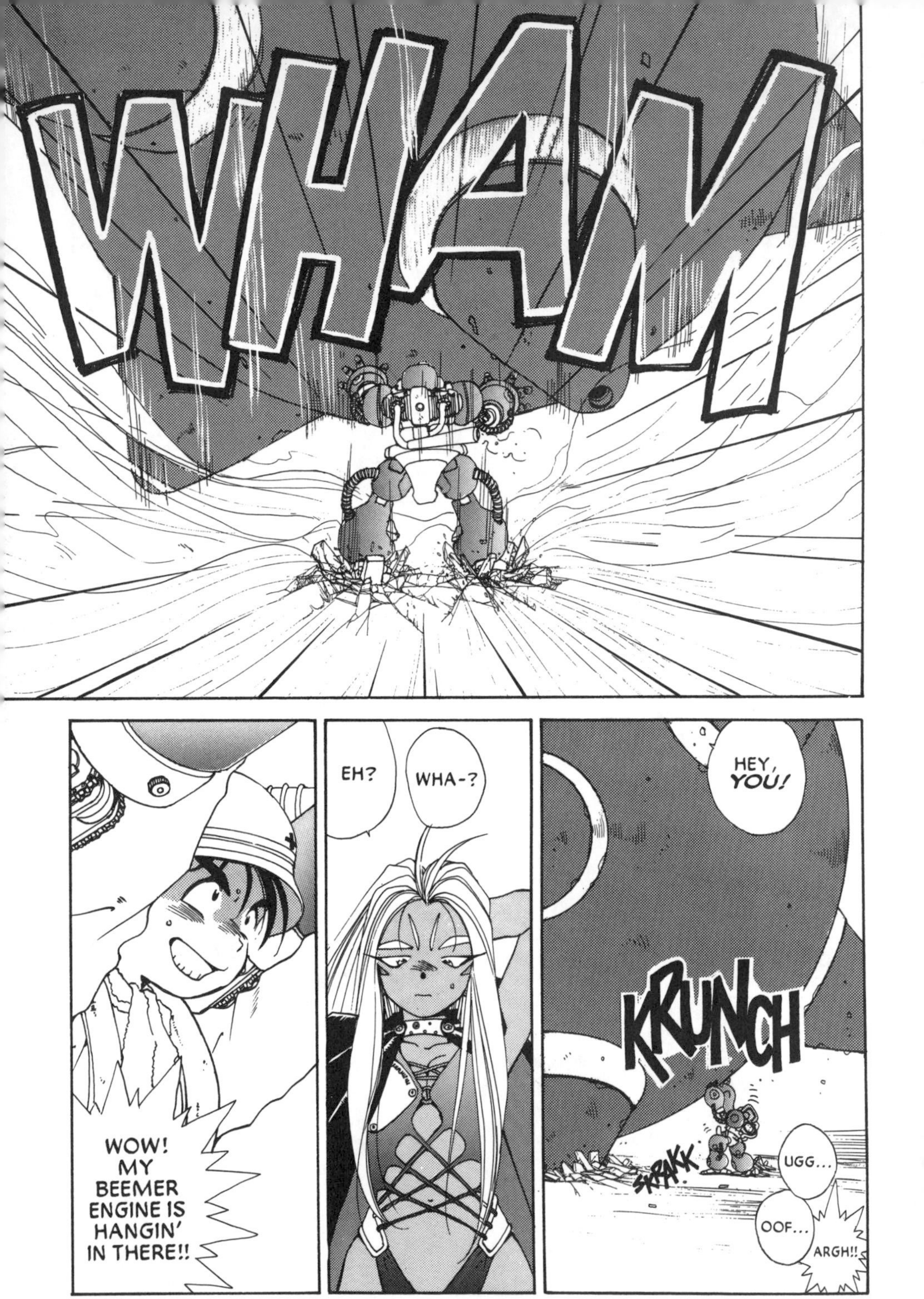
WHAM
WOW! MY BEEMER ENGINE IS HANGIN' IN THERE!!
EH?
WHA-?
HEY, YOU!
KRUNCH
SKRAKK
UGG...
OOF...
ARGH!!

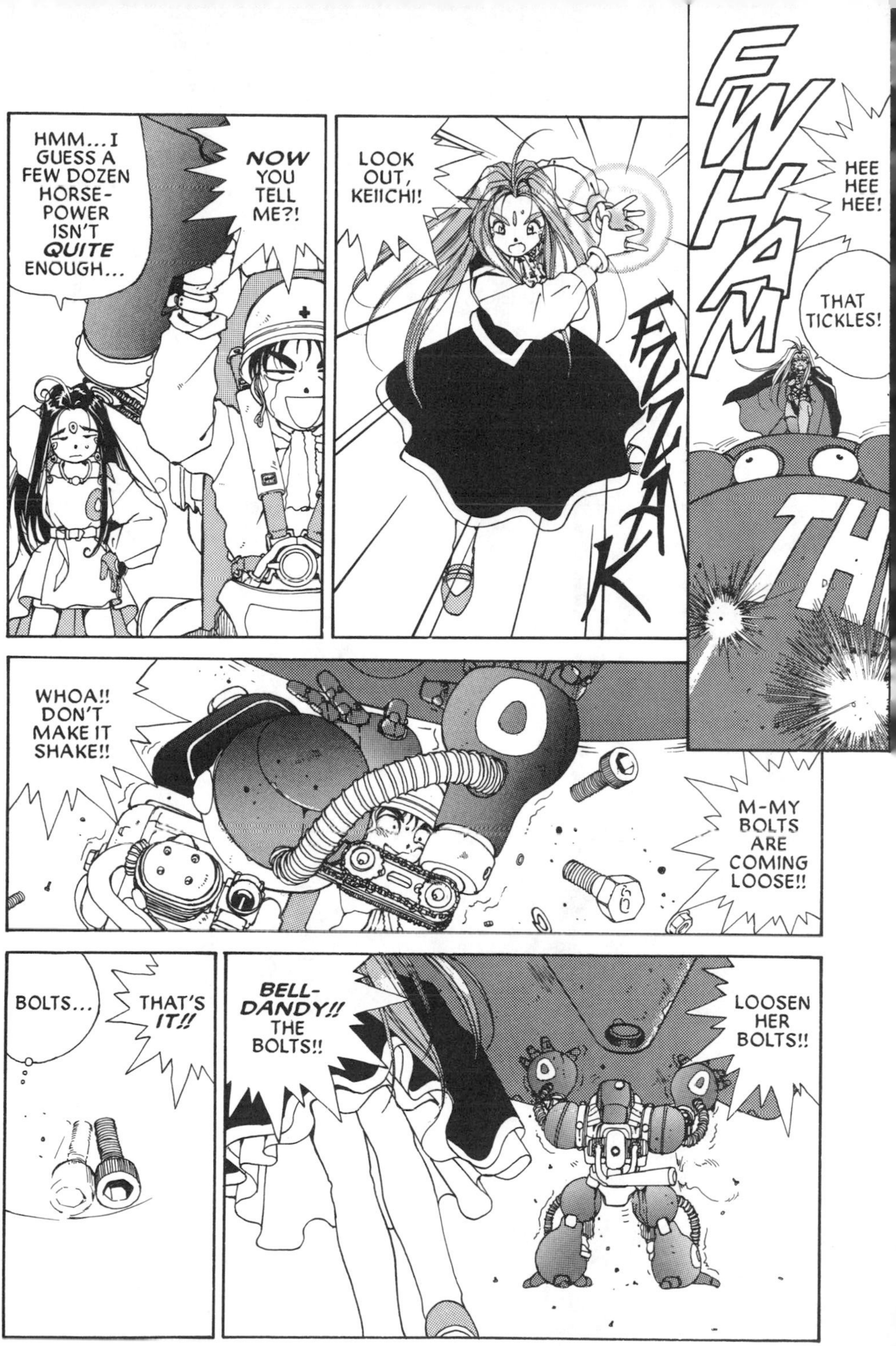
HMM...I GUESS A FEW DOZEN HORSE-POWER ISN'T *QUITE* ENOUGH...
NOW YOU TELL ME?!
LOOK OUT, KEIICHI!
FZZZAK
FWHAM
HEE HEE HEE!
THAT TICKLES!
TH
WHOA!! DON'T MAKE IT SHAKE!!
M-MY BOLTS ARE COMING LOOSE!!
BOLTS...
THAT'S *IT!!*
BELL-DANDY!! THE BOLTS!!
LOOSEN HER BOLTS!!

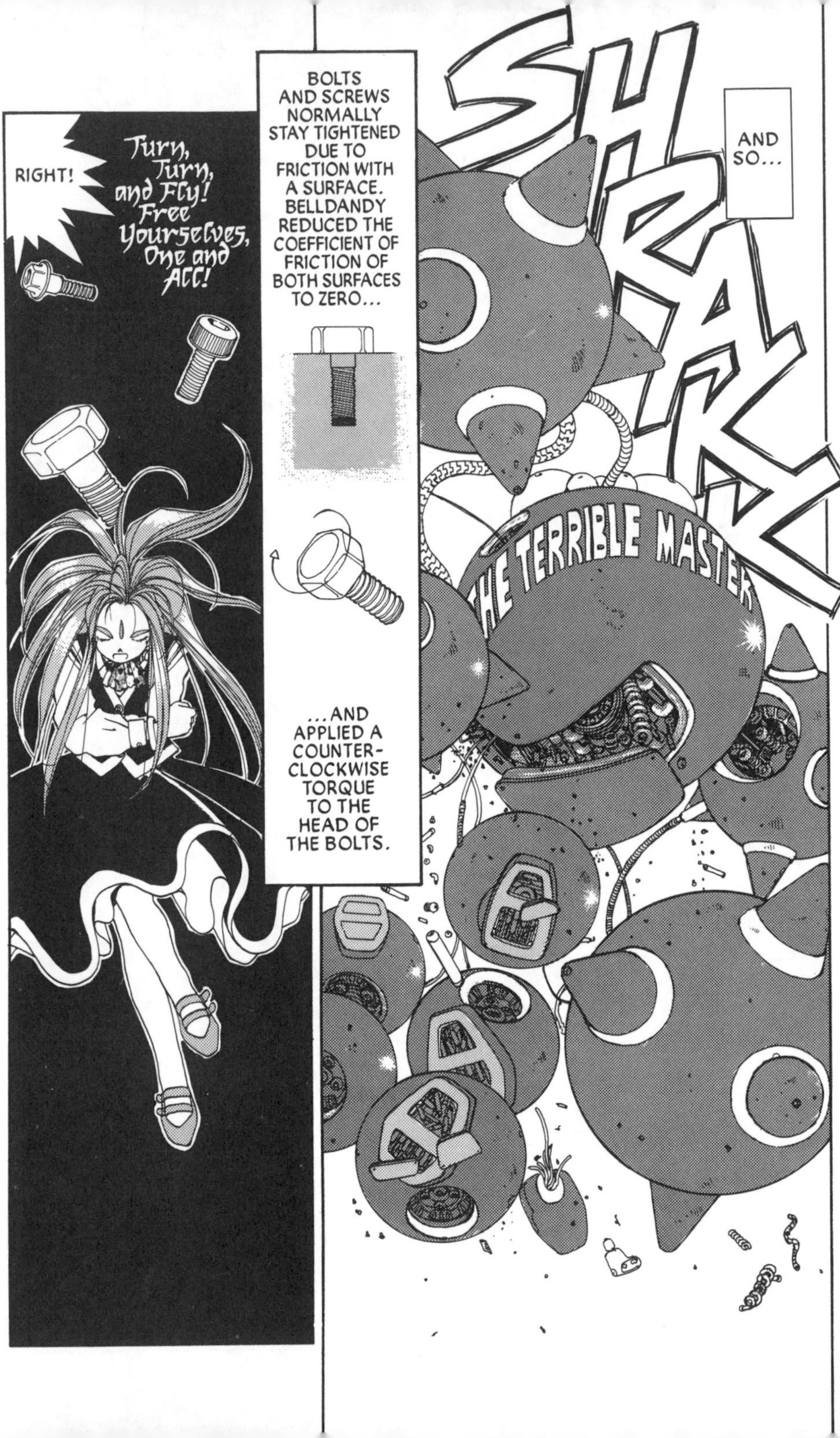
RIGHT!
Turn, Turn, and Fly! Free Yourselves, One and All!
BOLTS AND SCREWS NORMALLY STAY TIGHTENED DUE TO FRICTION WITH A SURFACE. BELLDANDY REDUCED THE COEFFICIENT OF FRICTION OF BOTH SURFACES TO ZERO...
...AND APPLIED A COUNTER-CLOCKWISE TORQUE TO THE HEAD OF THE BOLTS.
AND SO...
SHRAKY
THE TERRIBLE MASTER

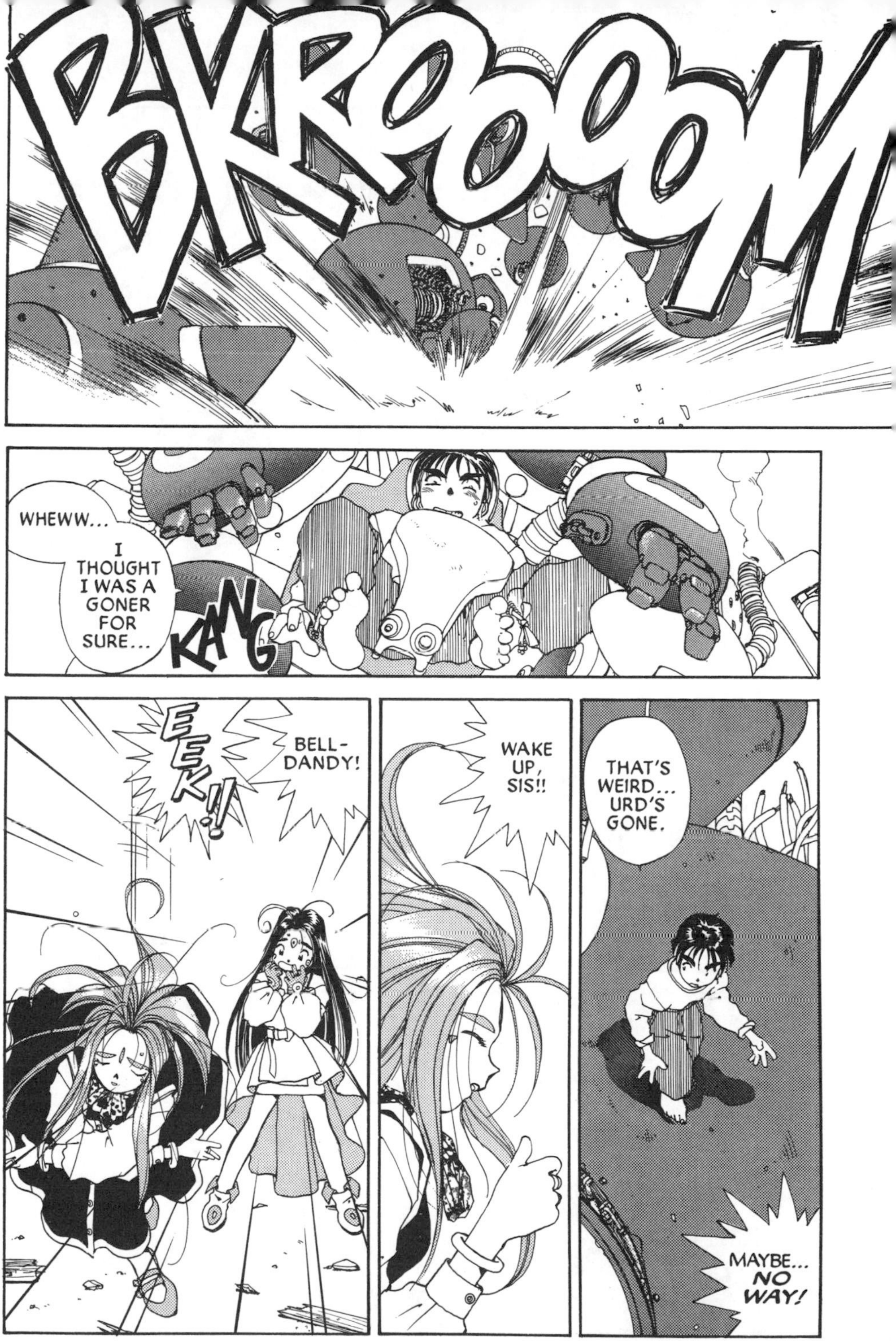
BKROOOOM
WHEWW... I THOUGHT I WAS A GONER FOR SURE...
KANG
EEEK!!
BELL-DANDY!
WAKE UP, SIS!!
THAT'S WEIRD... URD'S GONE.
MAYBE... NO WAY!

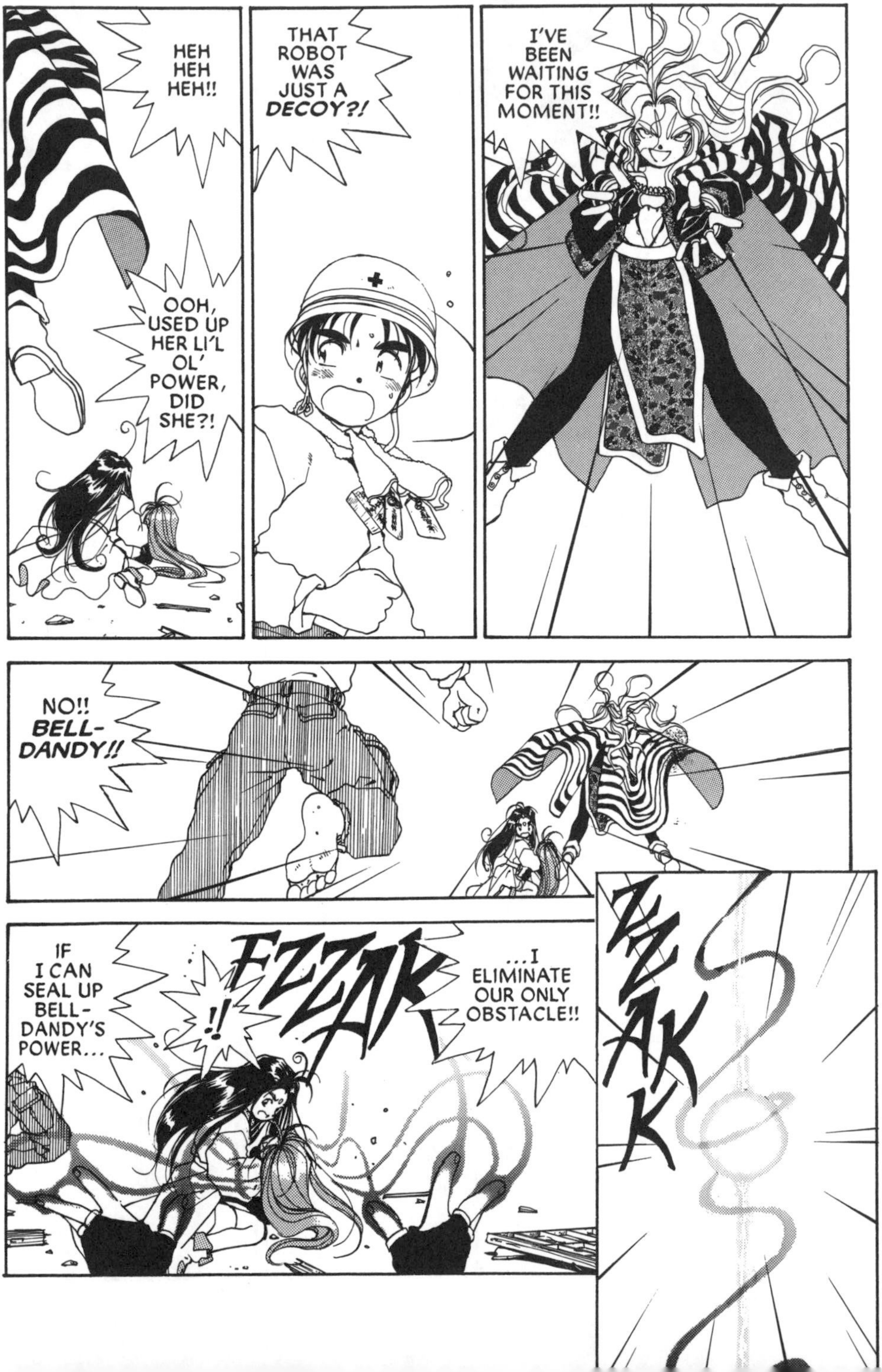
HEH HEH HEH!!
OOH, USED UP HER LI'L OL' POWER, DID SHE?!
THAT ROBOT WAS JUST A *DECOY?!*
I'VE BEEN WAITING FOR THIS MOMENT!!
NO!! *BELL-DANDY!!*
IF I CAN SEAL UP BELL-DANDY'S POWER...
!!
FZZAK
...I ELIMINATE OUR ONLY OBSTACLE!!
ZZZAKK

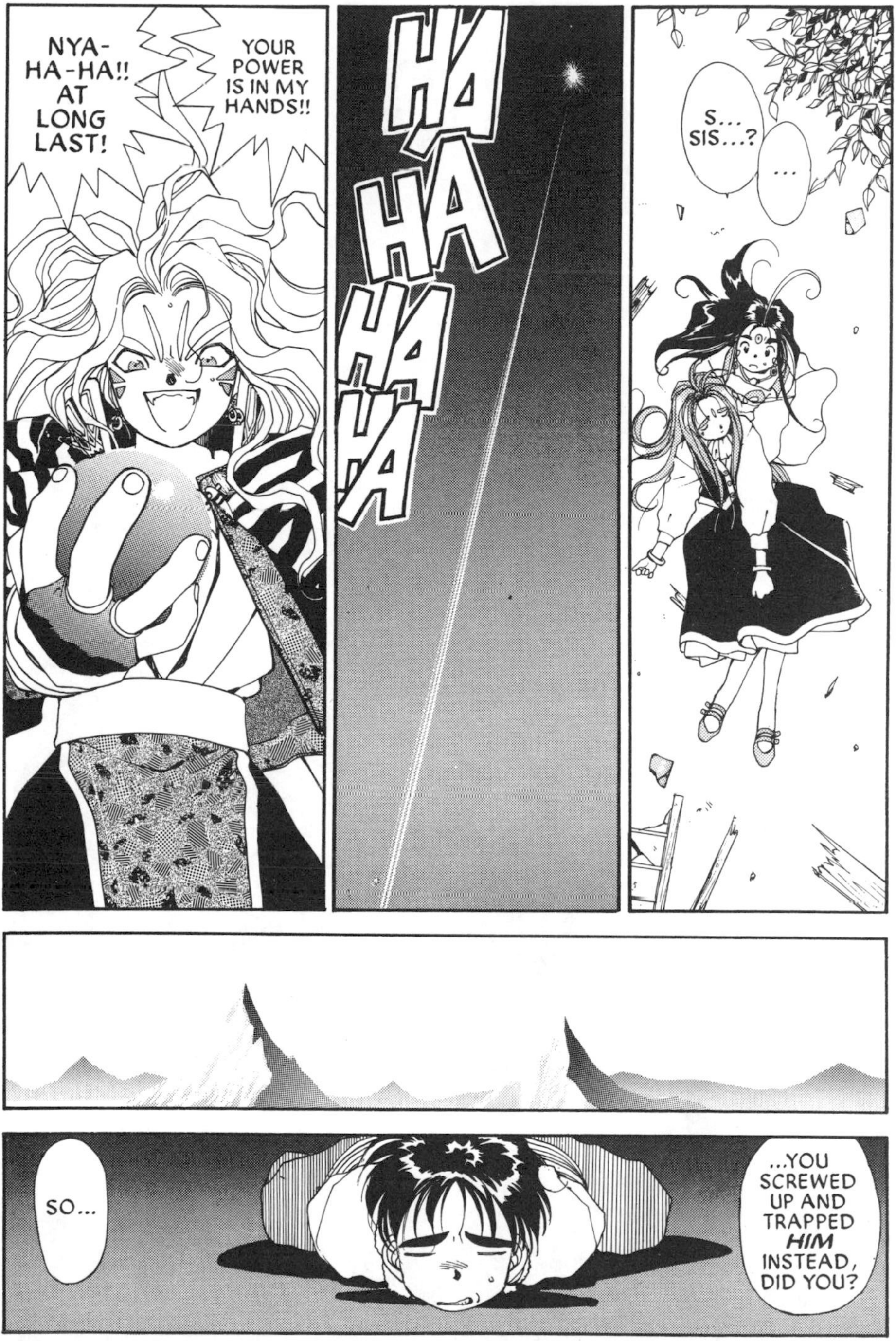
NYA-HA-HA!! AT LONG LAST!
YOUR POWER IS IN MY HANDS!!
HA HA HA HA HA
S... SIS...?
...
SO...
...YOU SCREWED UP AND TRAPPED HIM INSTEAD, DID YOU?

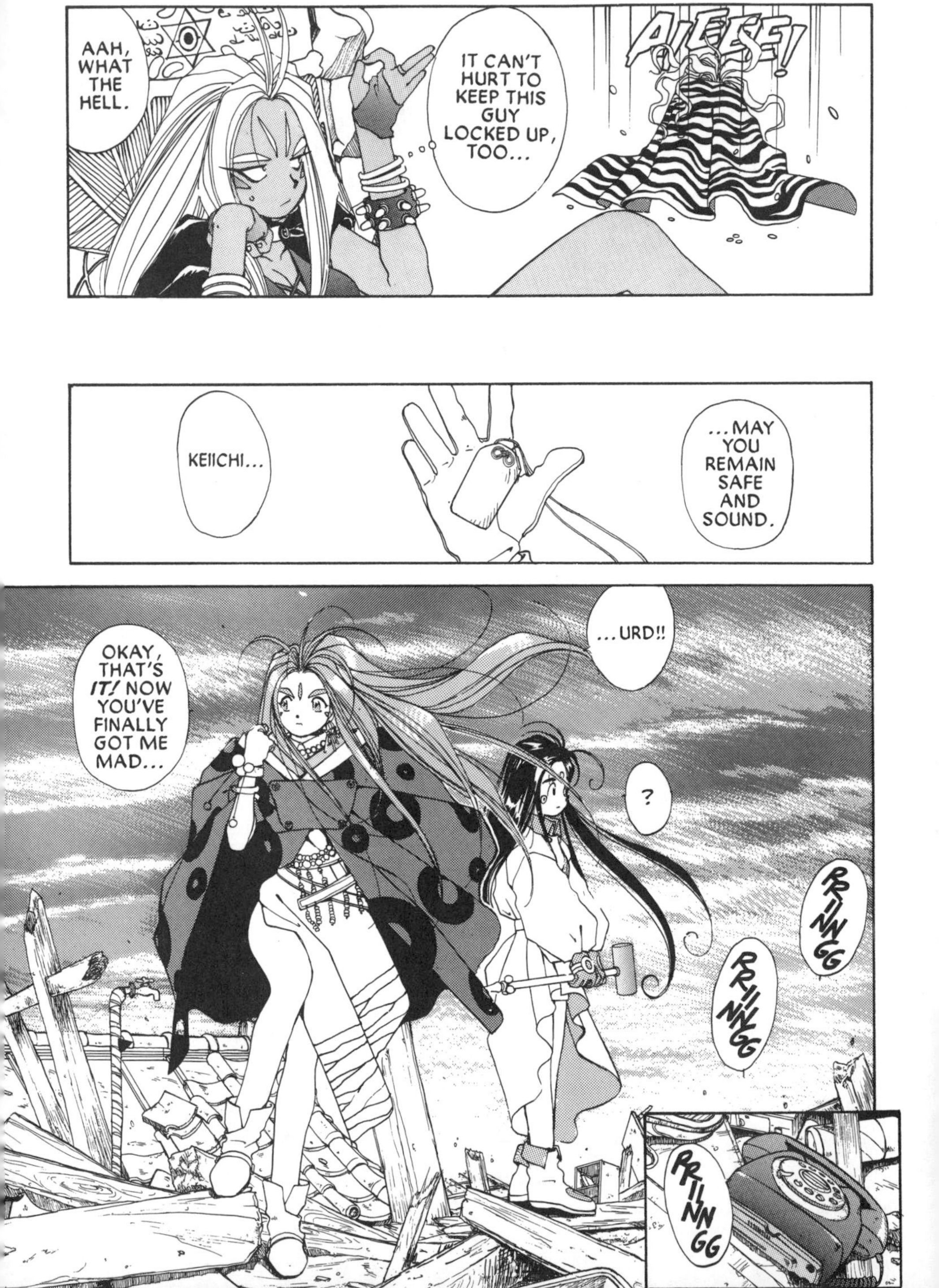
AAH, WHAT THE HELL.
IT CAN'T HURT TO KEEP THIS GUY LOCKED UP, TOO...
AIEEE!
KEIICHI...
...MAY YOU REMAIN SAFE AND SOUND.
OKAY, THAT'S *IT!* NOW YOU'VE FINALLY GOT ME MAD...
...URD!!
?
RRIINNGG
RRIINNGG
RRIINNGG

The Ultimate Destruction Program

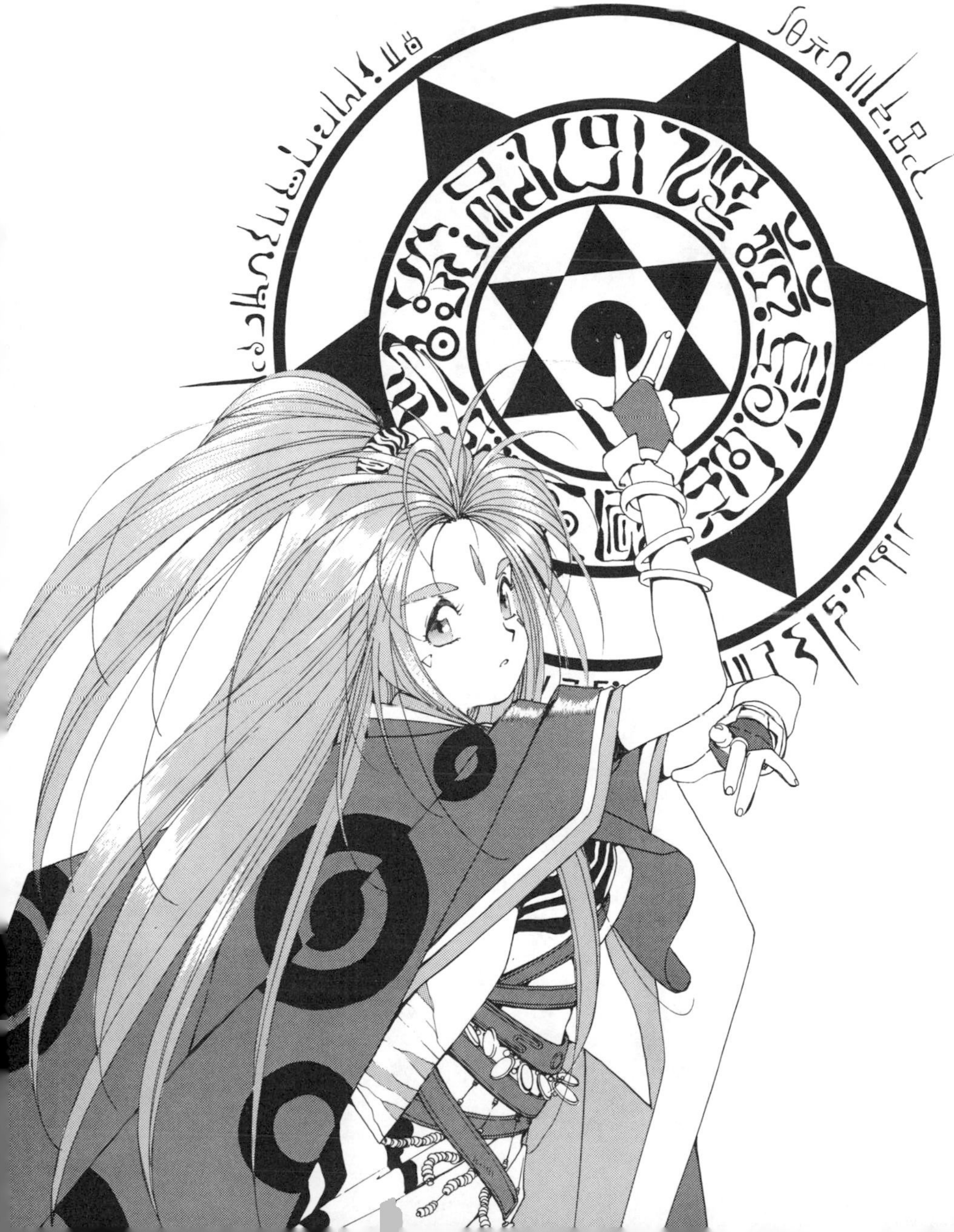

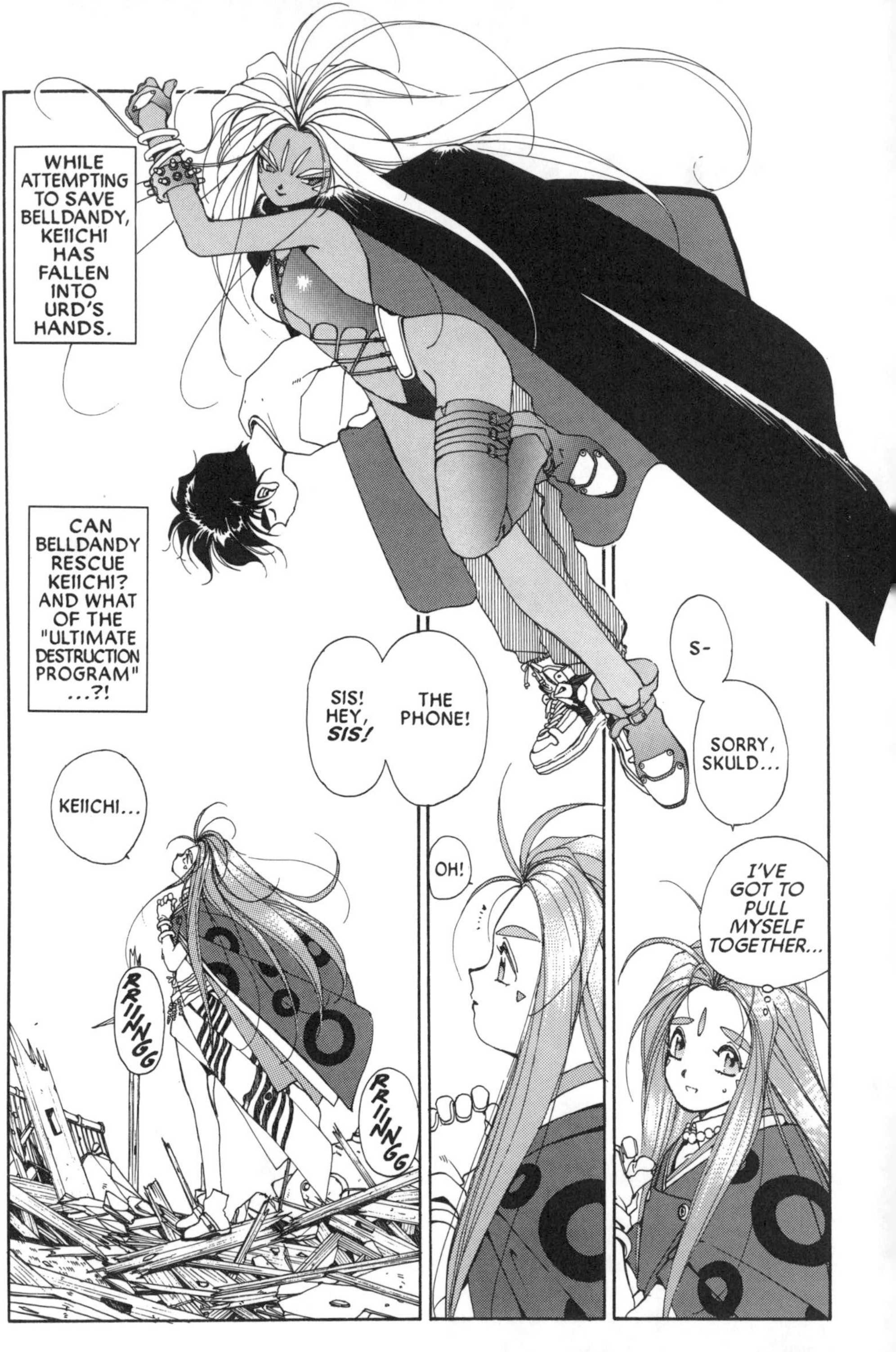
WHILE ATTEMPTING TO SAVE BELLDANDY, KEIICHI HAS FALLEN INTO URD'S HANDS.
CAN BELLDANDY RESCUE KEIICHI? AND WHAT OF THE "ULTIMATE DESTRUCTION PROGRAM" ...?!
KEIICHI...
RRIINGG
RRIINGG
SIS! HEY, *SIS!*
THE PHONE!
OH!
...
S-
SORRY, SKULD...
I'VE GOT TO PULL MYSELF TOGETHER...

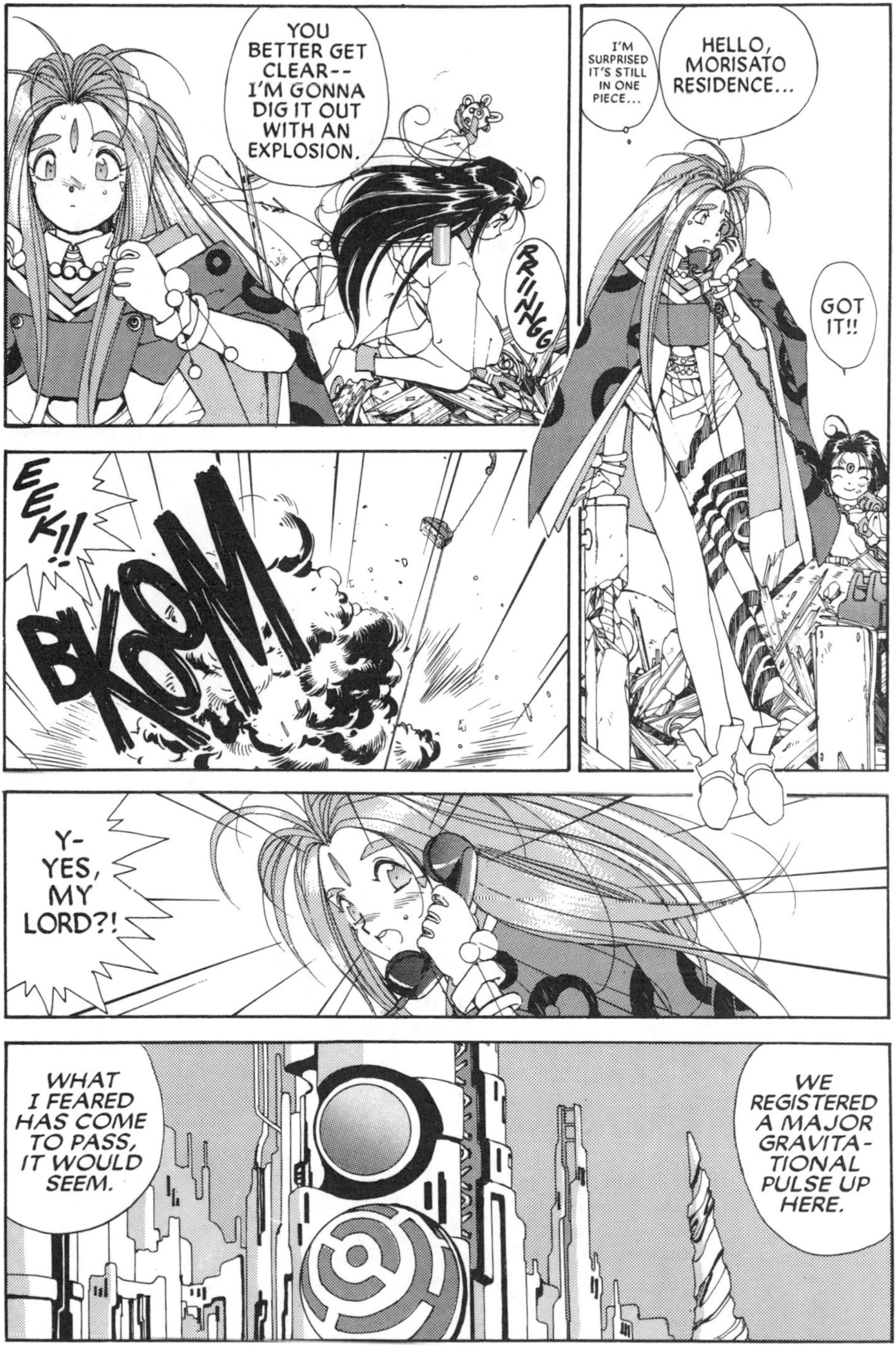
YOU BETTER GET CLEAR-- I'M GONNA DIG IT OUT WITH AN EXPLOSION.
RRIINNGG
EEK!!
BKOOM
I'M SURPRISED IT'S STILL IN ONE PIECE...
HELLO, MORISATO RESIDENCE...
GOT IT!!
Y-YES, MY LORD?!
WHAT I FEARED HAS COME TO PASS, IT WOULD SEEM.
WE REGISTERED A MAJOR GRAVITA-TIONAL PULSE UP HERE.

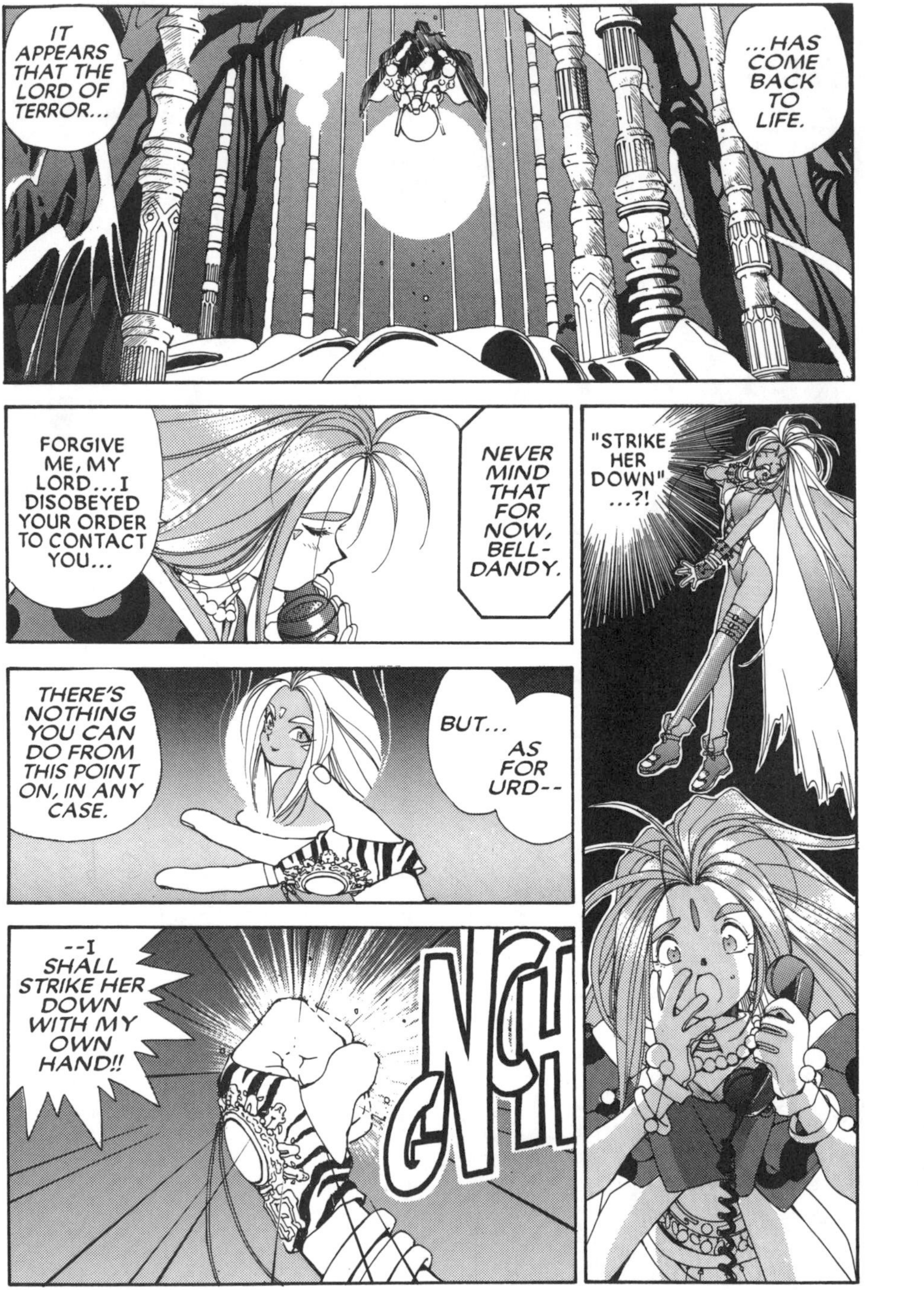
IT APPEARS THAT THE LORD OF TERROR...
...HAS COME BACK TO LIFE.
FORGIVE ME, MY LORD... I DISOBEYED YOUR ORDER TO CONTACT YOU...
NEVER MIND THAT FOR NOW, BELL-DANDY.
THERE'S NOTHING YOU CAN DO FROM THIS POINT ON, IN ANY CASE.
BUT... AS FOR URD--
--I SHALL STRIKE HER DOWN WITH MY OWN HAND!!
GNCH
"STRIKE HER DOWN" ...?!

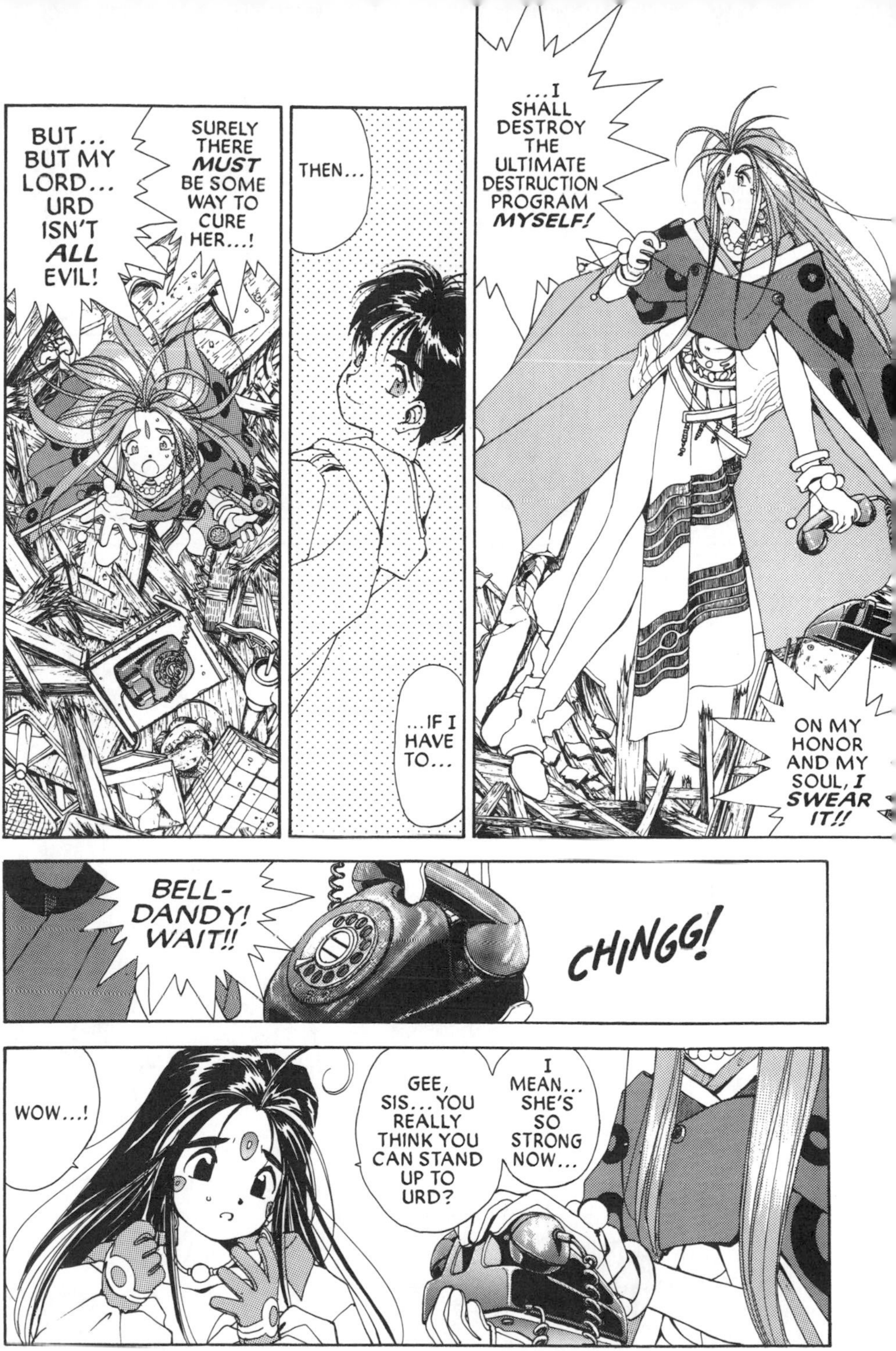
BUT... BUT MY LORD... URD ISN'T ALL EVIL!
SURELY THERE MUST BE SOME WAY TO CURE HER...!
THEN...
...IF I HAVE TO...
...I SHALL DESTROY THE ULTIMATE DESTRUCTION PROGRAM MYSELF!
ON MY HONOR AND MY SOUL, I SWEAR IT!!
BELL-DANDY! WAIT!!
CHINGG!
WOW...!
GEE, SIS... YOU REALLY THINK YOU CAN STAND UP TO URD?
I MEAN... SHE'S SO STRONG NOW...

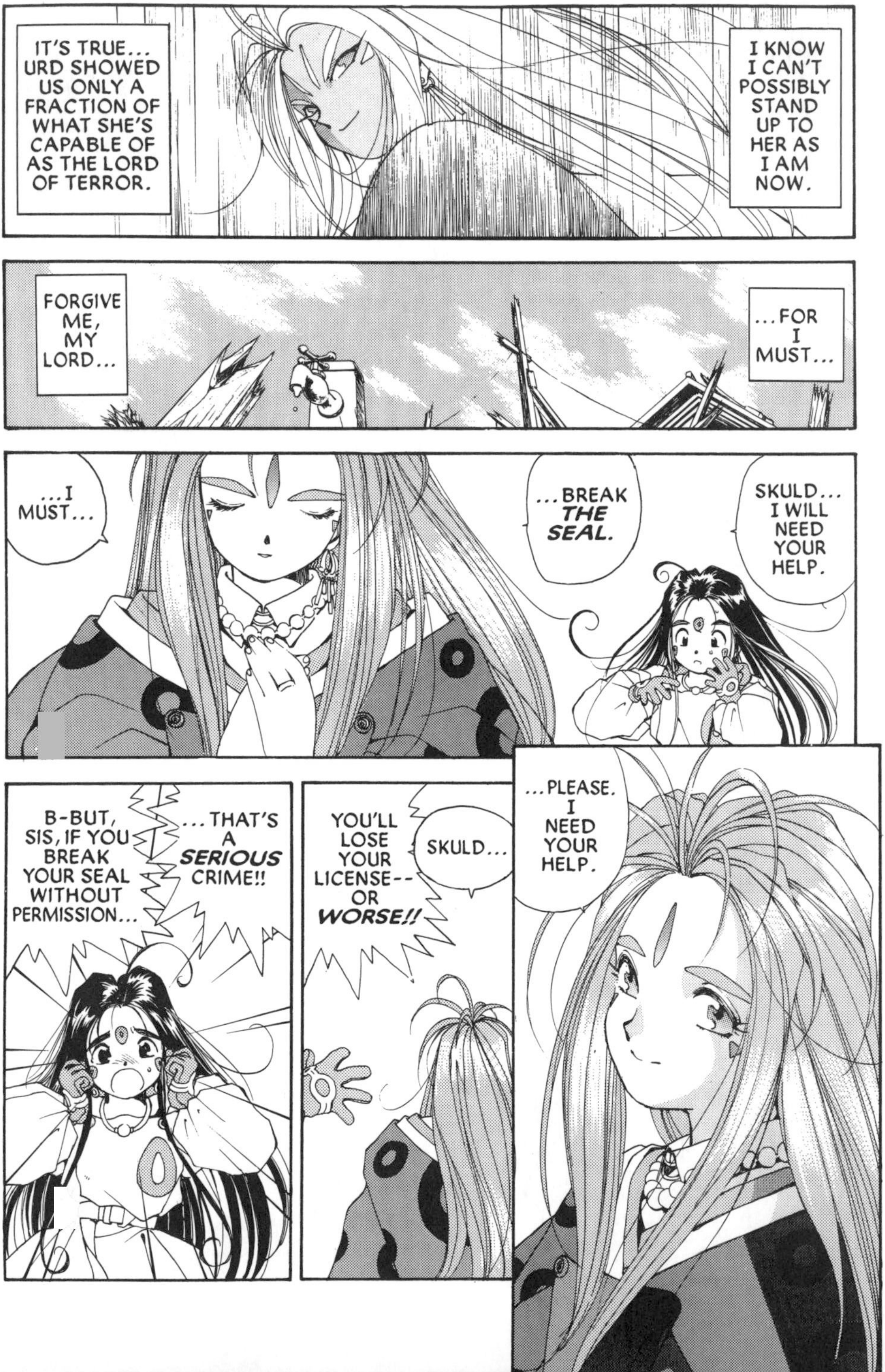
IT'S TRUE... URD SHOWED US ONLY A FRACTION OF WHAT SHE'S CAPABLE OF AS THE LORD OF TERROR.
I KNOW I CAN'T POSSIBLY STAND UP TO HER AS I AM NOW.
FORGIVE ME, MY LORD...
...FOR I MUST...
...I MUST...
...BREAK THE SEAL.
SKULD... I WILL NEED YOUR HELP.
B-BUT, SIS, IF YOU BREAK YOUR SEAL WITHOUT PERMISSION...
...THAT'S A SERIOUS CRIME!!
YOU'LL LOSE YOUR LICENSE-- OR WORSE!!
SKULD...
...PLEASE. I NEED YOUR HELP.

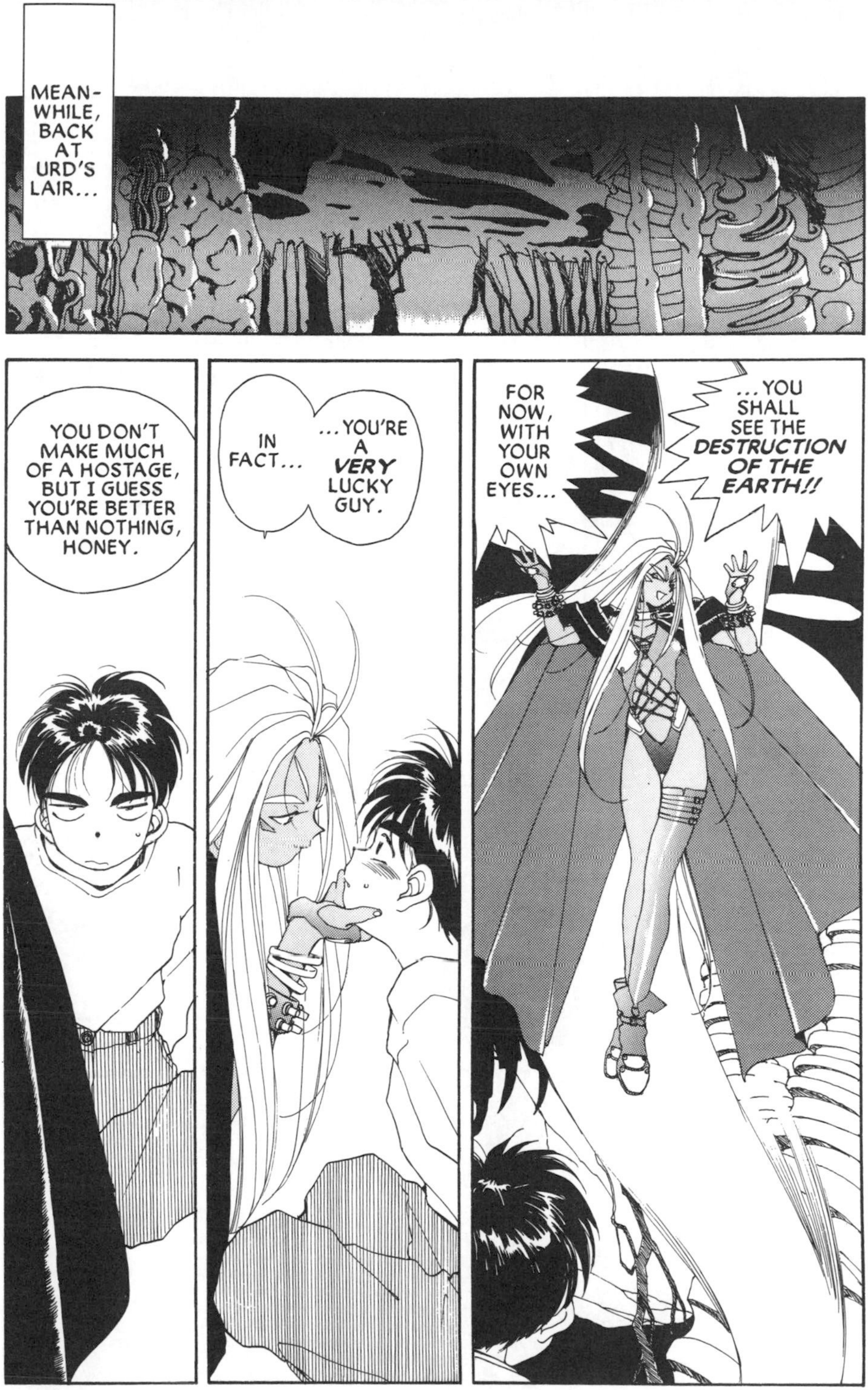
MEAN-WHILE, BACK AT URD'S LAIR...
YOU DON'T MAKE MUCH OF A HOSTAGE, BUT I GUESS YOU'RE BETTER THAN NOTHING, HONEY.
IN FACT...
...YOU'RE A VERY LUCKY GUY.
FOR NOW, WITH YOUR OWN EYES...
...YOU SHALL SEE THE DESTRUCTION OF THE EARTH!!

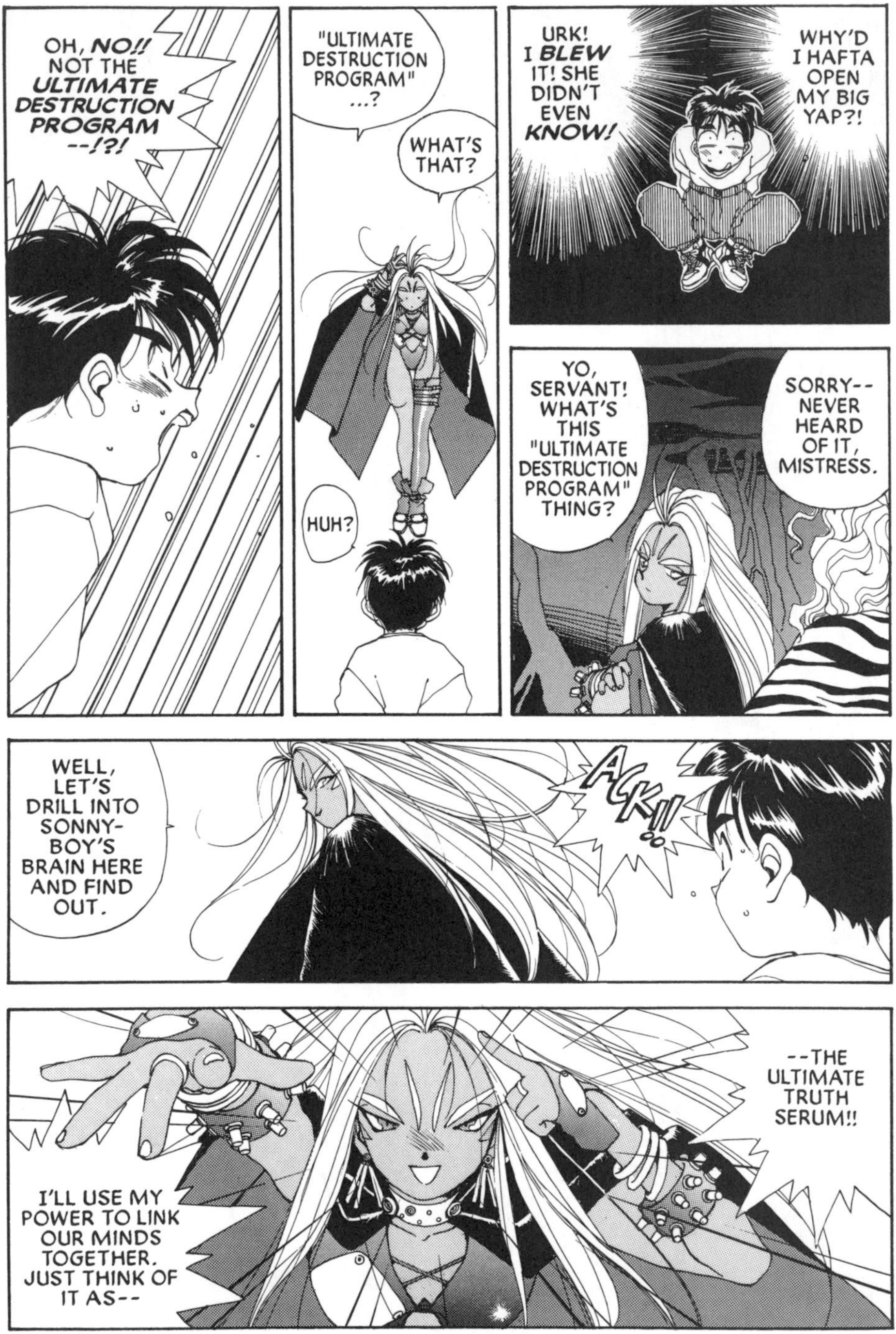
OH, NO!! NOT THE ULTIMATE DESTRUCTION PROGRAM --!?!
"ULTIMATE DESTRUCTION PROGRAM" ...?
WHAT'S THAT?
HUH?
URK! I BLEW IT! SHE DIDN'T EVEN KNOW!
WHY'D I HAFTA OPEN MY BIG YAP?!
YO, SERVANT! WHAT'S THIS "ULTIMATE DESTRUCTION PROGRAM" THING?
SORRY-- NEVER HEARD OF IT, MISTRESS.
WELL, LET'S DRILL INTO SONNY-BOY'S BRAIN HERE AND FIND OUT.
ACK!!
I'LL USE MY POWER TO LINK OUR MINDS TOGETHER. JUST THINK OF IT AS--
--THE ULTIMATE TRUTH SERUM!!

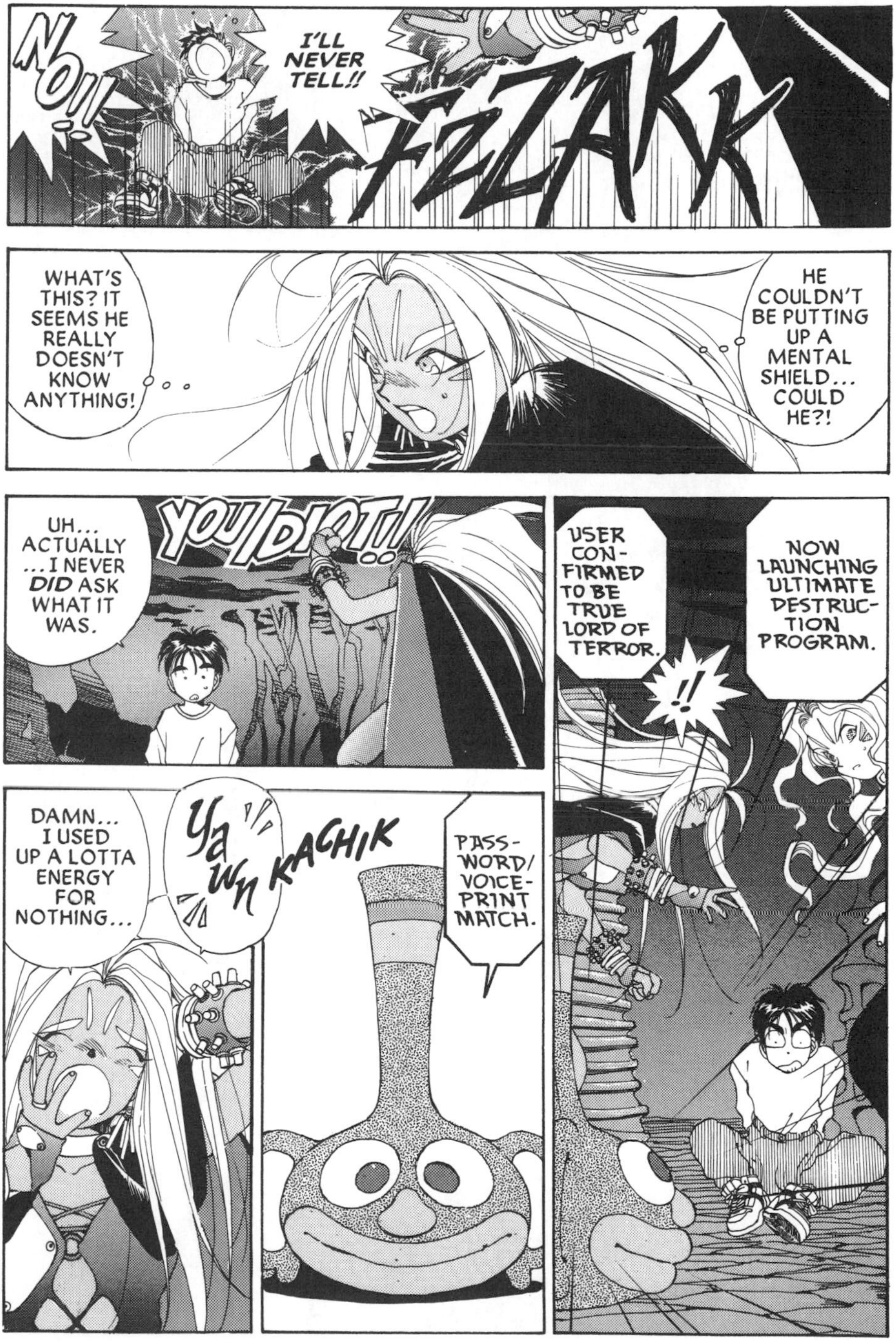
NO!!
I'LL NEVER TELL!!
FZZAKK
WHAT'S THIS? IT SEEMS HE REALLY DOESN'T KNOW ANYTHING!
HE COULDN'T BE PUTTING UP A MENTAL SHIELD... COULD HE?!
UH... ACTUALLY ...I NEVER DID ASK WHAT IT WAS.
YOU IDIOT!!
USER CONFIRMED TO BE TRUE LORD OF TERROR.
NOW LAUNCHING ULTIMATE DESTRUCTION PROGRAM.
!!
DAMN... I USED UP A LOTTA ENERGY FOR NOTHING...
Yawn
KACHIK
PASSWORD/VOICEPRINT MATCH.

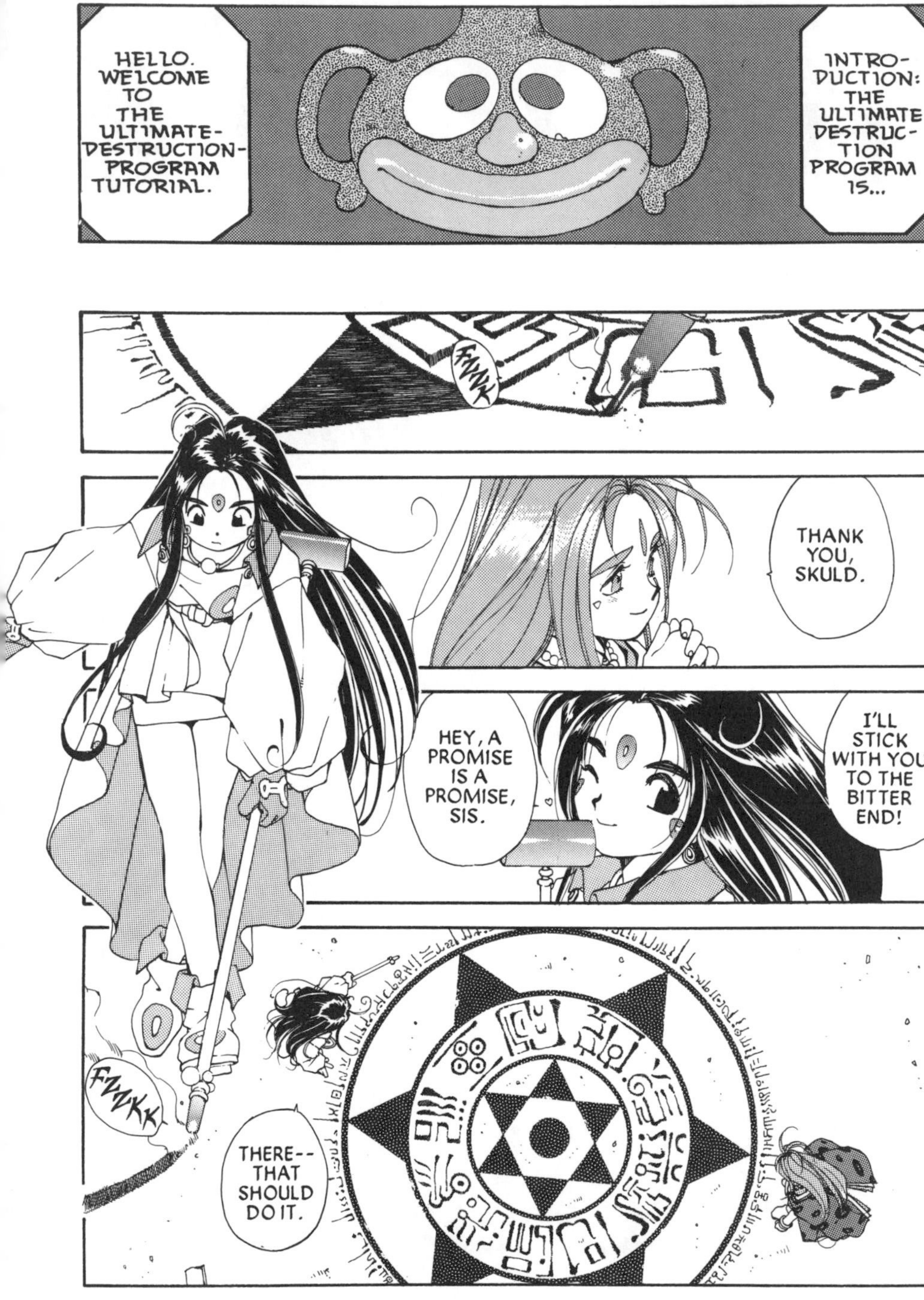
HELLO. WELCOME TO THE ULTIMATE-DESTRUCTION-PROGRAM TUTORIAL.
INTRO-DUCTION: THE ULTIMATE DESTRUC-TION PROGRAM IS...
FZZZK
THANK YOU, SKULD.
HEY, A PROMISE IS A PROMISE, SIS.
I'LL STICK WITH YOU TO THE BITTER END!
FZZZKK
THERE--THAT SHOULD DO IT.

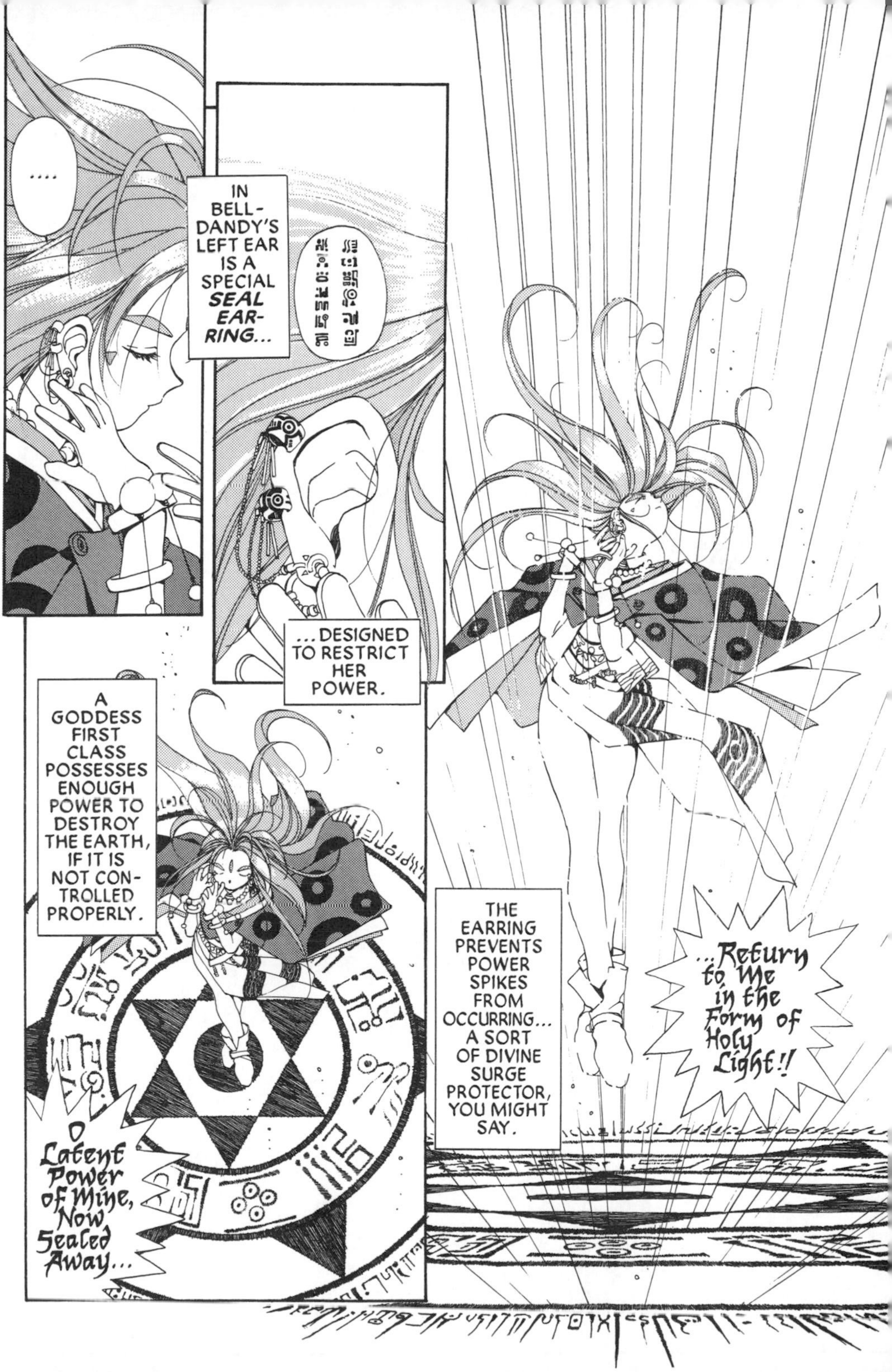
....
IN BELL-DANDY'S LEFT EAR IS A SPECIAL SEAL EAR-RING...
...DESIGNED TO RESTRICT HER POWER.
A GODDESS FIRST CLASS POSSESSES ENOUGH POWER TO DESTROY THE EARTH, IF IT IS NOT CON-TROLLED PROPERLY.
O Latent Power of Mine, Now Sealed Away...
THE EARRING PREVENTS POWER SPIKES FROM OCCURRING... A SORT OF DIVINE SURGE PROTECTOR, YOU MIGHT SAY.
...Return to Me in the Form of Holy Light!!

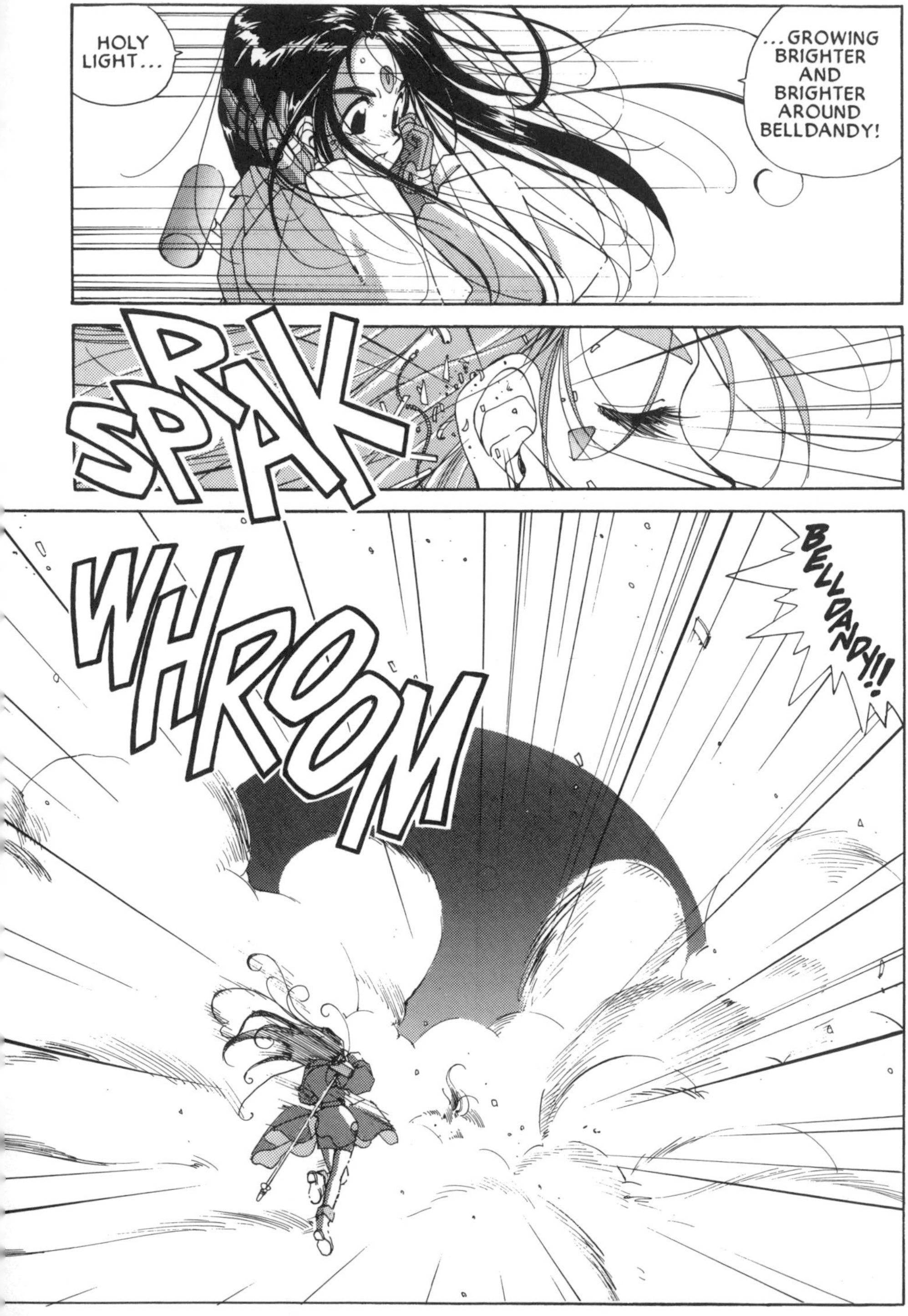
HOLY LIGHT...
...GROWING BRIGHTER AND BRIGHTER AROUND BELLDANDY!
SPRAK
WHROOM
BELLDANDY!!!

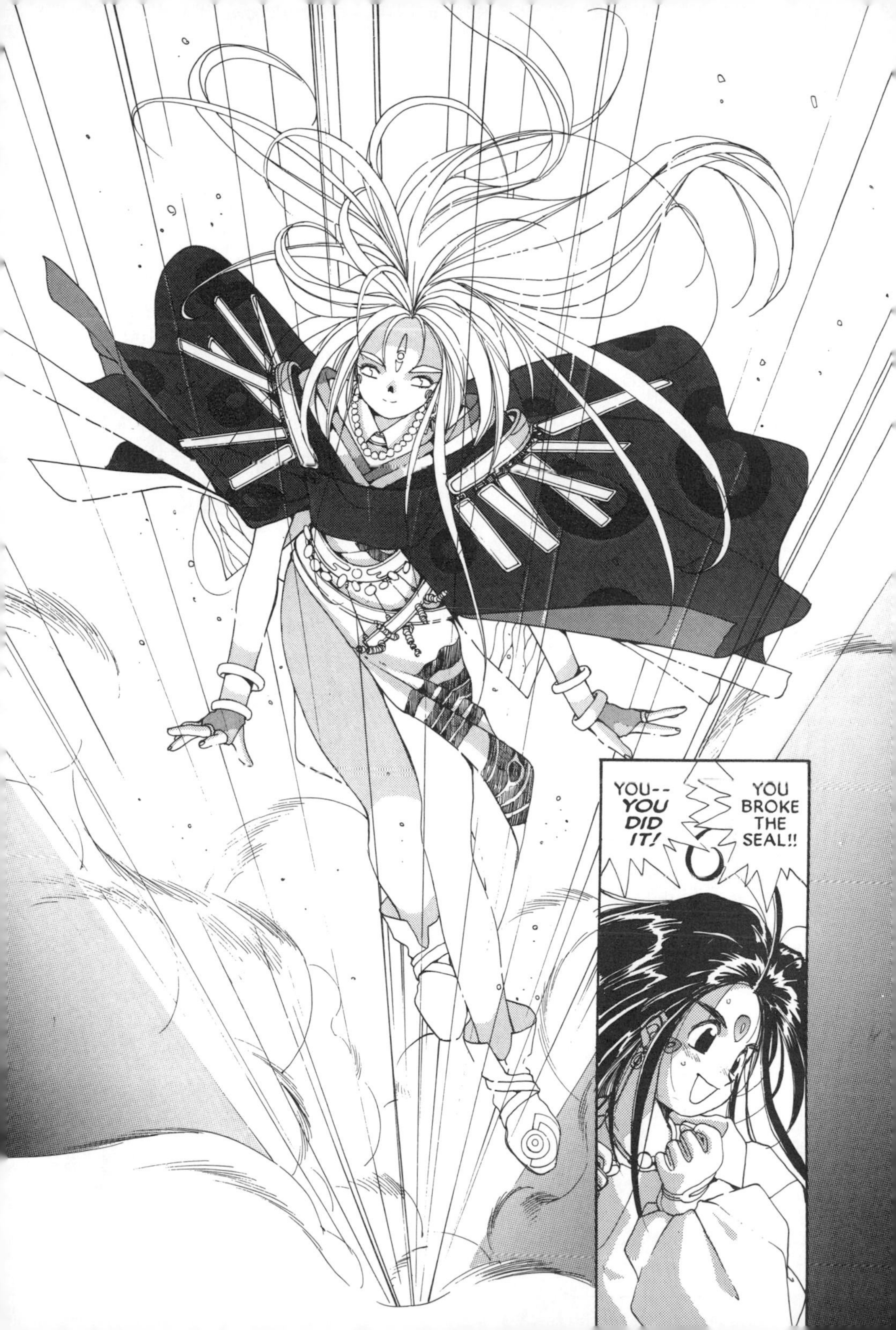
YOU-- *YOU DID IT!*
YOU BROKE THE SEAL!!

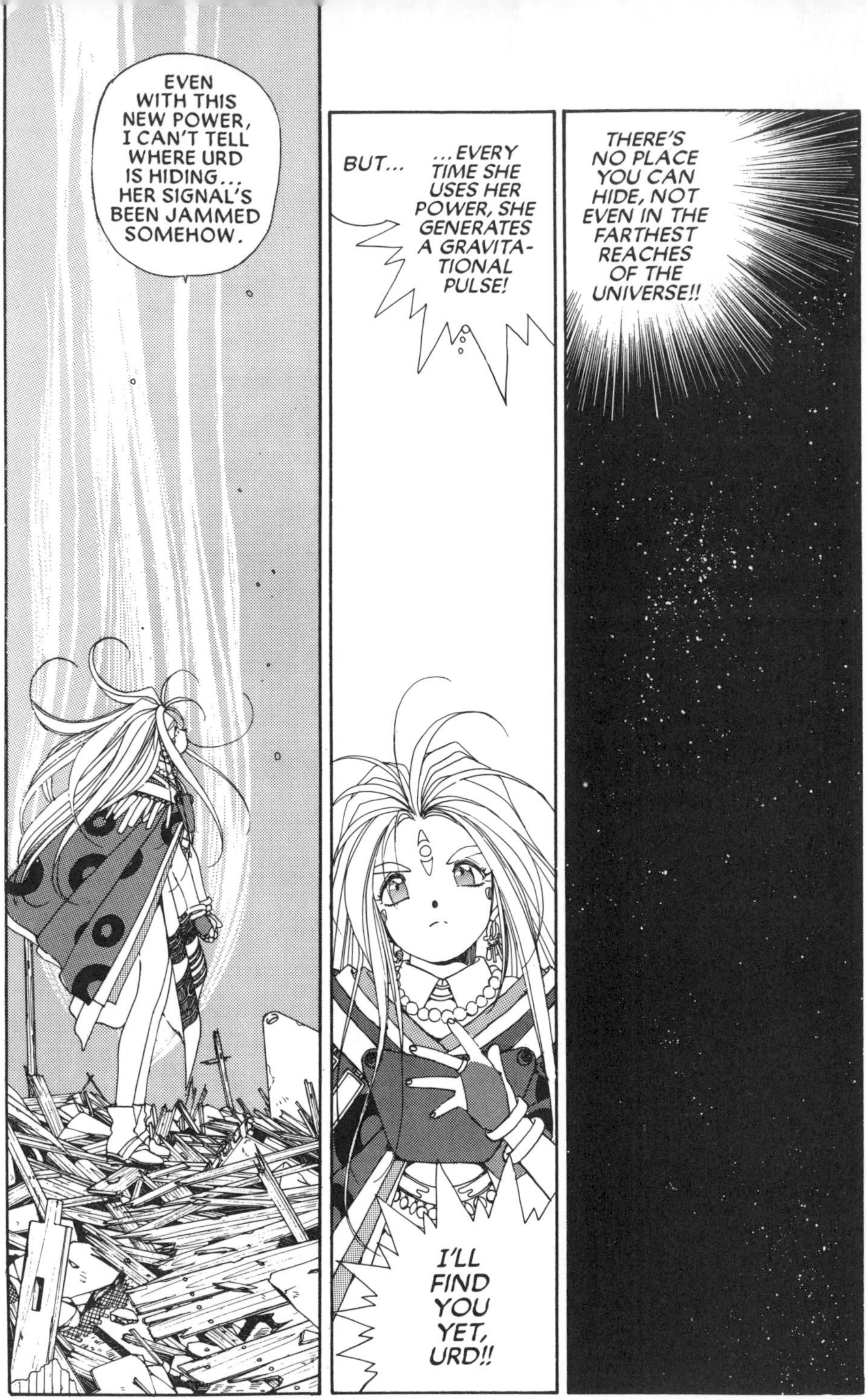
EVEN WITH THIS NEW POWER, I CAN'T TELL WHERE URD IS HIDING... HER SIGNAL'S BEEN JAMMED SOMEHOW.
BUT...
...EVERY TIME SHE USES HER POWER, SHE GENERATES A GRAVITA-TIONAL PULSE!
I'LL FIND YOU YET, URD!!
THERE'S NO PLACE YOU CAN HIDE, NOT EVEN IN THE FARTHEST REACHES OF THE UNIVERSE!!

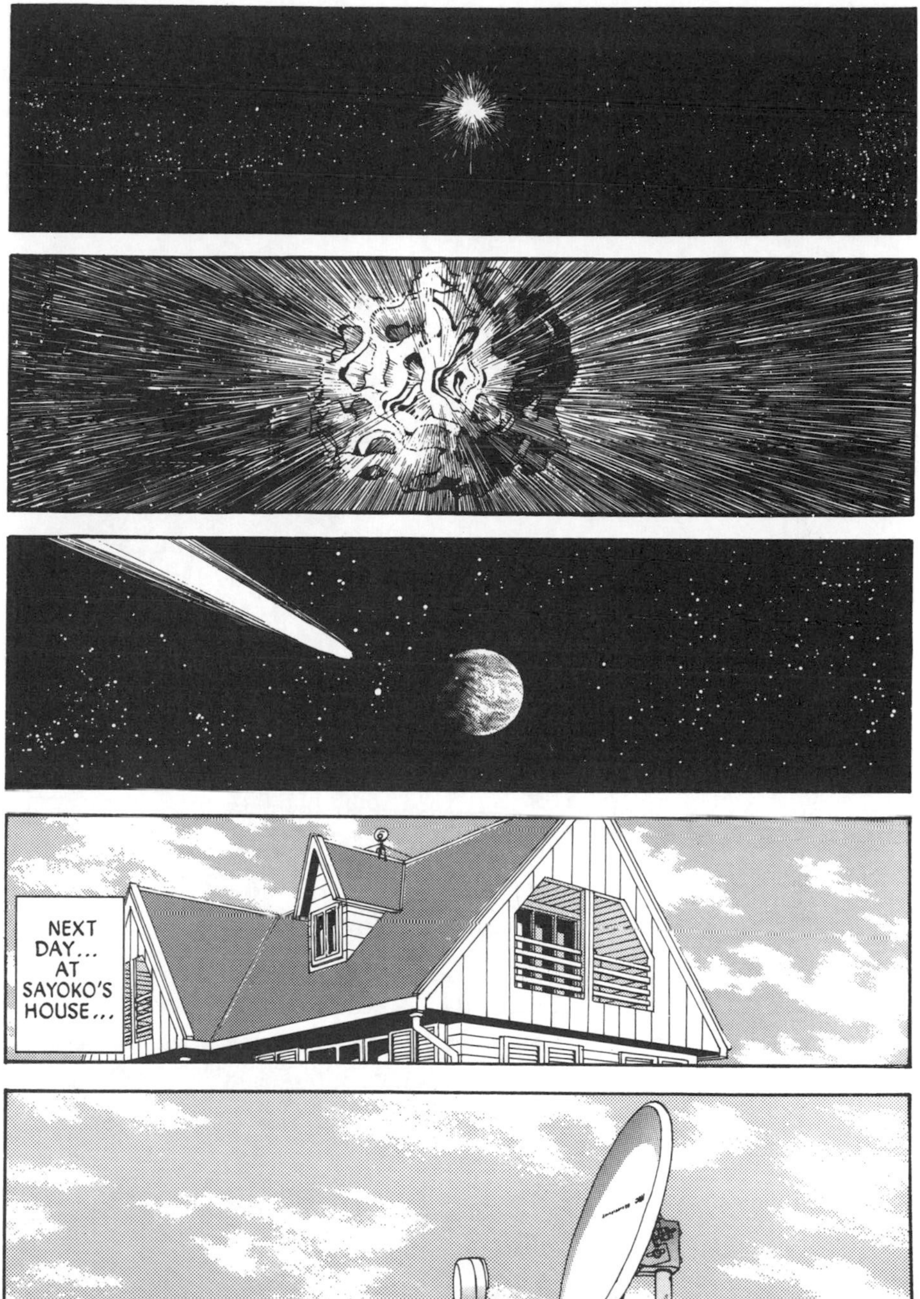
NEXT DAY... AT SAYOKO'S HOUSE...

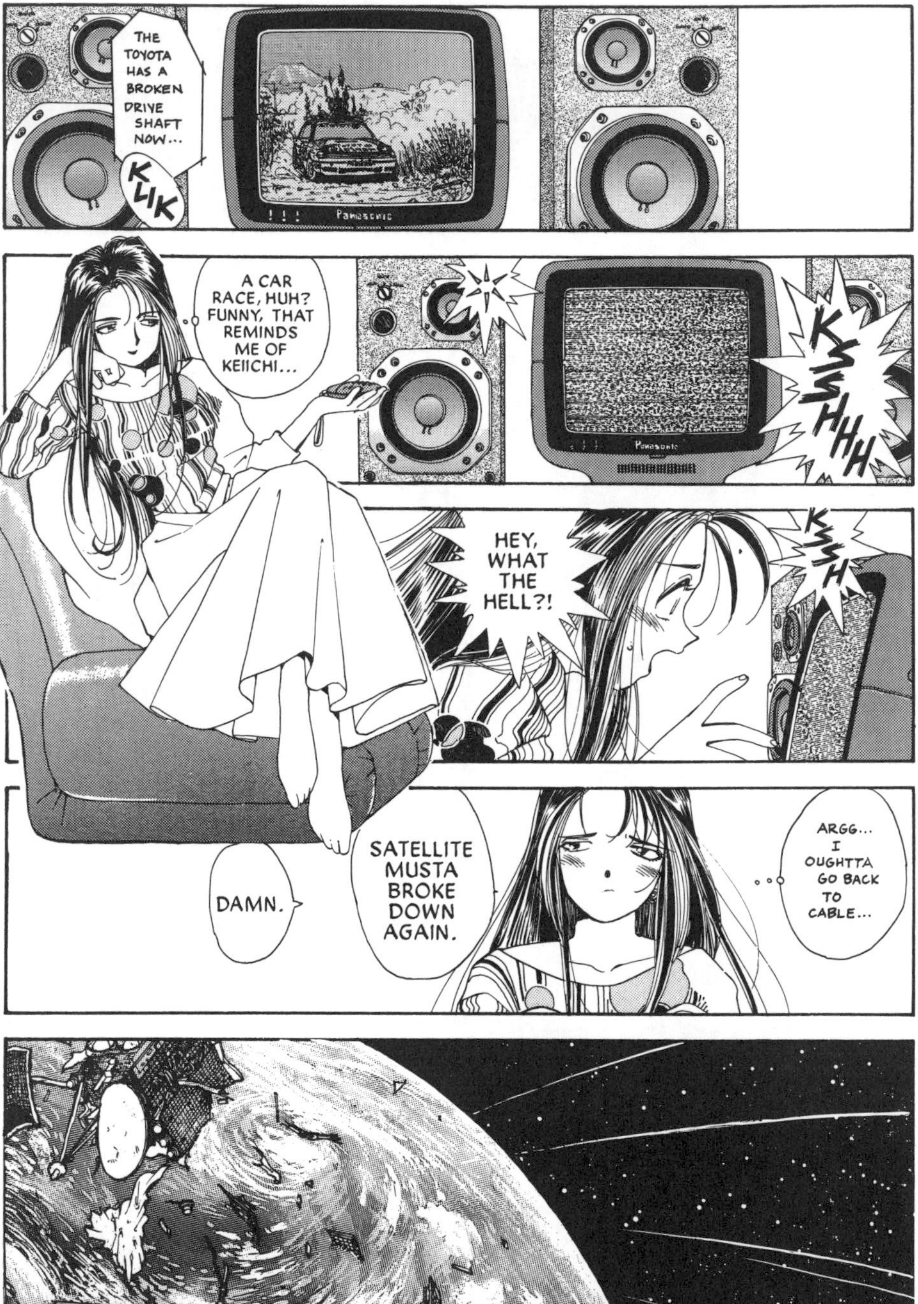
THE TOYOTA HAS A BROKEN DRIVE SHAFT NOW...
KLIK
A CAR RACE, HUH? FUNNY, THAT REMINDS ME OF KEIICHI...
KSSHHH
HEY, WHAT THE HELL?!
KSSH
DAMN.
SATELLITE MUSTA BROKE DOWN AGAIN.
ARGG... I OUGHTTA GO BACK TO CABLE...

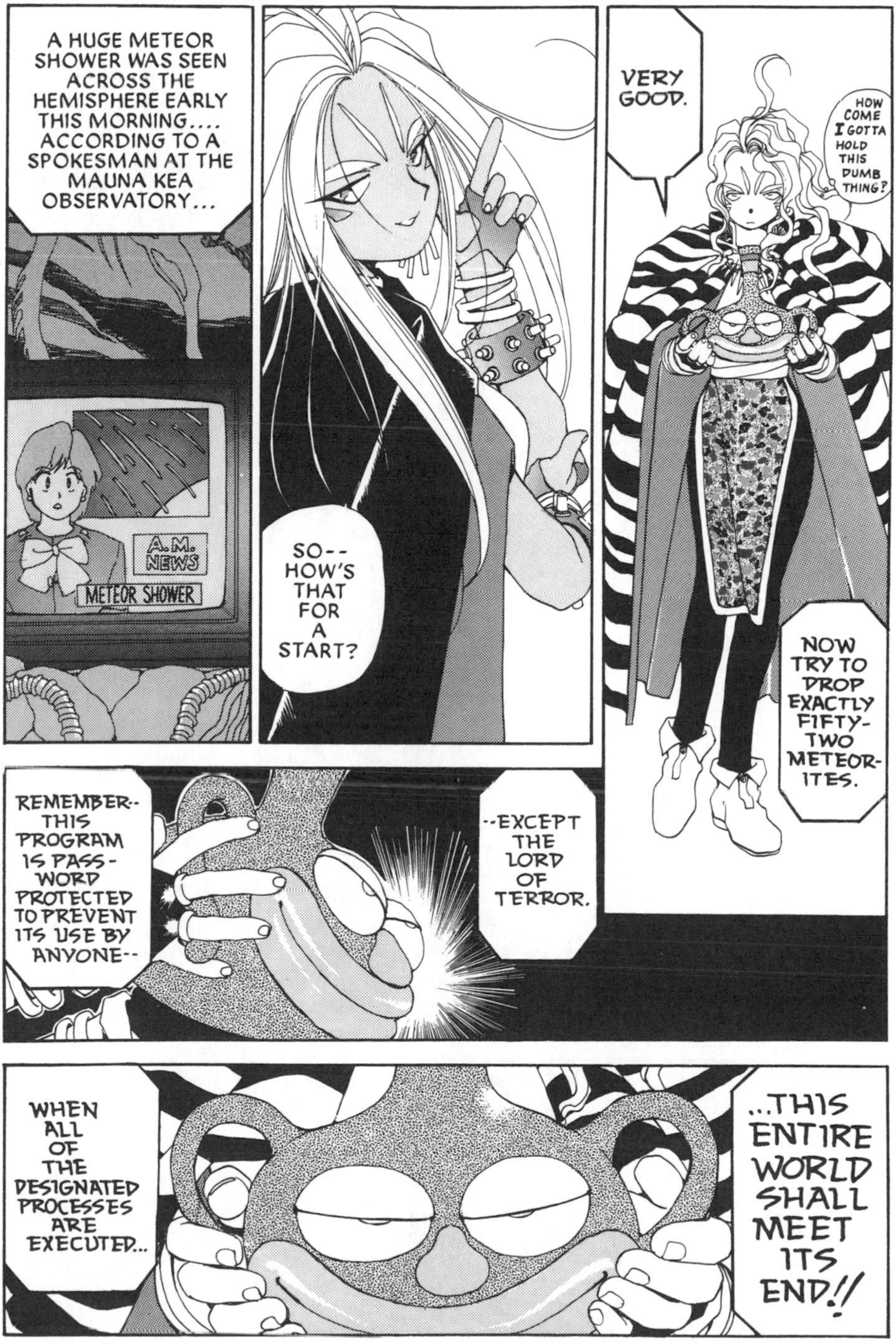
A HUGE METEOR SHOWER WAS SEEN ACROSS THE HEMISPHERE EARLY THIS MORNING.... ACCORDING TO A SPOKESMAN AT THE MAUNA KEA OBSERVATORY...
A.M. NEWS
METEOR SHOWER
SO--HOW'S THAT FOR A START?
VERY GOOD.
HOW COME I GOTTA HOLD THIS DUMB THING?
NOW TRY TO DROP EXACTLY FIFTY-TWO METEOR-ITES.
REMEMBER--THIS PROGRAM IS PASS-WORD PROTECTED TO PREVENT ITS USE BY ANYONE--
--EXCEPT THE LORD OF TERROR.
WHEN ALL OF THE DESIGNATED PROCESSES ARE EXECUTED...
...THIS ENTIRE WORLD SHALL MEET ITS END!!

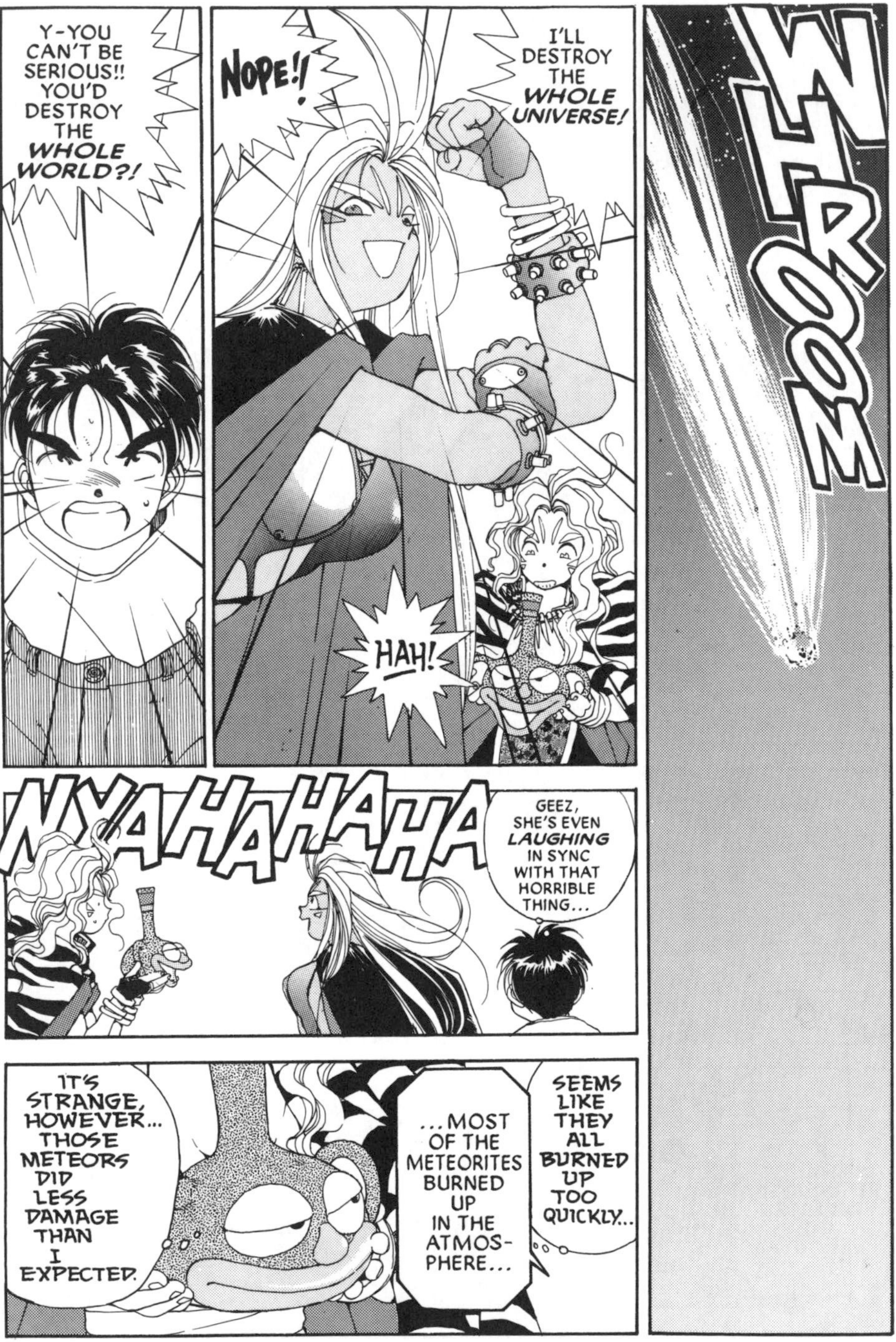
Y-YOU CAN'T BE SERIOUS!! YOU'D DESTROY THE WHOLE WORLD?!
NOPE!!
I'LL DESTROY THE WHOLE UNIVERSE!
HAH!
WHROOM
NYAHAHAHAHA
GEEZ, SHE'S EVEN LAUGHING IN SYNC WITH THAT HORRIBLE THING...
IT'S STRANGE, HOWEVER... THOSE METEORS DID LESS DAMAGE THAN I EXPECTED.
...MOST OF THE METEORITES BURNED UP IN THE ATMOSPHERE...
SEEMS LIKE THEY ALL BURNED UP TOO QUICKLY...

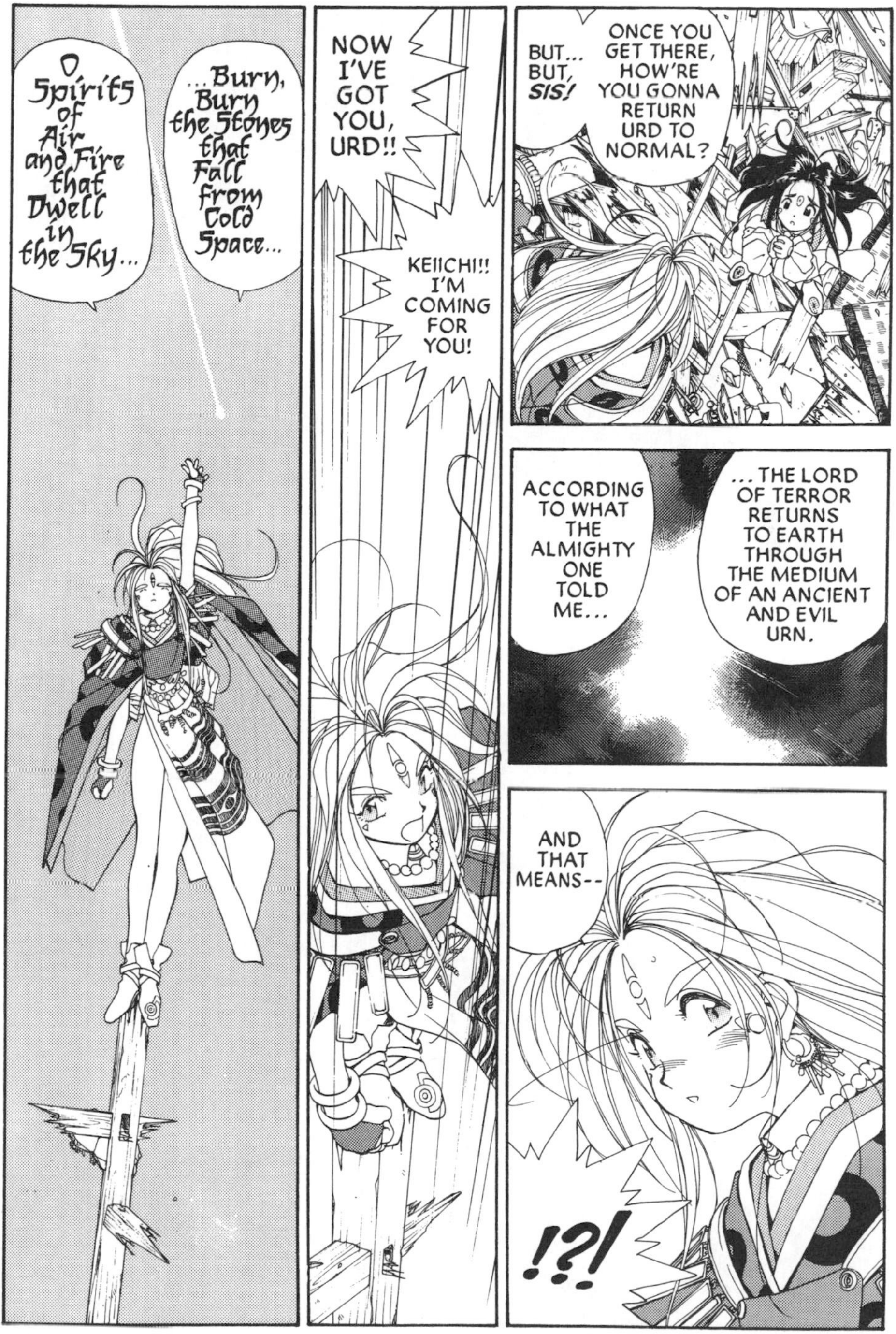
O, Spirits of Air and Fire that Dwell in the Sky...
...Burn, Burn the Stones that Fall from Cold Space...
NOW I'VE GOT YOU, URD!!
KEIICHI!! I'M COMING FOR YOU!
BUT... BUT, *SIS!*
ONCE YOU GET THERE, HOW'RE YOU GONNA RETURN URD TO NORMAL?
ACCORDING TO WHAT THE ALMIGHTY ONE TOLD ME...
...THE LORD OF TERROR RETURNS TO EARTH THROUGH THE MEDIUM OF AN ANCIENT AND EVIL URN.
AND THAT MEANS--
!?!

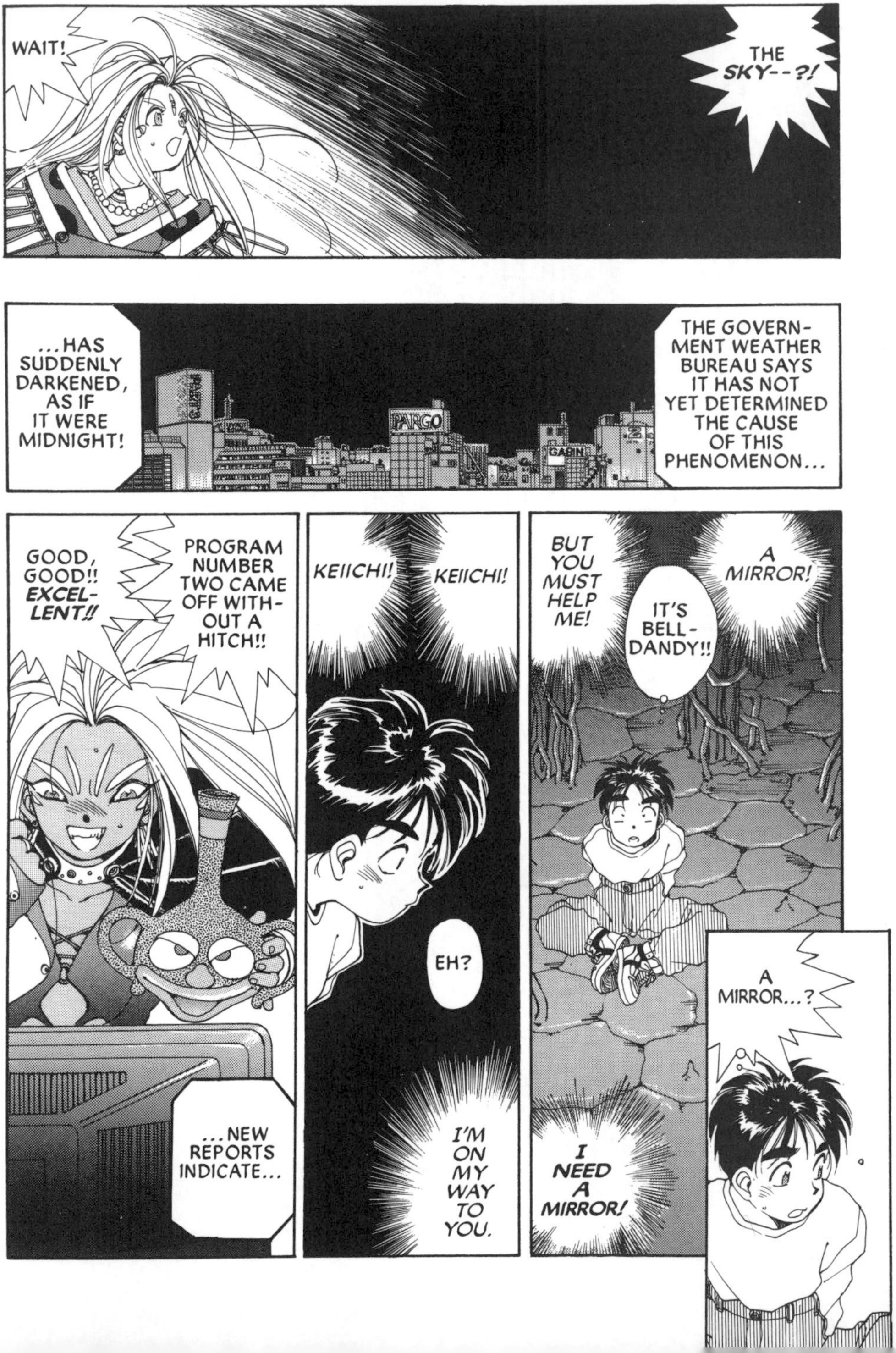
WAIT!
THE SKY--?!
...HAS SUDDENLY DARKENED, AS IF IT WERE MIDNIGHT!
THE GOVERN-MENT WEATHER BUREAU SAYS IT HAS NOT YET DETERMINED THE CAUSE OF THIS PHENOMENON...
PARGO
GOOD, GOOD!! EXCEL-LENT!!
PROGRAM NUMBER TWO CAME OFF WITH-OUT A HITCH!!
...NEW REPORTS INDICATE...
KEIICHI!
KEIICHI!
EH?
I'M ON MY WAY TO YOU.
BUT YOU MUST HELP ME!
A MIRROR!
IT'S BELL-DANDY!!
I NEED A MIRROR!
A MIRROR...?

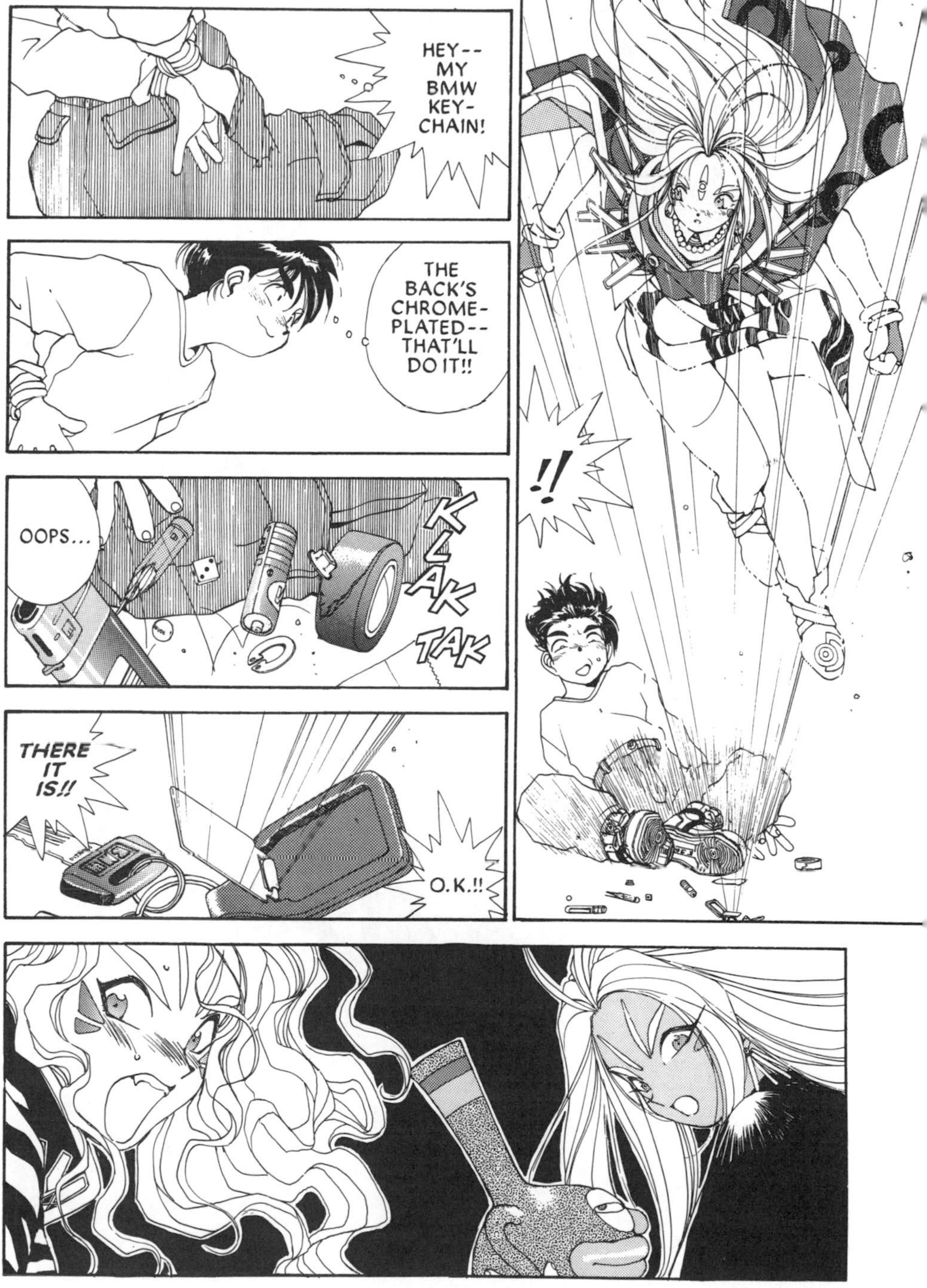
HEY-- MY BMW KEY-CHAIN!
THE BACK'S CHROME-PLATED-- THAT'LL DO IT!!
OOPS...
KLAK
TAK
THERE IT IS!!
O.K.!!
!!

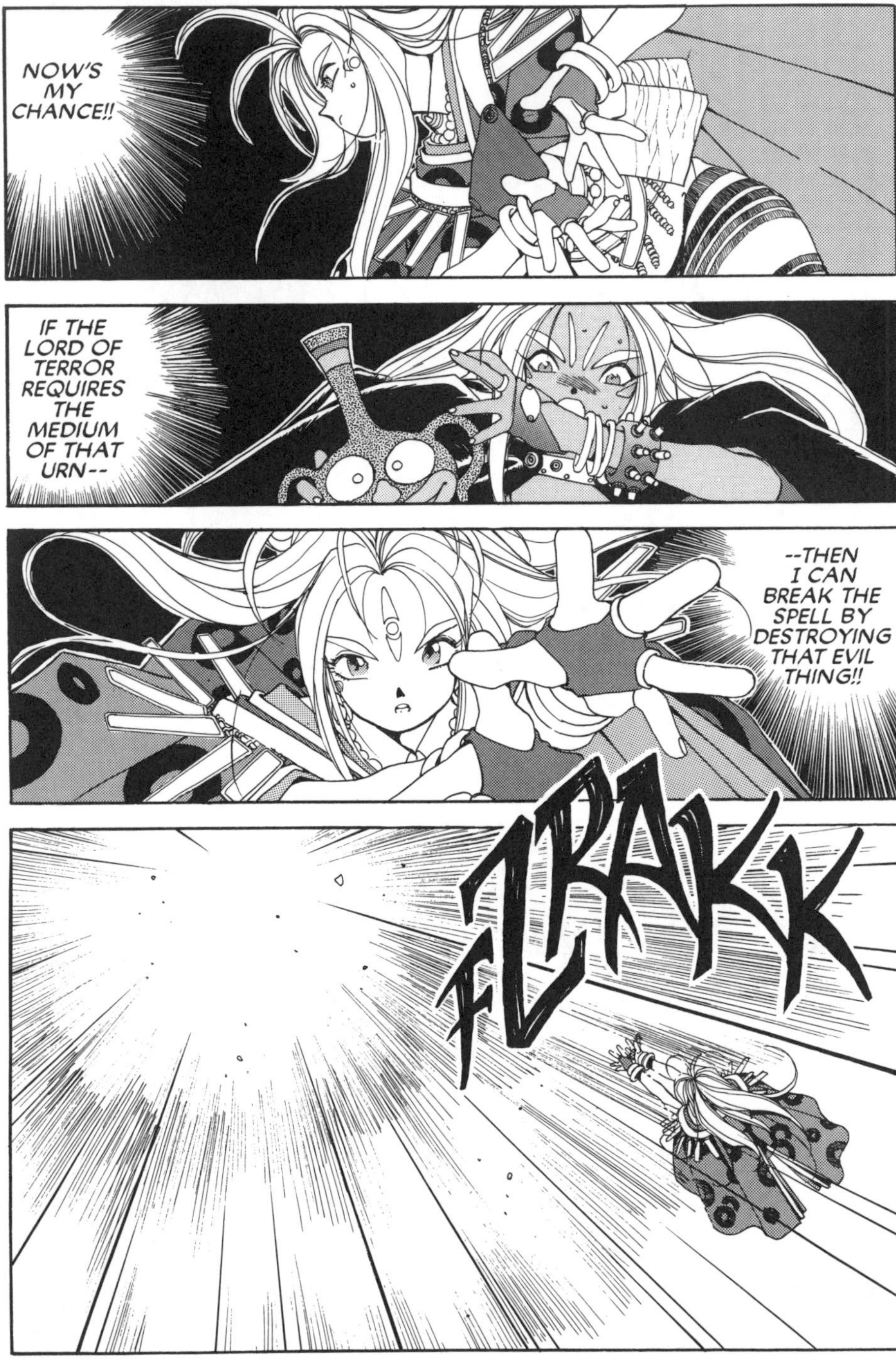
NOW'S MY CHANCE!!
IF THE LORD OF TERROR REQUIRES THE MEDIUM OF THAT URN--
--THEN I CAN BREAK THE SPELL BY DESTROYING THAT EVIL THING!!
FZRAKK

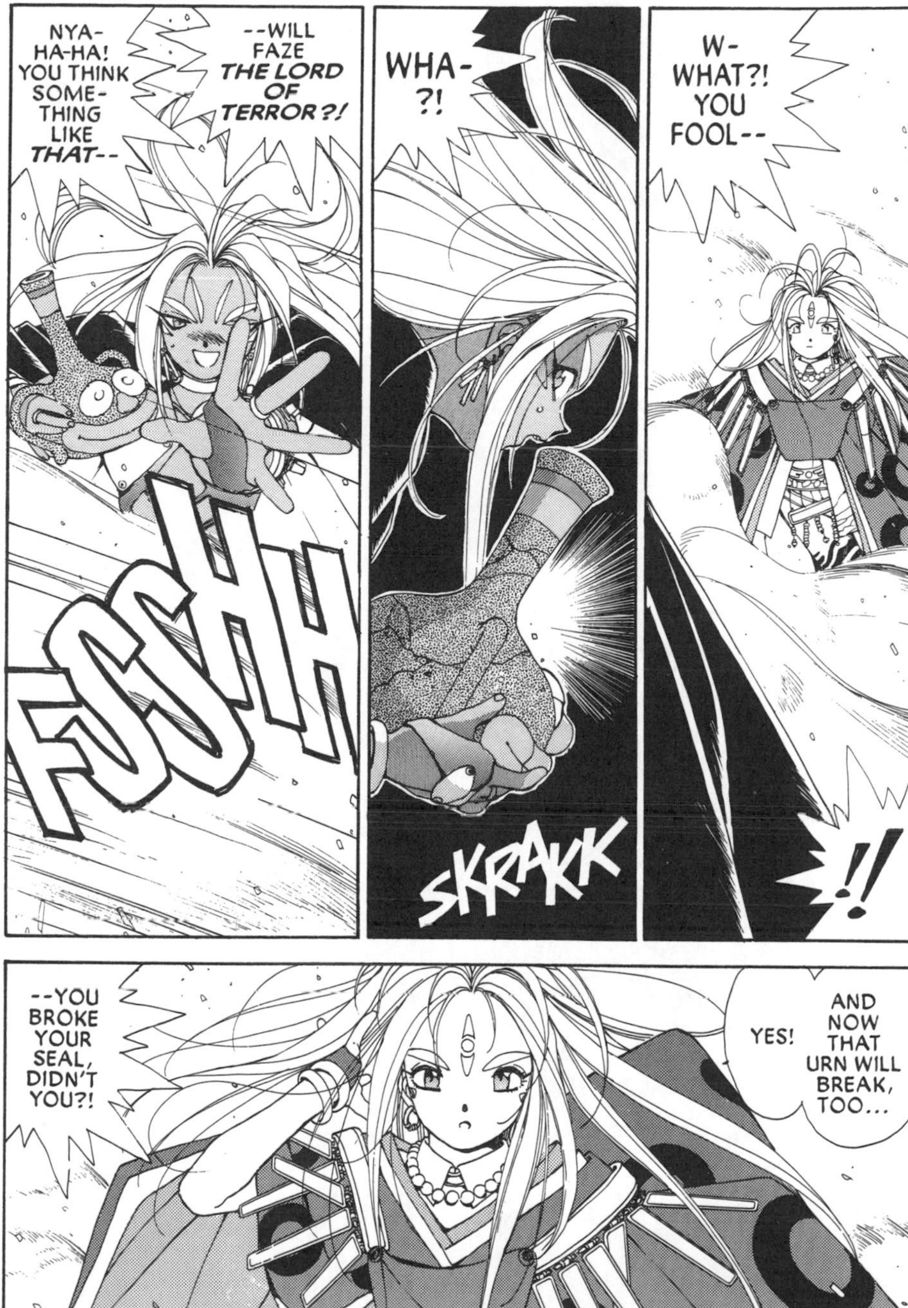
NYA-HA-HA! YOU THINK SOME-THING LIKE *THAT*--
--WILL FAZE *THE LORD OF TERROR?!*
FOSSHH
WHA-?!
SKRAKK
W-WHAT?! YOU FOOL--
!!
--YOU BROKE YOUR SEAL, DIDN'T YOU?!
YES!
AND NOW THAT URN WILL BREAK, TOO...

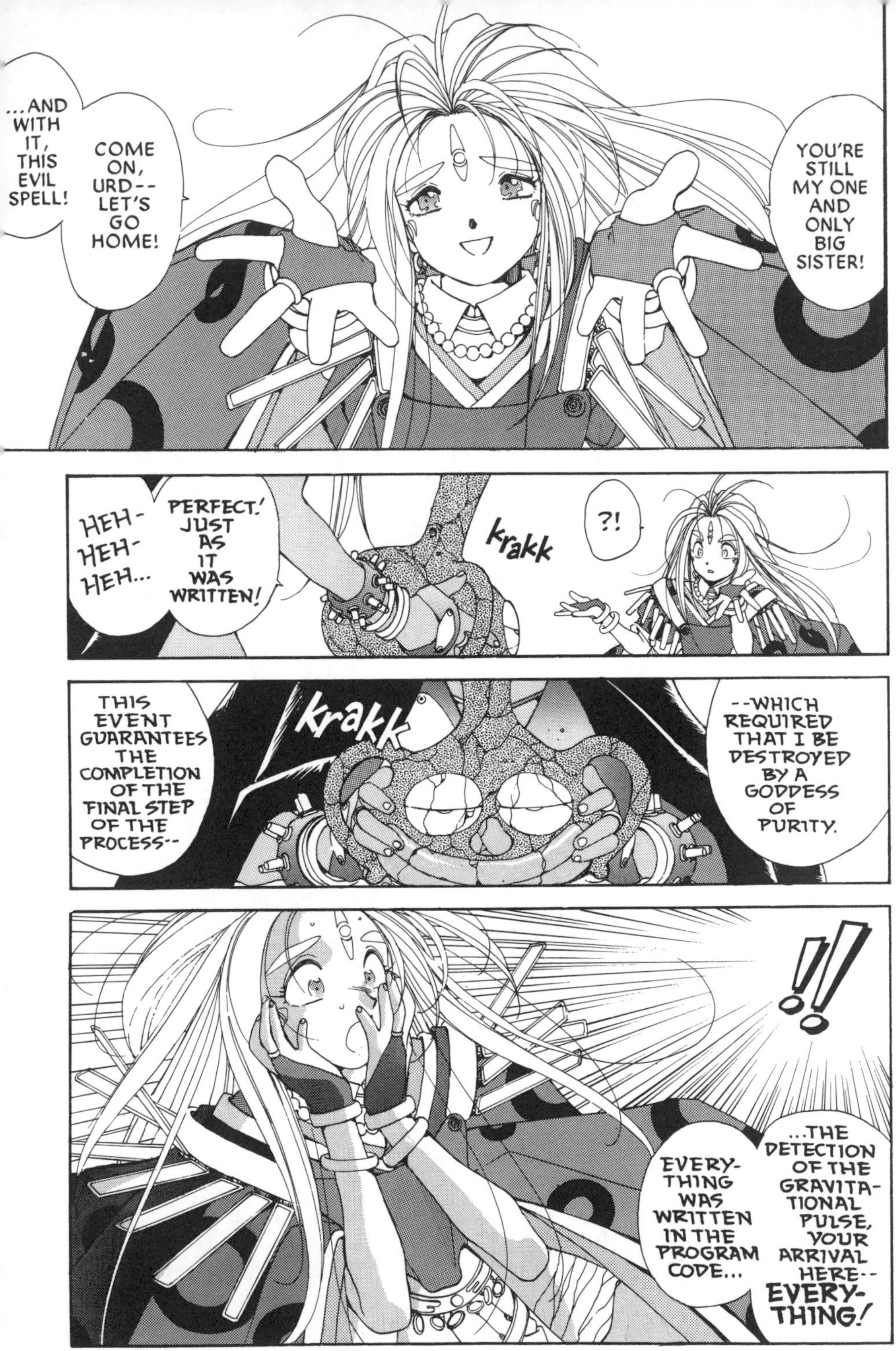
...AND WITH IT, THIS EVIL SPELL!
COME ON, URD-- LET'S GO HOME!
YOU'RE STILL MY ONE AND ONLY BIG SISTER!
HEH-HEH-HEH...
PERFECT! JUST AS IT WAS WRITTEN!
krakk
?!
THIS EVENT GUARANTEES THE COMPLETION OF THE FINAL STEP OF THE PROCESS--
krakk
--WHICH REQUIRED THAT I BE DESTROYED BY A GODDESS OF PURITY.
!!
...THE DETECTION OF THE GRAVITATIONAL PULSE, YOUR ARRIVAL HERE-- EVERYTHING!
EVERYTHING WAS WRITTEN IN THE PROGRAM CODE...

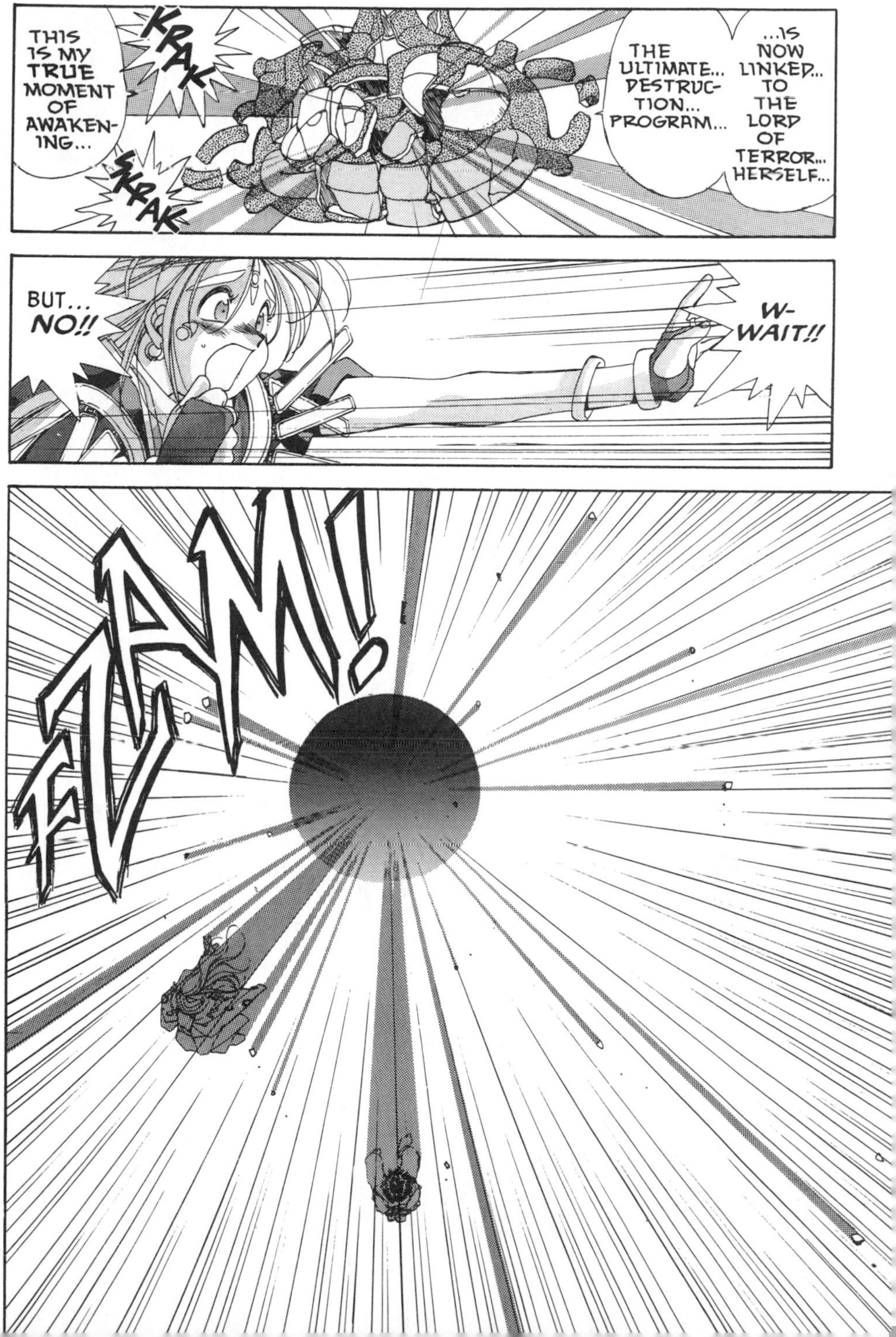
THIS IS MY TRUE MOMENT OF AWAKENING...
KRAK
SKRAK
THE ULTIMATE... DESTRUCTION... PROGRAM...
...IS NOW LINKED... TO THE LORD OF TERROR... HERSELF...
BUT... NO!!
W-WAIT!!
FZAM!!

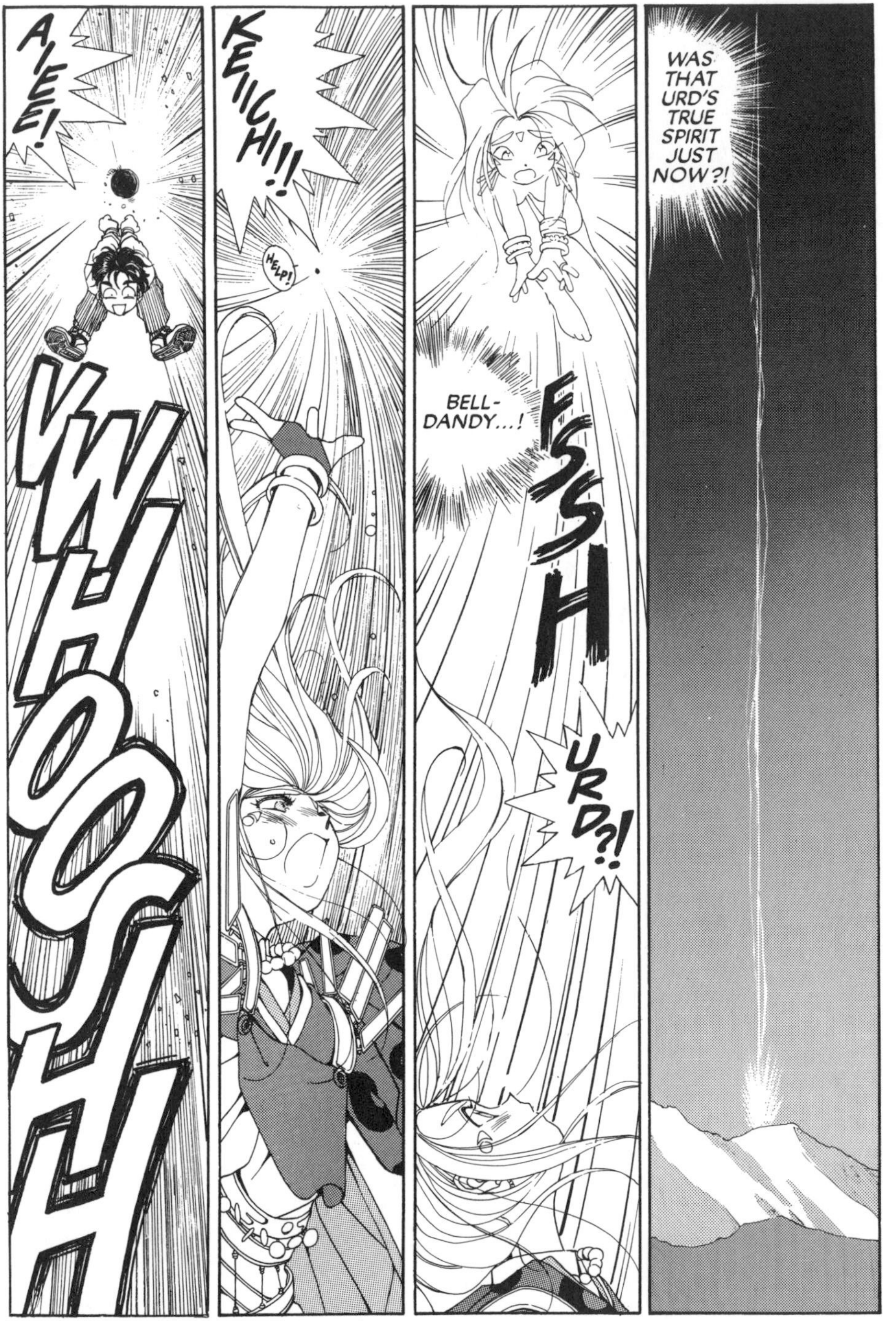
AIEEE!
WHOOSHH
KEIICHI!!
HELP!
BELL-DANDY...!
FSSH
URD?!
WAS THAT URD'S TRUE SPIRIT JUST NOW?!

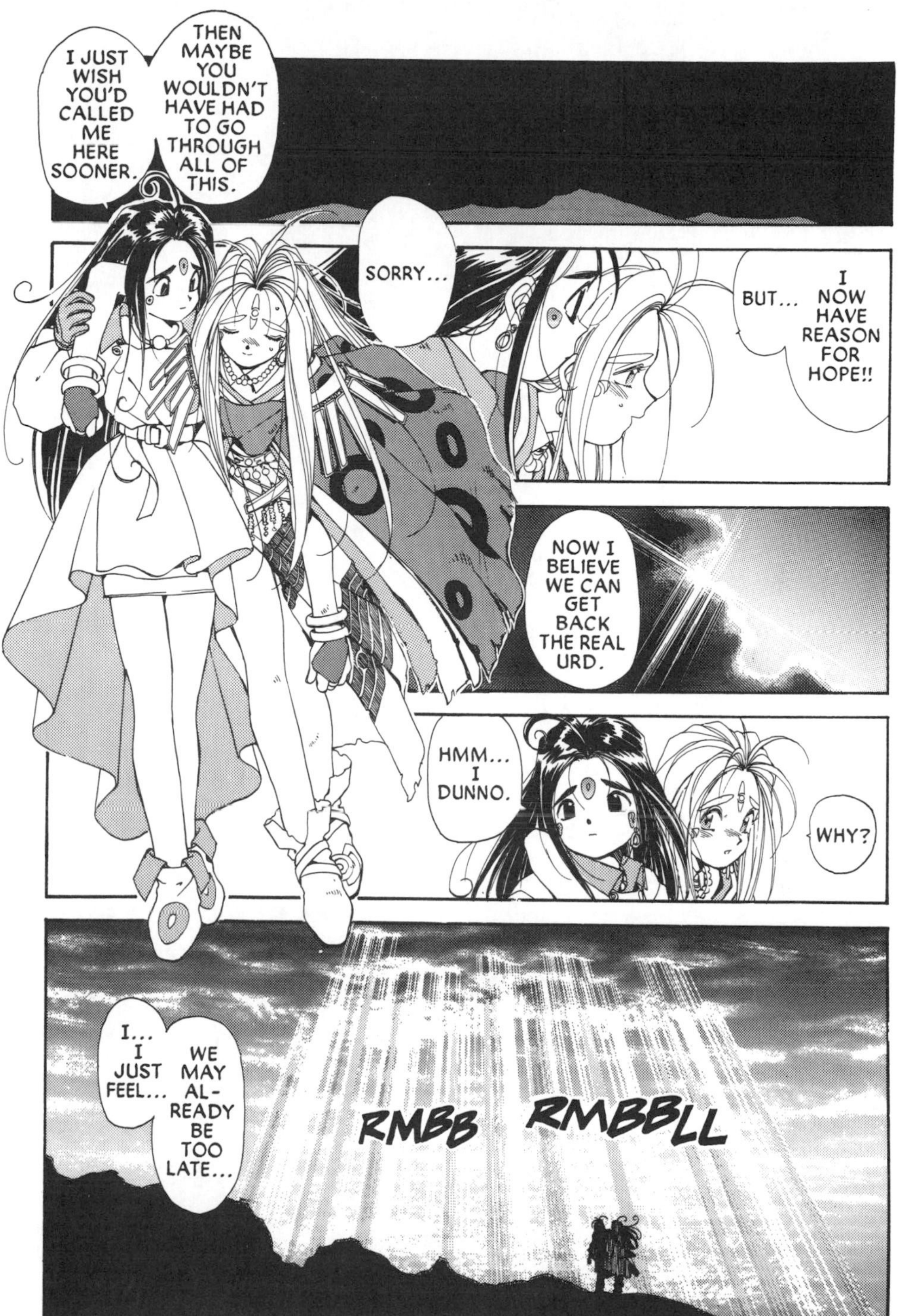
I JUST WISH YOU'D CALLED ME HERE SOONER.
THEN MAYBE YOU WOULDN'T HAVE HAD TO GO THROUGH ALL OF THIS.
SORRY...
BUT...
I NOW HAVE REASON FOR HOPE!!
NOW I BELIEVE WE CAN GET BACK THE REAL URD.
HMM... I DUNNO.
WHY?
I... I JUST FEEL...
WE MAY AL- READY BE TOO LATE...
RMBB RMBBLL

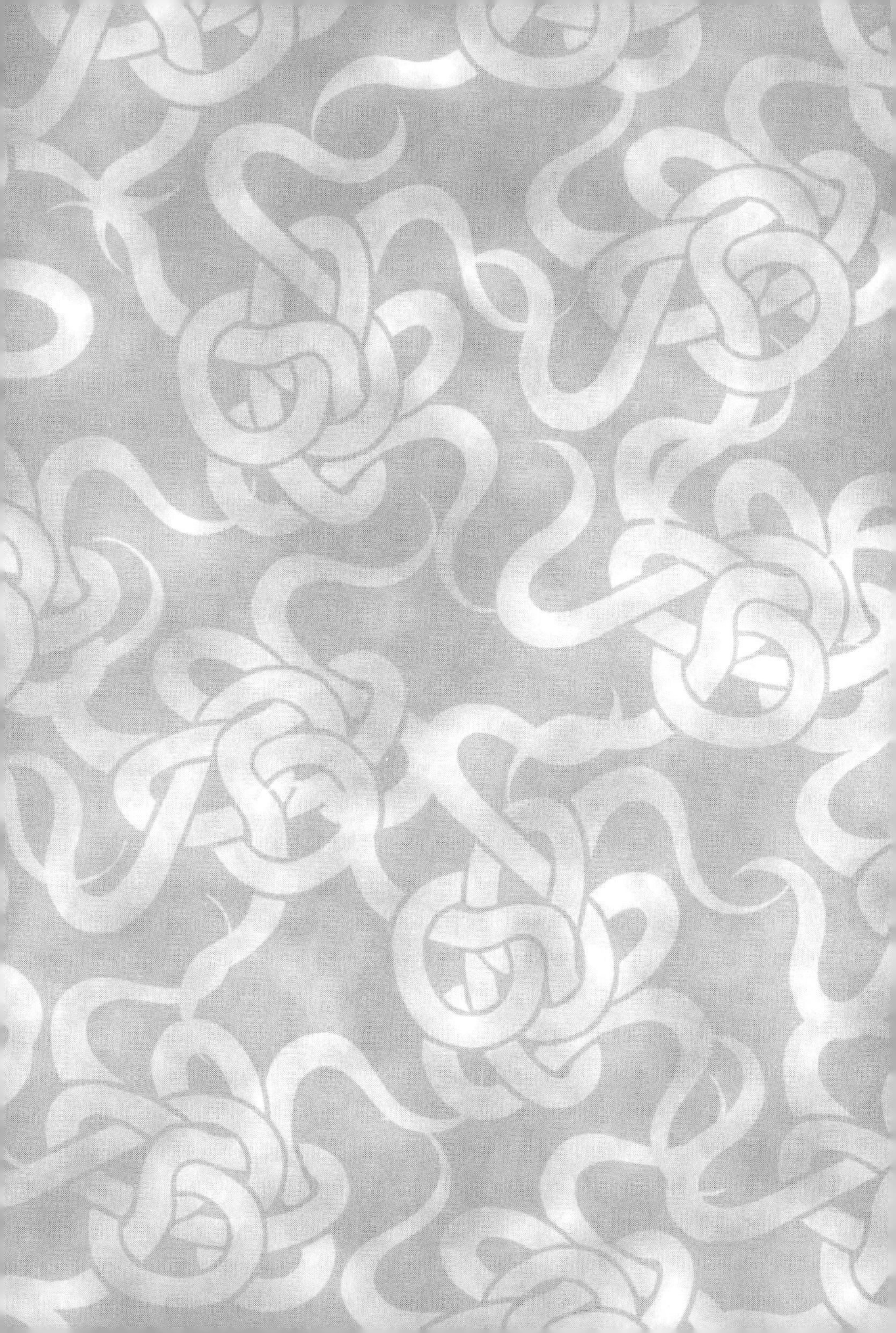

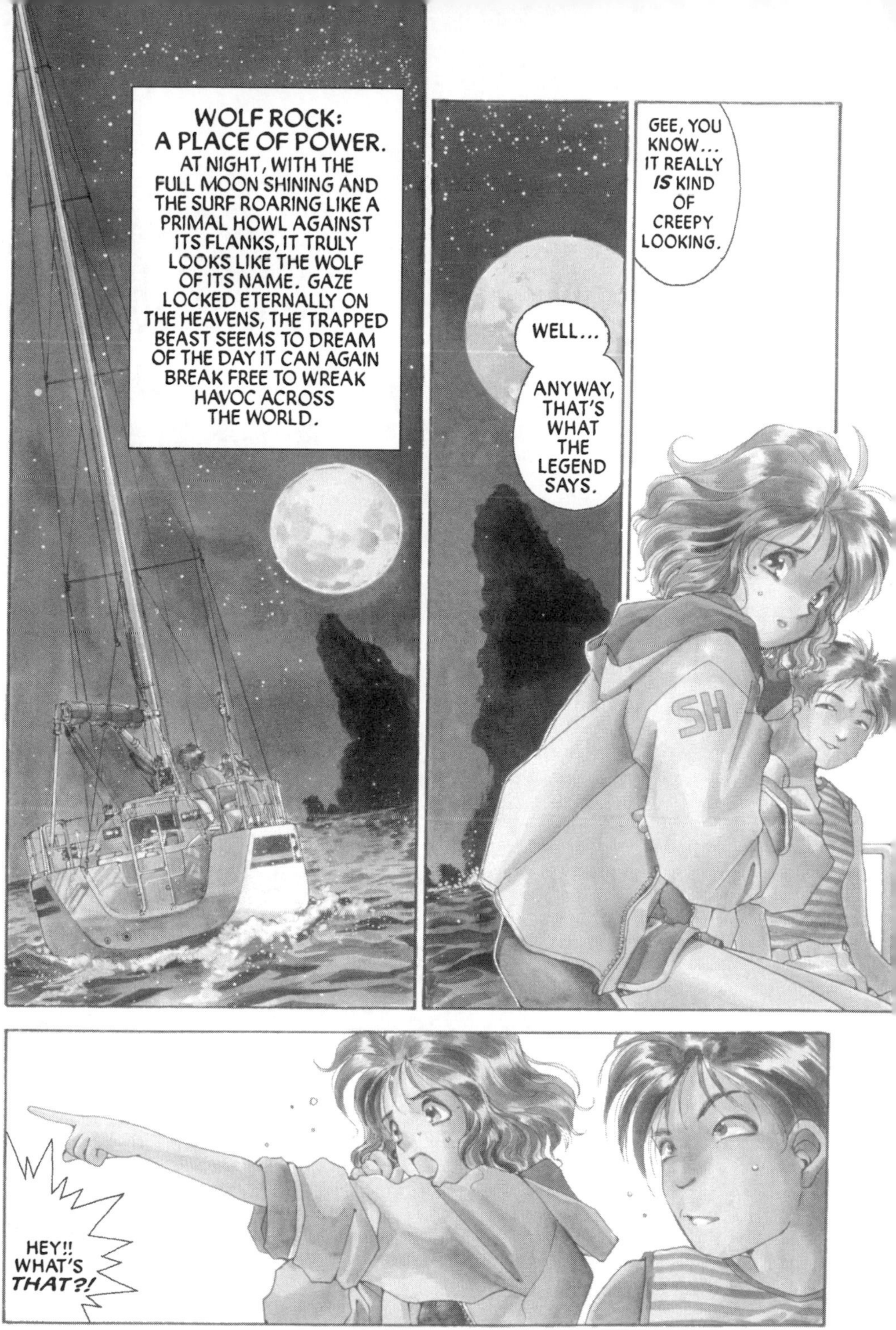
WOLF ROCK: A PLACE OF POWER.
AT NIGHT, WITH THE FULL MOON SHINING AND THE SURF ROARING LIKE A PRIMAL HOWL AGAINST ITS FLANKS, IT TRULY LOOKS LIKE THE WOLF OF ITS NAME. GAZE LOCKED ETERNALLY ON THE HEAVENS, THE TRAPPED BEAST SEEMS TO DREAM OF THE DAY IT CAN AGAIN BREAK FREE TO WREAK HAVOC ACROSS THE WORLD.
GEE, YOU KNOW... IT REALLY *IS* KIND OF CREEPY LOOKING.
WELL...
ANYWAY, THAT'S WHAT THE LEGEND SAYS.
HEY!! WHAT'S *THAT?!*

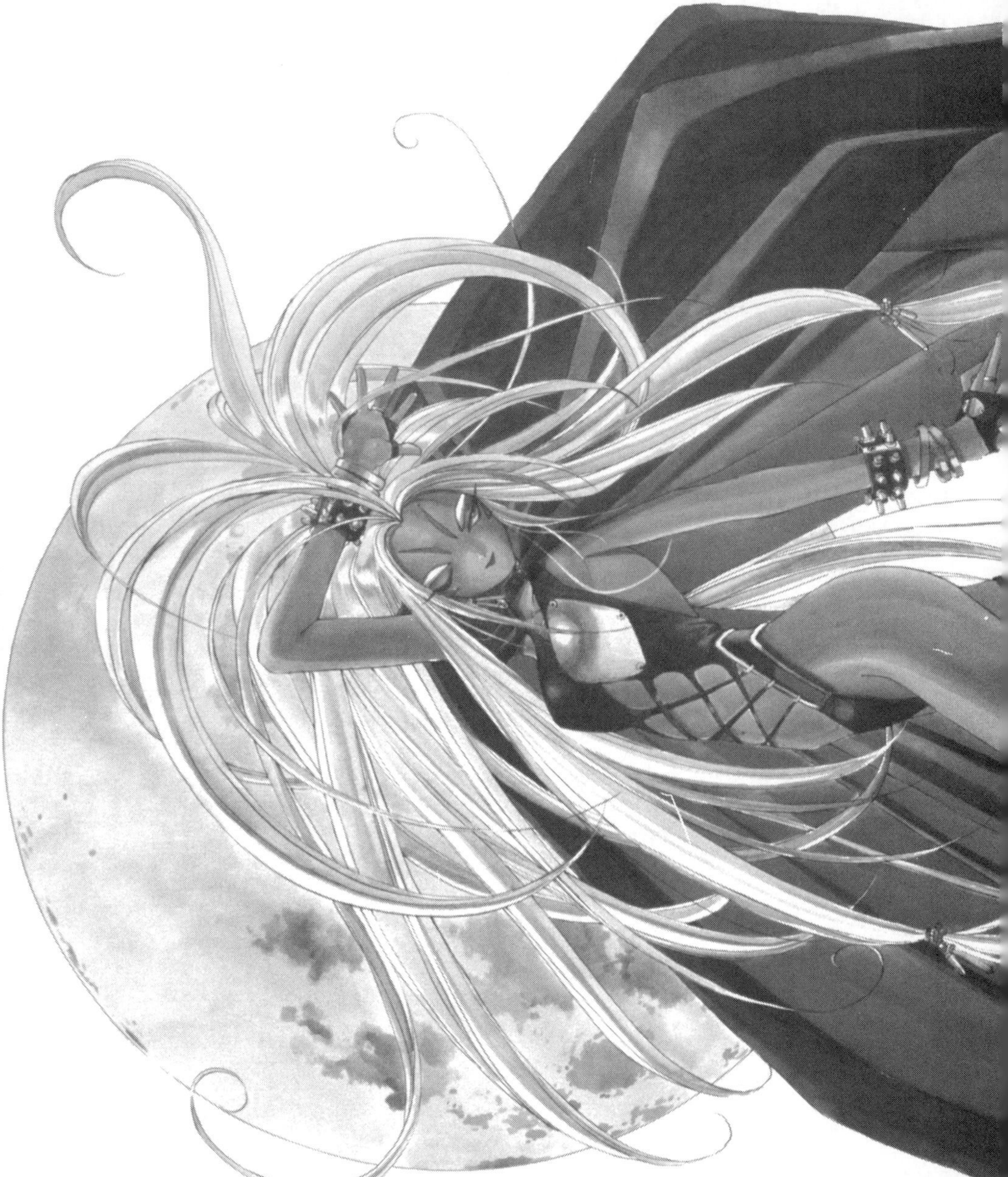

Urd Calls Forth the Beast

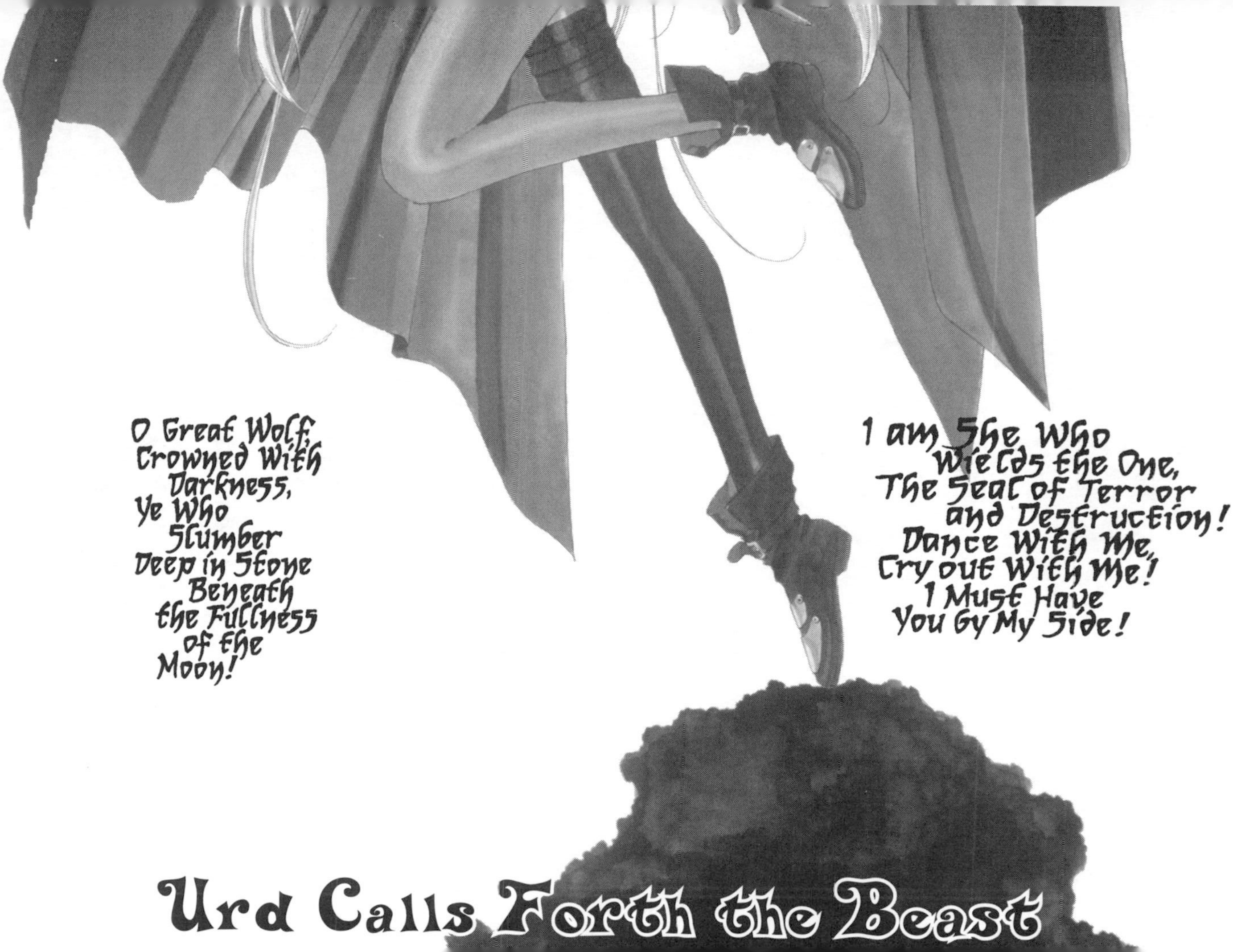
O Great Wolf,
Crowned With
Darkness,
Ye Who
Slumber
Deep in Stone
Beneath
the Fullness
of the
Moon!
I am She Who
Wields the One,
The Seal of Terror
and Destruction!
Dance With Me,
Cry out With Me!
I Must Have
You by My Side!

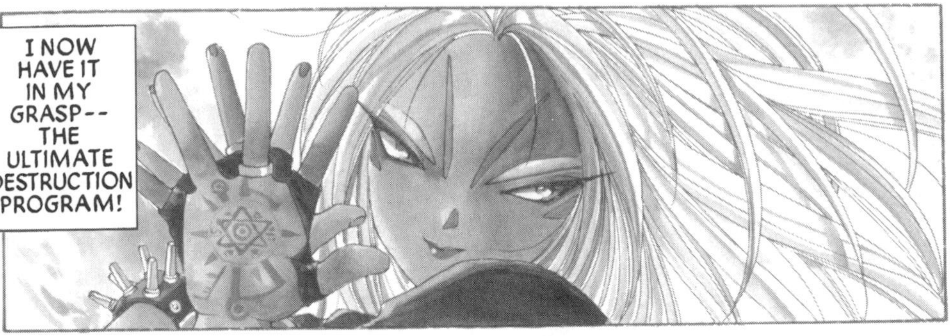
I NOW HAVE IT IN MY GRASP-- THE ULTIMATE DESTRUCTION PROGRAM!

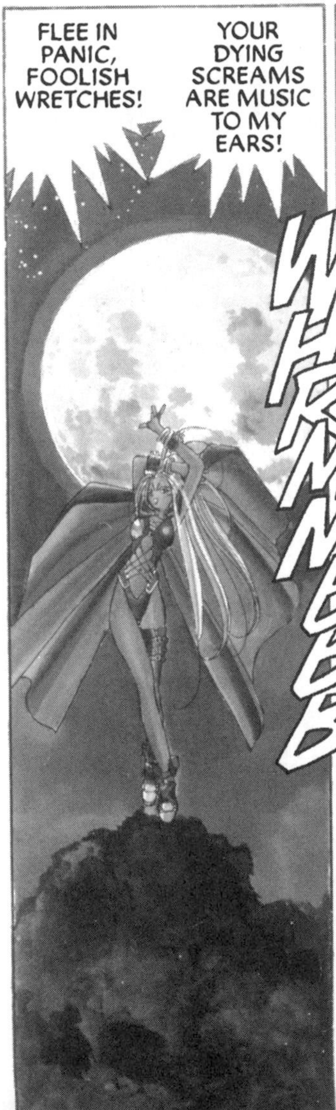
FLEE IN PANIC, FOOLISH WRETCHES!
YOUR DYING SCREAMS ARE MUSIC TO MY EARS!
WHRMMBBB

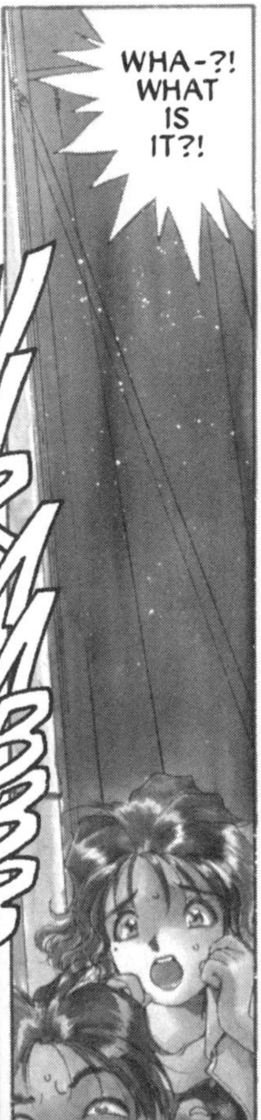
WHA-?! WHAT IS IT?!

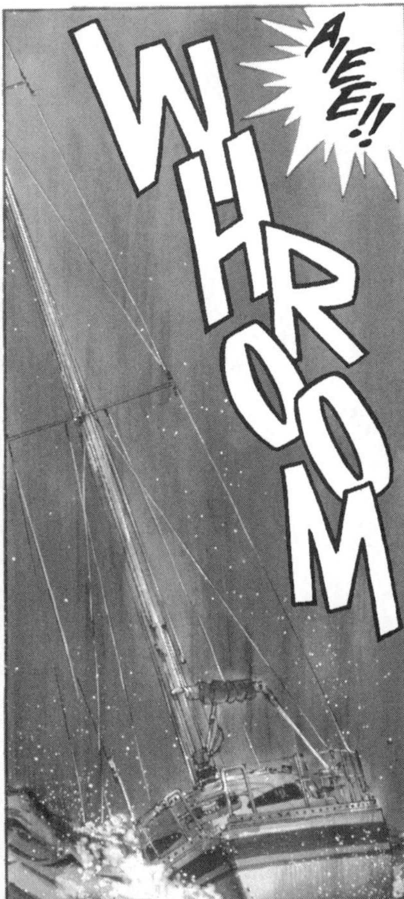
WHROOM
AIEE!!

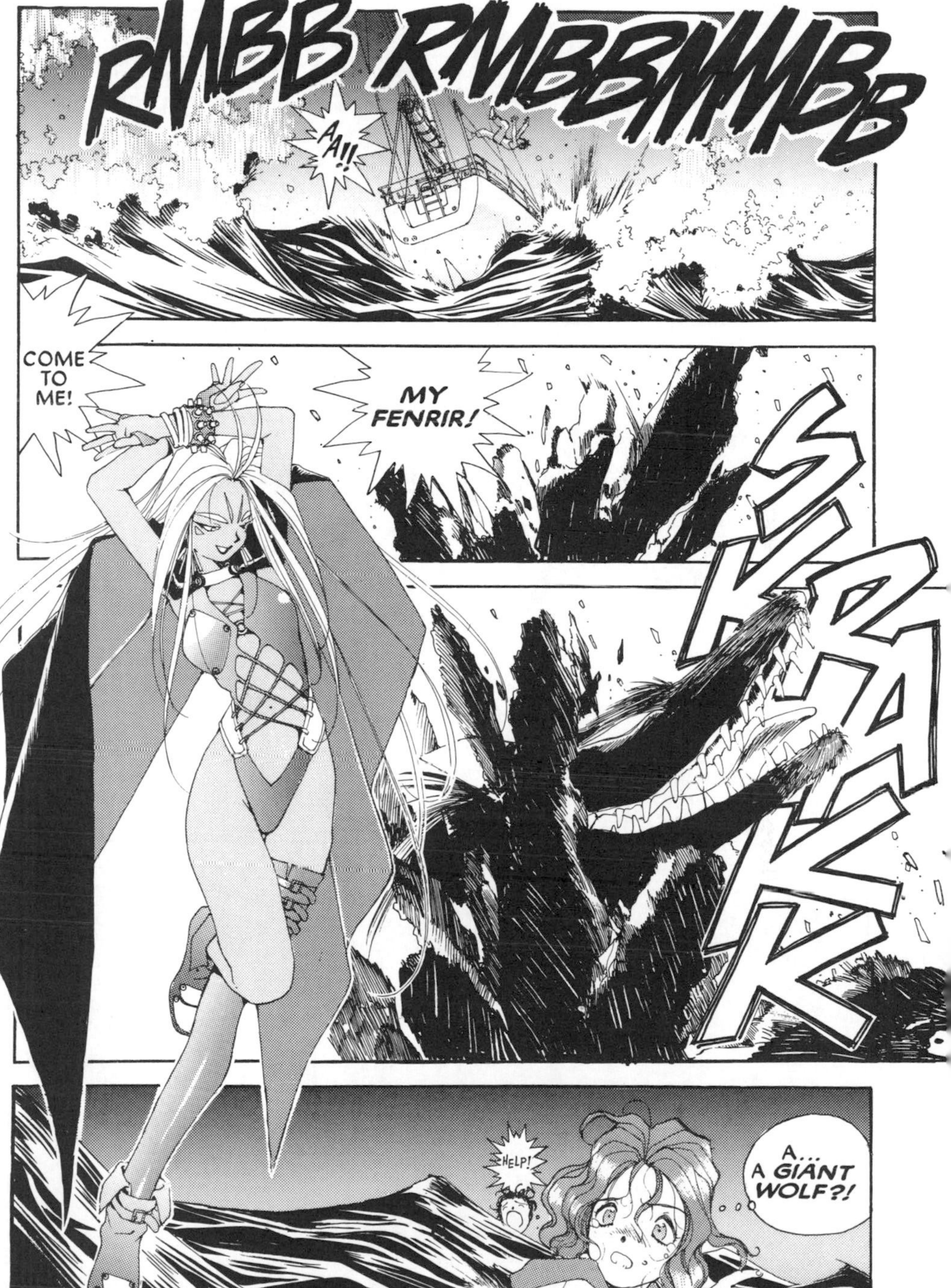
RMBB RMBBMMBB
AA!!
COME TO ME!
MY FENRIR!
SKRAKK
HELP!
A... A GIANT WOLF?!

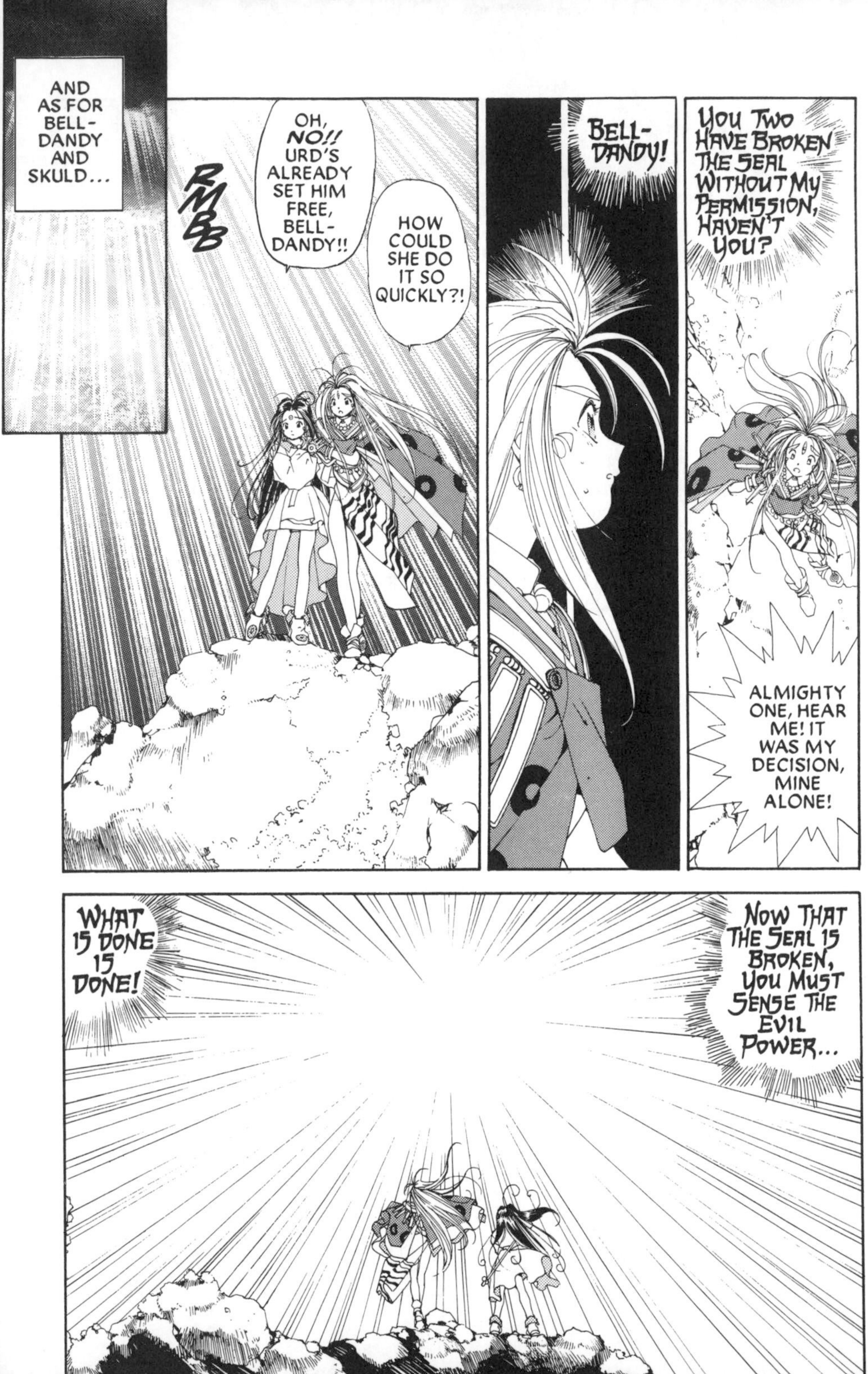
AND AS FOR BELL-DANDY AND SKULD...
RMBB
OH, NO!! URD'S ALREADY SET HIM FREE, BELL-DANDY!!
HOW COULD SHE DO IT SO QUICKLY?!
BELL-DANDY!
YOU TWO HAVE BROKEN THE SEAL WITHOUT MY PERMISSION, HAVEN'T YOU?
ALMIGHTY ONE, HEAR ME! IT WAS MY DECISION, MINE ALONE!
WHAT IS DONE IS DONE!
NOW THAT THE SEAL IS BROKEN, YOU MUST SENSE THE EVIL POWER...

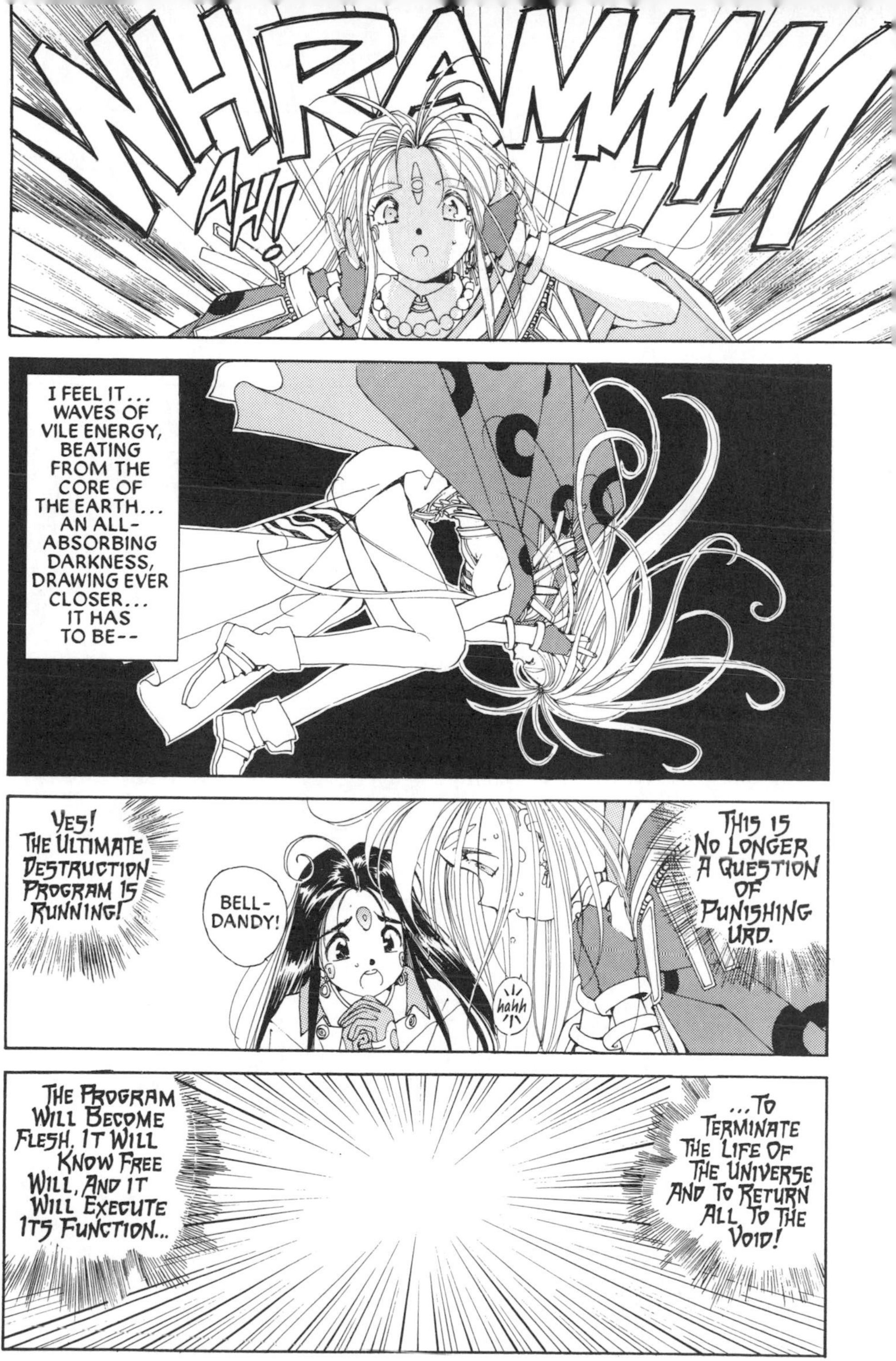
WHRAMMM
AH!
I FEEL IT... WAVES OF VILE ENERGY, BEATING FROM THE CORE OF THE EARTH... AN ALL-ABSORBING DARKNESS, DRAWING EVER CLOSER... IT HAS TO BE--
YES! THE ULTIMATE DESTRUCTION PROGRAM IS RUNNING!
BELL-DANDY!
hahh
THIS IS NO LONGER A QUESTION OF PUNISHING URD.
THE PROGRAM WILL BECOME FLESH, IT WILL KNOW FREE WILL, AND IT WILL EXECUTE ITS FUNCTION...
...TO TERMINATE THE LIFE OF THE UNIVERSE AND TO RETURN ALL TO THE VOID!

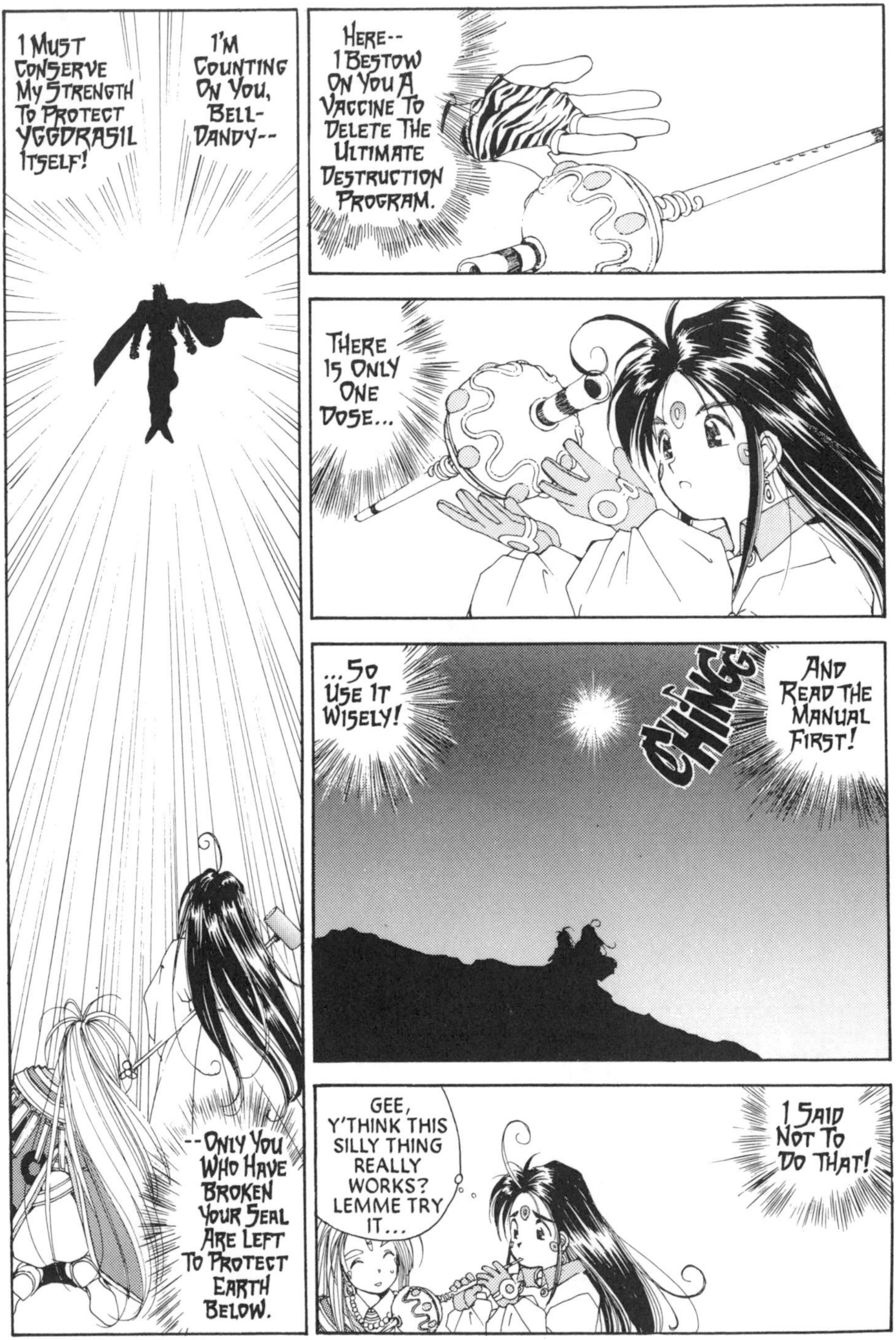
I MUST CONSERVE MY STRENGTH TO PROTECT YGGDRASIL ITSELF!
I'M COUNTING ON YOU, BELL-DANDY--
--ONLY YOU WHO HAVE BROKEN YOUR SEAL ARE LEFT TO PROTECT EARTH BELOW.
HERE-- I BESTOW ON YOU A VACCINE TO DELETE THE ULTIMATE DESTRUCTION PROGRAM.
THERE IS ONLY ONE DOSE...
...SO USE IT WISELY!
CHING
AND READ THE MANUAL FIRST!
GEE, Y'THINK THIS SILLY THING REALLY WORKS? LEMME TRY IT...
I SAID NOT TO DO THAT!

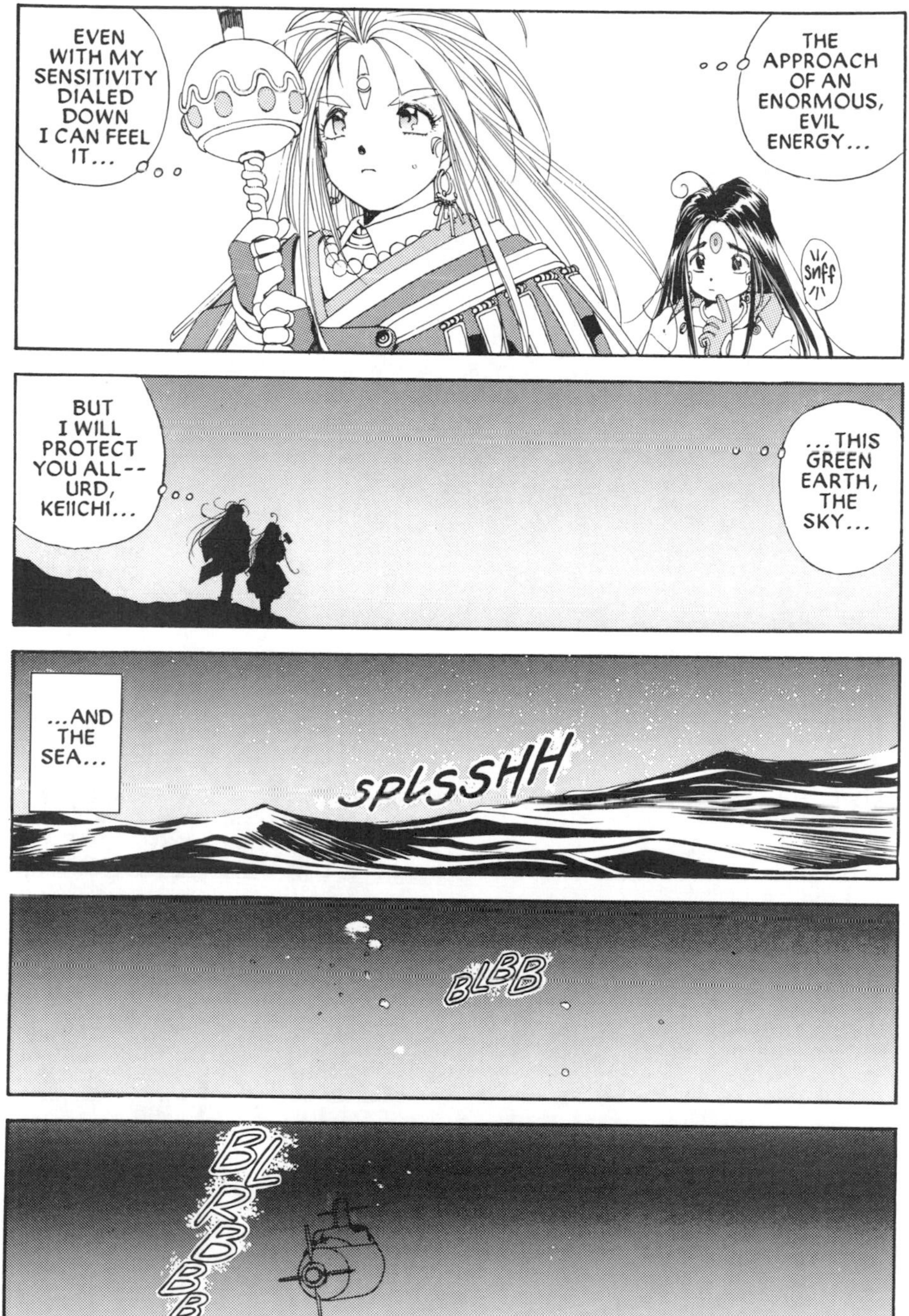
EVEN WITH MY SENSITIVITY DIALED DOWN I CAN FEEL IT...
THE APPROACH OF AN ENORMOUS, EVIL ENERGY...
SNFF
BUT I WILL PROTECT YOU ALL--URD, KEIICHI...
...THIS GREEN EARTH, THE SKY...
...AND THE SEA...
SPLSSHH
BLBB
BLRBBB

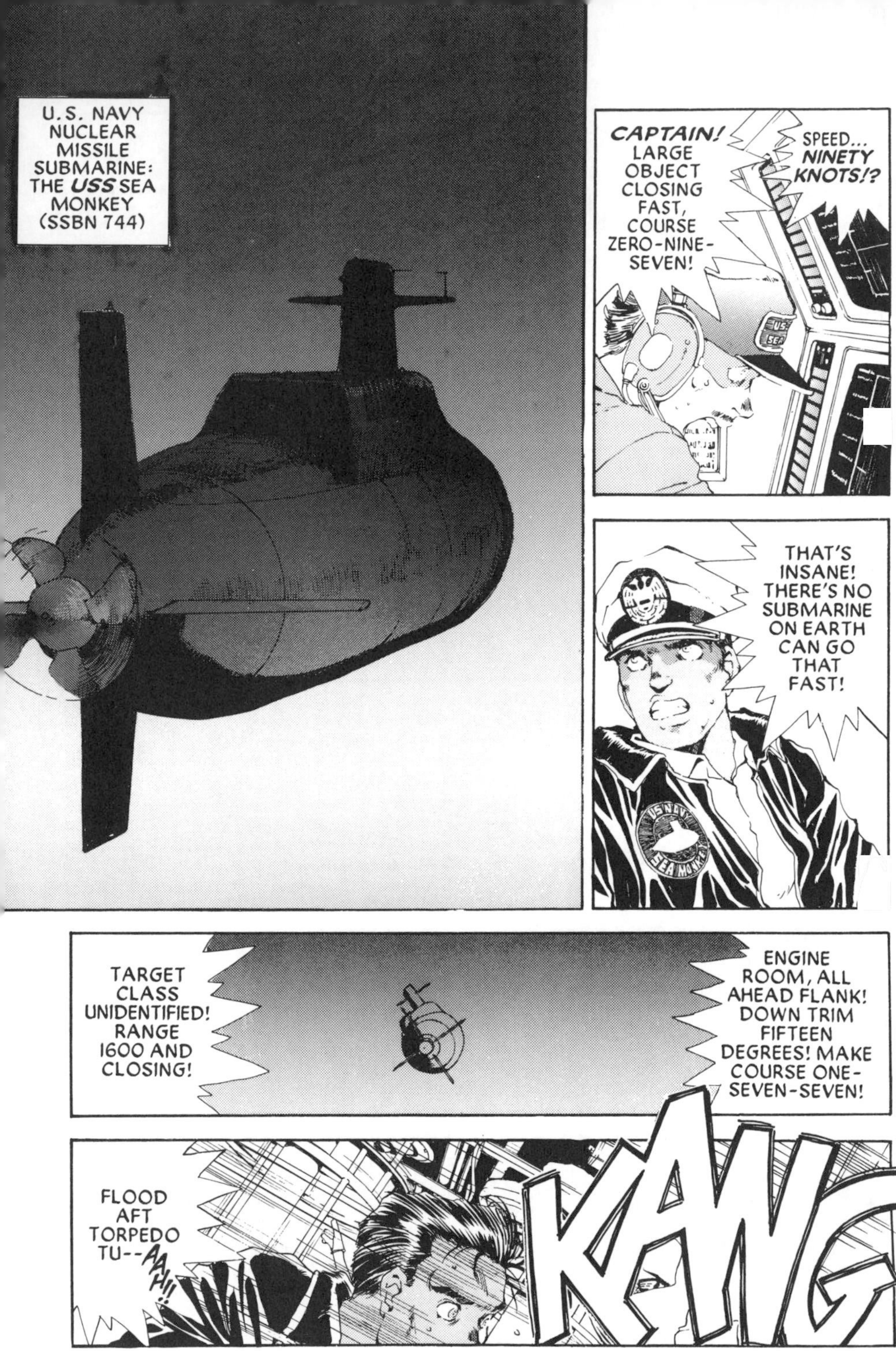
U.S. NAVY NUCLEAR MISSILE SUBMARINE: THE USS SEA MONKEY (SSBN 744)
CAPTAIN! LARGE OBJECT CLOSING FAST, COURSE ZERO-NINE-SEVEN!
SPEED... NINETY KNOTS!?
THAT'S INSANE! THERE'S NO SUBMARINE ON EARTH CAN GO THAT FAST!
TARGET CLASS UNIDENTIFIED! RANGE 1600 AND CLOSING!
ENGINE ROOM, ALL AHEAD FLANK! DOWN TRIM FIFTEEN DEGREES! MAKE COURSE ONE-SEVEN-SEVEN!
FLOOD AFT TORPEDO TU--AAH!!
KANG

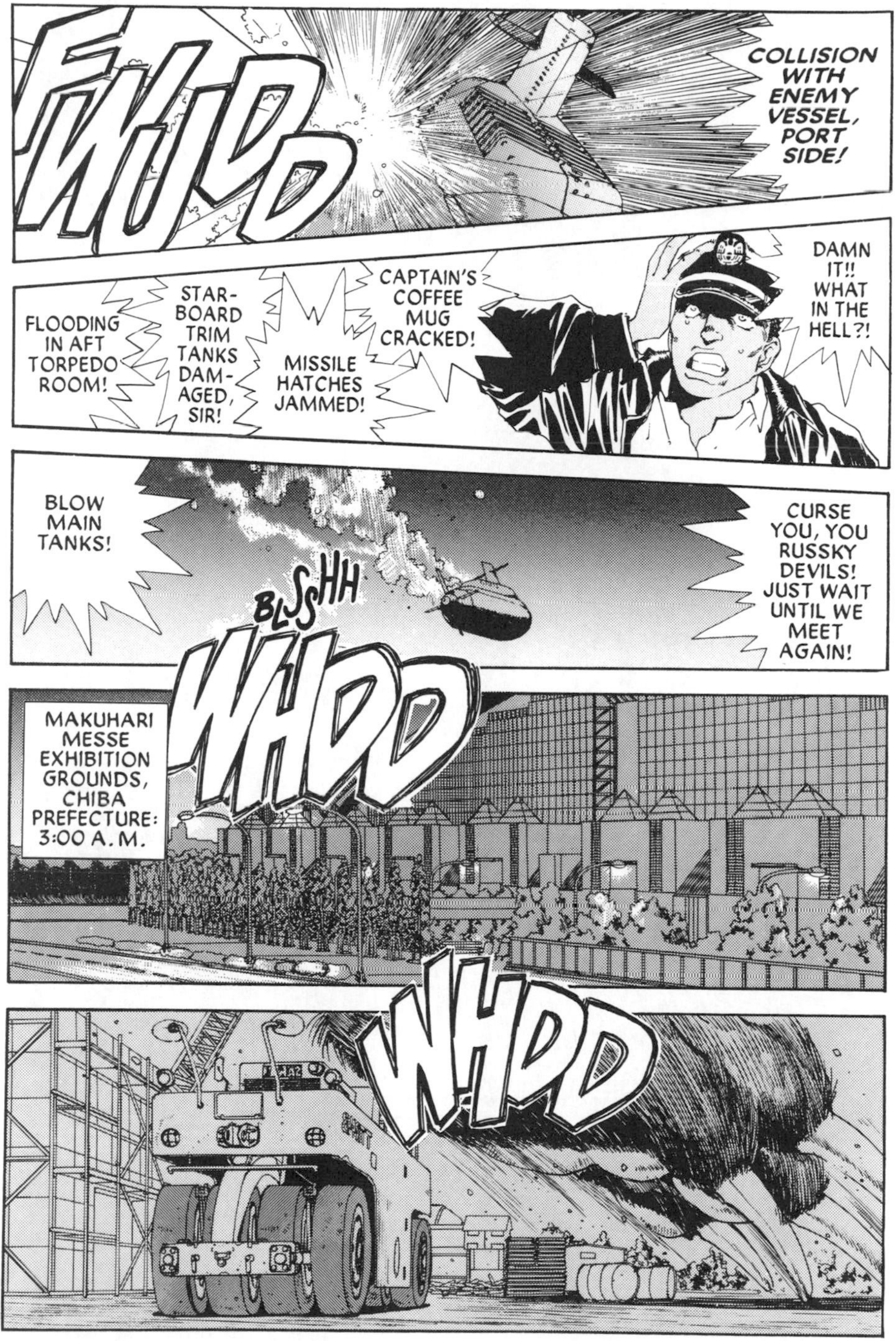
COLLISION WITH ENEMY VESSEL, PORT SIDE!
FLOODING IN AFT TORPEDO ROOM!
STAR-BOARD TRIM TANKS DAM-AGED, SIR!
MISSILE HATCHES JAMMED!
CAPTAIN'S COFFEE MUG CRACKED!
DAMN IT!! WHAT IN THE HELL?!
BLOW MAIN TANKS!
BLSSHH
CURSE YOU, YOU RUSSKY DEVILS! JUST WAIT UNTIL WE MEET AGAIN!
WHDD
MAKUHARI MESSE EXHIBITION GROUNDS, CHIBA PREFECTURE: 3:00 A. M.
WHDD

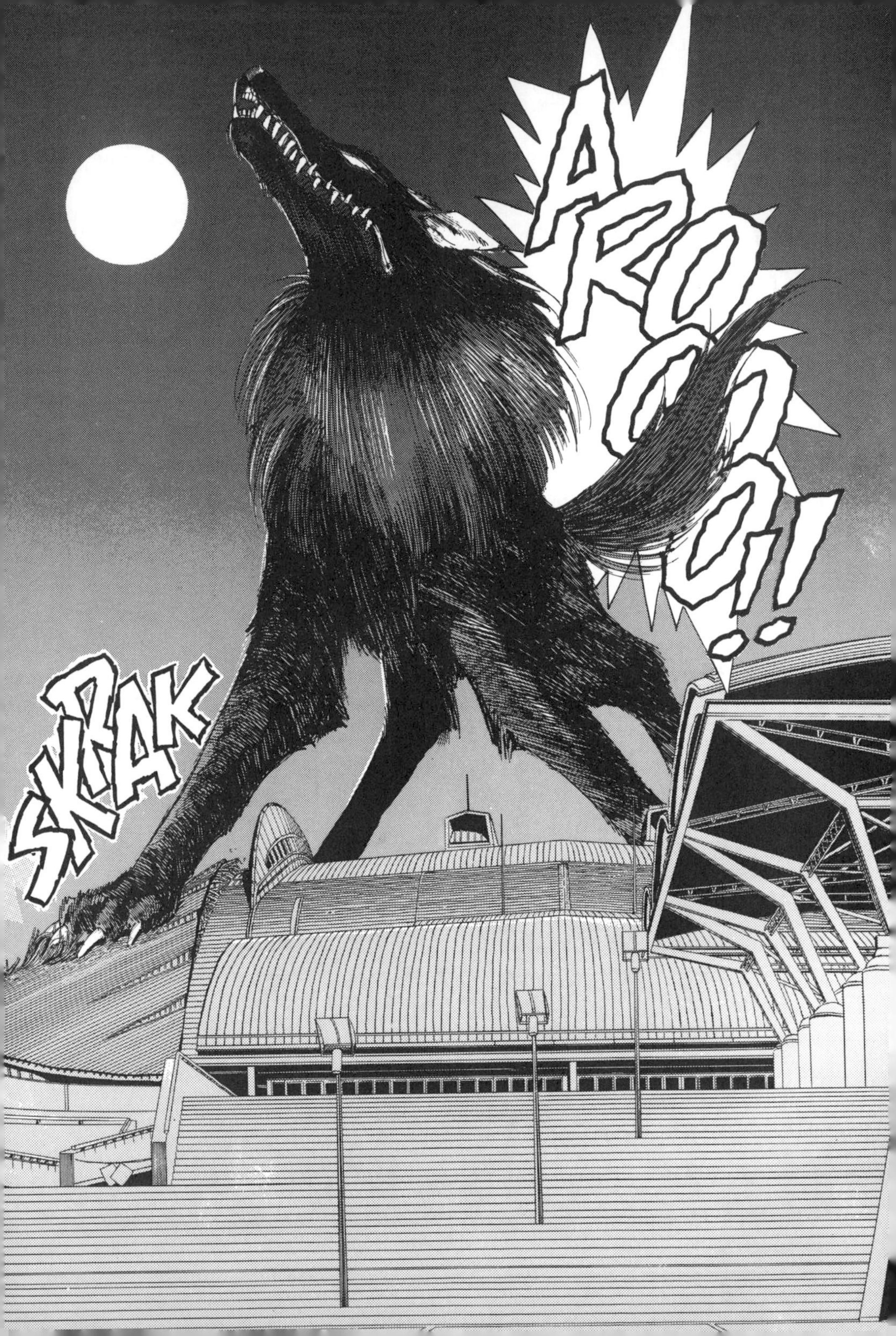
AROOOO!!
SKRAK

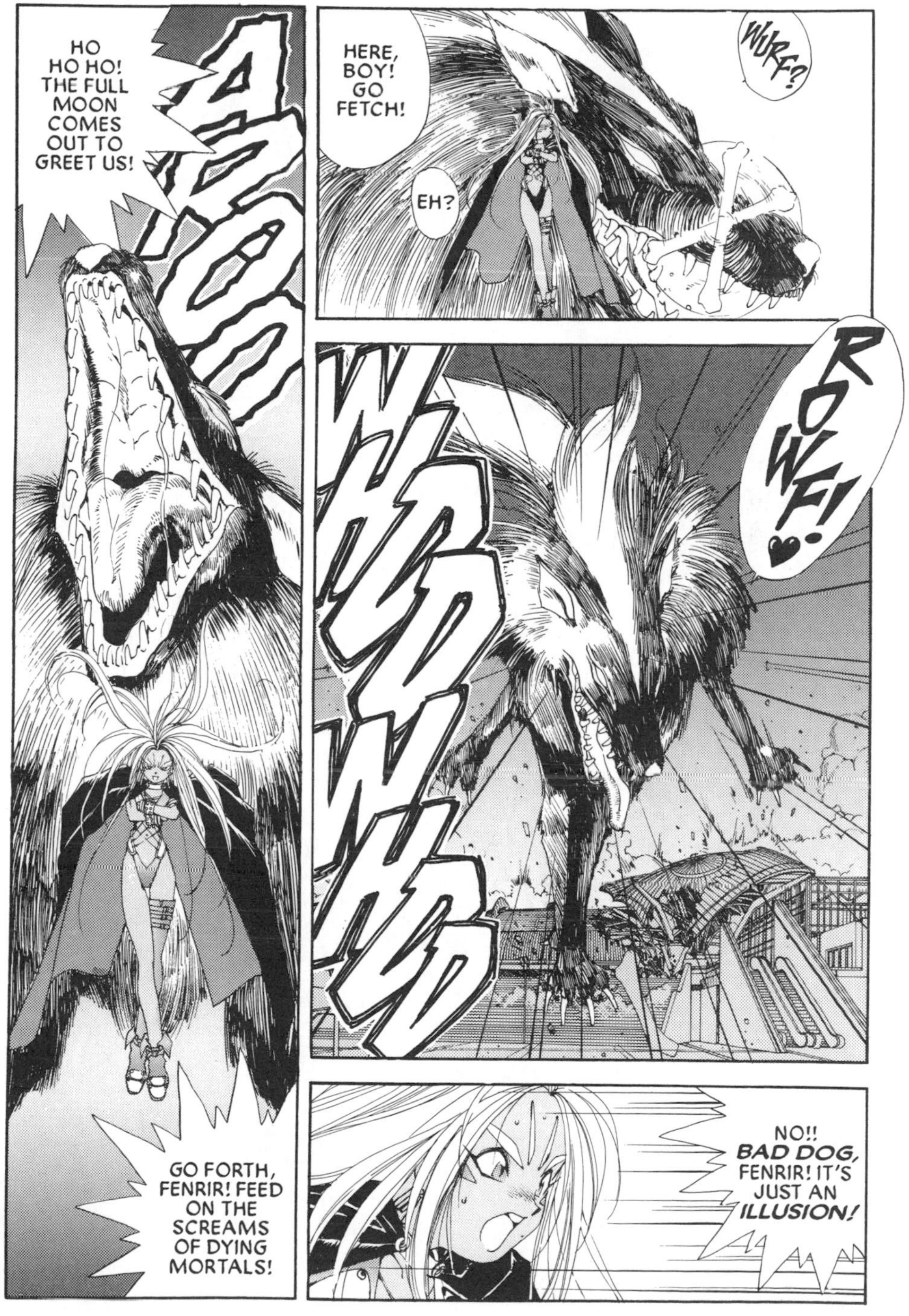
HO HO HO! THE FULL MOON COMES OUT TO GREET US!
GO FORTH, FENRIR! FEED ON THE SCREAMS OF DYING MORTALS!
HERE, BOY! GO FETCH!
EH?
WURF?
ROWF! ♥
NO!! BAD DOG, FENRIR! IT'S JUST AN ILLUSION!

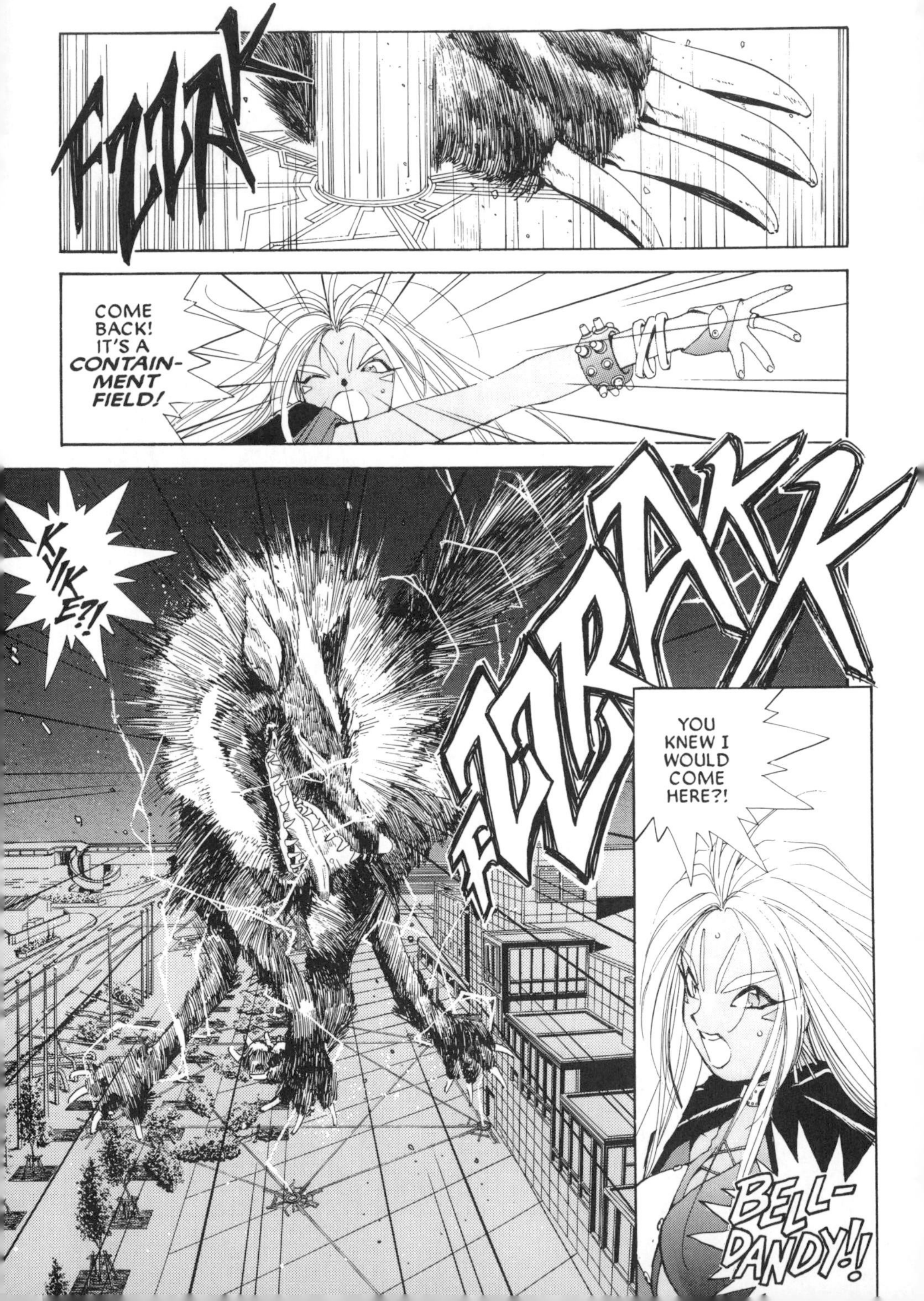
FZZAK
COME BACK! IT'S A CONTAINMENT FIELD!
KYIKE?!
ZZRAKK
YOU KNEW I WOULD COME HERE?!
BELL-DANDY!!

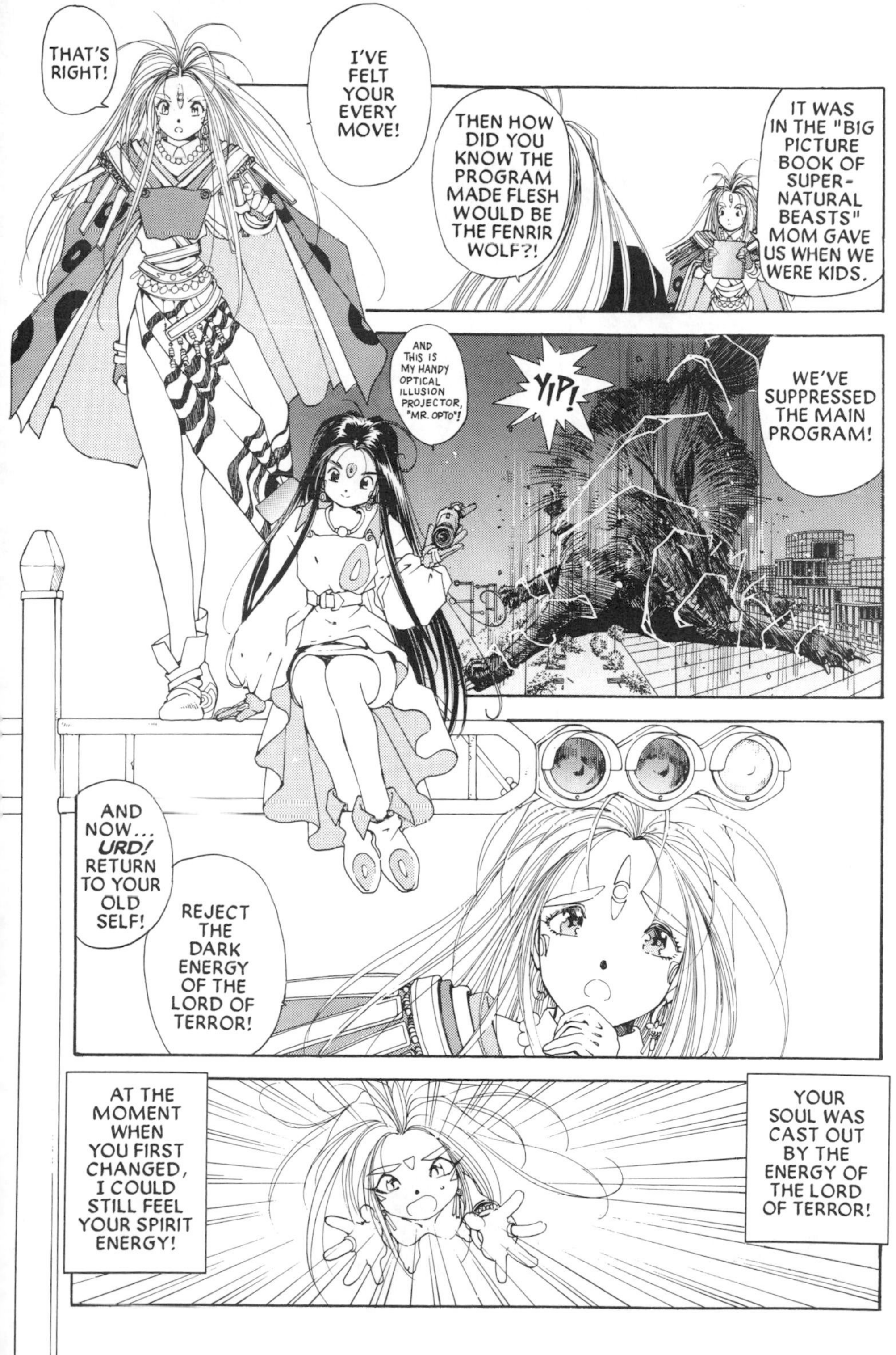
THAT'S RIGHT!
I'VE FELT YOUR EVERY MOVE!
THEN HOW DID YOU KNOW THE PROGRAM MADE FLESH WOULD BE THE FENRIR WOLF?!
IT WAS IN THE "BIG PICTURE BOOK OF SUPER-NATURAL BEASTS" MOM GAVE US WHEN WE WERE KIDS.
AND THIS IS MY HANDY OPTICAL ILLUSION PROJECTOR, "MR. OPTO"!
YIP!
WE'VE SUPPRESSED THE MAIN PROGRAM!
AND NOW... URD! RETURN TO YOUR OLD SELF!
REJECT THE DARK ENERGY OF THE LORD OF TERROR!
AT THE MOMENT WHEN YOU FIRST CHANGED, I COULD STILL FEEL YOUR SPIRIT ENERGY!
YOUR SOUL WAS CAST OUT BY THE ENERGY OF THE LORD OF TERROR!

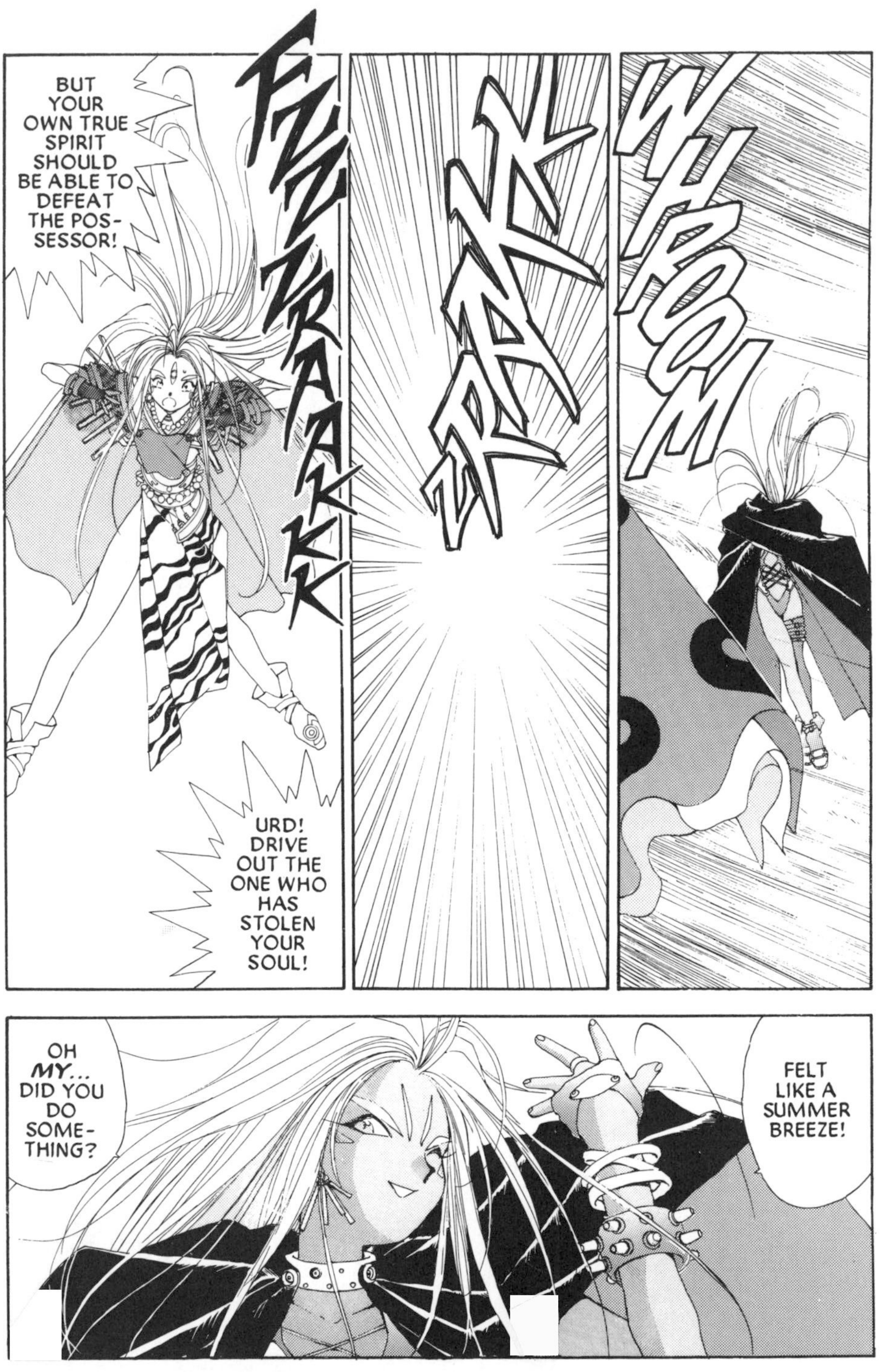
BUT YOUR OWN TRUE SPIRIT SHOULD BE ABLE TO DEFEAT THE POS-SESSOR!
FZZZRAKKK
URD! DRIVE OUT THE ONE WHO HAS STOLEN YOUR SOUL!
ZRAK
WHOOM
OH MY... DID YOU DO SOME-THING?
FELT LIKE A SUMMER BREEZE!

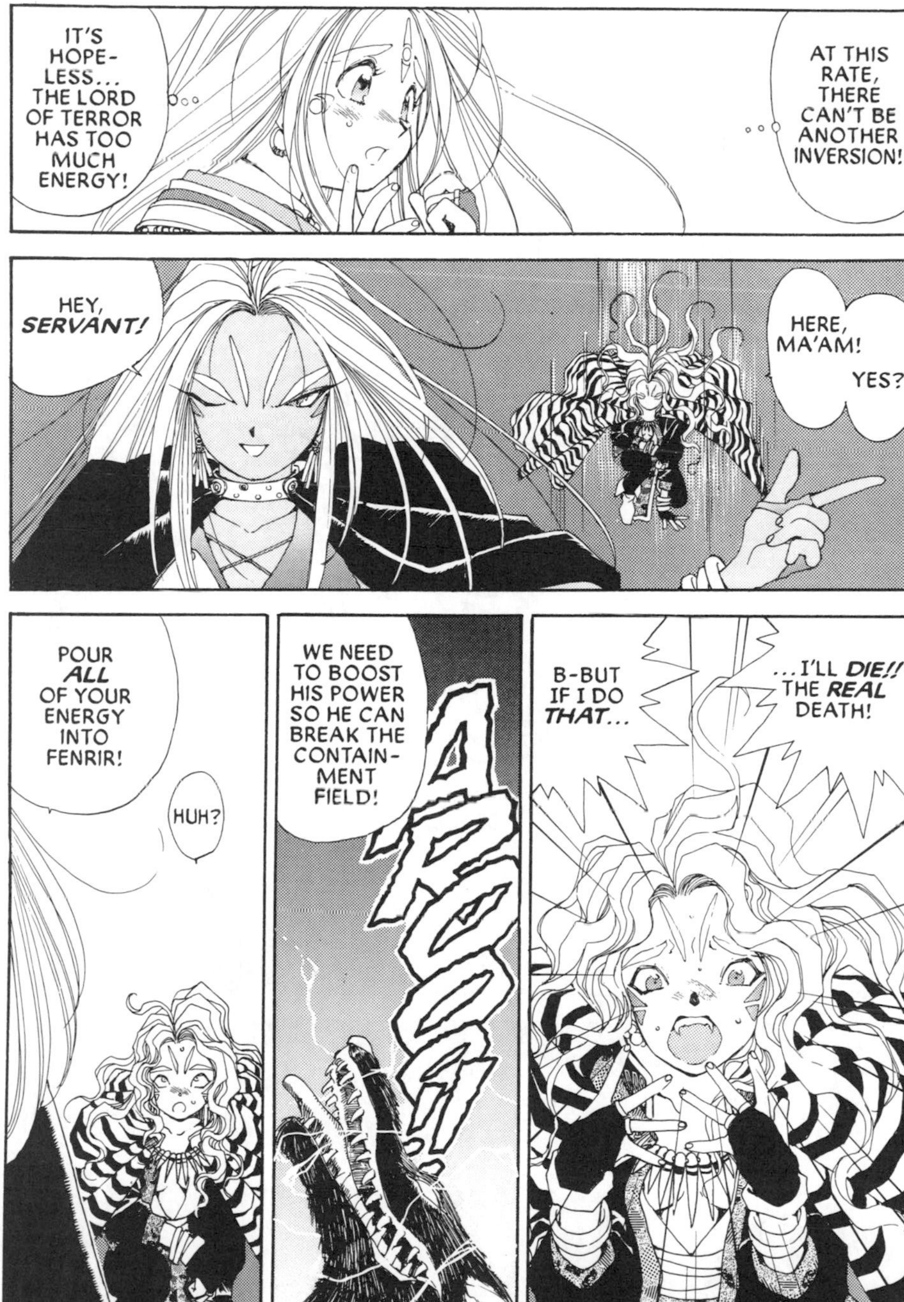
IT'S HOPE-LESS... THE LORD OF TERROR HAS TOO MUCH ENERGY!
AT THIS RATE, THERE CAN'T BE ANOTHER INVERSION!
HEY, *SERVANT!*
HERE, MA'AM!
YES?
POUR *ALL* OF YOUR ENERGY INTO FENRIR!
HUH?
WE NEED TO BOOST HIS POWER SO HE CAN BREAK THE CONTAIN-MENT FIELD!
B-BUT IF I DO *THAT*...
...I'LL *DIE!!* THE *REAL* DEATH!

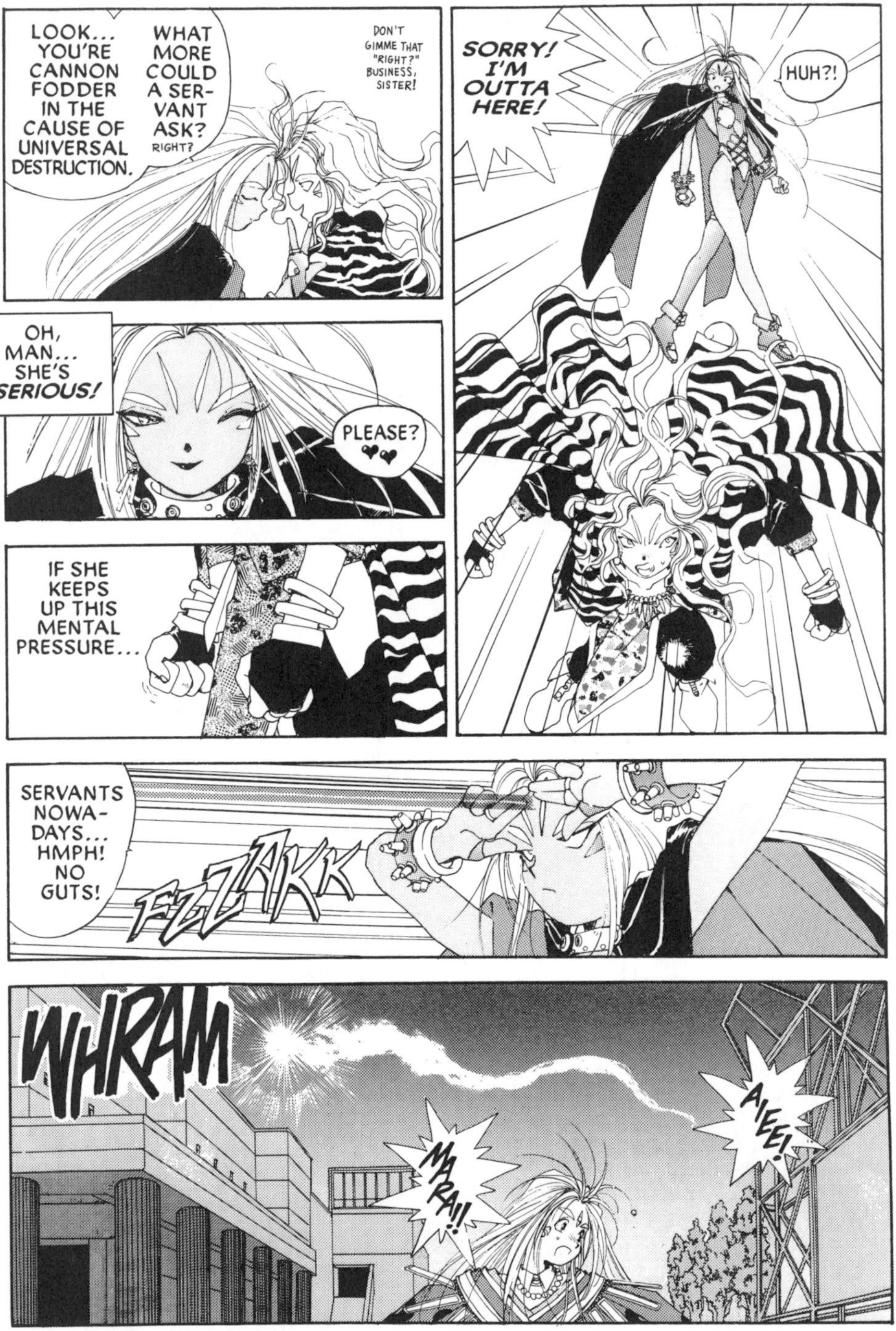
LOOK... YOU'RE CANNON FODDER IN THE CAUSE OF UNIVERSAL DESTRUCTION.
WHAT MORE COULD A SERVANT ASK? RIGHT?
DON'T GIMME THAT "RIGHT?" BUSINESS, SISTER!
OH, MAN... SHE'S SERIOUS!
PLEASE? ❤❤
IF SHE KEEPS UP THIS MENTAL PRESSURE...
SORRY! I'M OUTTA HERE!
HUH?!
SERVANTS NOWADAYS... HMPH! NO GUTS!
FZZZAKK
WHRAM
MARA!!
AIEEE!

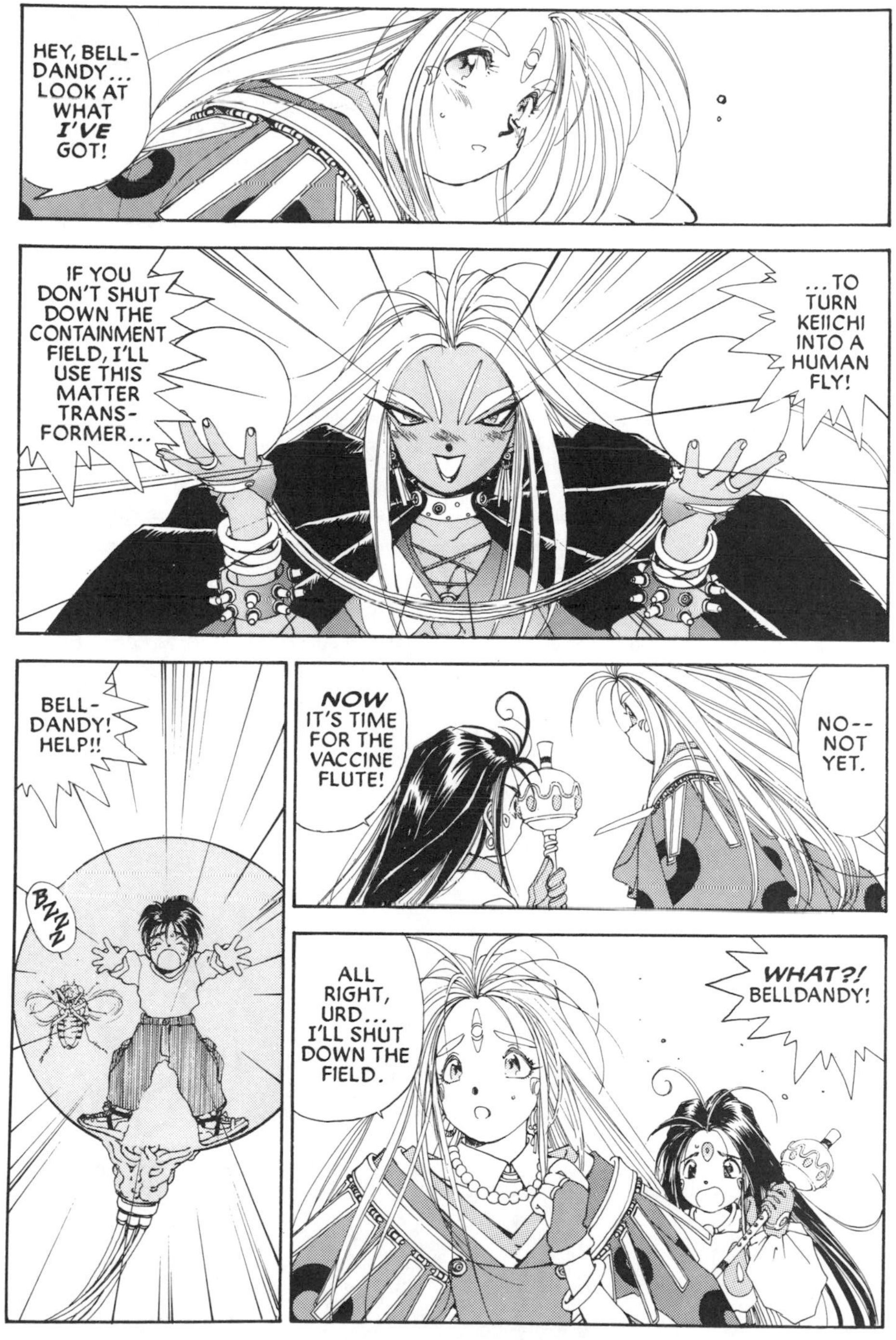
HEY, BELL-DANDY... LOOK AT WHAT *I'VE* GOT!
IF YOU DON'T SHUT DOWN THE CONTAINMENT FIELD, I'LL USE THIS MATTER TRANS-FORMER...
...TO TURN KEIICHI INTO A HUMAN FLY!
BELL-DANDY! HELP!!
BZZZ
NOW IT'S TIME FOR THE VACCINE FLUTE!
NO-- NOT YET.
ALL RIGHT, URD... I'LL SHUT DOWN THE FIELD.
WHAT?! BELLDANDY!

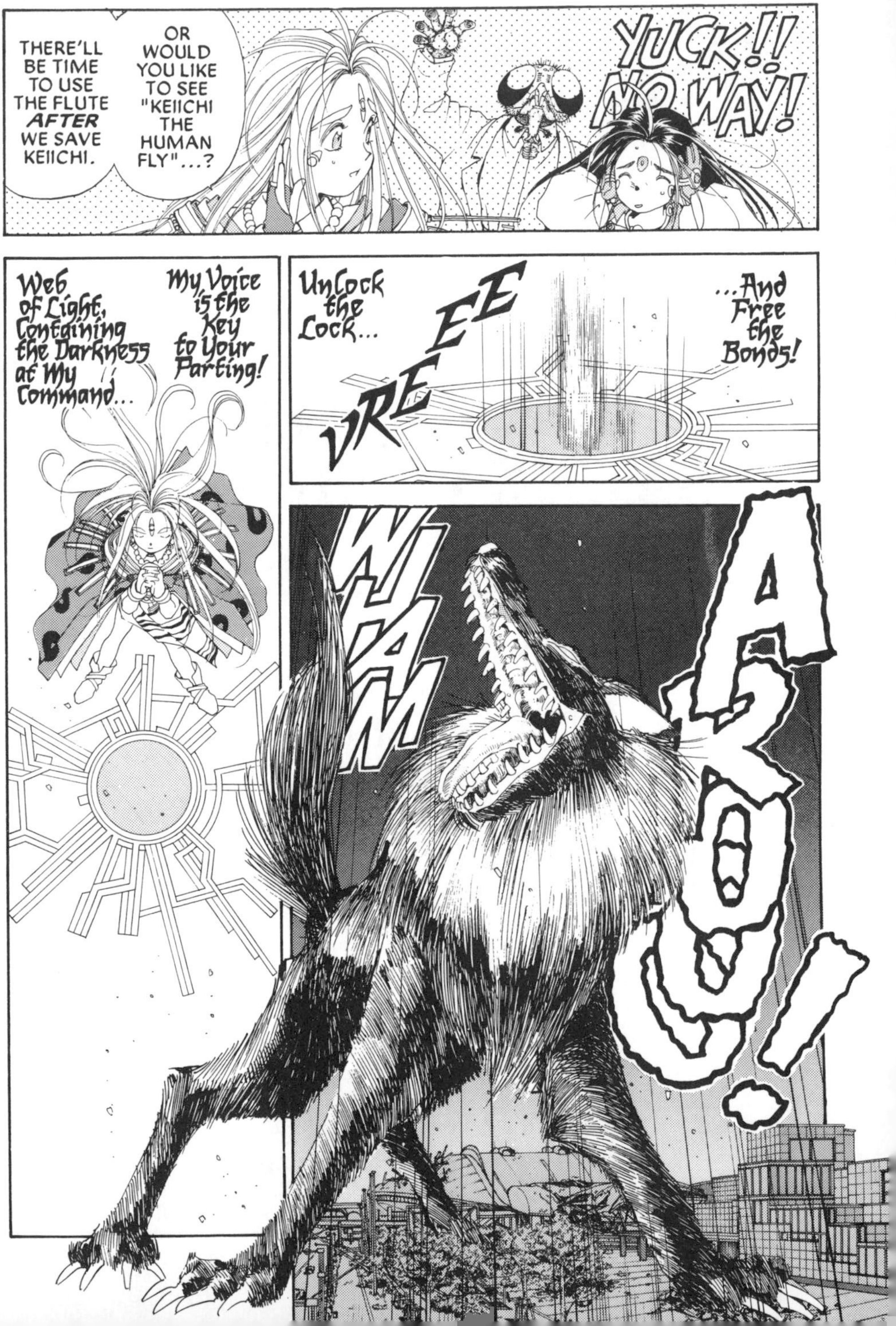
THERE'LL BE TIME TO USE THE FLUTE *AFTER* WE SAVE KEIICHI.
OR WOULD YOU LIKE TO SEE "KEIICHI THE HUMAN FLY"...?
YUCK!! NO WAY!
Web of Light, Containing the Darkness at My Command...
My Voice is the Key to Your Parting!
Unlock the Lock...
VREEEE
...And Free the Bonds!
WHAM
AROOO!

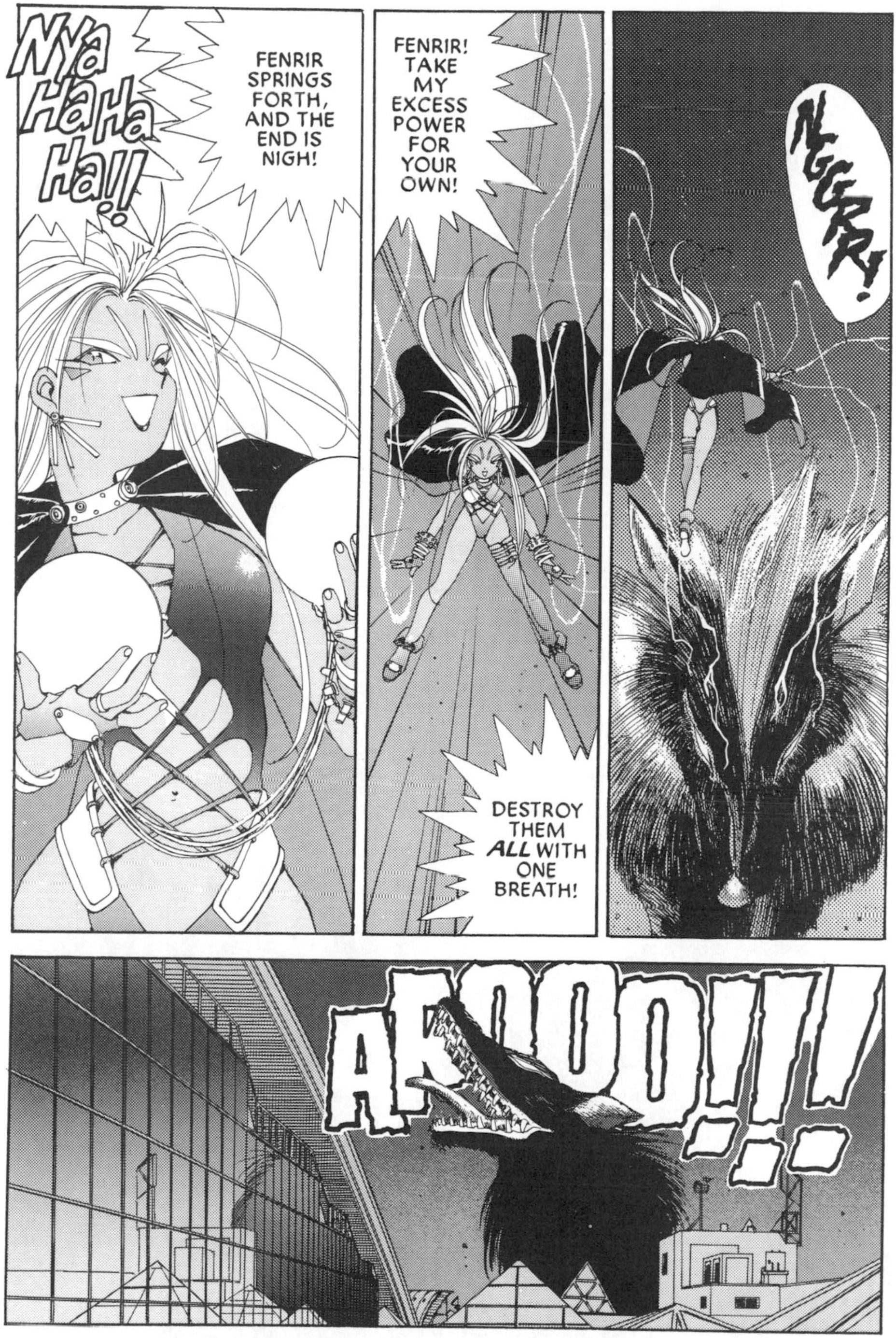

NYA HA HA HA HA!!
FENRIR SPRINGS FORTH, AND THE END IS NIGH!
FENRIR! TAKE MY EXCESS POWER FOR YOUR OWN!
DESTROY THEM ALL WITH ONE BREATH!
NGGRR!
AROOO!!!

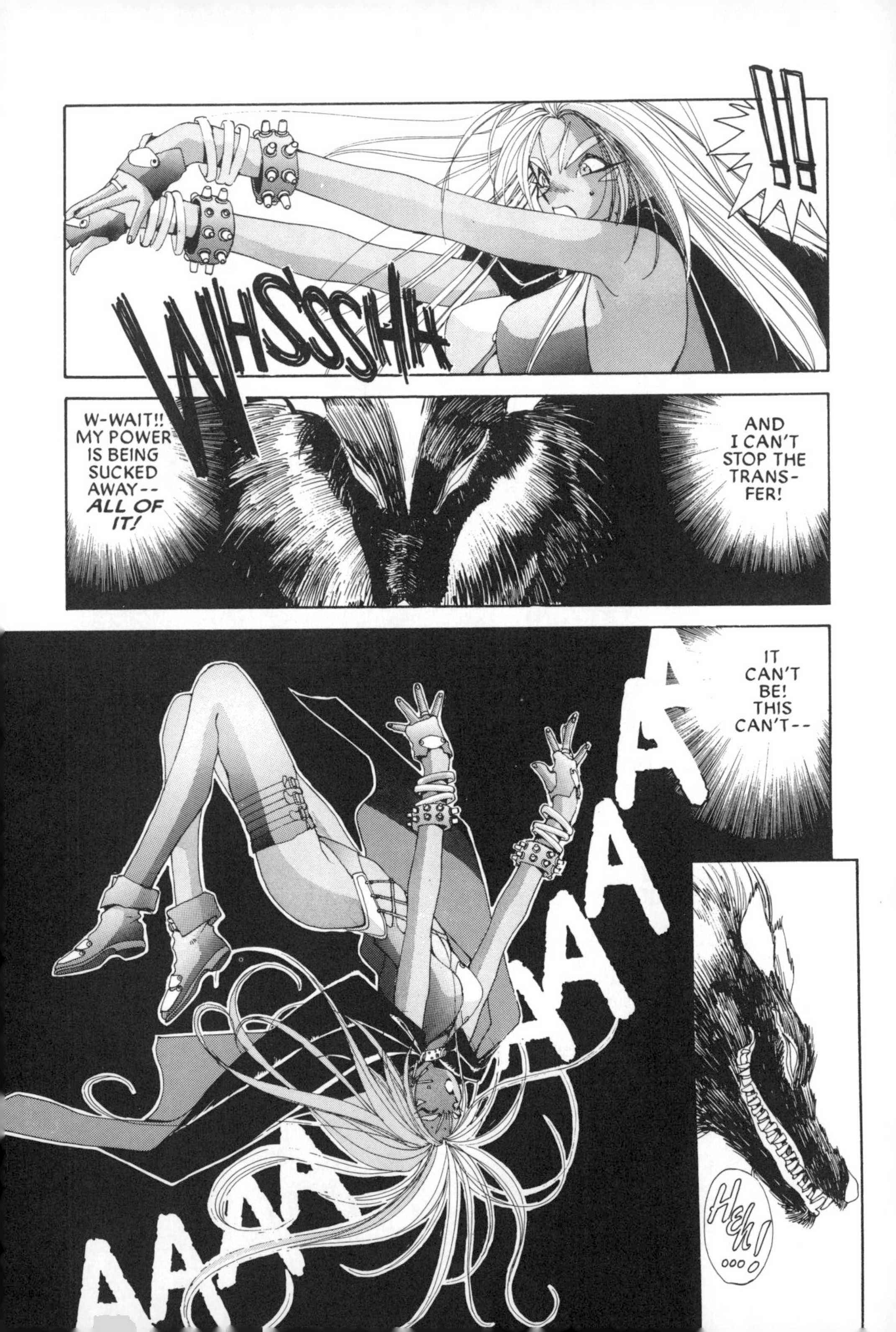
!!
WHSSSHA
W-WAIT!! MY POWER IS BEING SUCKED AWAY-- ALL OF IT!
AND I CAN'T STOP THE TRANS-FER!
IT CAN'T BE! THIS CAN'T--
AAAAAAAAA
HEH! ...

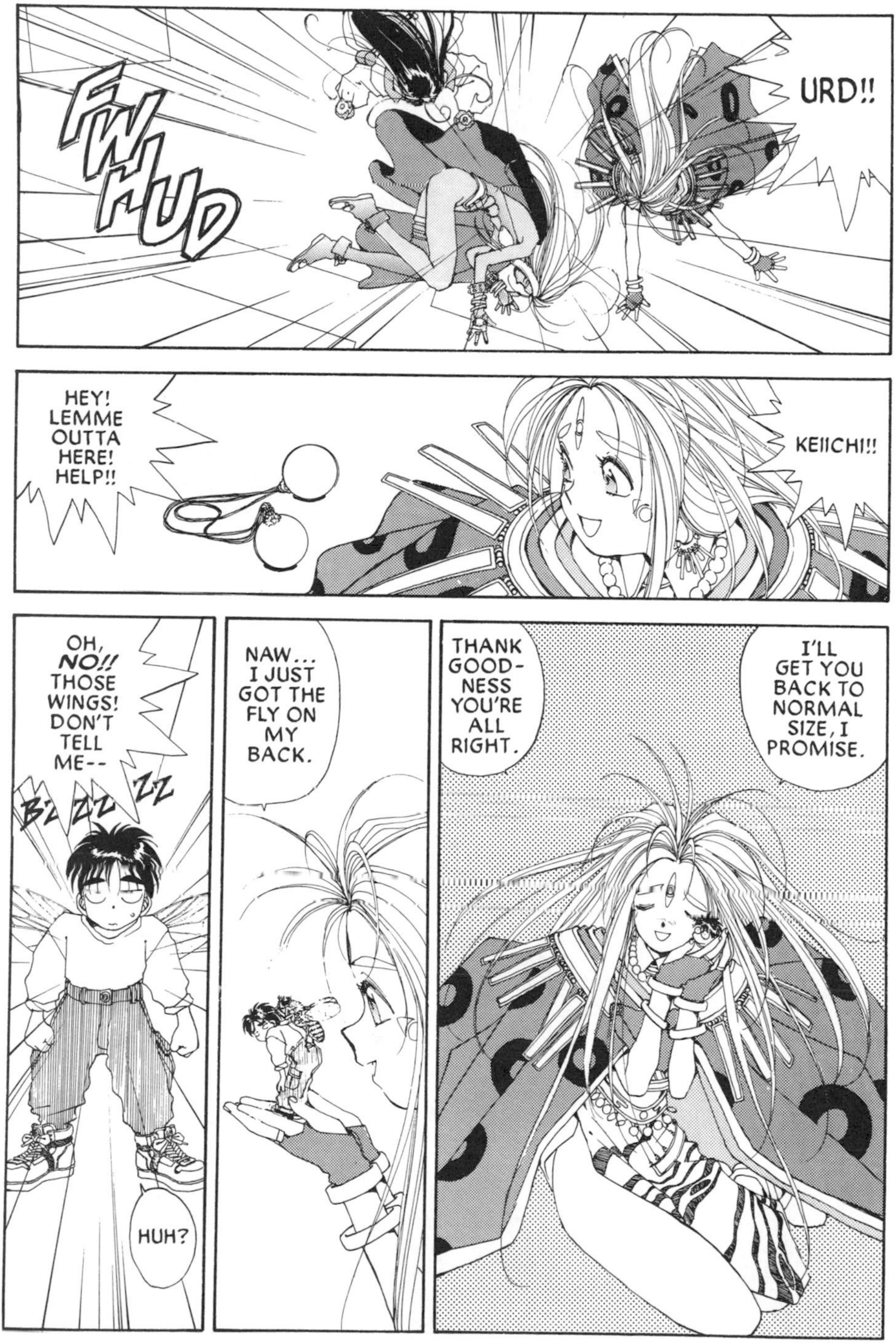
FWHUD
URD!!
HEY! LEMME OUTTA HERE! HELP!!
KEIICHI!!
OH, ***NO!!*** THOSE WINGS! DON'T TELL ME--
BZZZZZ
HUH?
NAW... I JUST GOT THE FLY ON MY BACK.
THANK GOOD-NESS YOU'RE ALL RIGHT.
I'LL GET YOU BACK TO NORMAL SIZE, I PROMISE.

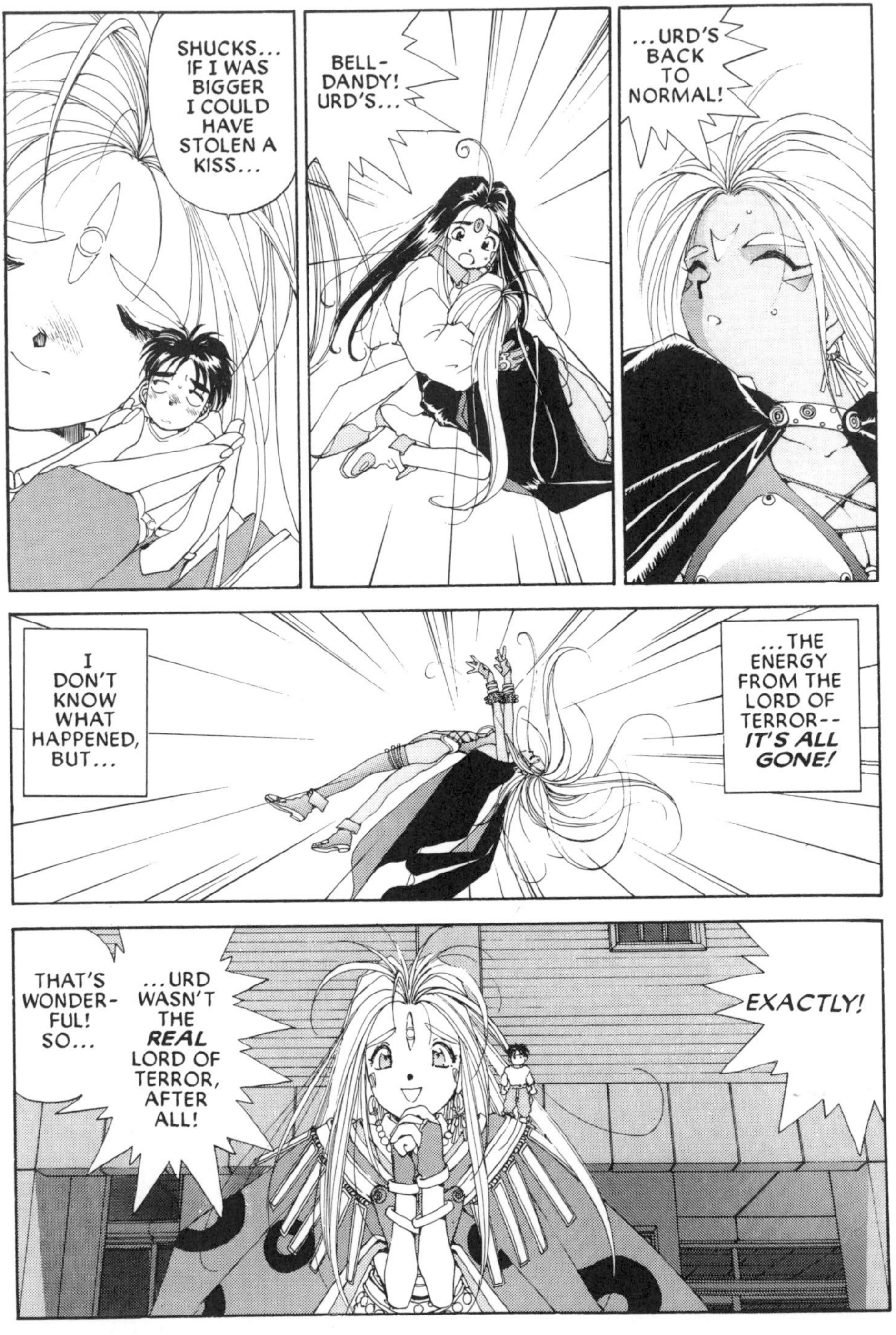
SHUCKS... IF I WAS BIGGER I COULD HAVE STOLEN A KISS...
BELL-DANDY! URD'S...
...URD'S BACK TO NORMAL!
I DON'T KNOW WHAT HAPPENED, BUT...
...THE ENERGY FROM THE LORD OF TERROR-- *IT'S ALL GONE!*
THAT'S WONDERFUL! SO...
...URD WASN'T THE *REAL* LORD OF TERROR, AFTER ALL!
EXACTLY!

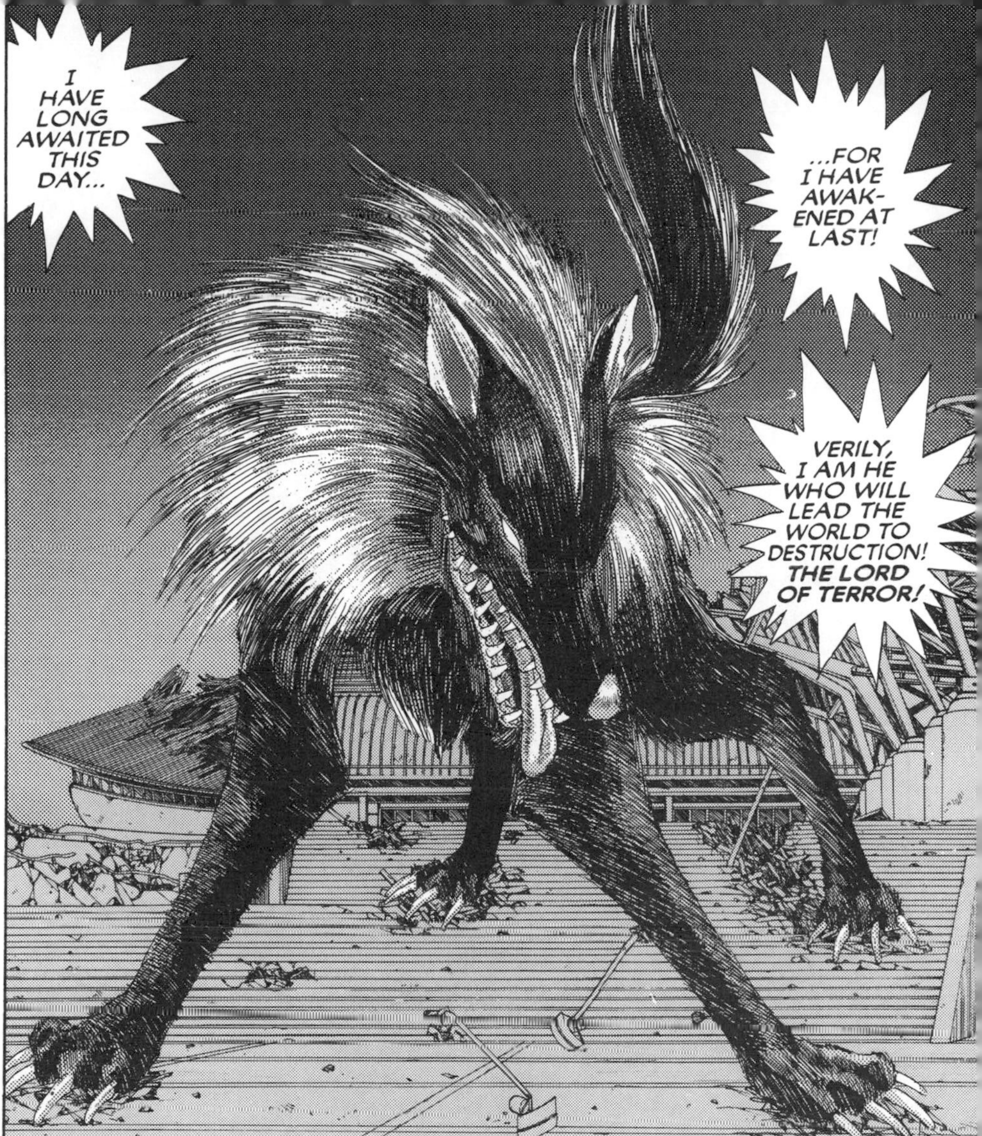
I HAVE LONG AWAITED THIS DAY...
...FOR I HAVE AWAKENED AT LAST!
VERILY, I AM HE WHO WILL LEAD THE WORLD TO DESTRUCTION! THE LORD OF TERROR!

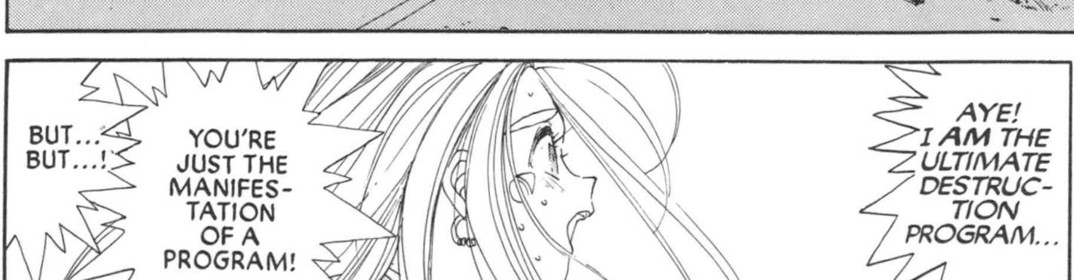
BUT... BUT...!
YOU'RE JUST THE MANIFESTATION OF A PROGRAM!
AYE! I AM THE ULTIMATE DESTRUCTION PROGRAM...

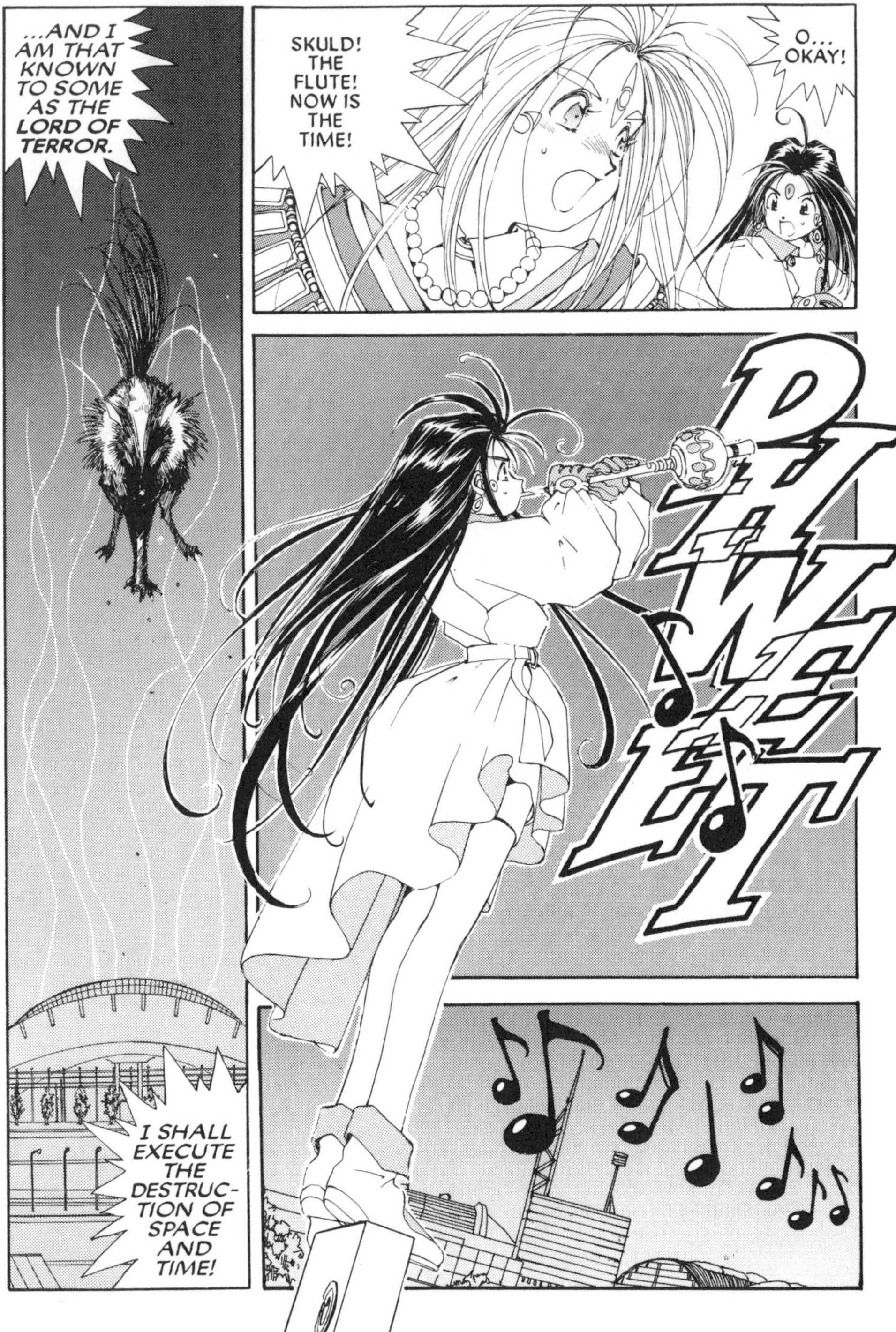
...AND I AM THAT KNOWN TO SOME AS THE **LORD OF TERROR.**
I SHALL EXECUTE THE DESTRUC-TION OF SPACE AND TIME!
SKULD! THE FLUTE! NOW IS THE TIME!
O... OKAY!
PIWEET

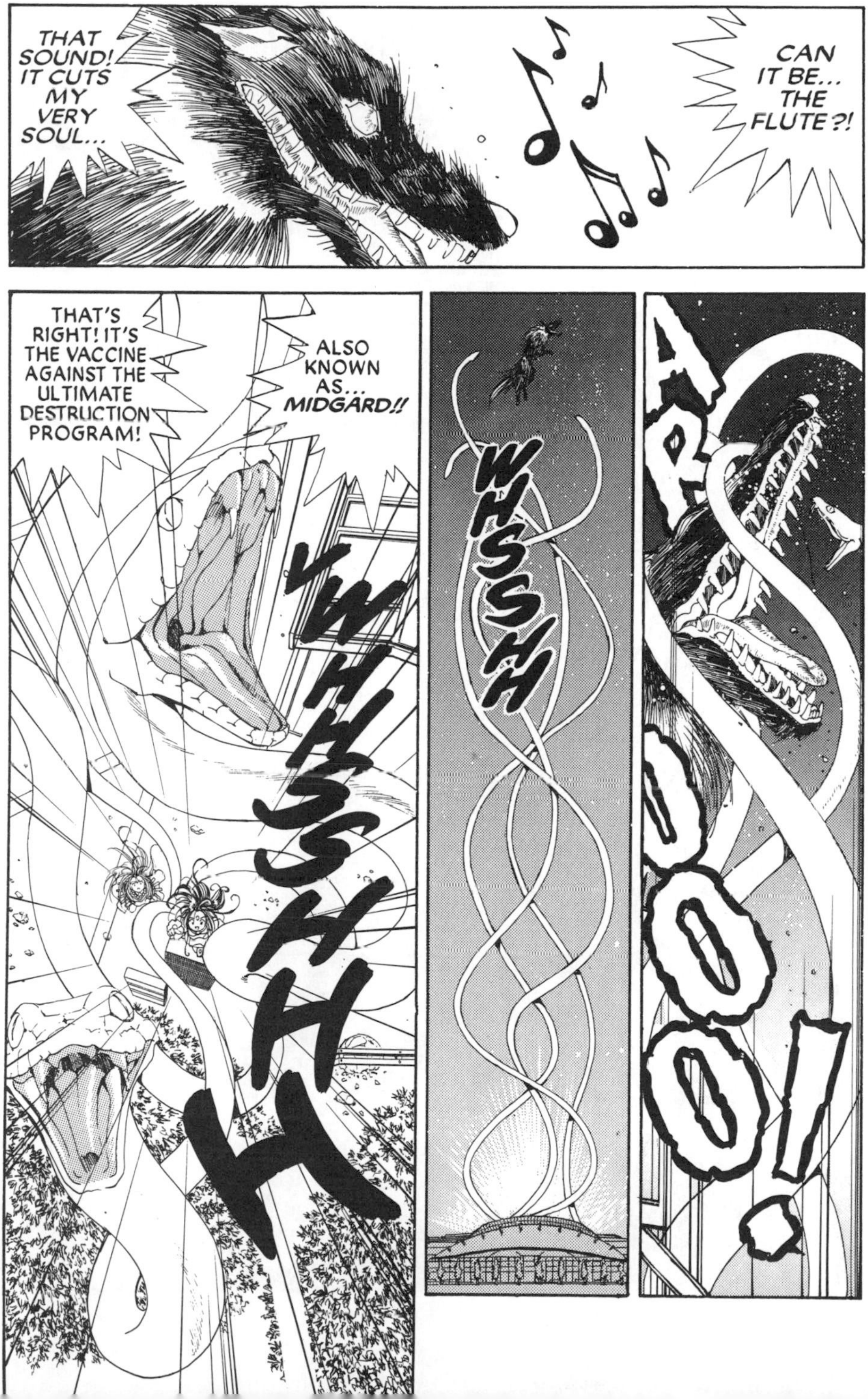
THAT SOUND! IT CUTS MY VERY SOUL...
CAN IT BE... THE FLUTE?!
THAT'S RIGHT! IT'S THE VACCINE AGAINST THE ULTIMATE DESTRUCTION PROGRAM!
ALSO KNOWN AS... MIDGARD!!
VWHHSSHHH
WHSSHH
AROOOO!

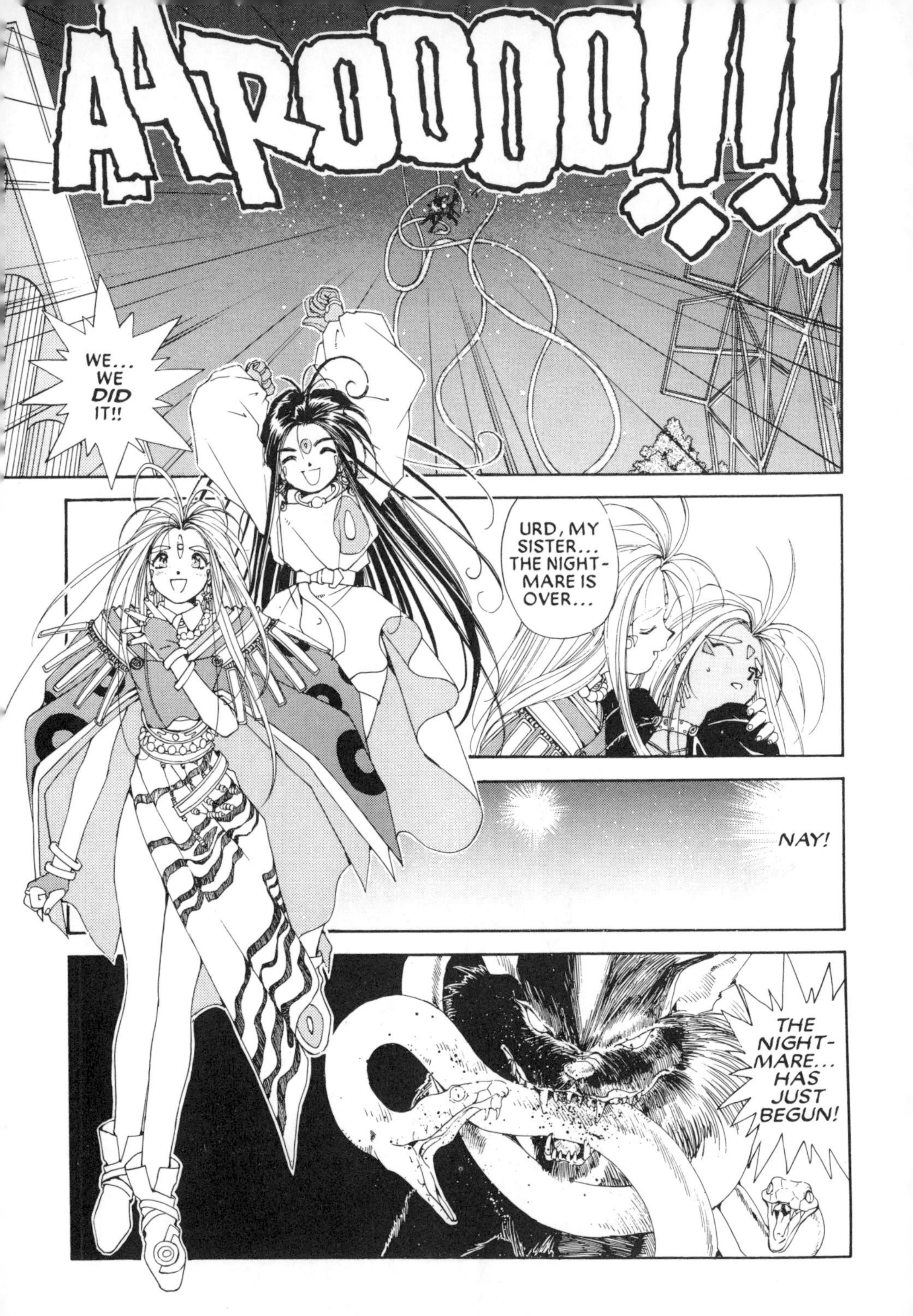

AAROOOO!!!
WE... WE DID IT!!
URD, MY SISTER... THE NIGHT-MARE IS OVER...
NAY!
THE NIGHT-MARE... HAS JUST BEGUN!

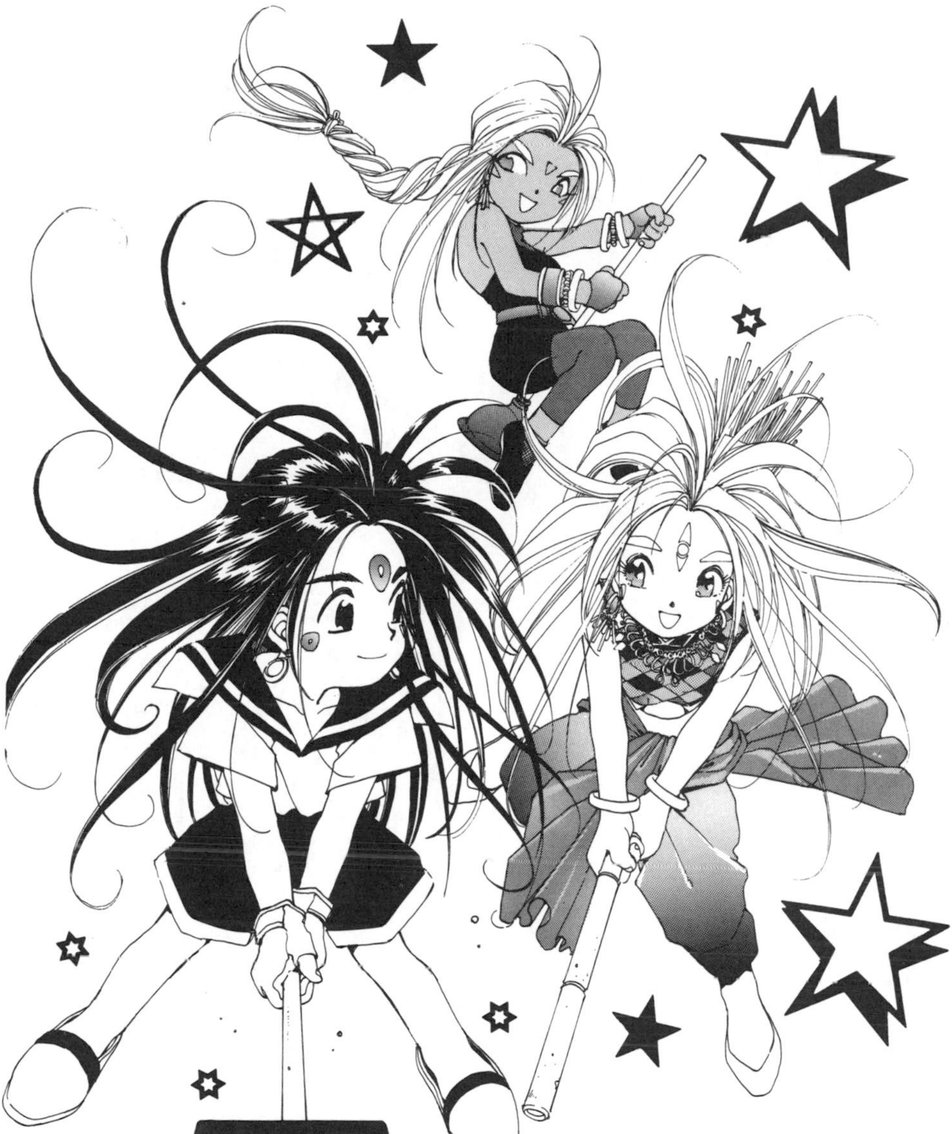

The Secret of the Lord of Terror

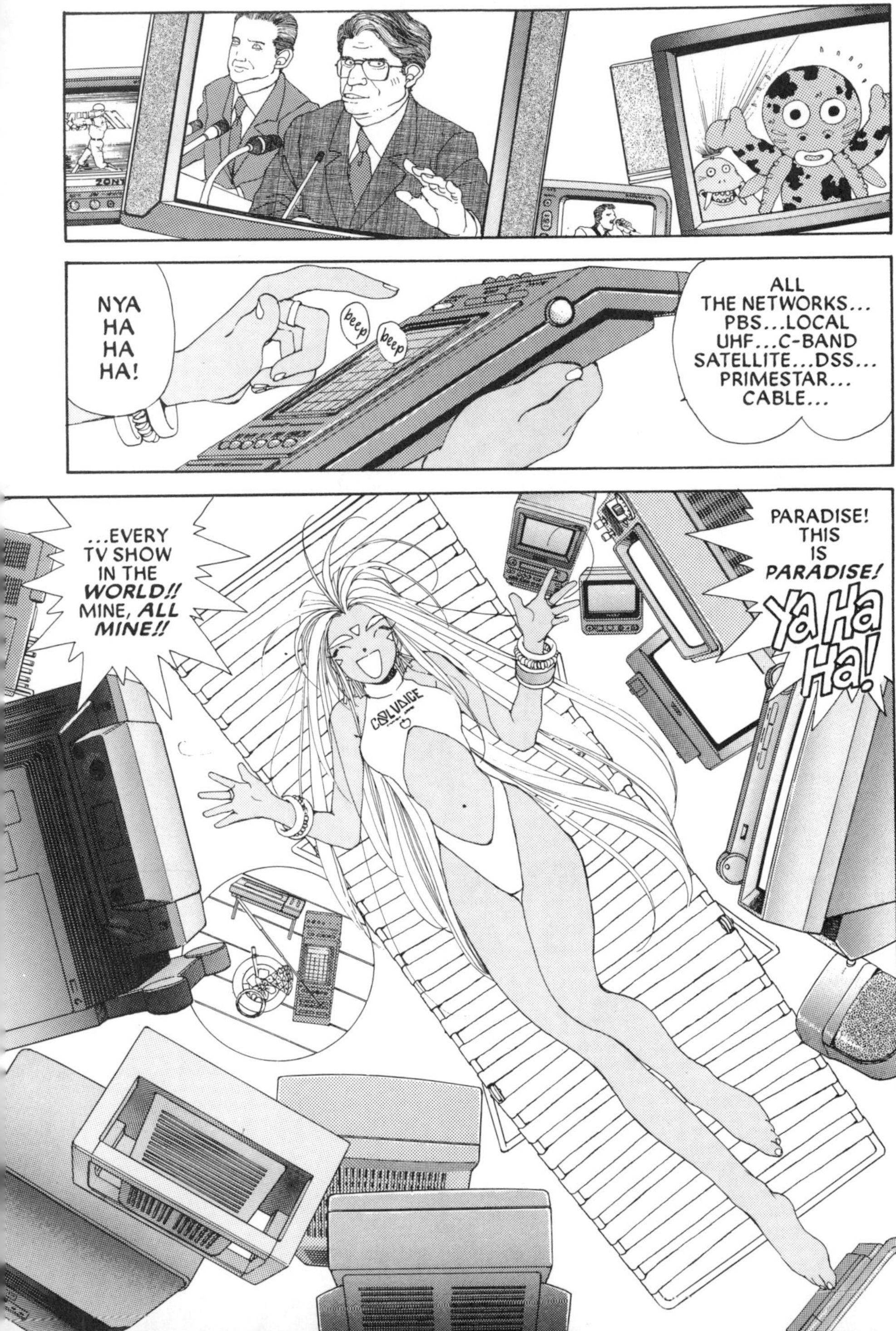
NYA HA HA HA!
beep
beep
ALL THE NETWORKS... PBS...LOCAL UHF...C-BAND SATELLITE...DSS... PRIMESTAR... CABLE...
...EVERY TV SHOW IN THE WORLD!! MINE, ALL MINE!!
PARADISE! THIS IS PARADISE!
Ya Ha Ha!

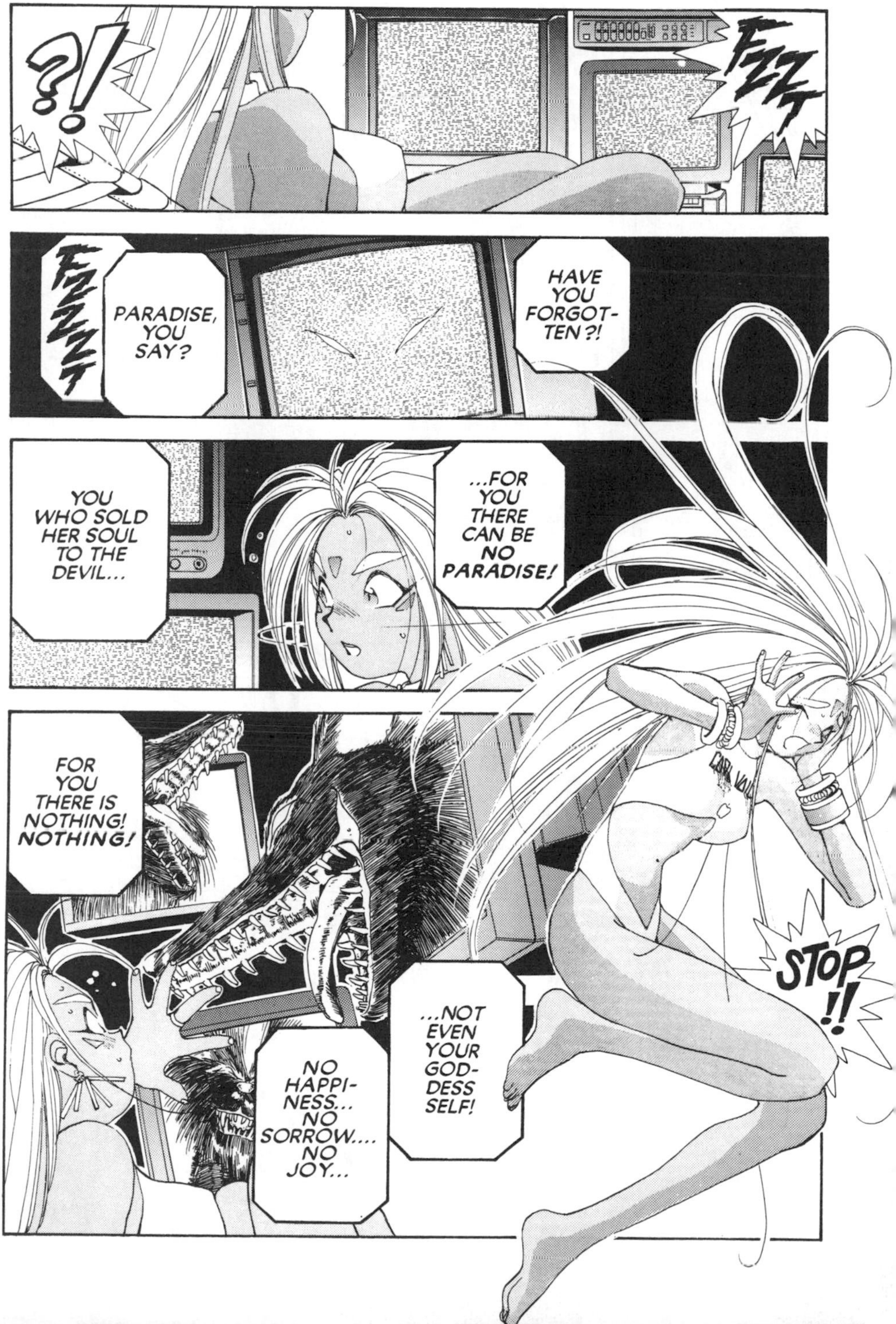
?!
FZZT
FZZZZT
PARADISE, YOU SAY?
HAVE YOU FORGOT-TEN?!
YOU WHO SOLD HER SOUL TO THE DEVIL...
...FOR YOU THERE CAN BE NO PARADISE!
FOR YOU THERE IS NOTHING! NOTHING!
NO HAPPI-NESS... NO SORROW.... NO JOY...
...NOT EVEN YOUR GOD-DESS SELF!
STOP!!

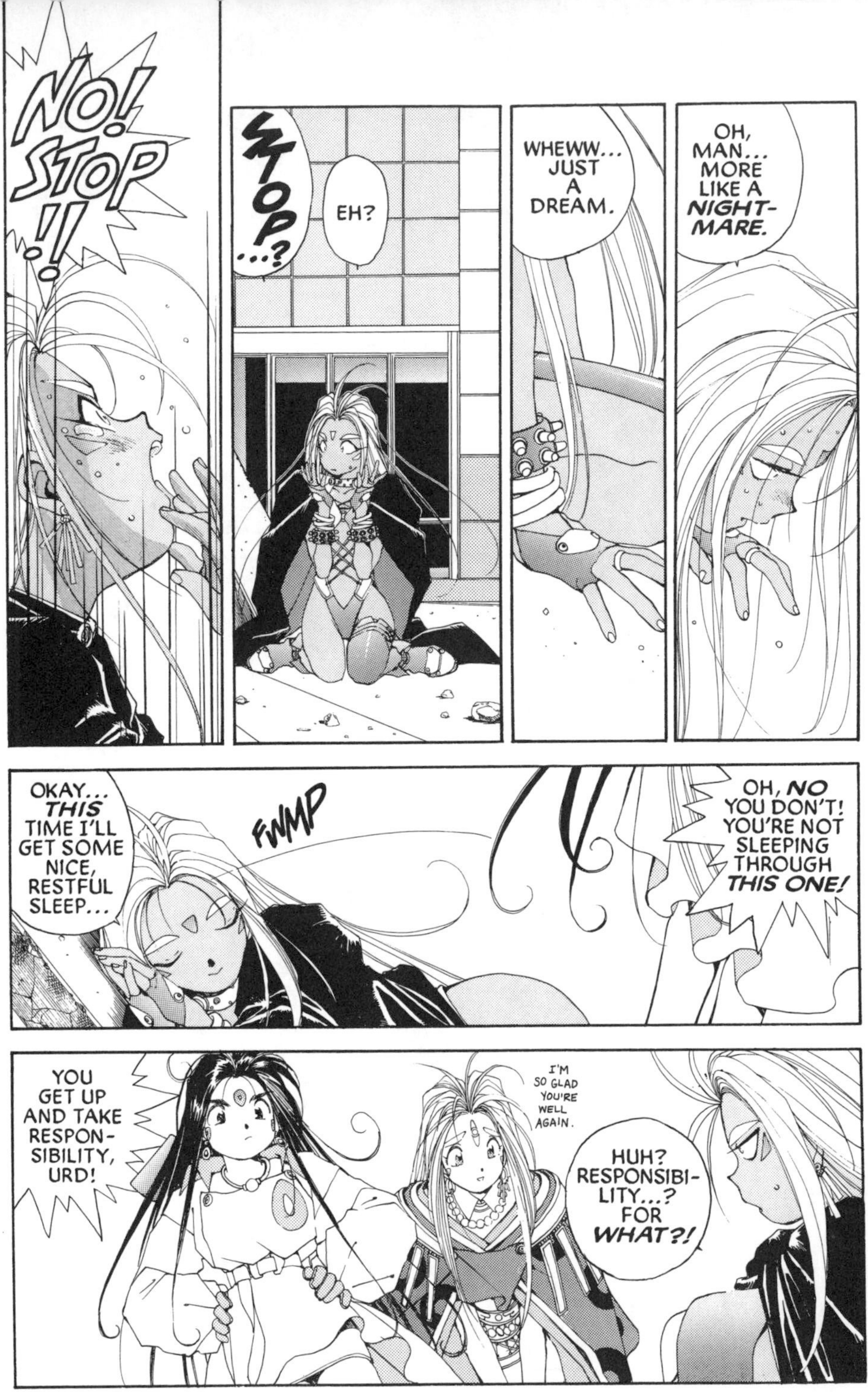
NO! STOP!!
STOP...?
EH?
WHEWW... JUST A DREAM.
OH, MAN... MORE LIKE A NIGHTMARE.
OKAY... THIS TIME I'LL GET SOME NICE, RESTFUL SLEEP...
FWMP
OH, NO YOU DON'T! YOU'RE NOT SLEEPING THROUGH THIS ONE!
YOU GET UP AND TAKE RESPONSIBILITY, URD!
I'M SO GLAD YOU'RE WELL AGAIN.
HUH? RESPONSIBILITY...? FOR WHAT?!

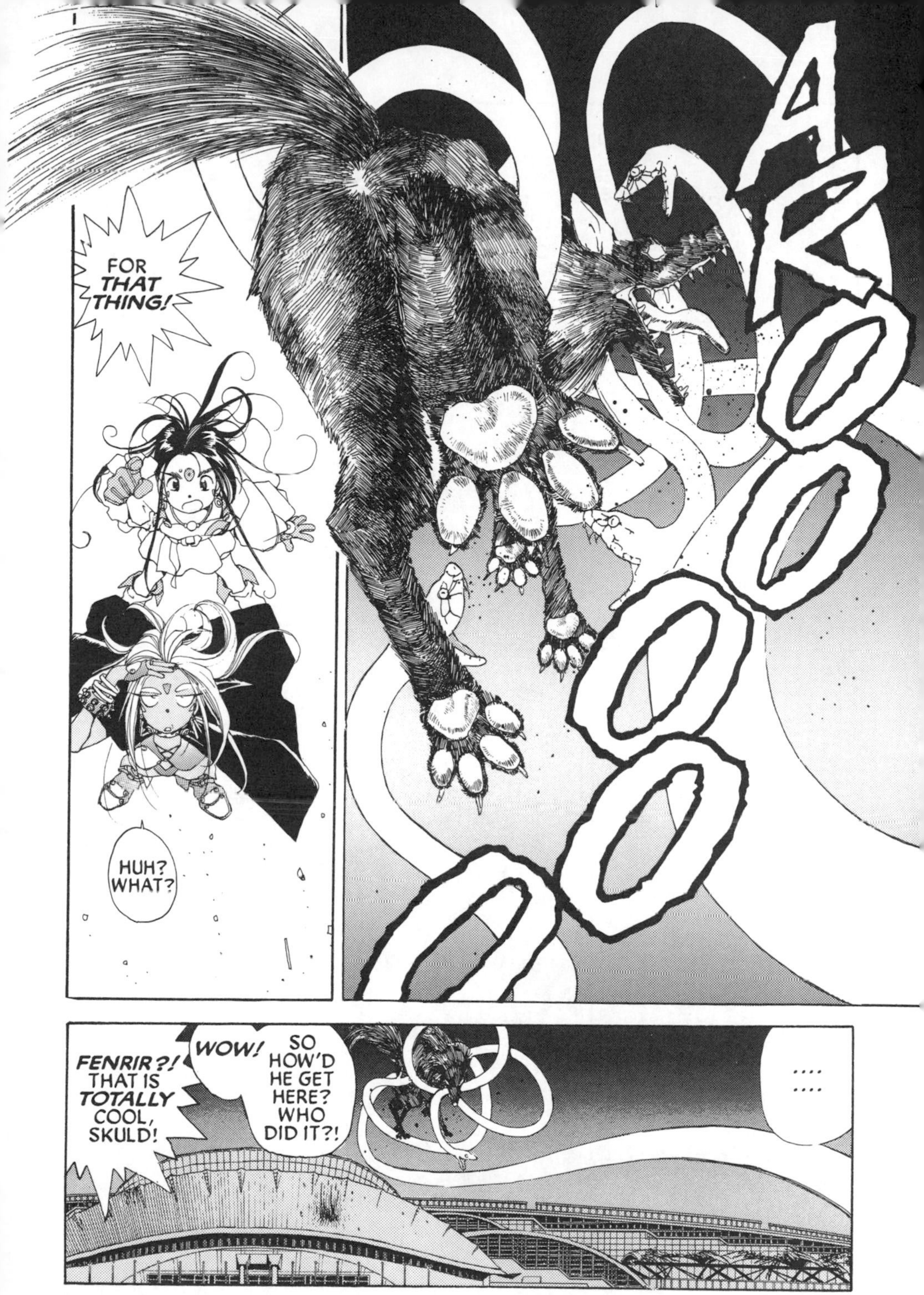
FOR *THAT THING!*
HUH? WHAT?
FENRIR?! THAT IS *TOTALLY* COOL, SKULD!
WOW!
SO HOW'D HE GET HERE? WHO DID IT?!
....
....

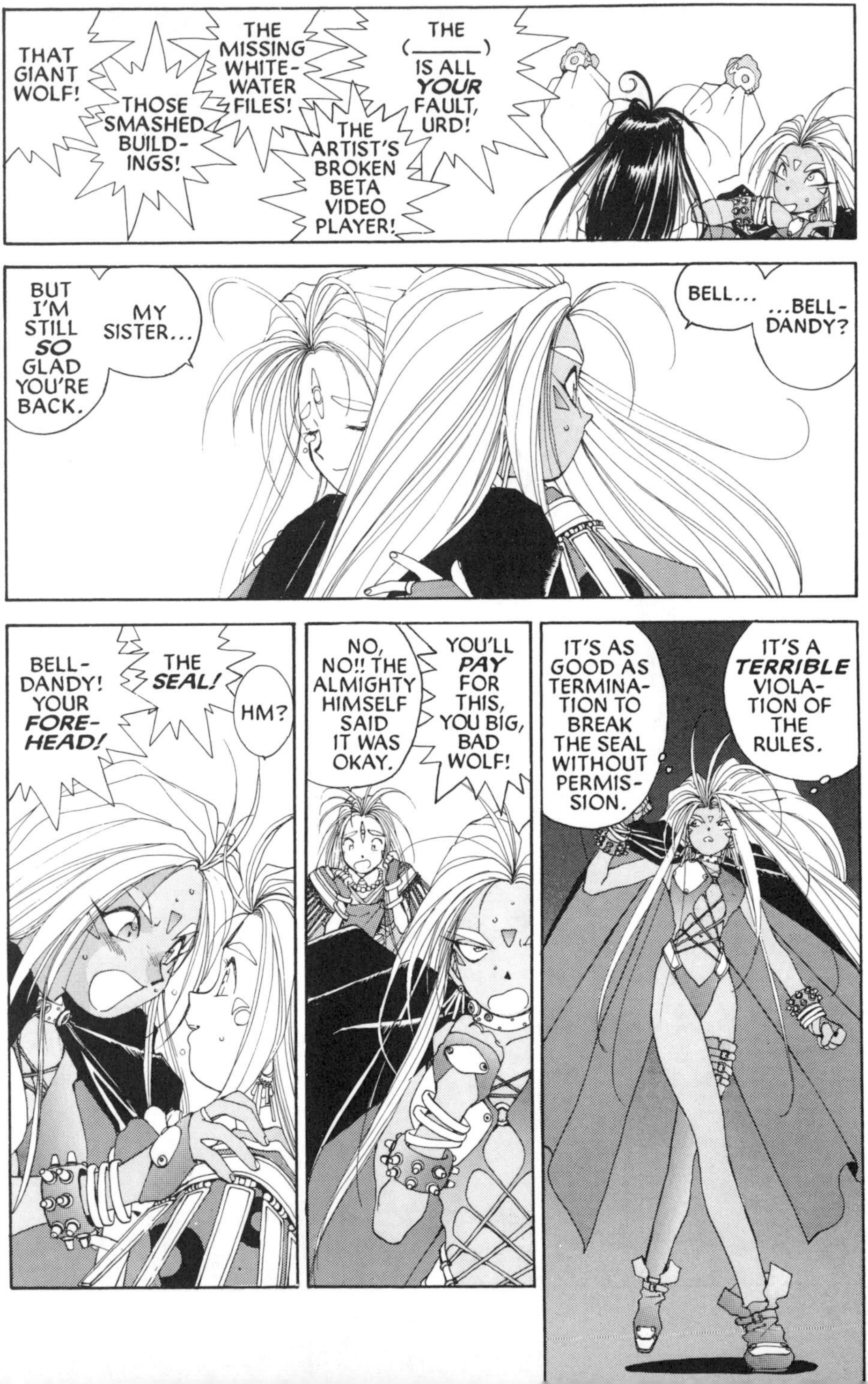
THAT GIANT WOLF!
THOSE SMASHED BUILD-INGS!
THE MISSING WHITE-WATER FILES!
THE ARTIST'S BROKEN BETA VIDEO PLAYER!
THE (______) IS ALL YOUR FAULT, URD!
BUT I'M STILL SO GLAD YOU'RE BACK.
MY SISTER...
BELL...
...BELL-DANDY?
BELL-DANDY! YOUR FORE-HEAD!
THE SEAL!
HM?
NO, NO!! THE ALMIGHTY HIMSELF SAID IT WAS OKAY.
YOU'LL PAY FOR THIS, YOU BIG, BAD WOLF!
IT'S AS GOOD AS TERMINA-TION TO BREAK THE SEAL WITHOUT PERMIS-SION.
IT'S A TERRIBLE VIOLA-TION OF THE RULES.

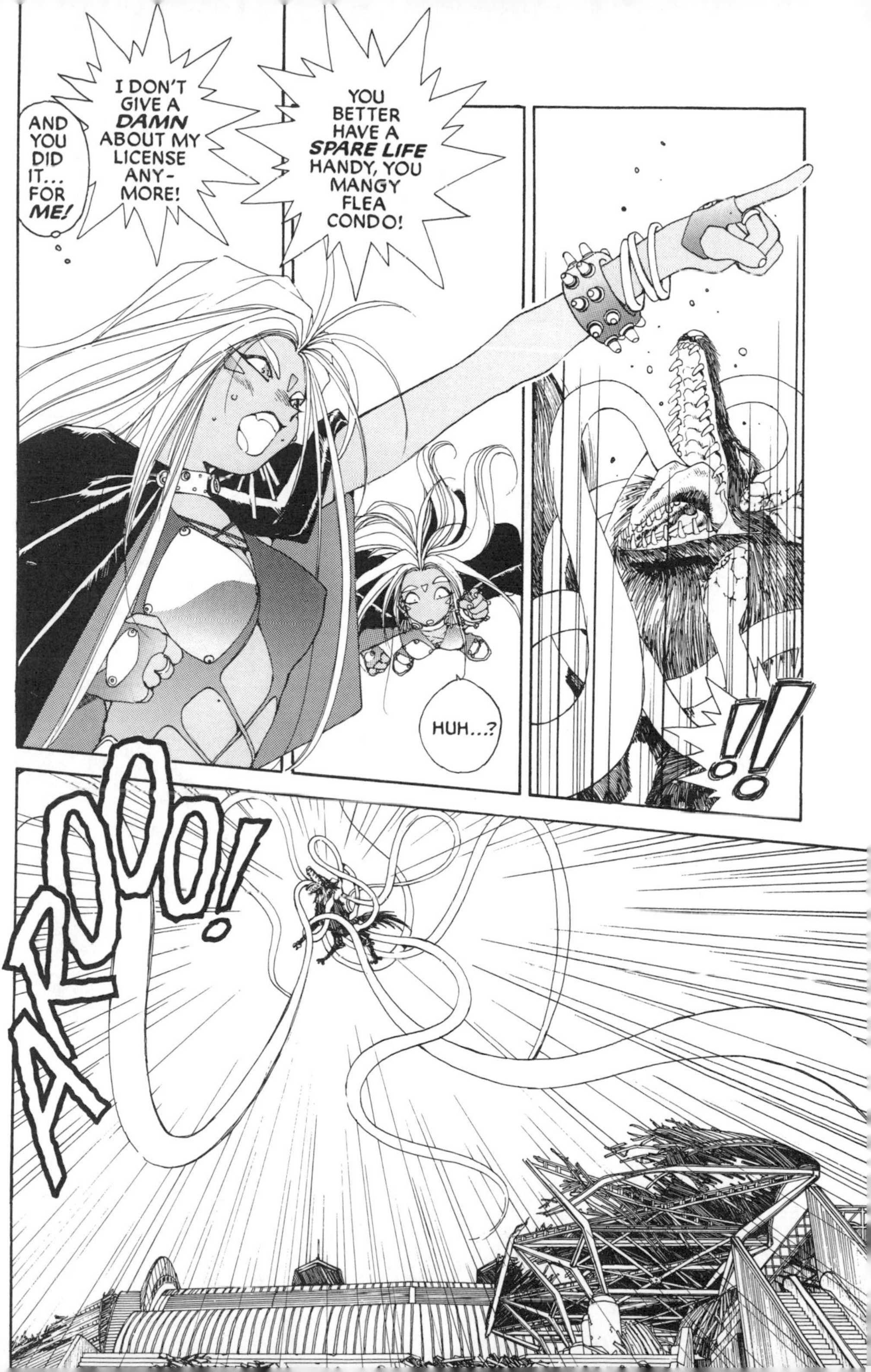
AND YOU DID IT... FOR *ME!*
I DON'T GIVE A ***DAMN*** ABOUT MY LICENSE ANY-MORE!
YOU BETTER HAVE A ***SPARE LIFE*** HANDY, YOU MANGY FLEA CONDO!
HUH...?
!!
AROOOO!

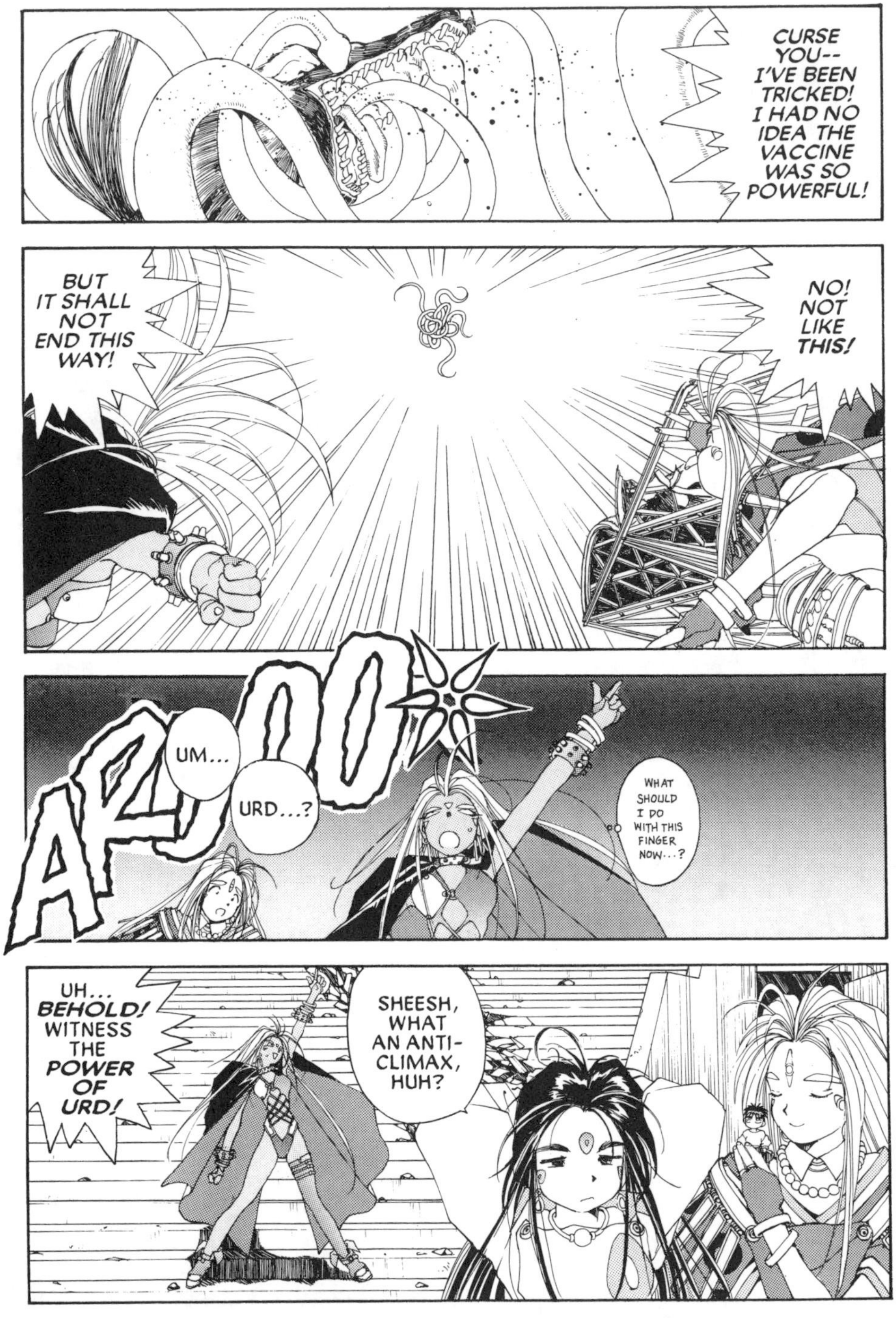
CURSE YOU-- I'VE BEEN TRICKED! I HAD NO IDEA THE VACCINE WAS SO POWERFUL!
BUT IT SHALL NOT END THIS WAY!
NO! NOT LIKE THIS!
UM...
URD...?
WHAT SHOULD I DO WITH THIS FINGER NOW...?
UH... BEHOLD! WITNESS THE POWER OF URD!
SHEESH, WHAT AN ANTI-CLIMAX, HUH?

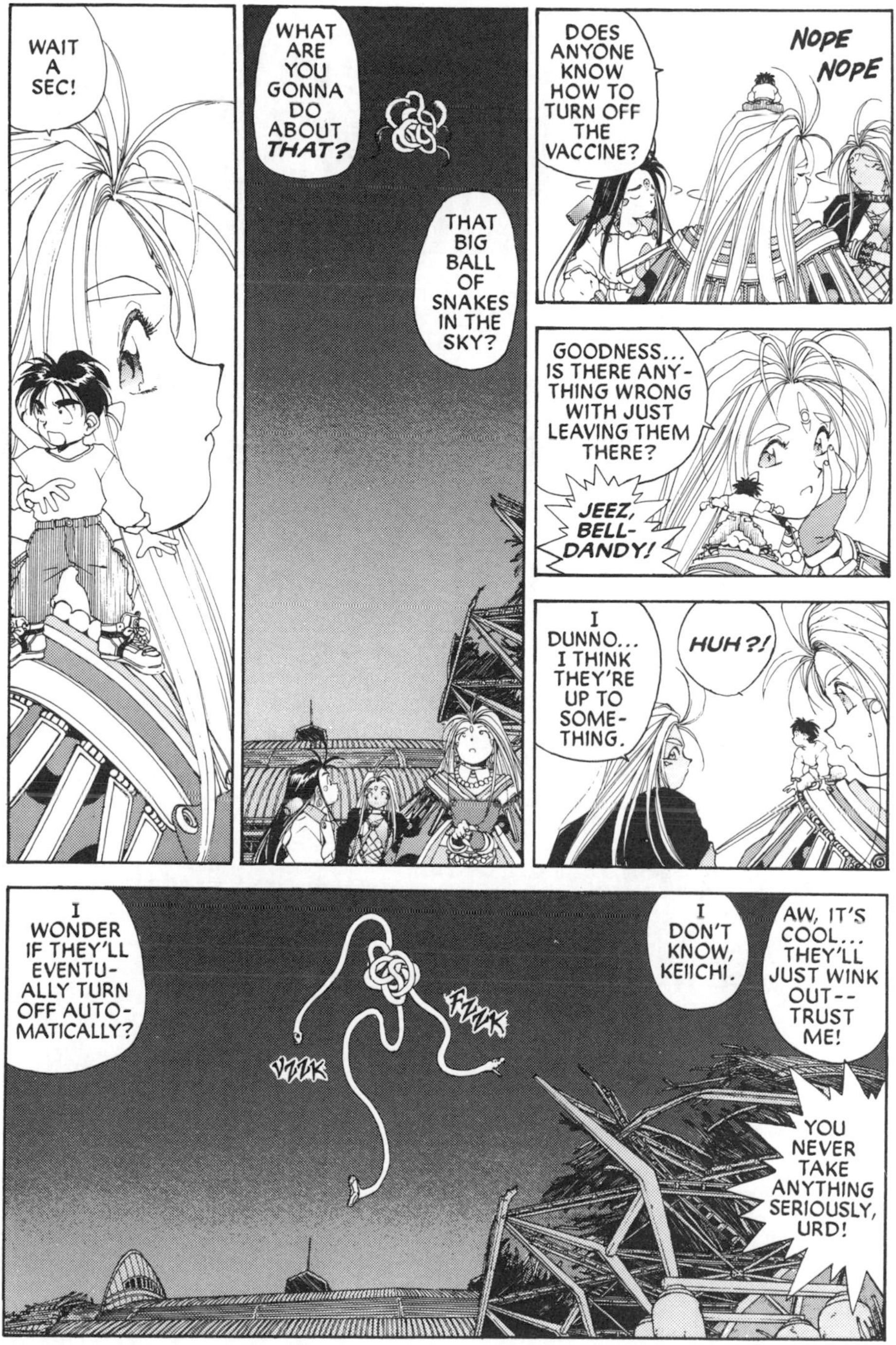
WAIT A SEC!
WHAT ARE YOU GONNA DO ABOUT *THAT?*
THAT BIG BALL OF SNAKES IN THE SKY?
DOES ANYONE KNOW HOW TO TURN OFF THE VACCINE?
NOPE
NOPE
GOODNESS... IS THERE ANYTHING WRONG WITH JUST LEAVING THEM THERE?
JEEZ, BELLDANDY!
I DUNNO... I THINK THEY'RE UP TO SOMETHING.
HUH?!
I WONDER IF THEY'LL EVENTUALLY TURN OFF AUTOMATICALLY?
VZZZK
FZZZK
I DON'T KNOW, KEIICHI.
AW, IT'S COOL... THEY'LL JUST WINK OUT-- TRUST ME!
YOU NEVER TAKE ANYTHING SERIOUSLY, URD!

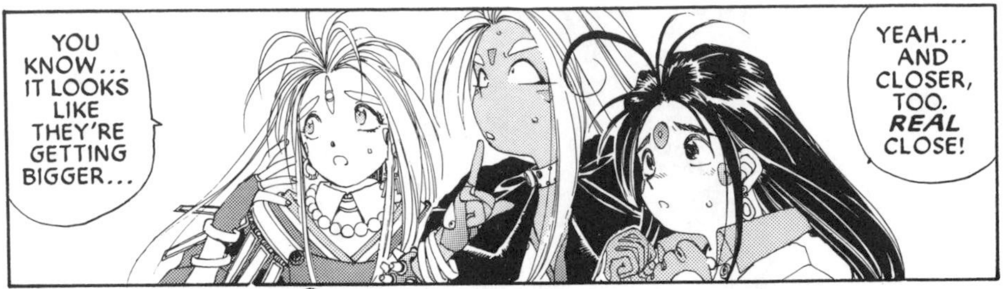
YOU KNOW... IT LOOKS LIKE THEY'RE GETTING BIGGER...
YEAH... AND CLOSER, TOO. *REAL* CLOSE!

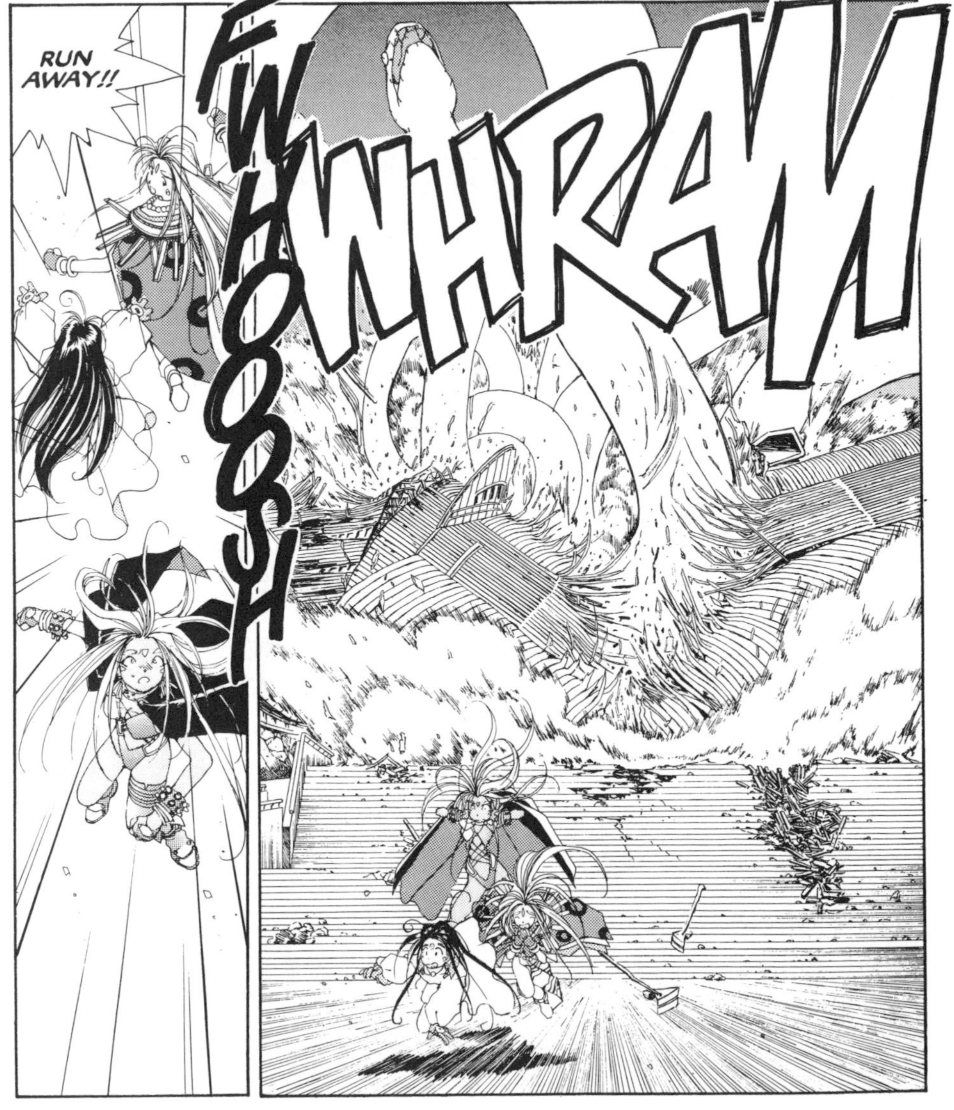
RUN AWAY!!
FWHOOOSH
WHRAM

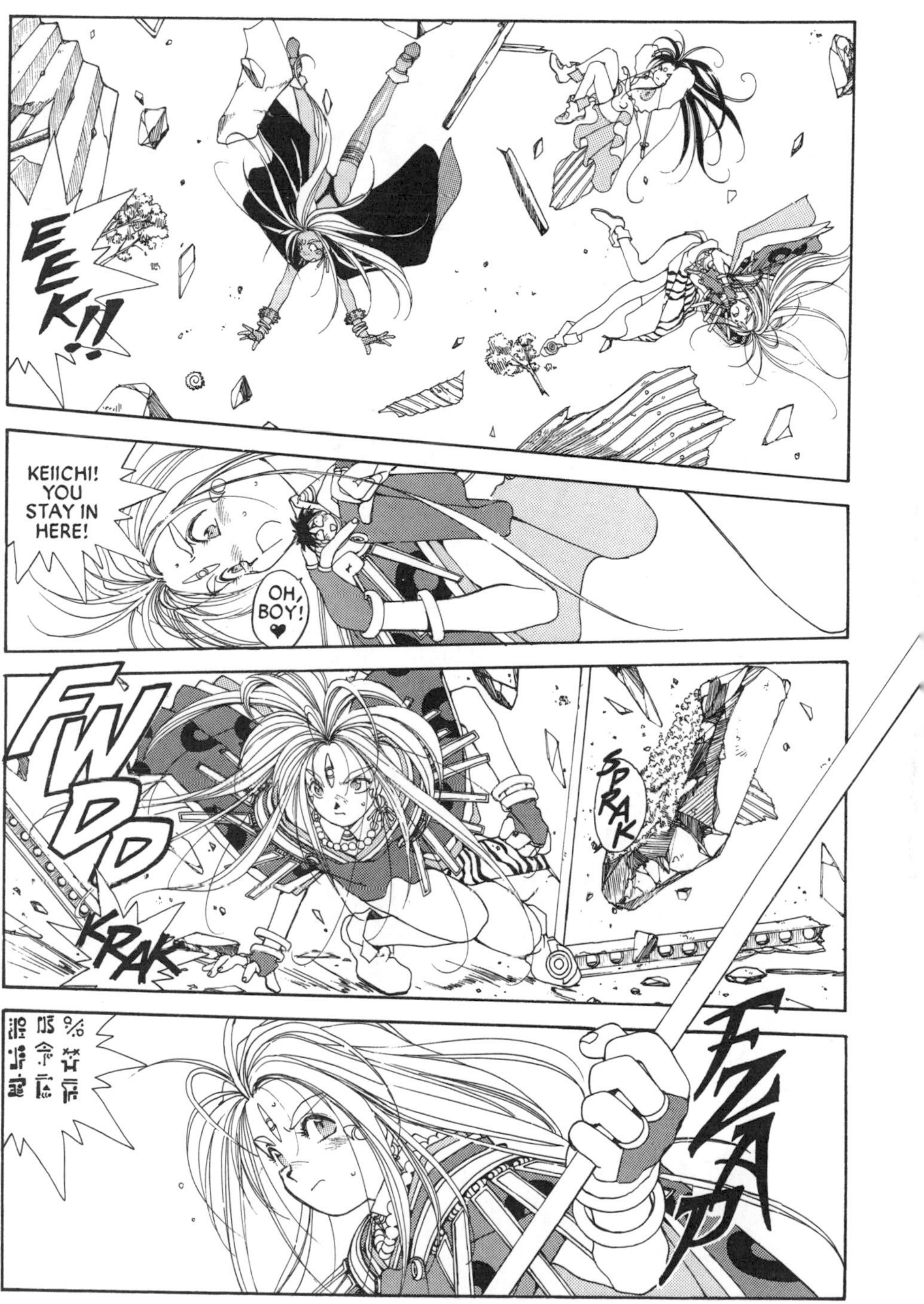
EEEK!!
KEIICHI! YOU STAY IN HERE!
OH, BOY!
FWDD
KRAK
SPRAK
FZAP

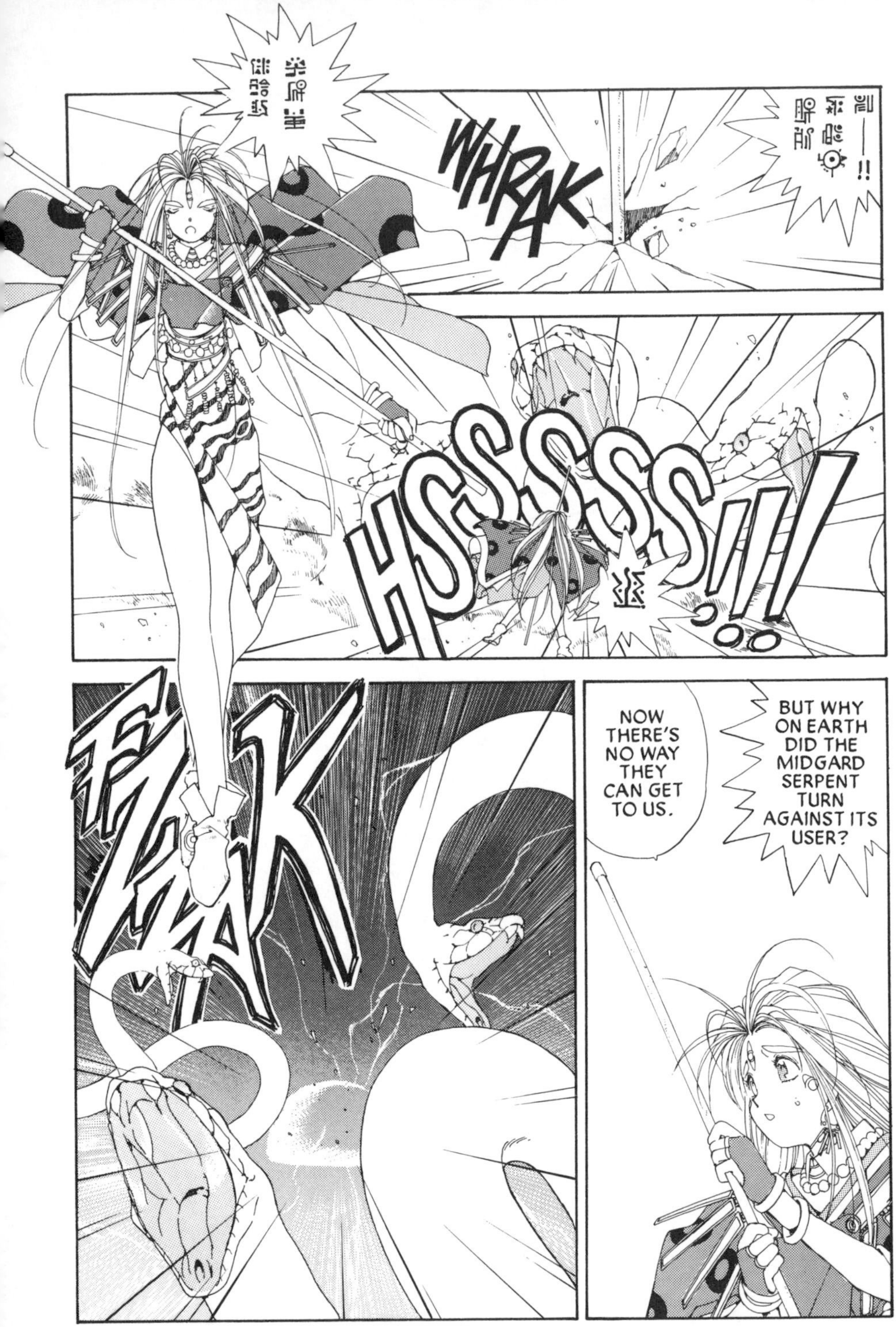
WHRAK
HSSSSSS!!!
NOW THERE'S NO WAY THEY CAN GET TO US.
BUT WHY ON EARTH DID THE MIDGARD SERPENT TURN AGAINST ITS USER?

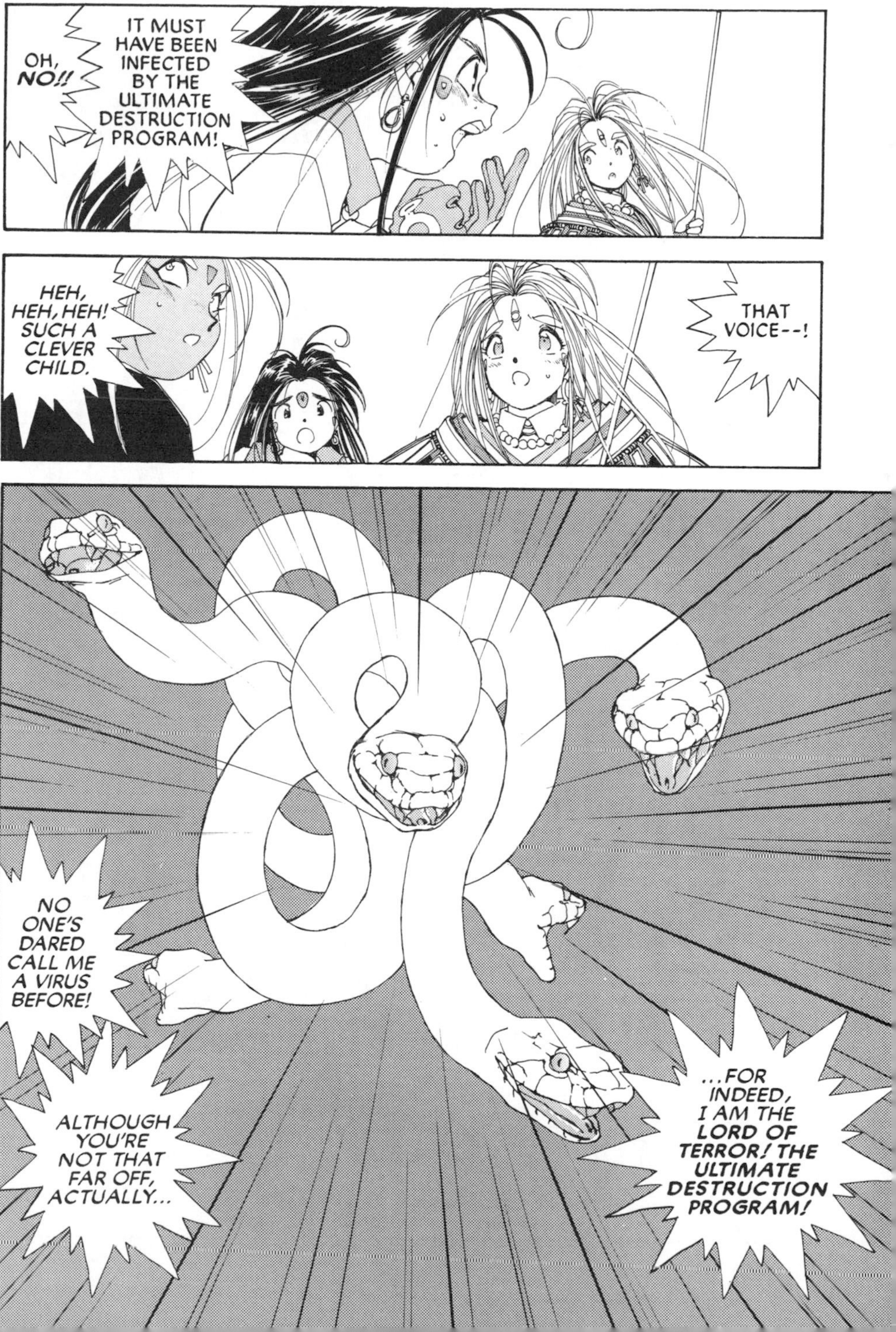
OH, NO!!
IT MUST HAVE BEEN INFECTED BY THE ULTIMATE DESTRUCTION PROGRAM!
HEH, HEH, HEH! SUCH A CLEVER CHILD.
THAT VOICE--!
NO ONE'S DARED CALL ME A VIRUS BEFORE!
ALTHOUGH YOU'RE NOT THAT FAR OFF, ACTUALLY...
...FOR INDEED, I AM THE LORD OF TERROR! THE ULTIMATE DESTRUCTION PROGRAM!

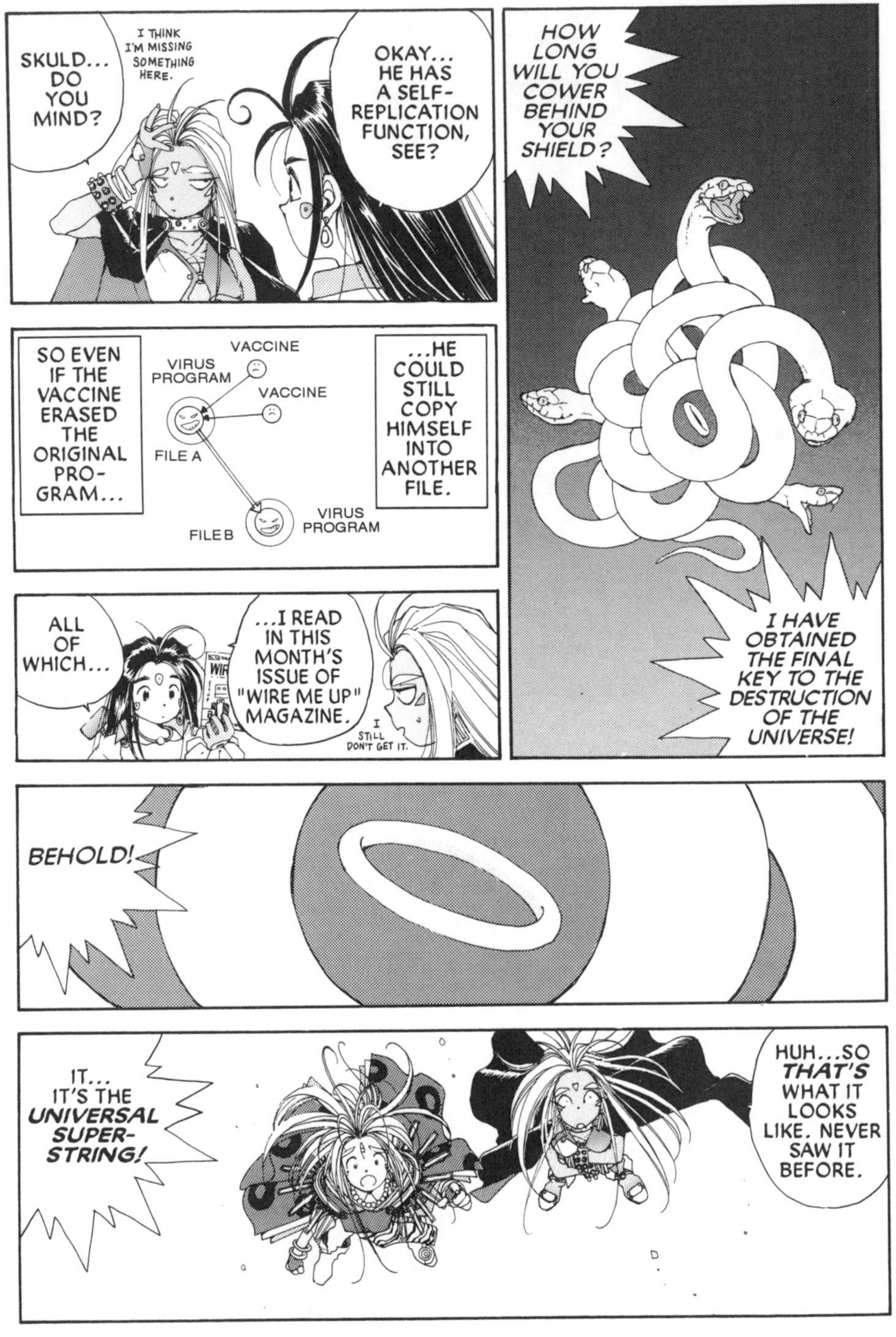
SKULD... DO YOU MIND?
I THINK I'M MISSING SOMETHING HERE.
OKAY... HE HAS A SELF-REPLICATION FUNCTION, SEE?
SO EVEN IF THE VACCINE ERASED THE ORIGINAL PROGRAM...
VACCINE
VIRUS PROGRAM
VACCINE
FILE A
VIRUS PROGRAM
FILE B
...HE COULD STILL COPY HIMSELF INTO ANOTHER FILE.
ALL OF WHICH...
...I READ IN THIS MONTH'S ISSUE OF "WIRE ME UP" MAGAZINE.
I STILL DON'T GET IT.
HOW LONG WILL YOU COWER BEHIND YOUR SHIELD?
I HAVE OBTAINED THE FINAL KEY TO THE DESTRUCTION OF THE UNIVERSE!
BEHOLD!
IT... IT'S THE UNIVERSAL SUPER-STRING!
HUH...SO THAT'S WHAT IT LOOKS LIKE. NEVER SAW IT BEFORE.

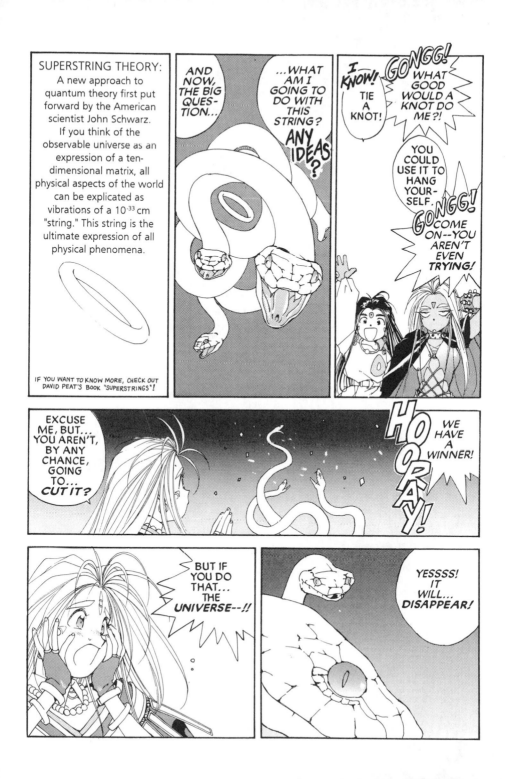

SUPERSTRING THEORY:

A new approach to quantum theory first put forward by the American scientist John Schwarz.

If you think of the observable universe as an expression of a ten-dimensional matrix, all physical aspects of the world can be explicated as vibrations of a 10^{-33} cm "string." This string is the ultimate expression of all physical phenomena.

IF YOU WANT TO KNOW MORE, CHECK OUT DAVID PEAT'S BOOK "SUPERSTRINGS"!

AND NOW, THE BIG QUESTION...

...WHAT AM I GOING TO DO WITH THIS STRING? ANY IDEAS?

I KNOW! TIE A KNOT!

GONGG! WHAT GOOD WOULD A KNOT DO ME?!

YOU COULD USE IT TO HANG YOURSELF.

GONGG! COME ON--YOU AREN'T EVEN TRYING!

EXCUSE ME, BUT... YOU AREN'T, BY ANY CHANCE, GOING TO... CUT IT?

HOORAY!

WE HAVE A WINNER!

BUT IF YOU DO THAT... THE UNIVERSE--!!

YESSSS! IT WILL... DISAPPEAR!

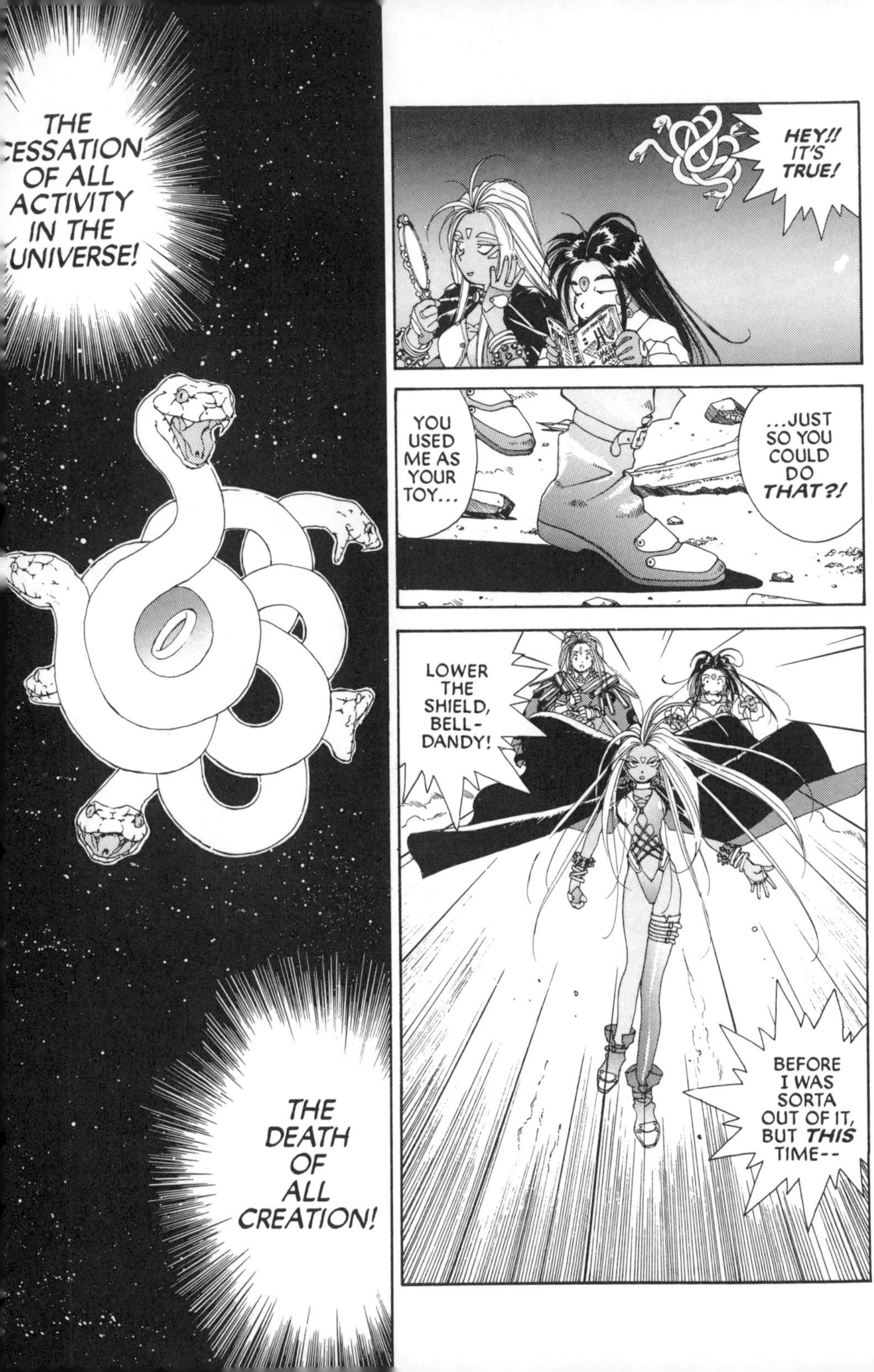

THE CESSATION OF ALL ACTIVITY IN THE UNIVERSE!
THE DEATH OF ALL CREATION!
HEY!! IT'S TRUE!
YOU USED ME AS YOUR TOY...
...JUST SO YOU COULD DO THAT?!
LOWER THE SHIELD, BELL-DANDY!
BEFORE I WAS SORTA OUT OF IT, BUT THIS TIME--

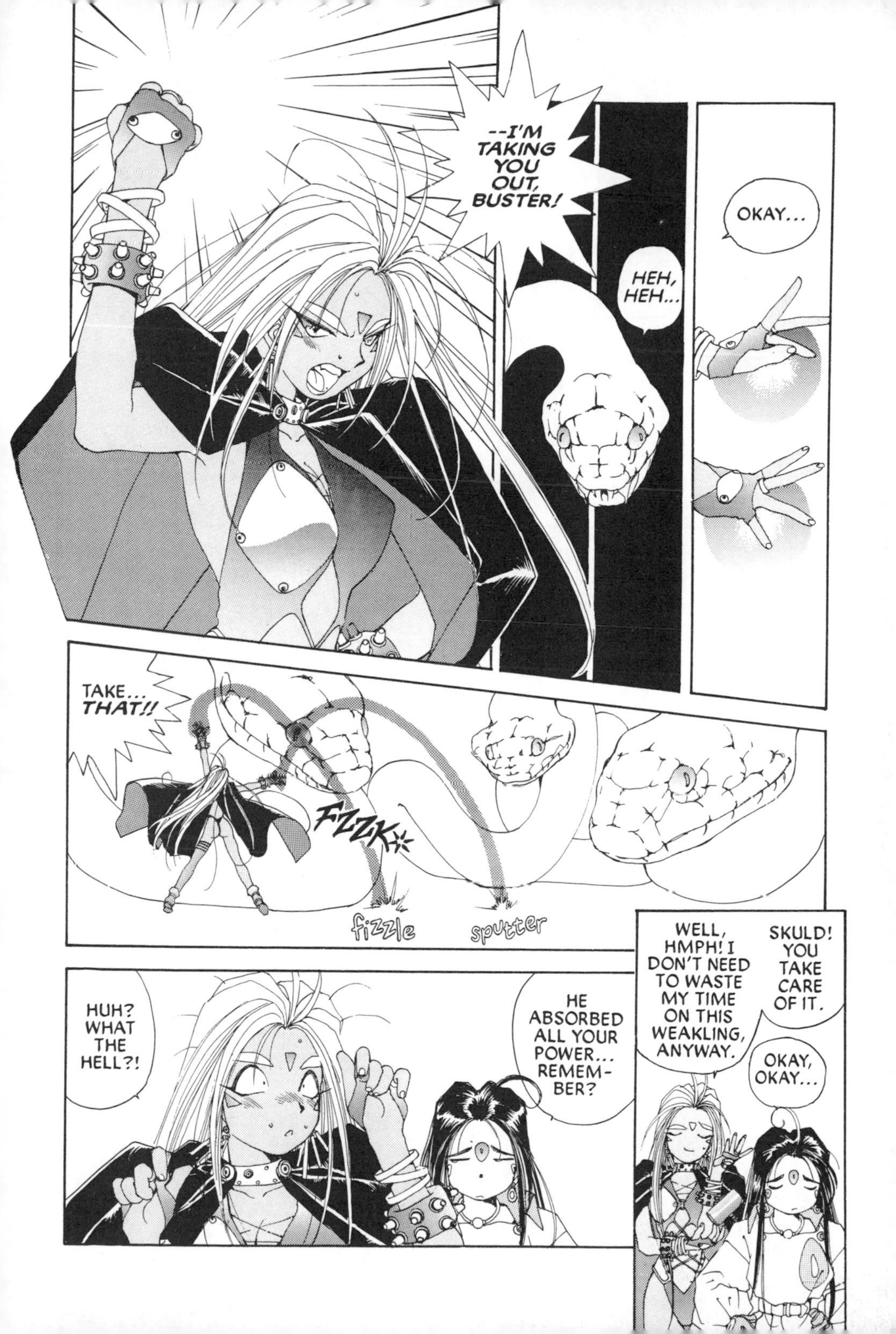
--I'M TAKING YOU OUT, BUSTER!
HEH, HEH...
OKAY...
TAKE... THAT!!
FZZK
fizzle
sputter
HUH? WHAT THE HELL?!
HE ABSORBED ALL YOUR POWER... REMEMBER?
WELL, HMPH! I DON'T NEED TO WASTE MY TIME ON THIS WEAKLING, ANYWAY.
SKULD! YOU TAKE CARE OF IT.
OKAY, OKAY...

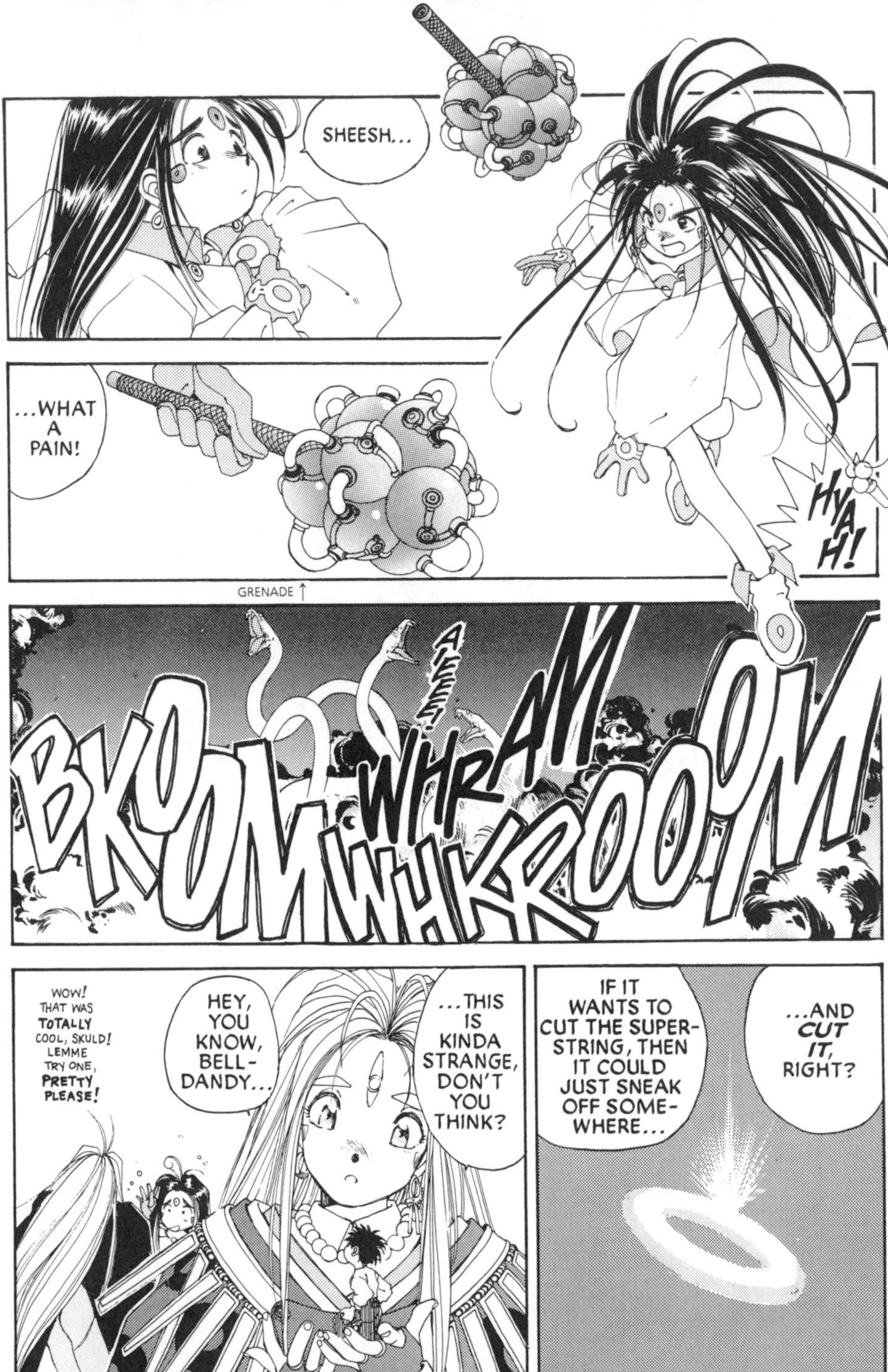
SHEESH...
...WHAT A PAIN!
HYAH!
GRENADE ↑
AEEE!
BKOOM
WHRAAM
WHKROOOM
WOW! THAT WAS **TOTALLY** COOL, SKULD! LEMME TRY ONE, **PRETTY PLEASE!**
HEY, YOU KNOW, BELL-DANDY...
...THIS IS KINDA STRANGE, DON'T YOU THINK?
IF IT WANTS TO CUT THE SUPER-STRING, THEN IT COULD JUST SNEAK OFF SOME-WHERE...
...AND ***CUT IT,*** RIGHT?

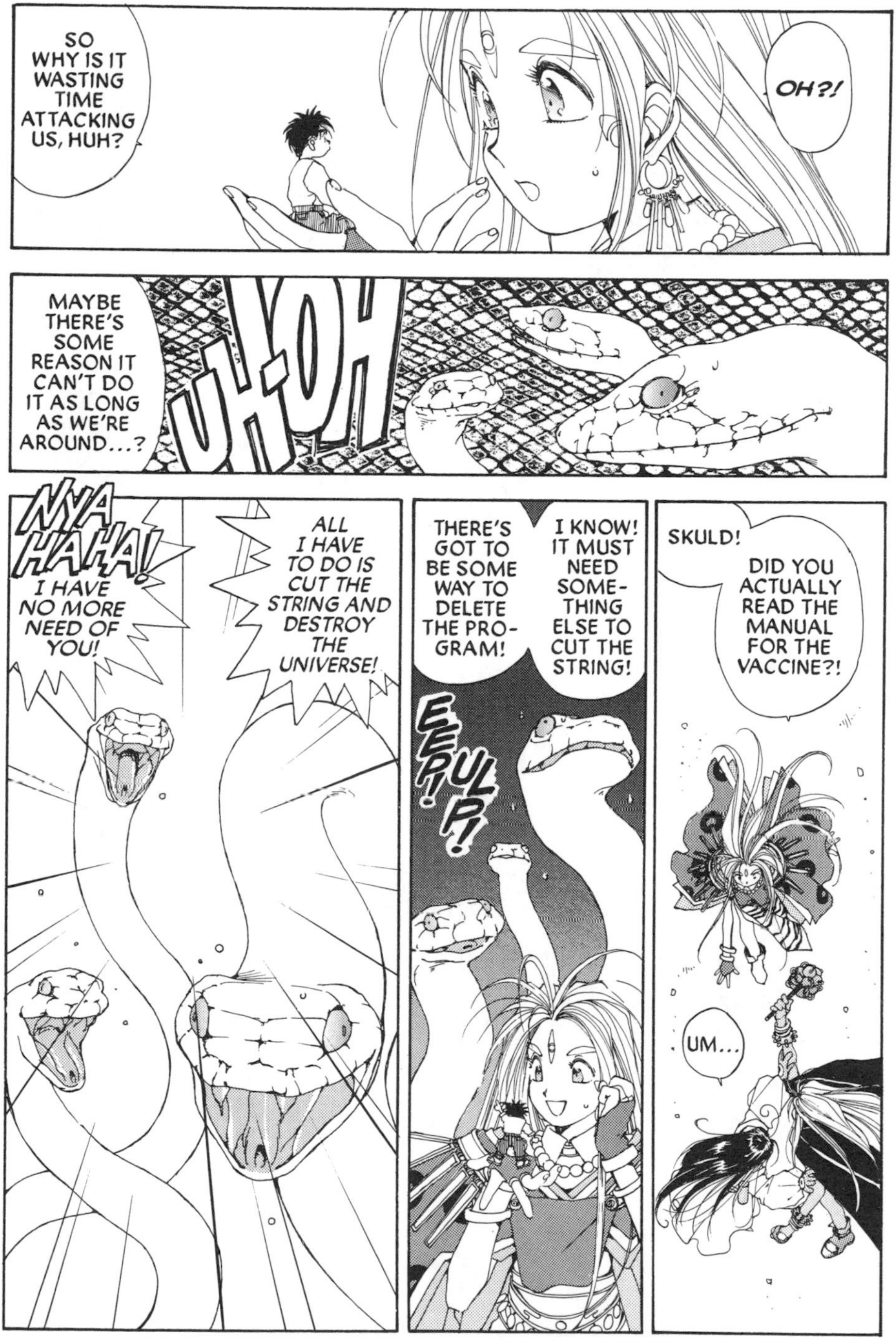
SO WHY IS IT WASTING TIME ATTACKING US, HUH?
OH?!
MAYBE THERE'S SOME REASON IT CAN'T DO IT AS LONG AS WE'RE AROUND...?
UH-OH
NYA HAHA!
I HAVE NO MORE NEED OF YOU!
ALL I HAVE TO DO IS CUT THE STRING AND DESTROY THE UNIVERSE!
THERE'S GOT TO BE SOME WAY TO DELETE THE PRO- GRAM!
I KNOW! IT MUST NEED SOME- THING ELSE TO CUT THE STRING!
EEP!
ULP!
SKULD!
DID YOU ACTUALLY READ THE MANUAL FOR THE VACCINE?!
UM...

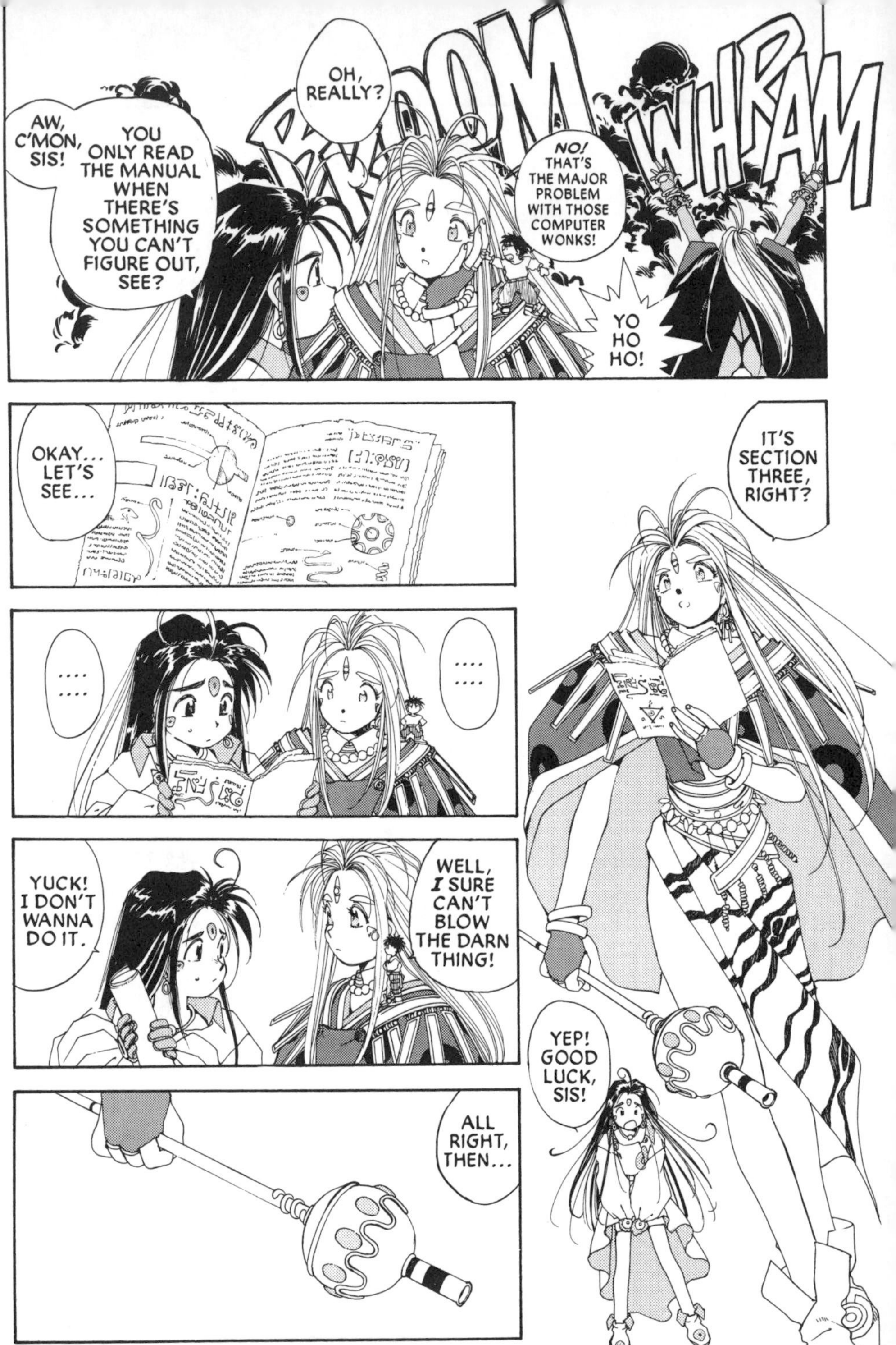
AW, C'MON, SIS!
YOU ONLY READ THE MANUAL WHEN THERE'S SOMETHING YOU CAN'T FIGURE OUT, SEE?
OH, REALLY?
NO! THAT'S THE MAJOR PROBLEM WITH THOSE COMPUTER WONKS!
WHRAM
YO HO HO!
OKAY... LET'S SEE...
....
....
....
....
YUCK! I DON'T WANNA DO IT.
WELL, *I* SURE CAN'T BLOW THE DARN THING!
ALL RIGHT, THEN...
IT'S SECTION THREE, RIGHT?
YEP! GOOD LUCK, SIS!

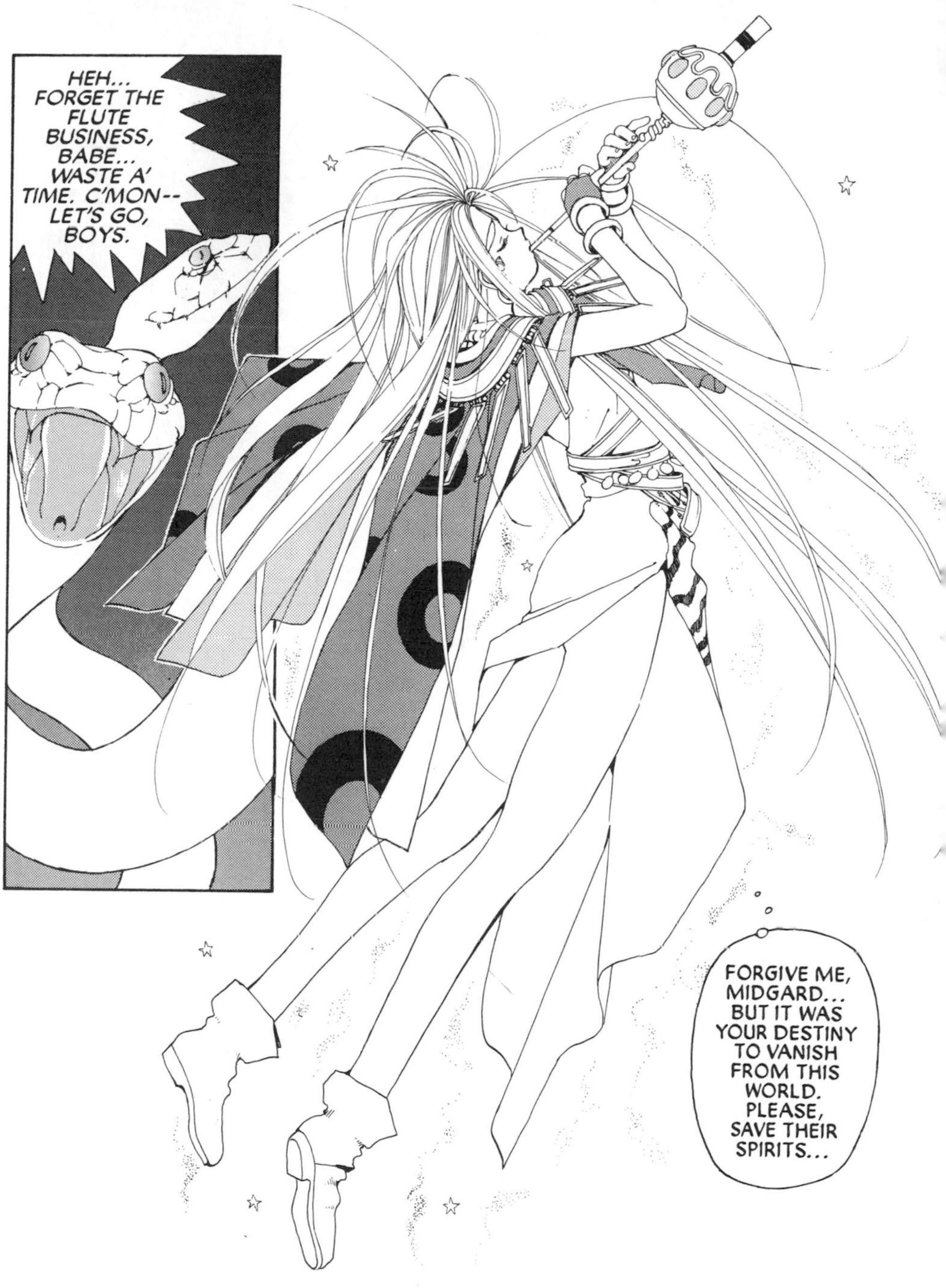
HEH... FORGET THE FLUTE BUSINESS, BABE... WASTE A' TIME. C'MON-- LET'S GO, BOYS.
FORGIVE ME, MIDGARD... BUT IT WAS YOUR DESTINY TO VANISH FROM THIS WORLD. PLEASE, SAVE THEIR SPIRITS...

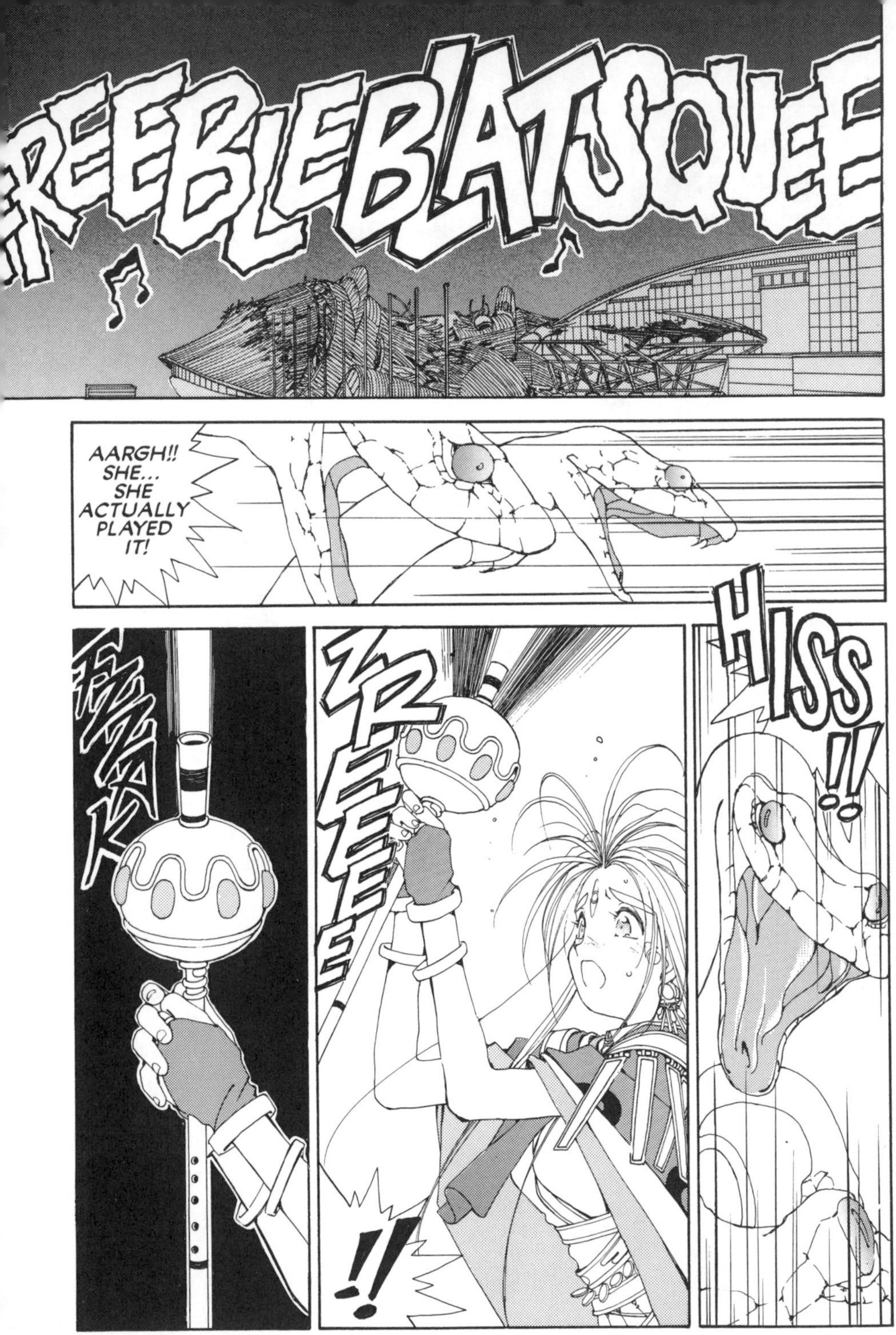
REEBLEBLATSQUEE
AARGH!! SHE... SHE ACTUALLY PLAYED IT!
!!
HISS!!

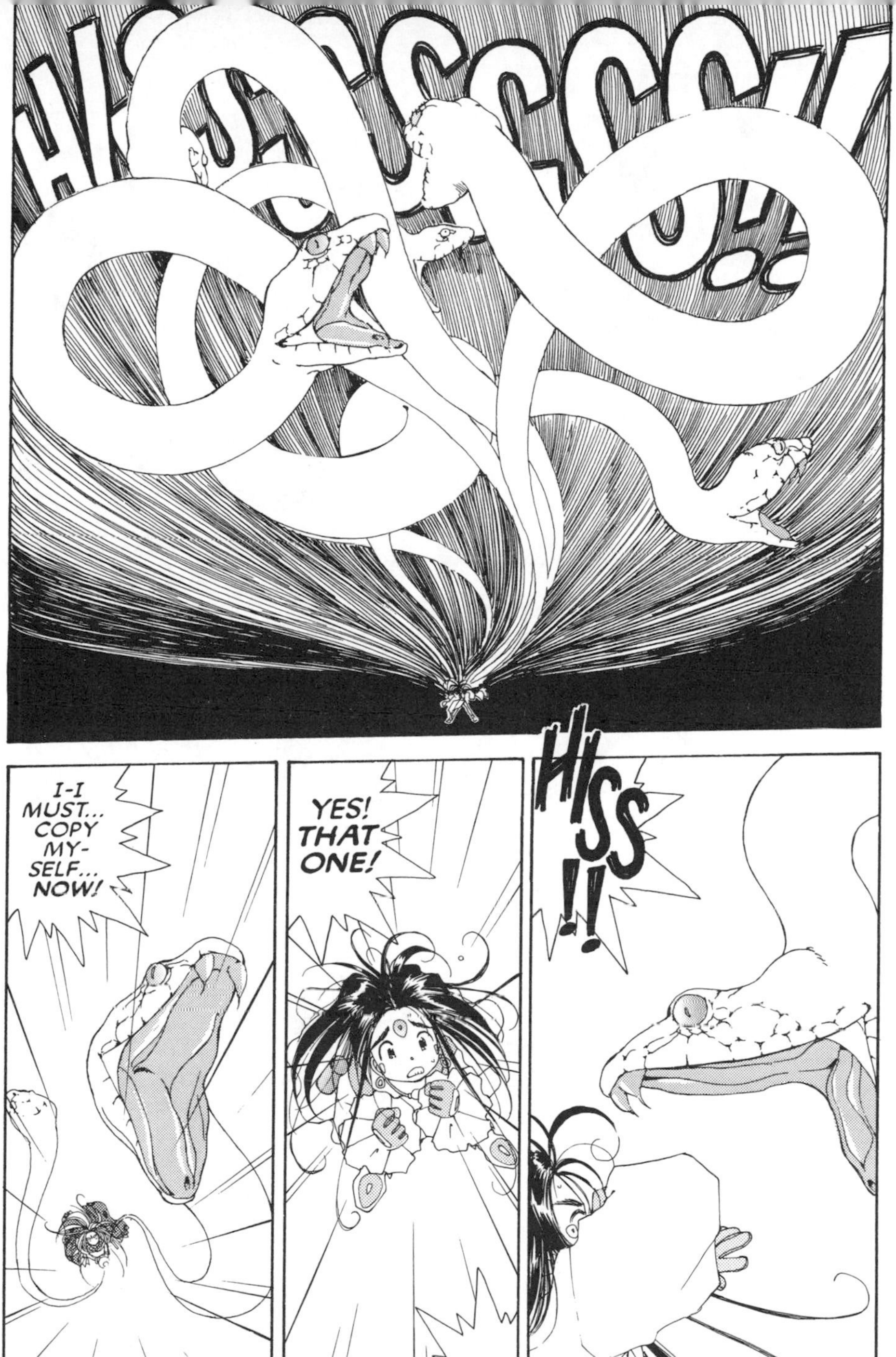
I-I MUST... COPY MY-SELF... NOW!
YES! THAT ONE!
EEK!
HISS!!

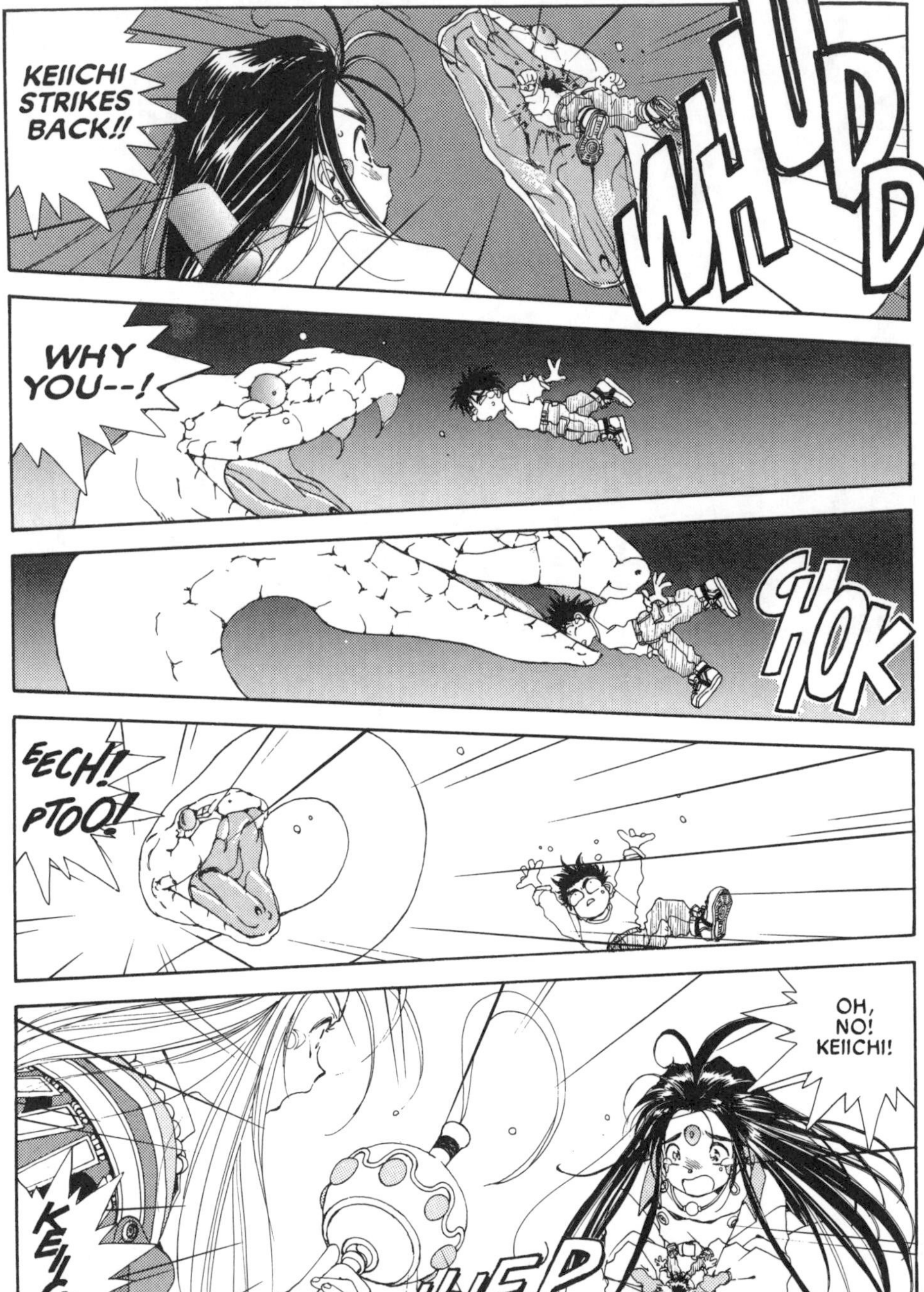
KEIICHI STRIKES BACK!!
WHUDD
WHY YOU--!
CHOK
EECH! PTOO!
KEIICHI!!
SHHFFP
OH, NO! KEIICHI!

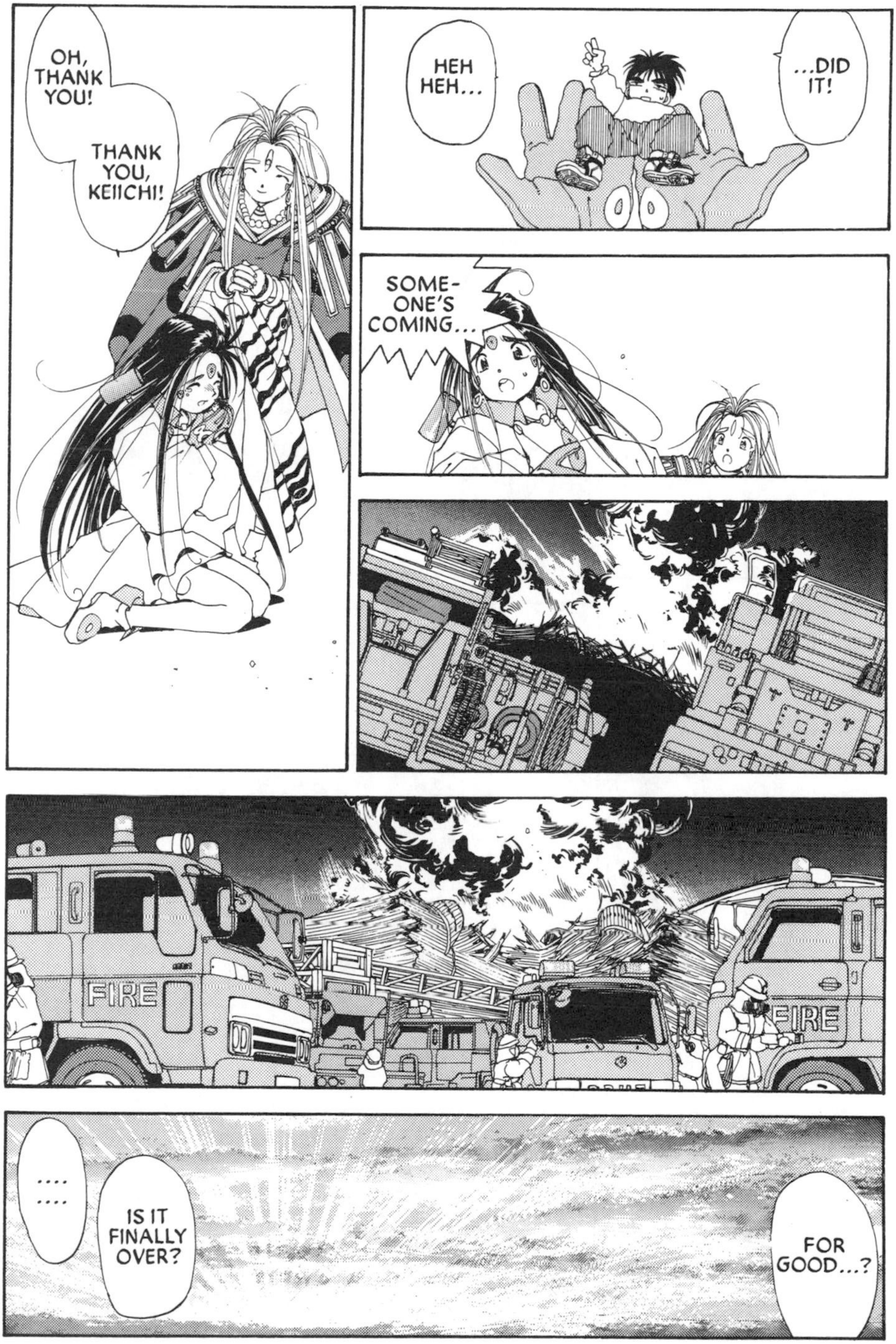
OH, THANK YOU!
THANK YOU, KEIICHI!
HEH HEH...
...DID IT!
SOME-ONE'S COMING...
....
....
IS IT FINALLY OVER?
FOR GOOD...?

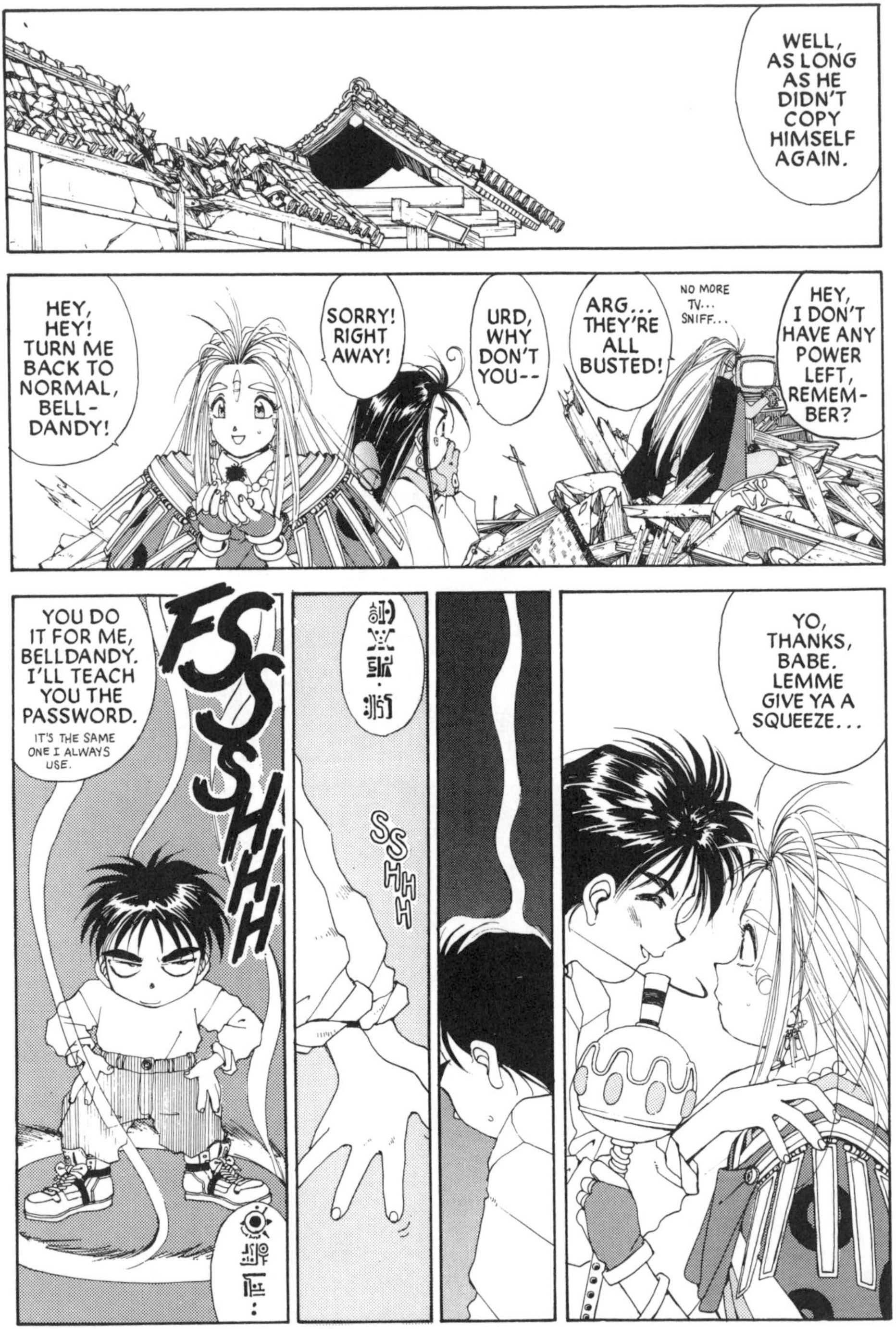
WELL, AS LONG AS HE DIDN'T COPY HIMSELF AGAIN.
HEY, HEY! TURN ME BACK TO NORMAL, BELL-DANDY!
SORRY! RIGHT AWAY!
URD, WHY DON'T YOU--
ARG... THEY'RE ALL BUSTED!
NO MORE TV... SNIFF...
HEY, I DON'T HAVE ANY POWER LEFT, REMEM-BER?
YOU DO IT FOR ME, BELLDANDY. I'LL TEACH YOU THE PASSWORD.
IT'S THE SAME ONE I ALWAYS USE.
FSSHHH
SSHHH
YO, THANKS, BABE. LEMME GIVE YA A SQUEEZE...

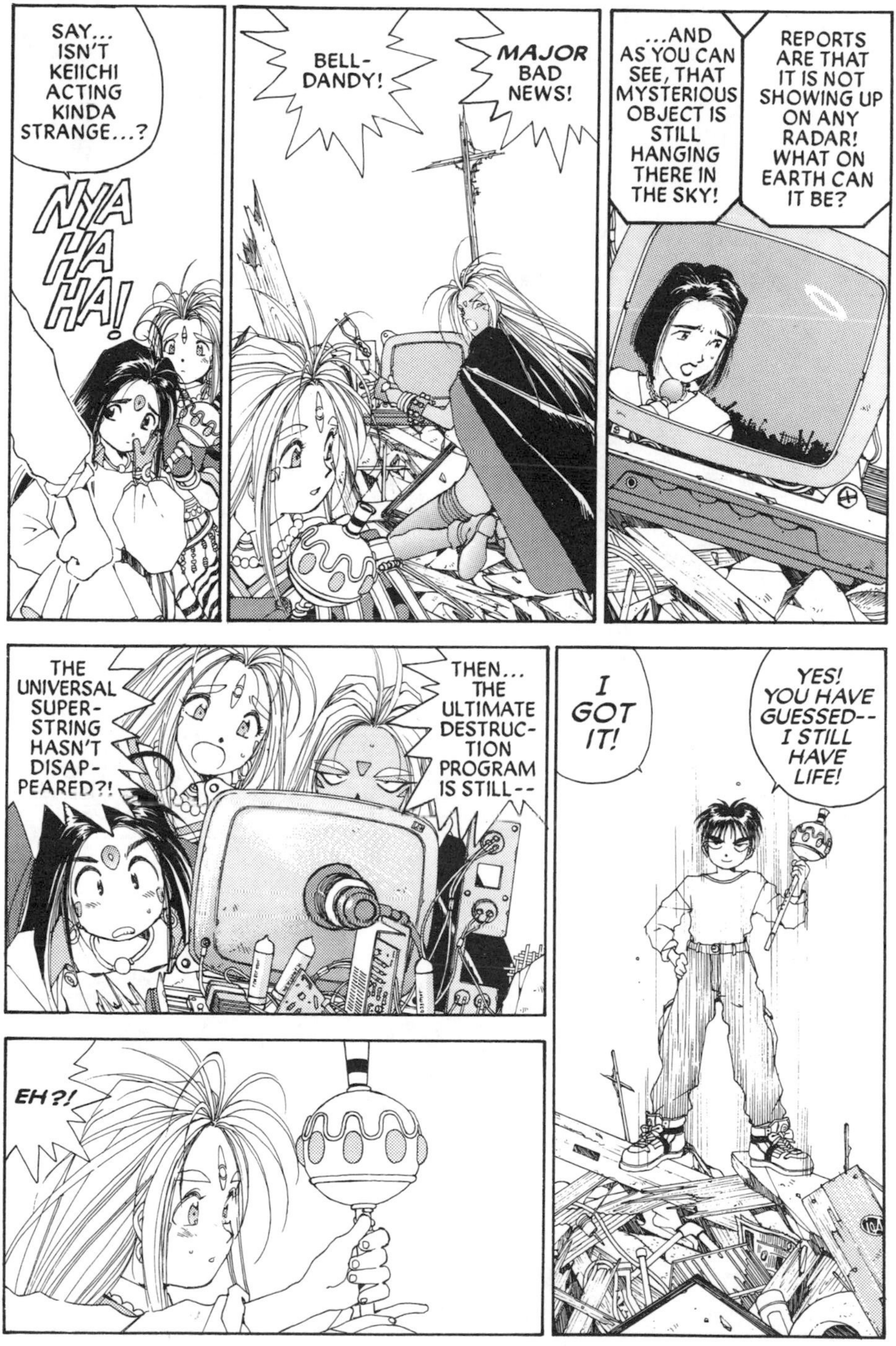
SAY... ISN'T KEIICHI ACTING KINDA STRANGE...?
NYA HA HA HA!
BELL-DANDY!
MAJOR BAD NEWS!
...AND AS YOU CAN SEE, THAT MYSTERIOUS OBJECT IS STILL HANGING THERE IN THE SKY!
REPORTS ARE THAT IT IS NOT SHOWING UP ON ANY RADAR! WHAT ON EARTH CAN IT BE?
THE UNIVERSAL SUPER-STRING HASN'T DISAP-PEARED?!
THEN... THE ULTIMATE DESTRUC-TION PROGRAM IS STILL--
EH?!
I GOT IT!
YES! YOU HAVE GUESSED-- I STILL HAVE LIFE!

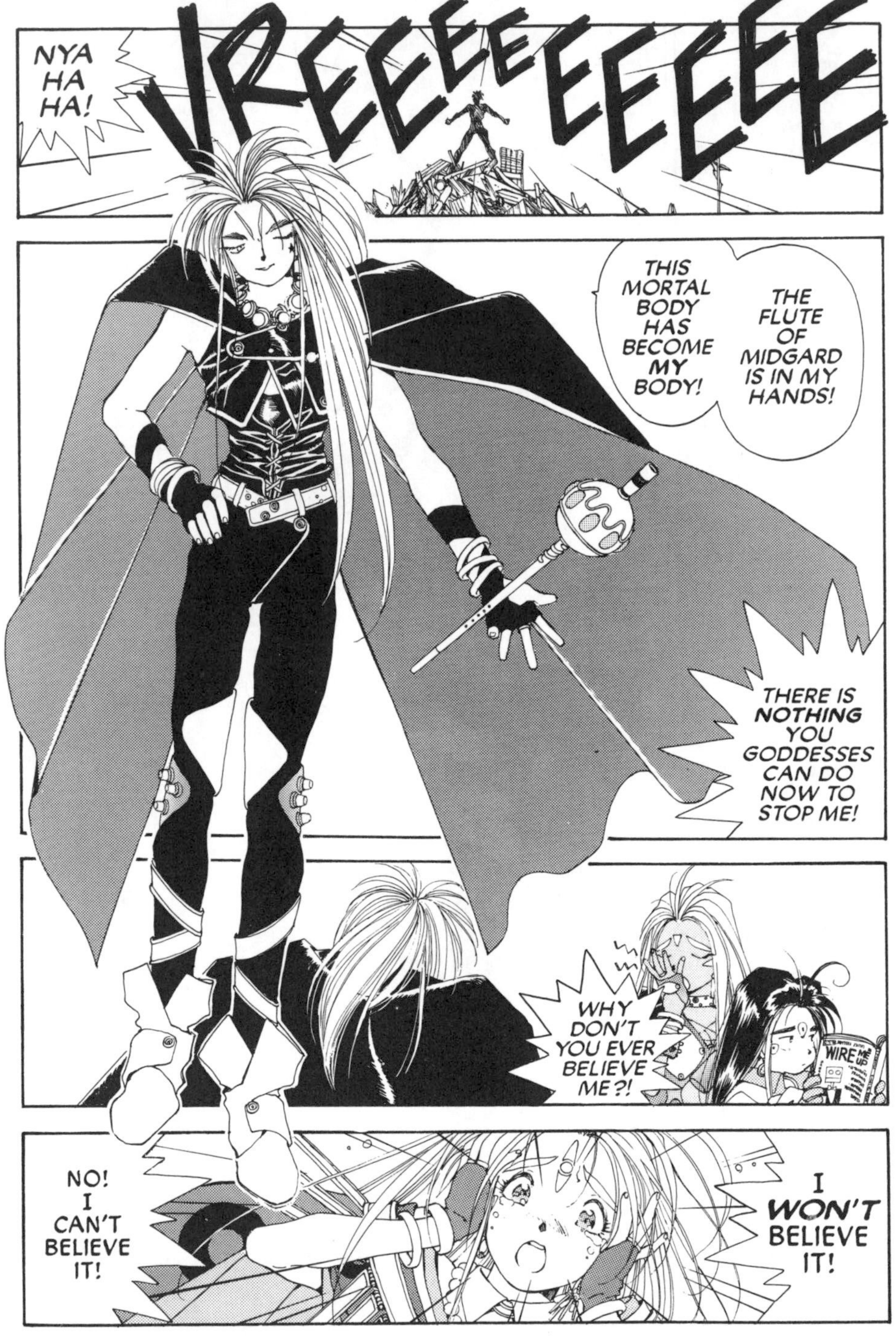
NYA HA HA!
VREEEEEEEEEE
THIS MORTAL BODY HAS BECOME MY BODY!
THE FLUTE OF MIDGARD IS IN MY HANDS!
THERE IS NOTHING YOU GODDESSES CAN DO NOW TO STOP ME!
WHY DON'T YOU EVER BELIEVE ME?!
WIRE
NO! I CAN'T BELIEVE IT!
I WON'T BELIEVE IT!

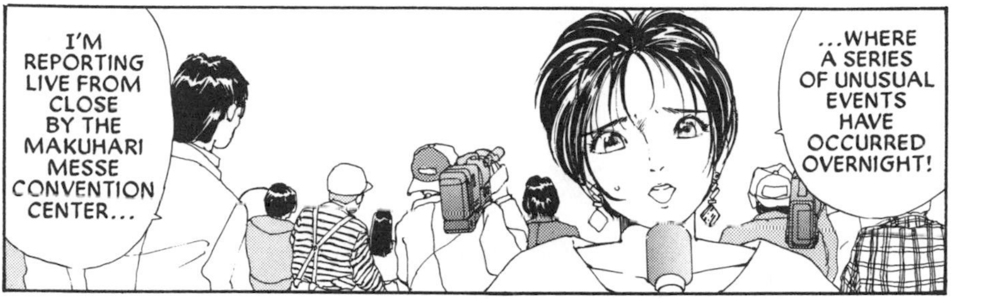
I'M REPORTING LIVE FROM CLOSE BY THE MAKUHARI MESSE CONVENTION CENTER...
...WHERE A SERIES OF UNUSUAL EVENTS HAVE OCCURRED OVERNIGHT!

Confession

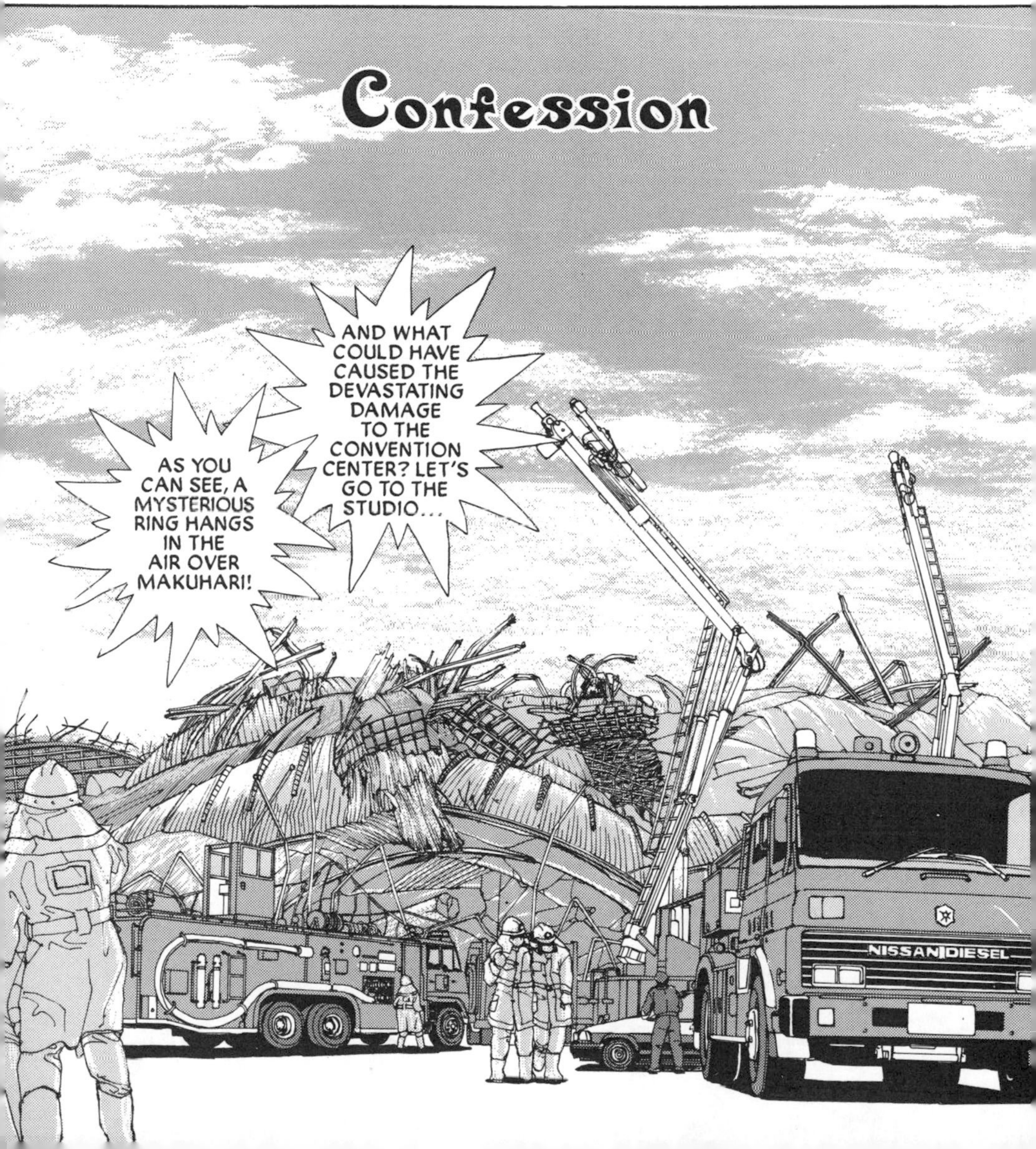
AS YOU CAN SEE, A MYSTERIOUS RING HANGS IN THE AIR OVER MAKUHARI!
AND WHAT COULD HAVE CAUSED THE DEVASTATING DAMAGE TO THE CONVENTION CENTER? LET'S GO TO THE STUDIO...
NISSAN DIESEL

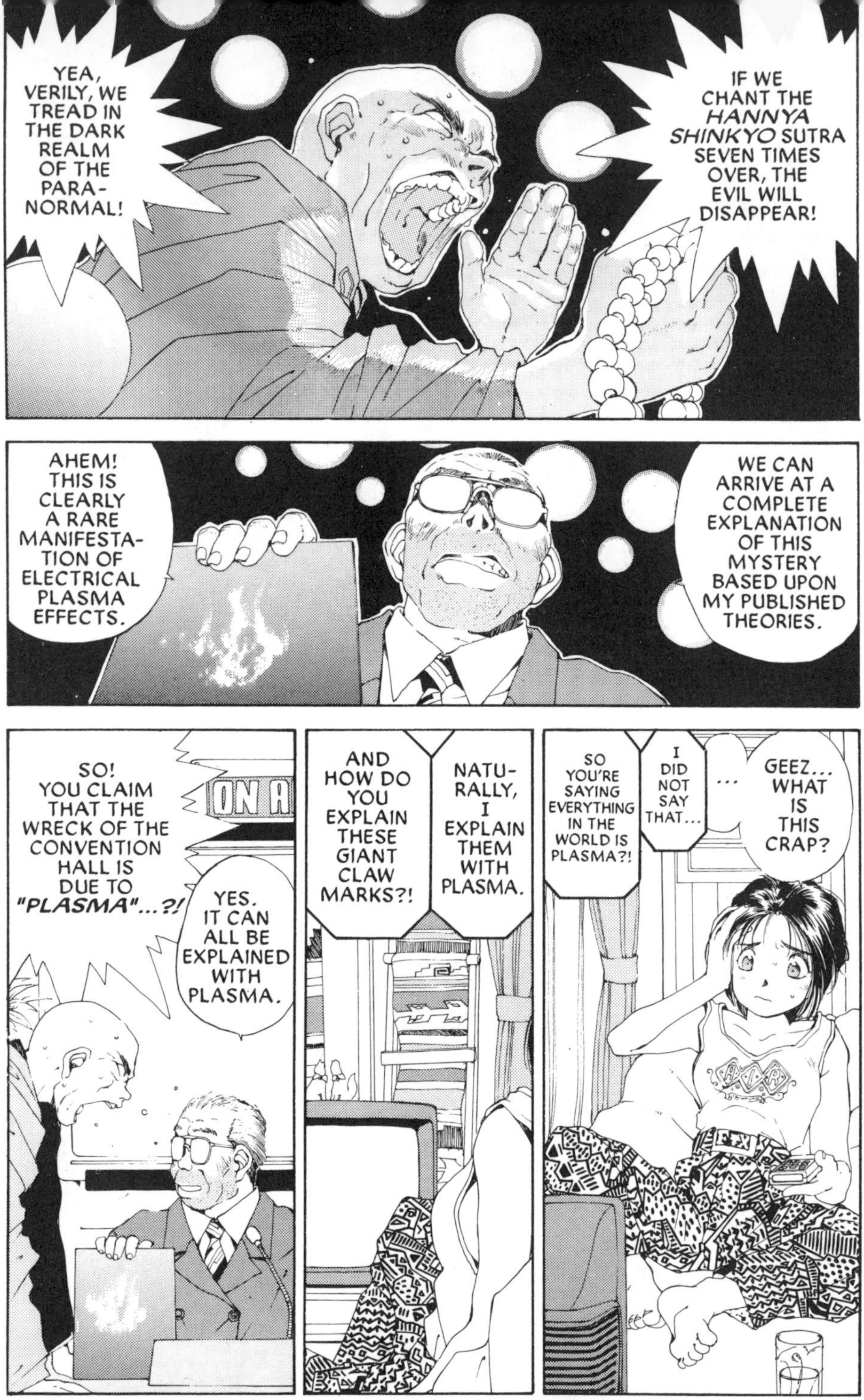
YEA, VERILY, WE TREAD IN THE DARK REALM OF THE PARA-NORMAL!
IF WE CHANT THE *HANNYA SHINKYO* SUTRA SEVEN TIMES OVER, THE EVIL WILL DISAPPEAR!
AHEM! THIS IS CLEARLY A RARE MANIFESTA-TION OF ELECTRICAL PLASMA EFFECTS.
WE CAN ARRIVE AT A COMPLETE EXPLANATION OF THIS MYSTERY BASED UPON MY PUBLISHED THEORIES.
SO! YOU CLAIM THAT THE WRECK OF THE CONVENTION HALL IS DUE TO ***"PLASMA"***...?!
YES. IT CAN ALL BE EXPLAINED WITH PLASMA.
AND HOW DO YOU EXPLAIN THESE GIANT CLAW MARKS?!
NATU-RALLY, I EXPLAIN THEM WITH PLASMA.
SO YOU'RE SAYING EVERYTHING IN THE WORLD IS PLASMA?!
I DID NOT SAY THAT...
...
GEEZ... WHAT IS THIS CRAP?

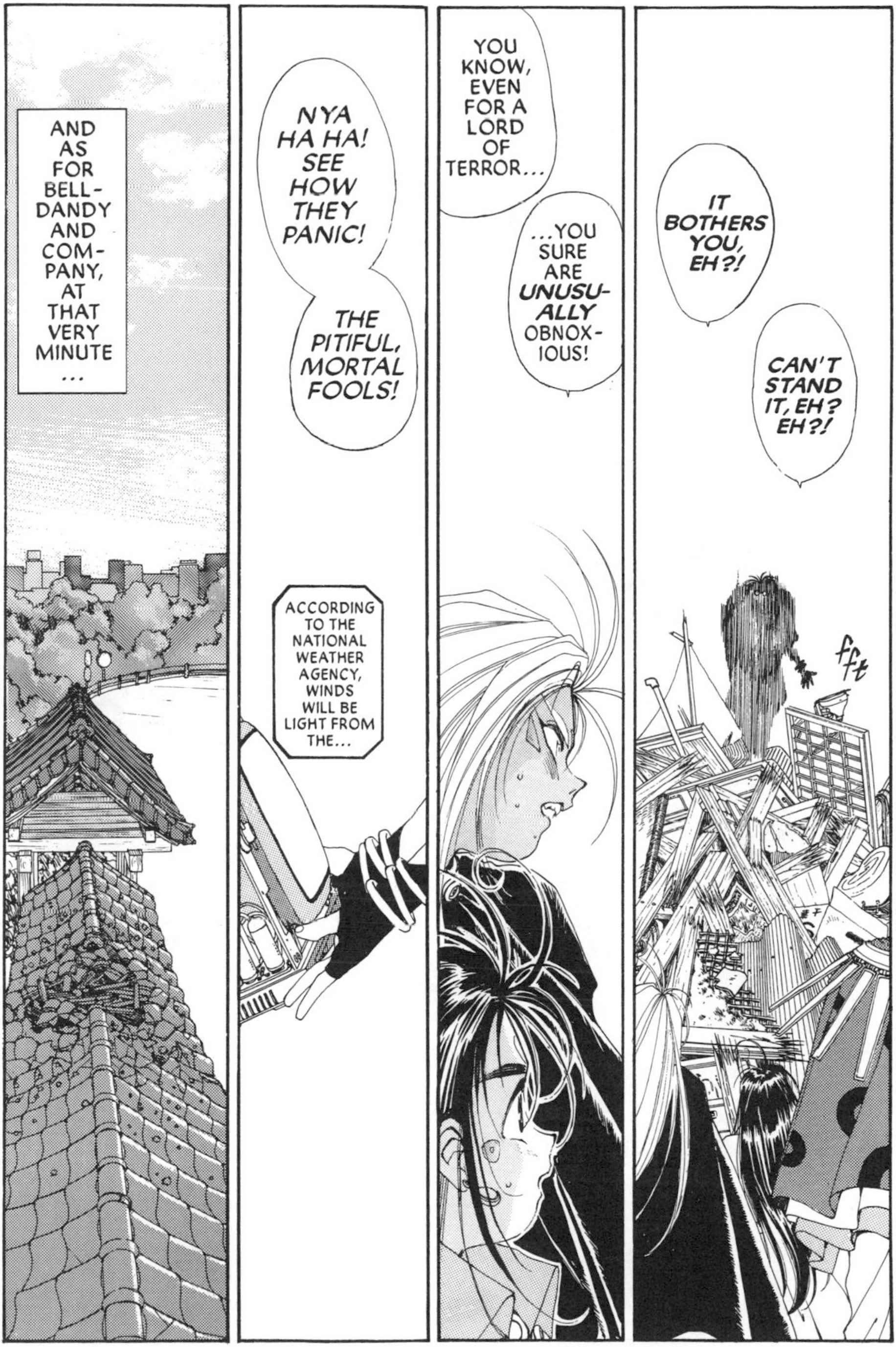
AND AS FOR BELL-DANDY AND COM-PANY, AT THAT VERY MINUTE...
NYA HA HA! SEE HOW THEY PANIC!
THE PITIFUL, MORTAL FOOLS!
ACCORDING TO THE NATIONAL WEATHER AGENCY, WINDS WILL BE LIGHT FROM THE...
YOU KNOW, EVEN FOR A LORD OF TERROR...
...YOU SURE ARE UNUSU-ALLY OBNOX-IOUS!
IT BOTHERS YOU, EH?!
CAN'T STAND IT, EH? EH?!
fft

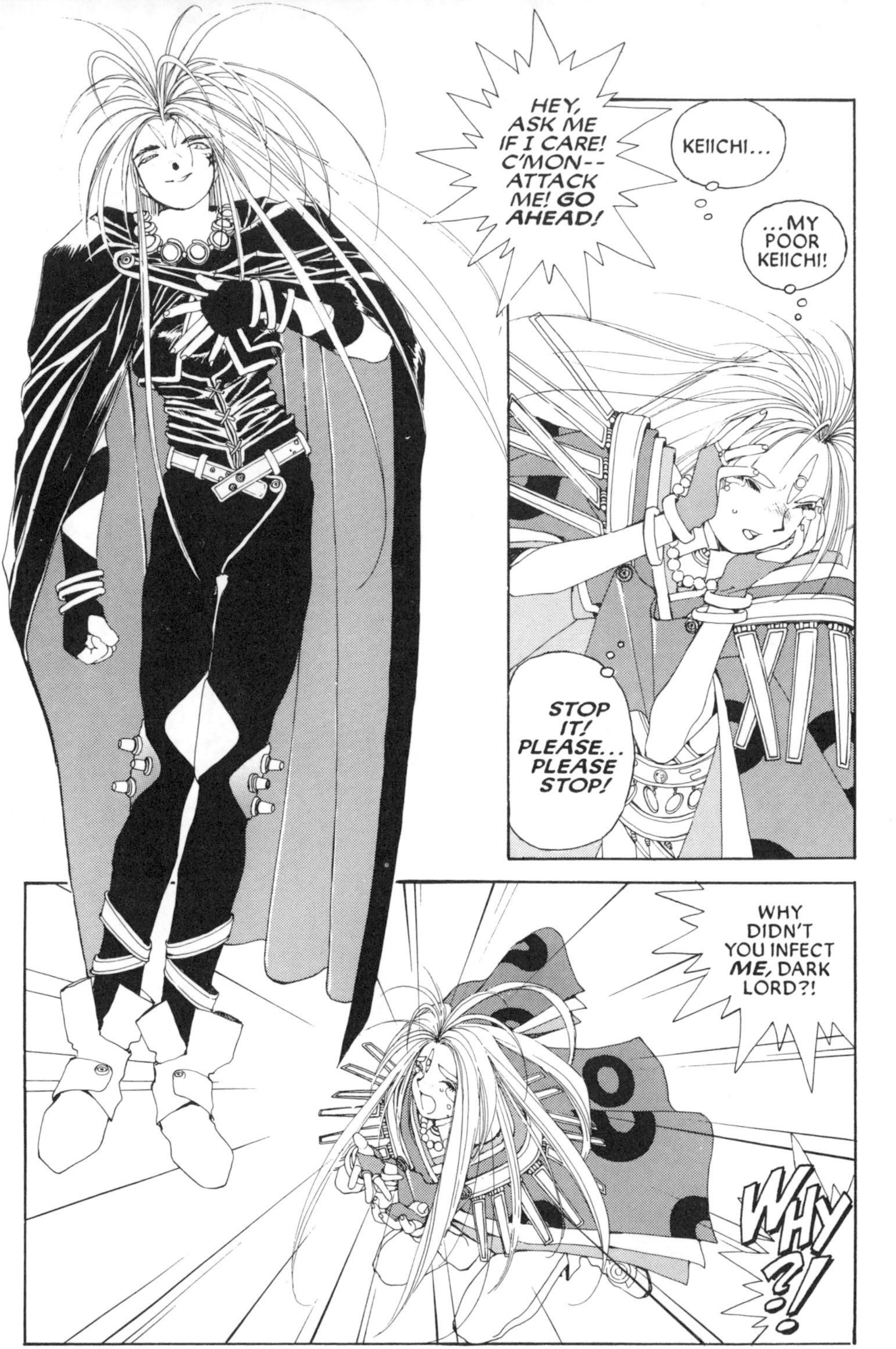

HEY, ASK ME IF I CARE! C'MON-- ATTACK ME! GO AHEAD!
KEIICHI...
...MY POOR KEIICHI!
STOP IT! PLEASE... PLEASE STOP!
WHY DIDN'T YOU INFECT ME, DARK LORD?!
WHY?!

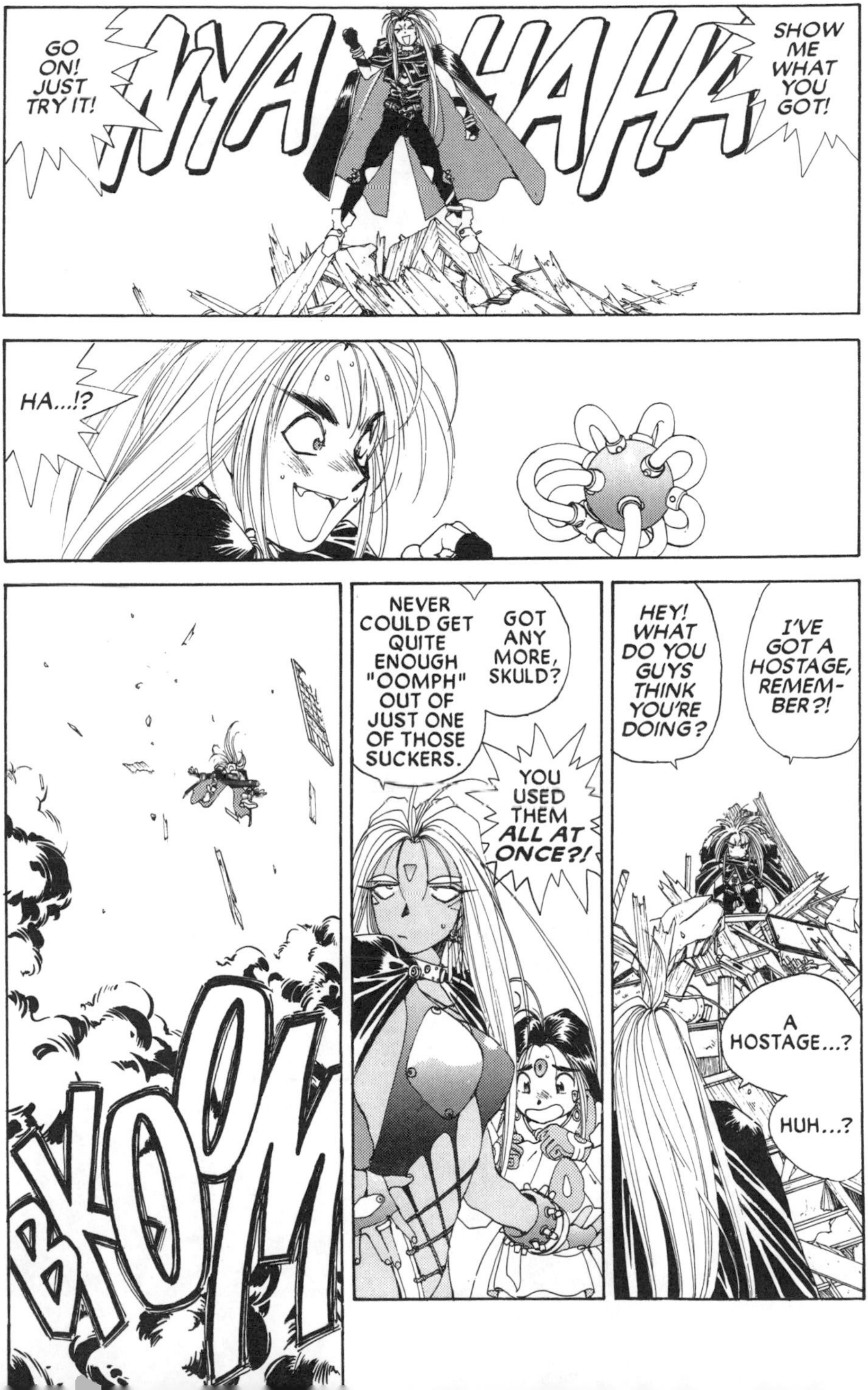
GO ON! JUST TRY IT!
NYA HAHAHA
SHOW ME WHAT YOU GOT!
HA...!?
BKOOM
NEVER COULD GET QUITE ENOUGH "OOMPH" OUT OF JUST ONE OF THOSE SUCKERS.
GOT ANY MORE, SKULD?
YOU USED THEM ALL AT ONCE?!
HEY! WHAT DO YOU GUYS THINK YOU'RE DOING?
I'VE GOT A HOSTAGE, REMEMBER?!
A HOSTAGE...?
HUH...?

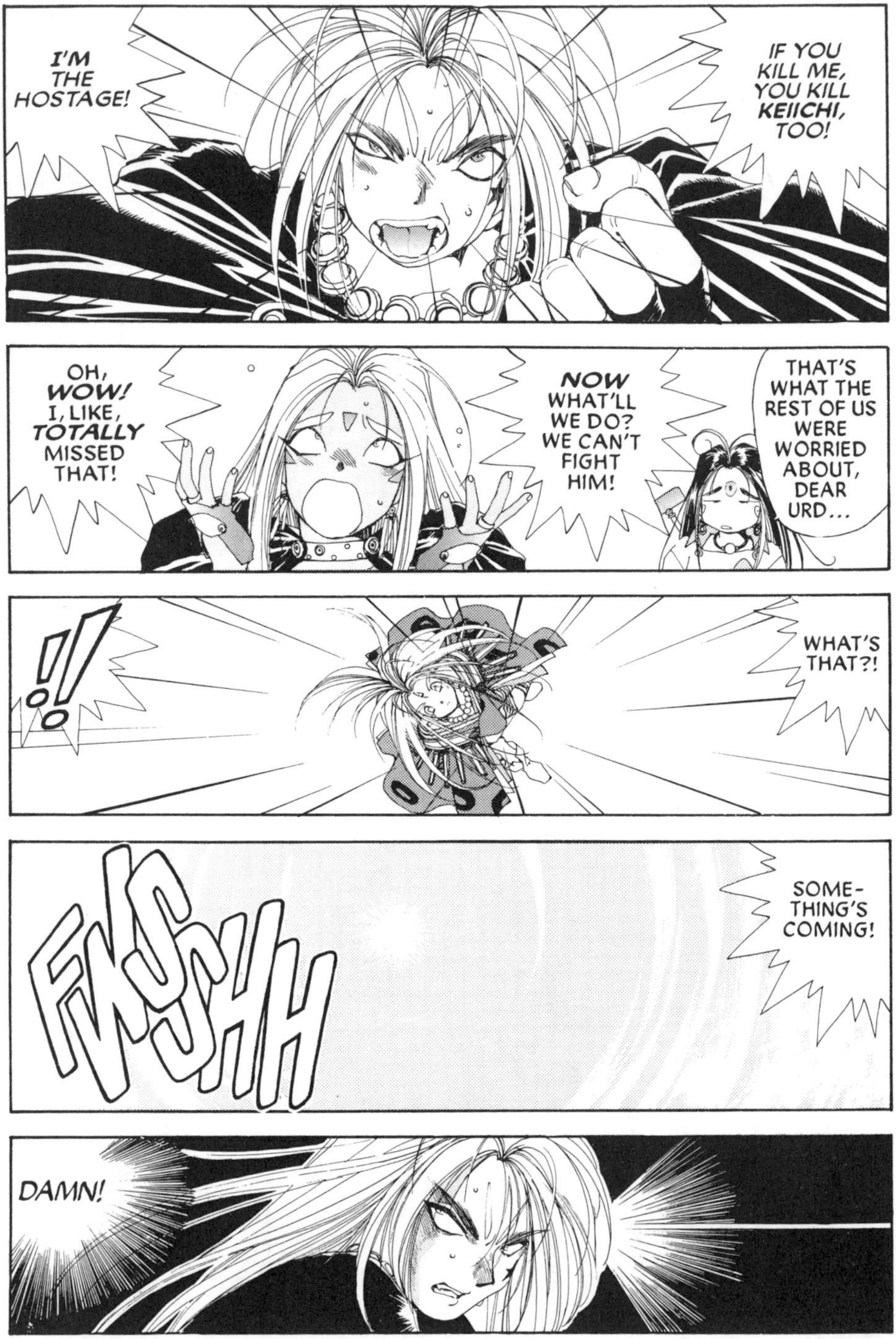
I'M THE HOSTAGE!
IF YOU KILL ME, YOU KILL KEIICHI, TOO!
OH, WOW! I, LIKE, TOTALLY MISSED THAT!
NOW WHAT'LL WE DO? WE CAN'T FIGHT HIM!
THAT'S WHAT THE REST OF US WERE WORRIED ABOUT, DEAR URD...
!!
WHAT'S THAT?!
FWSSHH
SOME-THING'S COMING!
DAMN!

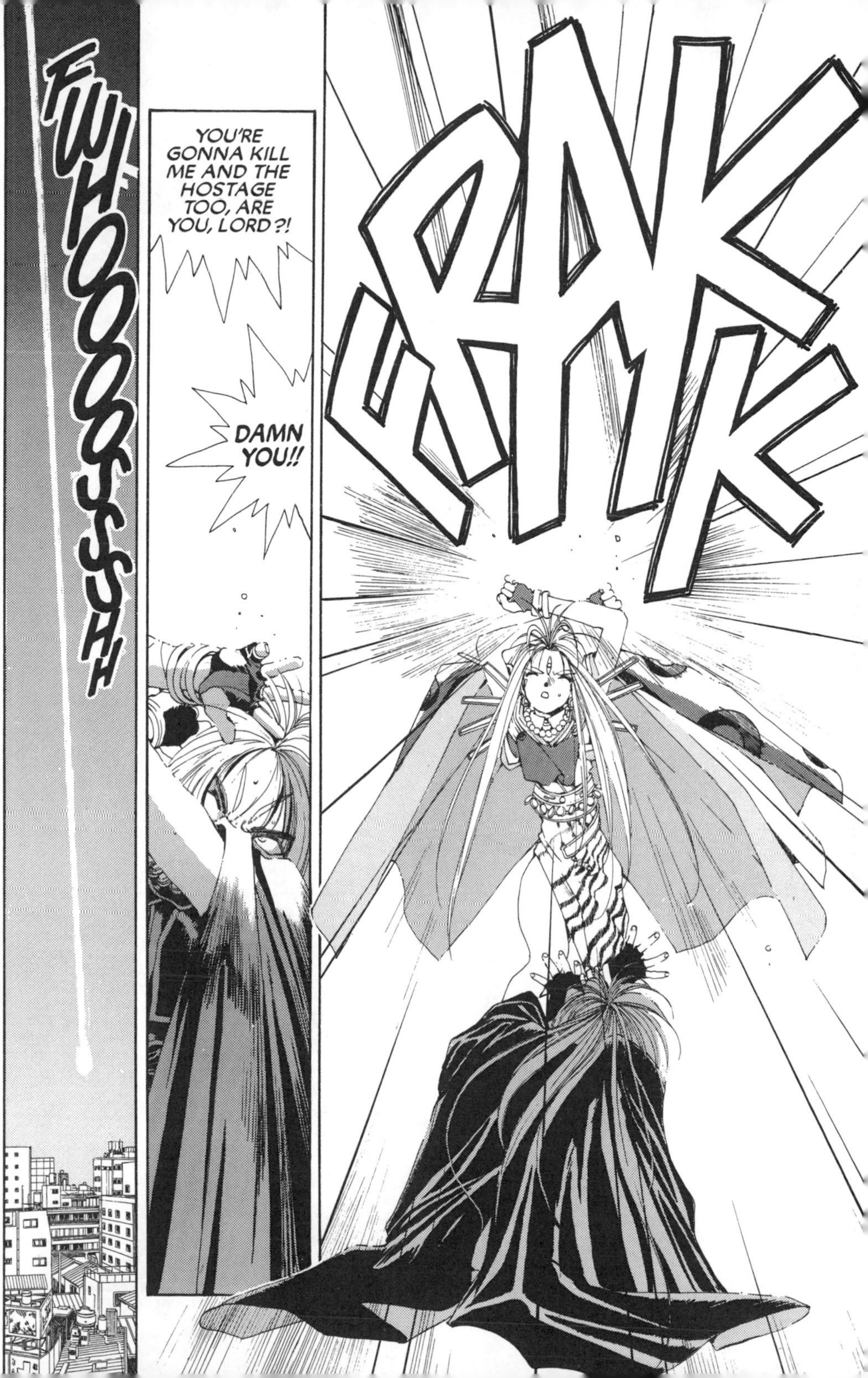
FWHOOOOOSSSHHH
YOU'RE GONNA KILL ME AND THE HOSTAGE TOO, ARE YOU, LORD?!
DAMN YOU!!

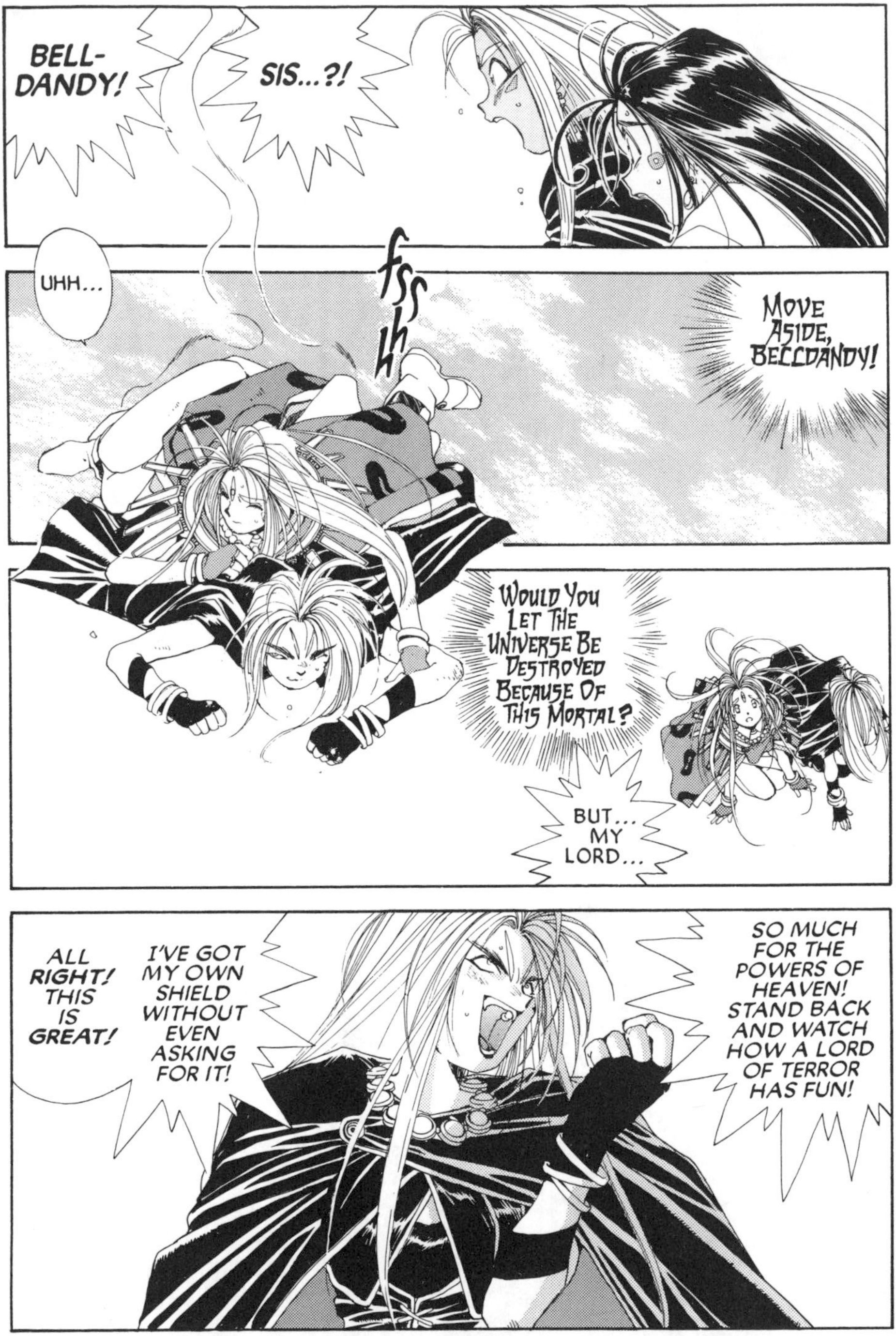
BELL-DANDY!
SIS...?!
UHH...
fssh
MOVE ASIDE, BELLDANDY!
WOULD YOU LET THE UNIVERSE BE DESTROYED BECAUSE OF THIS MORTAL?
BUT... MY LORD...
ALL RIGHT! THIS IS GREAT!
I'VE GOT MY OWN SHIELD WITHOUT EVEN ASKING FOR IT!
SO MUCH FOR THE POWERS OF HEAVEN! STAND BACK AND WATCH HOW A LORD OF TERROR HAS FUN!

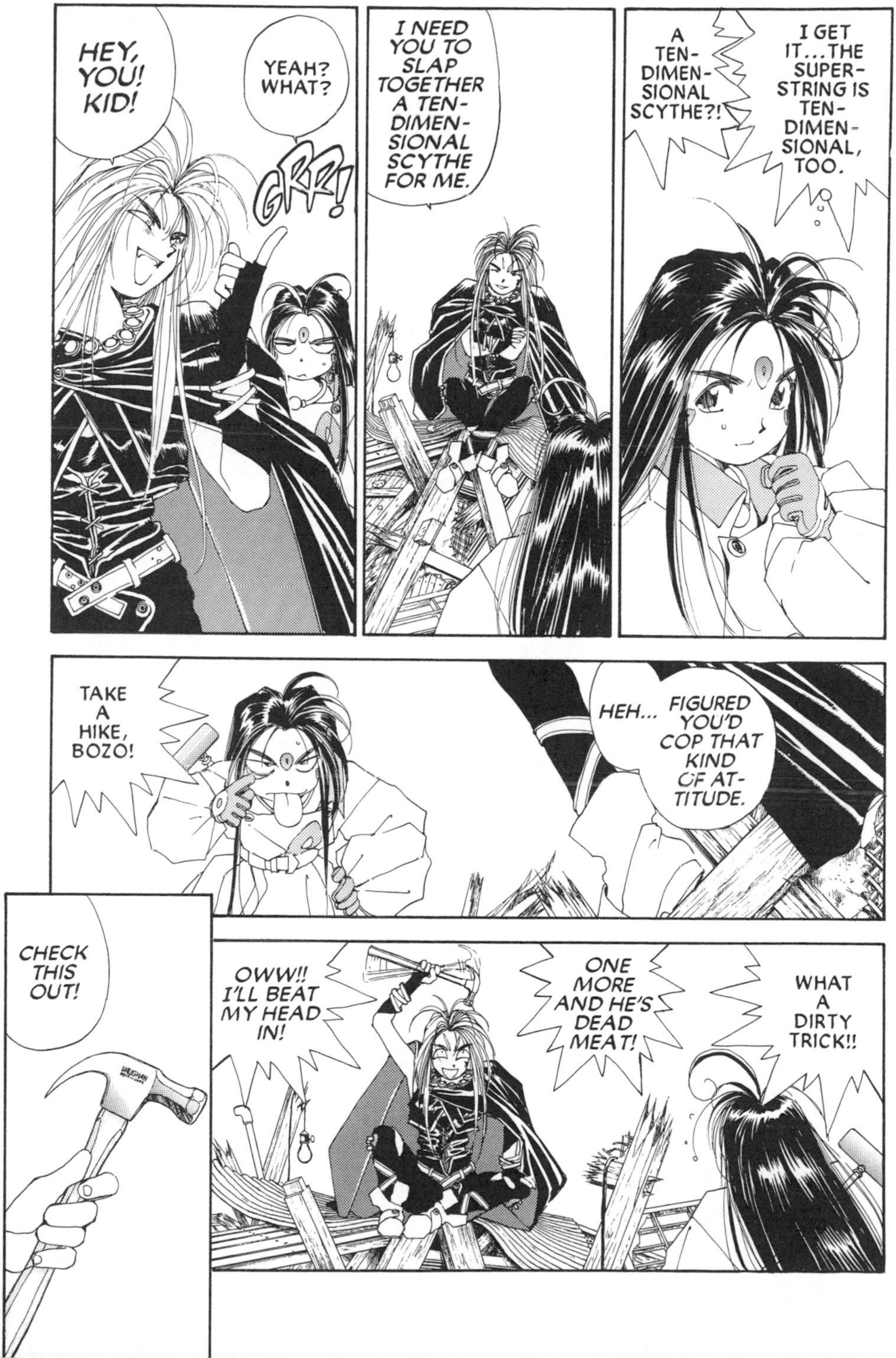
HEY, YOU! KID!
YEAH? WHAT?
GRR!
I NEED YOU TO SLAP TOGETHER A TEN-DIMENSIONAL SCYTHE FOR ME.
A TEN-DIMENSIONAL SCYTHE?!
I GET IT...THE SUPER-STRING IS TEN-DIMENSIONAL, TOO.
TAKE A HIKE, BOZO!
HEH...
FIGURED YOU'D COP THAT KIND OF AT-TITUDE.
CHECK THIS OUT!
OWW!! I'LL BEAT MY HEAD IN!
ONE MORE AND HE'S DEAD MEAT!
WHAT A DIRTY TRICK!!

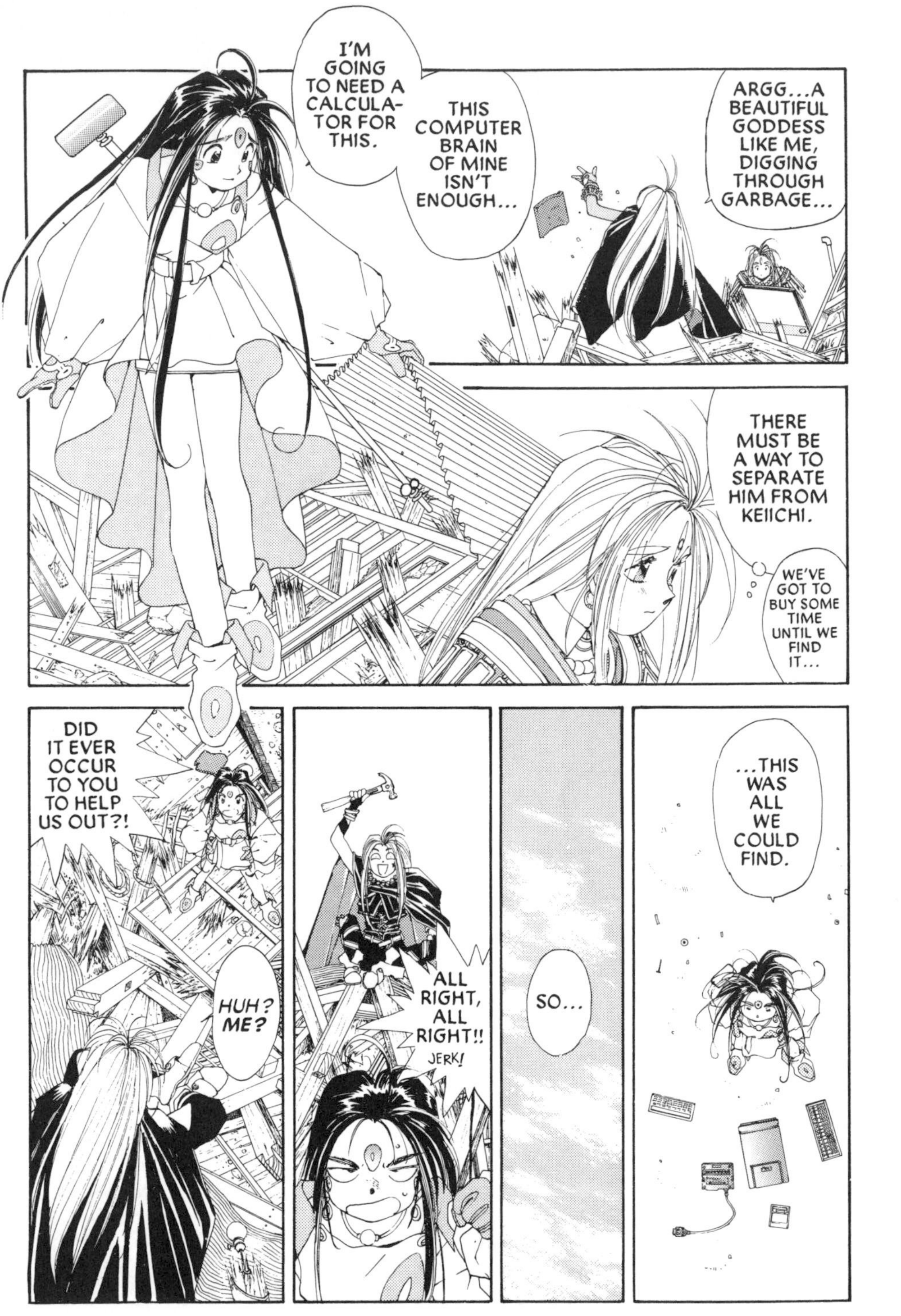
I'M GOING TO NEED A CALCULA-TOR FOR THIS.
THIS COMPUTER BRAIN OF MINE ISN'T ENOUGH...
ARGG...A BEAUTIFUL GODDESS LIKE ME, DIGGING THROUGH GARBAGE...
THERE MUST BE A WAY TO SEPARATE HIM FROM KEIICHI.
WE'VE GOT TO BUY SOME TIME UNTIL WE FIND IT...
DID IT EVER OCCUR TO YOU TO HELP US OUT?!
HUH? ME?
ALL RIGHT, ALL RIGHT!!
JERK!
SO...
...THIS WAS ALL WE COULD FIND.

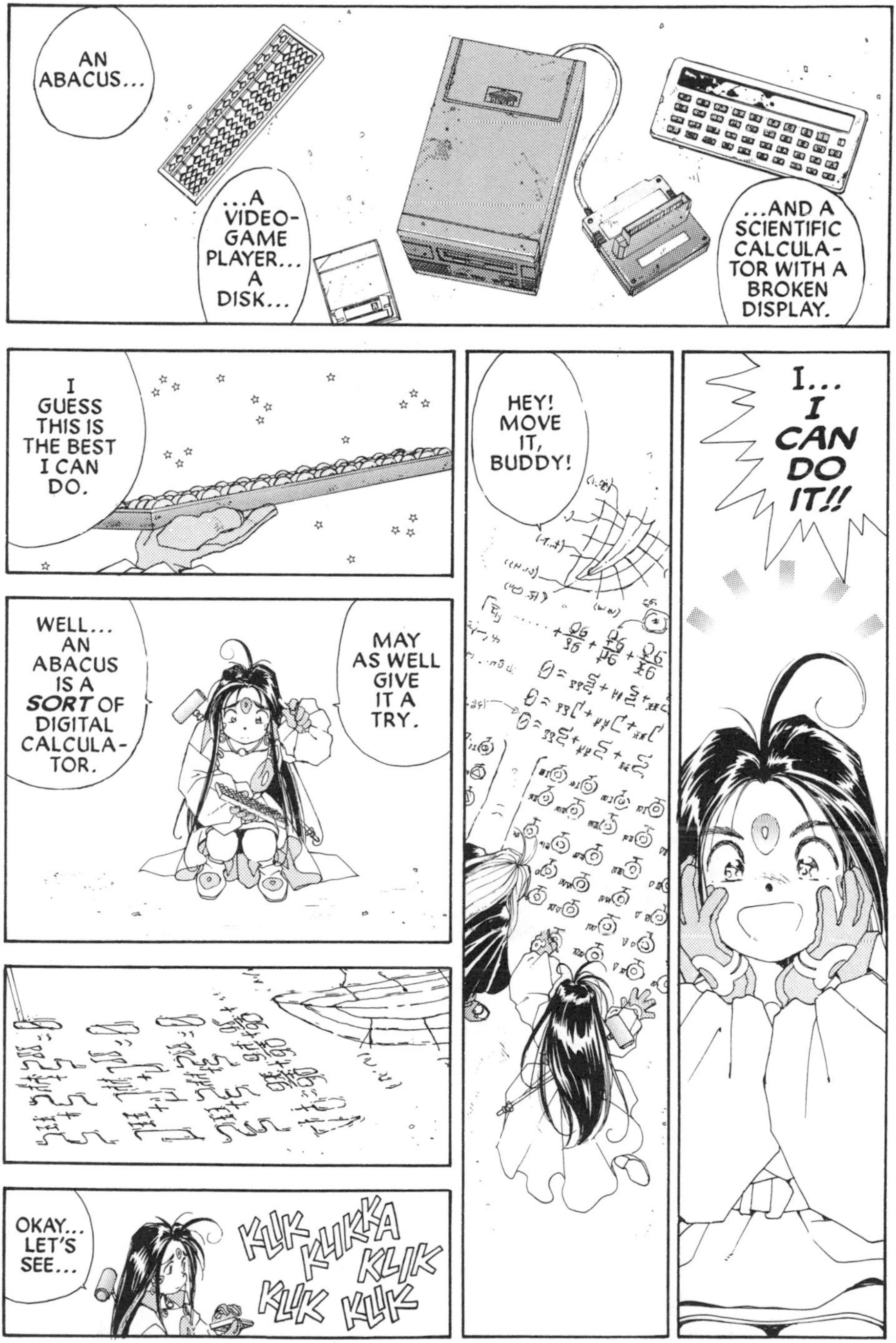
AN ABACUS...
...A VIDEO-GAME PLAYER... A DISK...
...AND A SCIENTIFIC CALCULATOR WITH A BROKEN DISPLAY.
I GUESS THIS IS THE BEST I CAN DO.
WELL... AN ABACUS IS A *SORT* OF DIGITAL CALCULATOR.
MAY AS WELL GIVE IT A TRY.
OKAY... LET'S SEE...
KLIK KLIKKA KLIK KLIK KLIK
HEY! MOVE IT, BUDDY!
I... *I CAN DO IT!!*

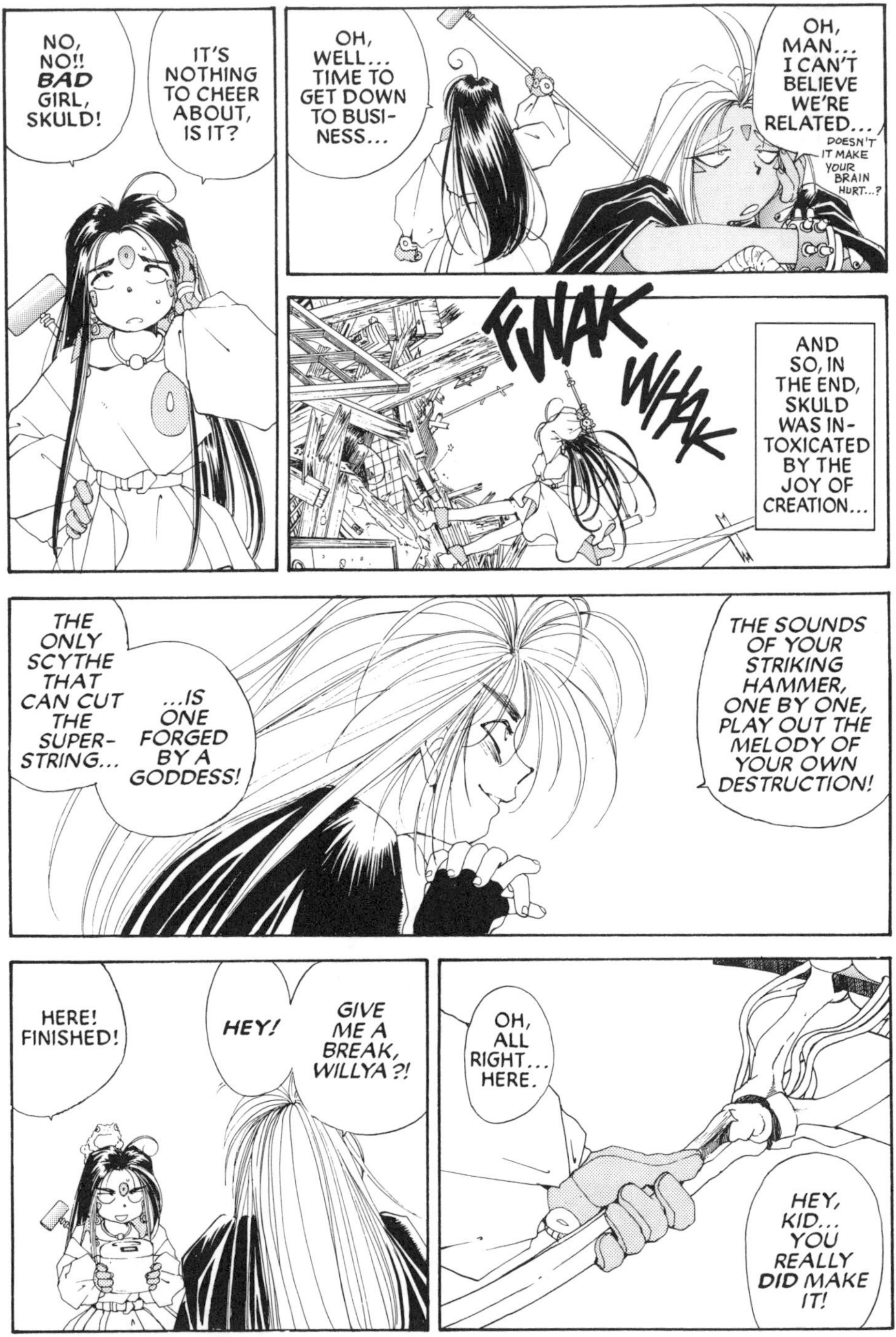
NO, NO!! BAD GIRL, SKULD!
IT'S NOTHING TO CHEER ABOUT, IS IT?
OH, WELL... TIME TO GET DOWN TO BUSI-NESS...
OH, MAN... I CAN'T BELIEVE WE'RE RELATED...
DOESN'T IT MAKE YOUR BRAIN HURT...?
FWAK
WHAK
AND SO, IN THE END, SKULD WAS IN-TOXICATED BY THE JOY OF CREATION...
THE ONLY SCYTHE THAT CAN CUT THE SUPER-STRING...
...IS ONE FORGED BY A GODDESS!
THE SOUNDS OF YOUR STRIKING HAMMER, ONE BY ONE, PLAY OUT THE MELODY OF YOUR OWN DESTRUCTION!
HERE! FINISHED!
HEY!
GIVE ME A BREAK, WILLYA?!
OH, ALL RIGHT... HERE.
HEY, KID... YOU REALLY DID MAKE IT!

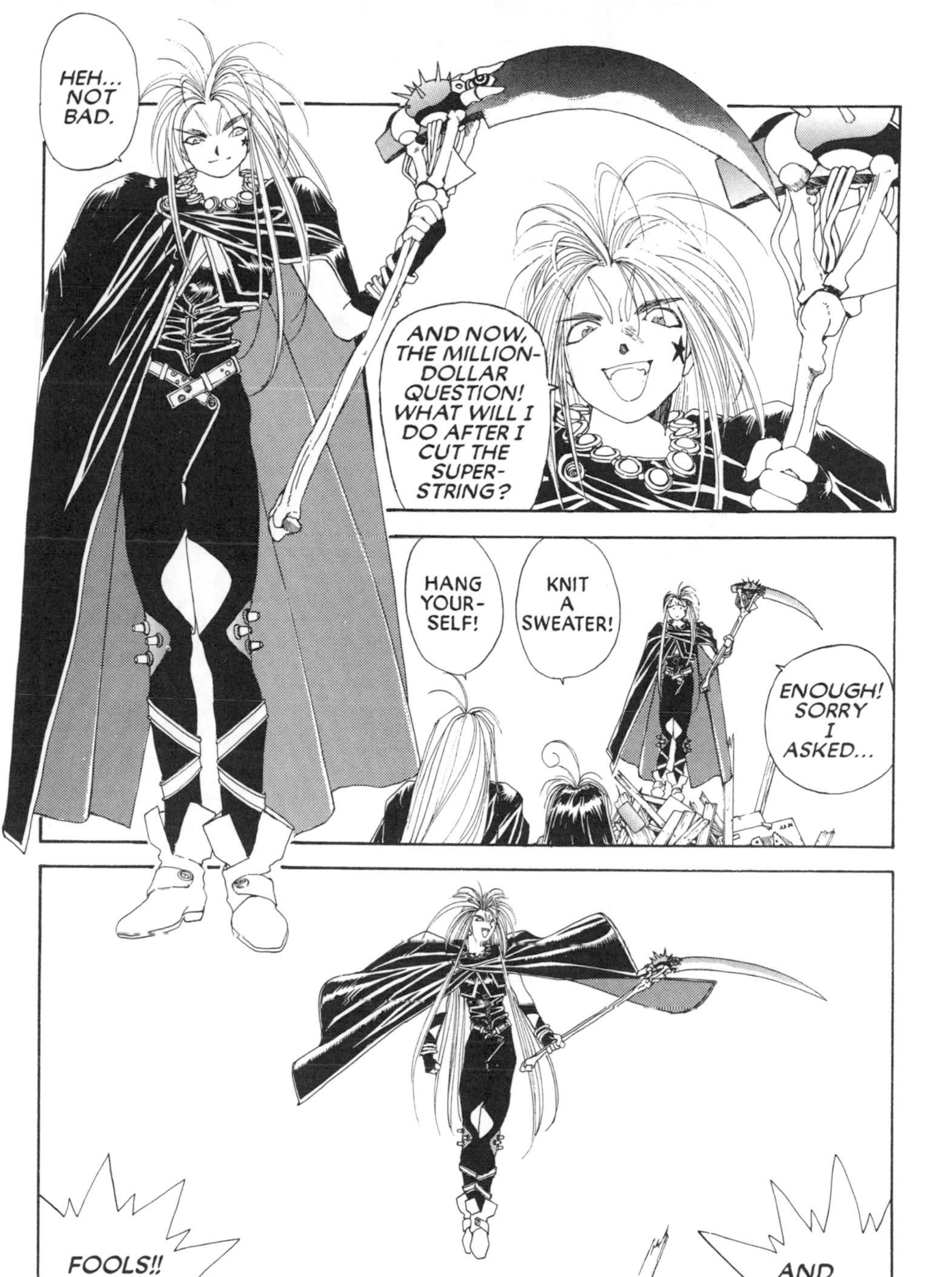
HEH... NOT BAD.
AND NOW, THE MILLION-DOLLAR QUESTION! WHAT WILL I DO AFTER I CUT THE SUPER-STRING?
HANG YOUR-SELF!
KNIT A SWEATER!
ENOUGH! SORRY I ASKED...
FOOLS!! I SHALL RE-CREATE THE UNIVERSE!
AND MAKE IT ONE OF MY OWN CONCEPTION!

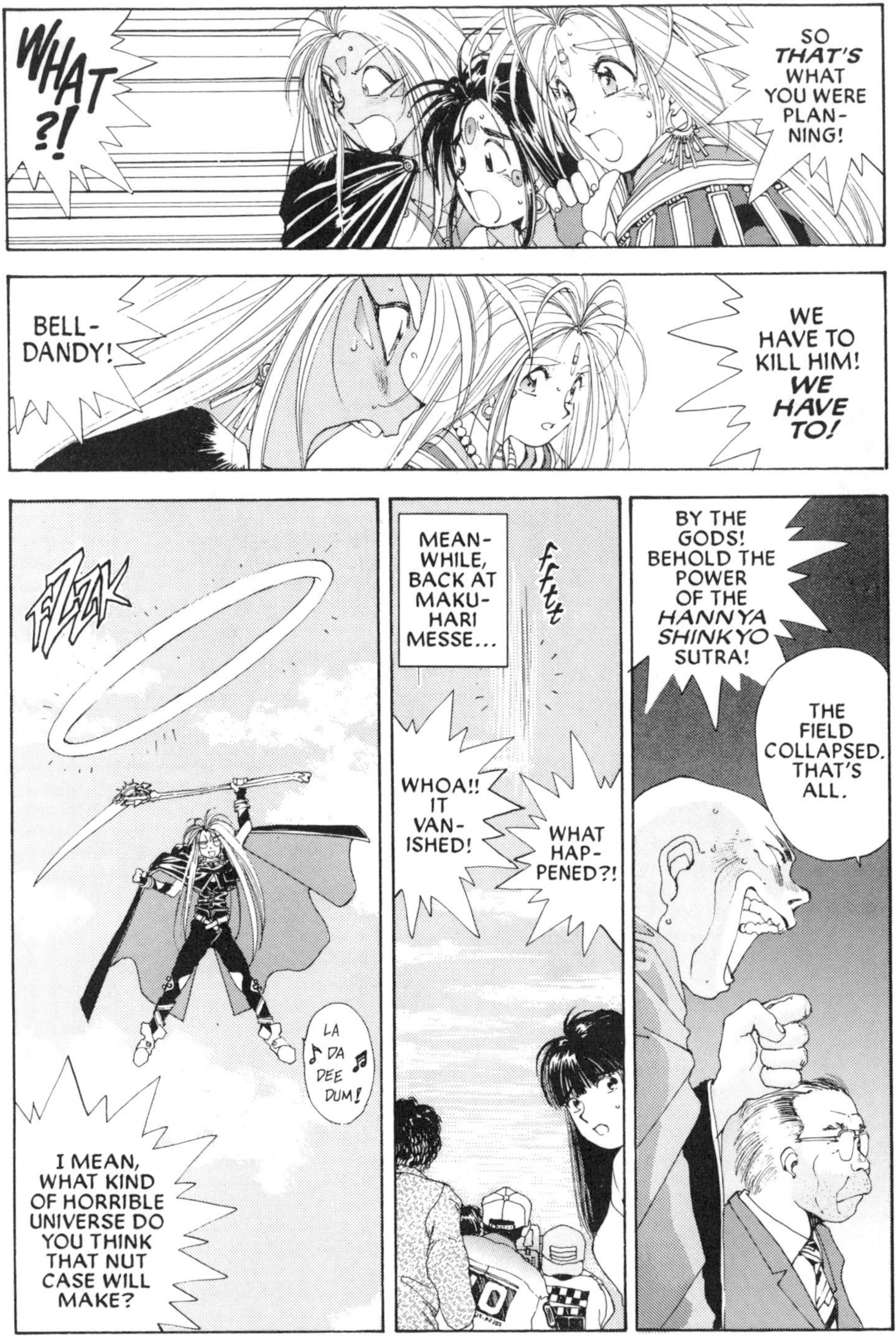
WHAT?!
SO THAT'S WHAT YOU WERE PLAN-NING!
BELL-DANDY!
WE HAVE TO KILL HIM! WE HAVE TO!
FZZK
LA DA DEE DUM!
I MEAN, WHAT KIND OF HORRIBLE UNIVERSE DO YOU THINK THAT NUT CASE WILL MAKE?
MEAN-WHILE, BACK AT MAKU-HARI MESSE...
fftt
WHOA!! IT VAN-ISHED!
WHAT HAP-PENED?!
BY THE GODS! BEHOLD THE POWER OF THE HANNYA SHINKYO SUTRA!
THE FIELD COLLAPSED. THAT'S ALL.

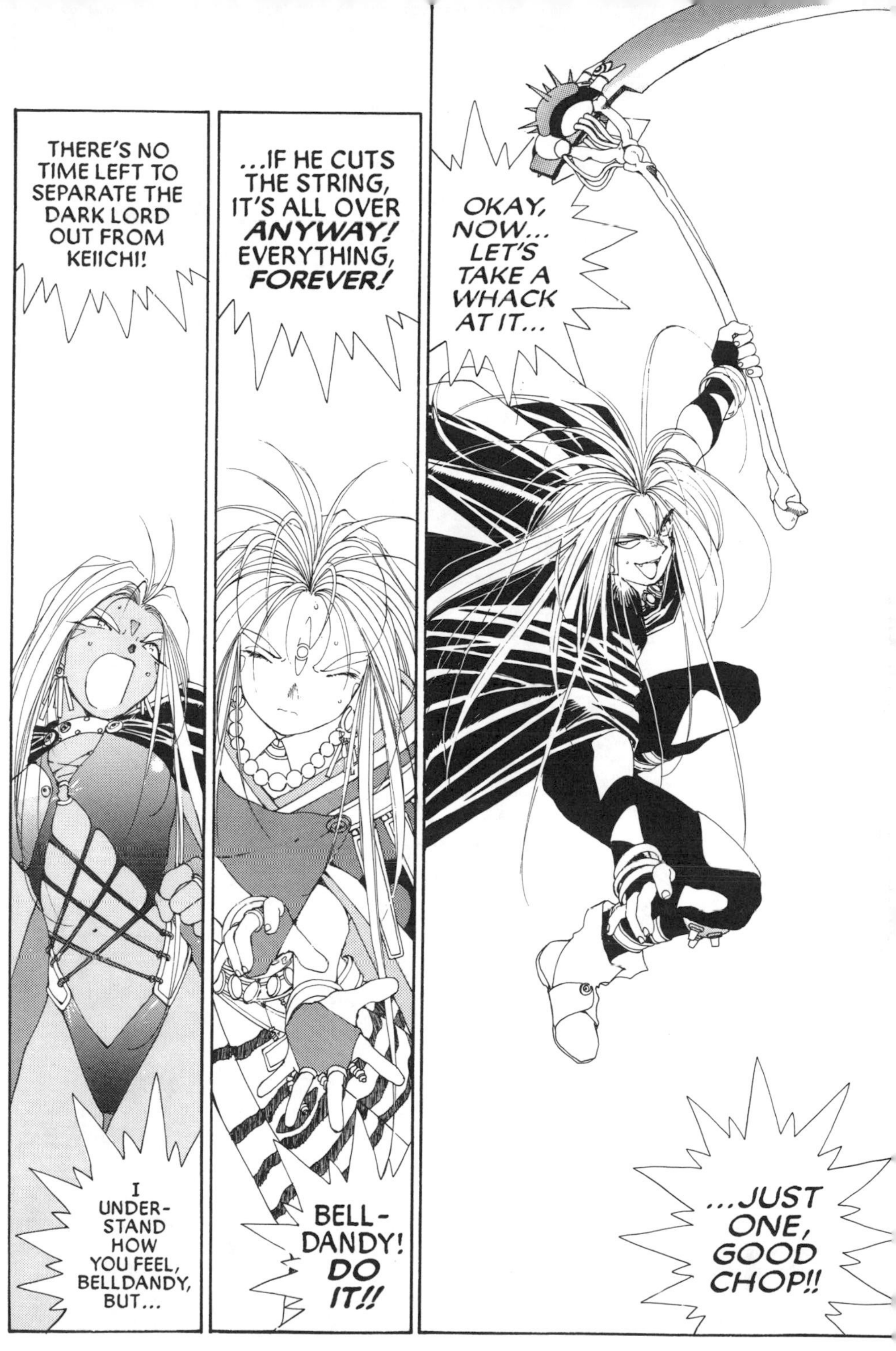
THERE'S NO TIME LEFT TO SEPARATE THE DARK LORD OUT FROM KEIICHI!
I UNDER-STAND HOW YOU FEEL, BELLDANDY, BUT...
...IF HE CUTS THE STRING, IT'S ALL OVER ANYWAY! EVERYTHING, FOREVER!
BELL-DANDY! DO IT!!
OKAY, NOW... LET'S TAKE A WHACK AT IT...
...JUST ONE, GOOD CHOP!!

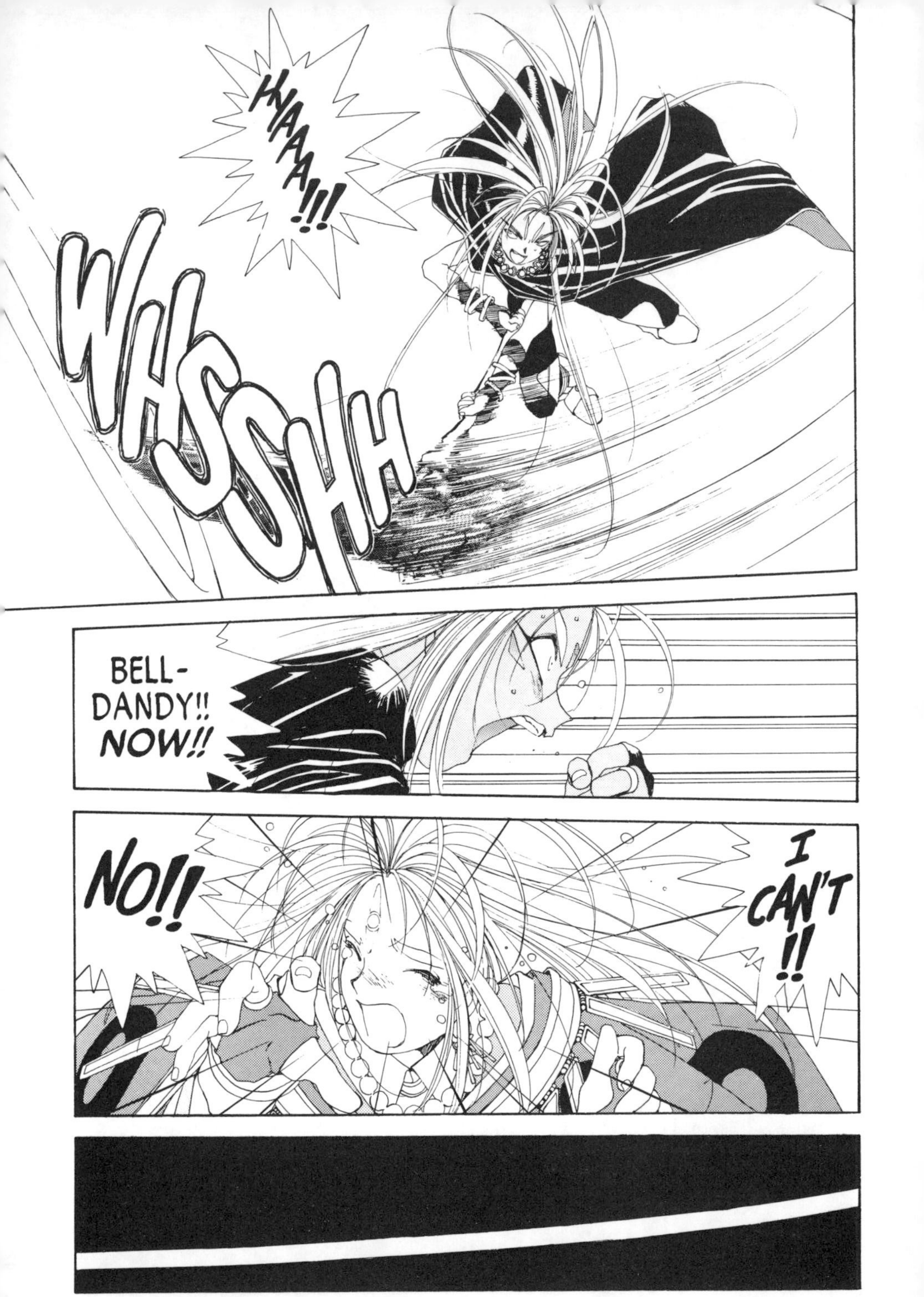
HYAAAA!!!
WHSSHH
BELL-DANDY!! NOW!!
NO!!
I CAN'T!!

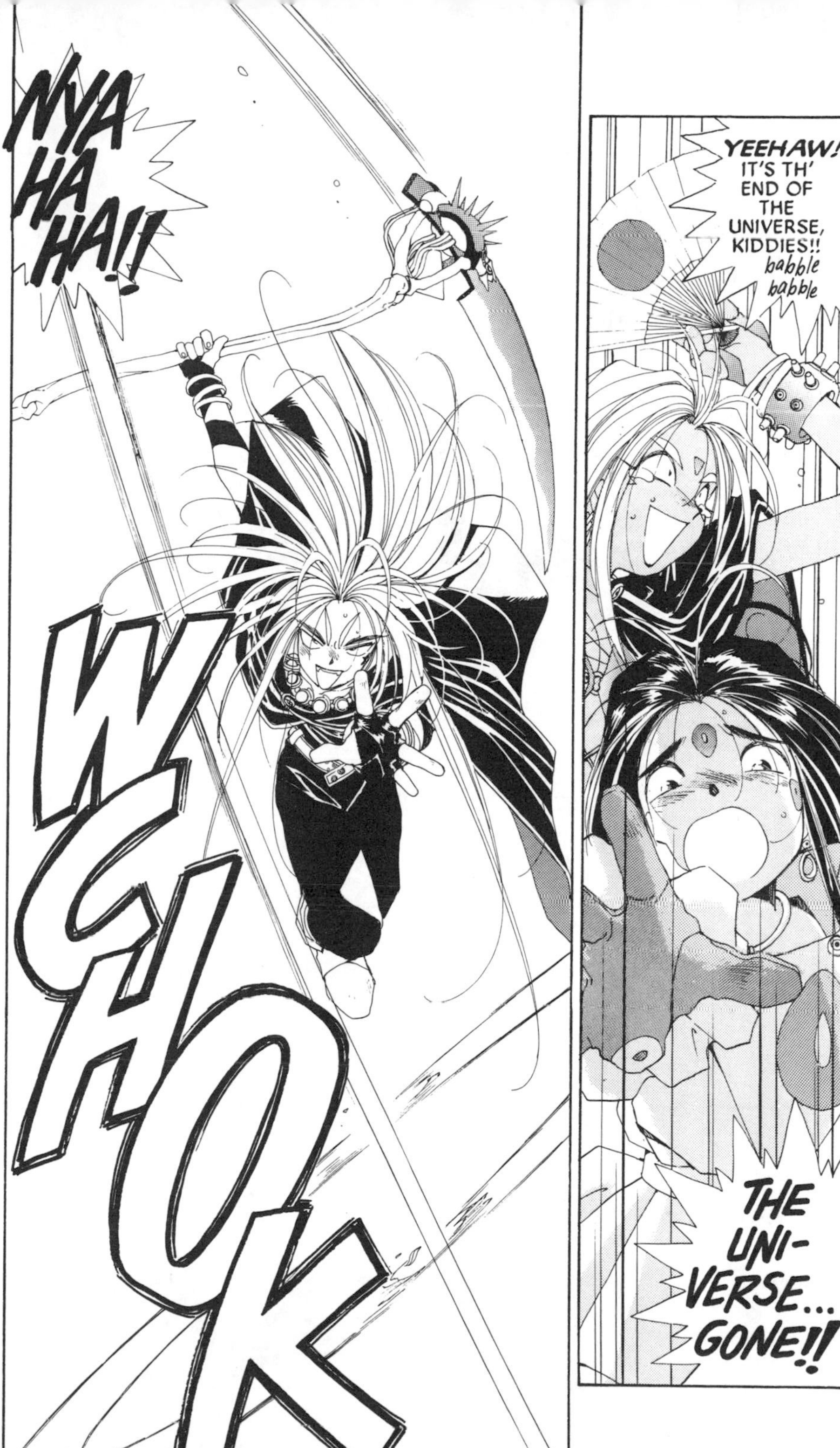
NYA HA HA!!
WHOCK
YEEHAW! IT'S TH' END OF THE UNIVERSE, KIDDIES!!
babble babble
THE UNI-VERSE... GONE!!

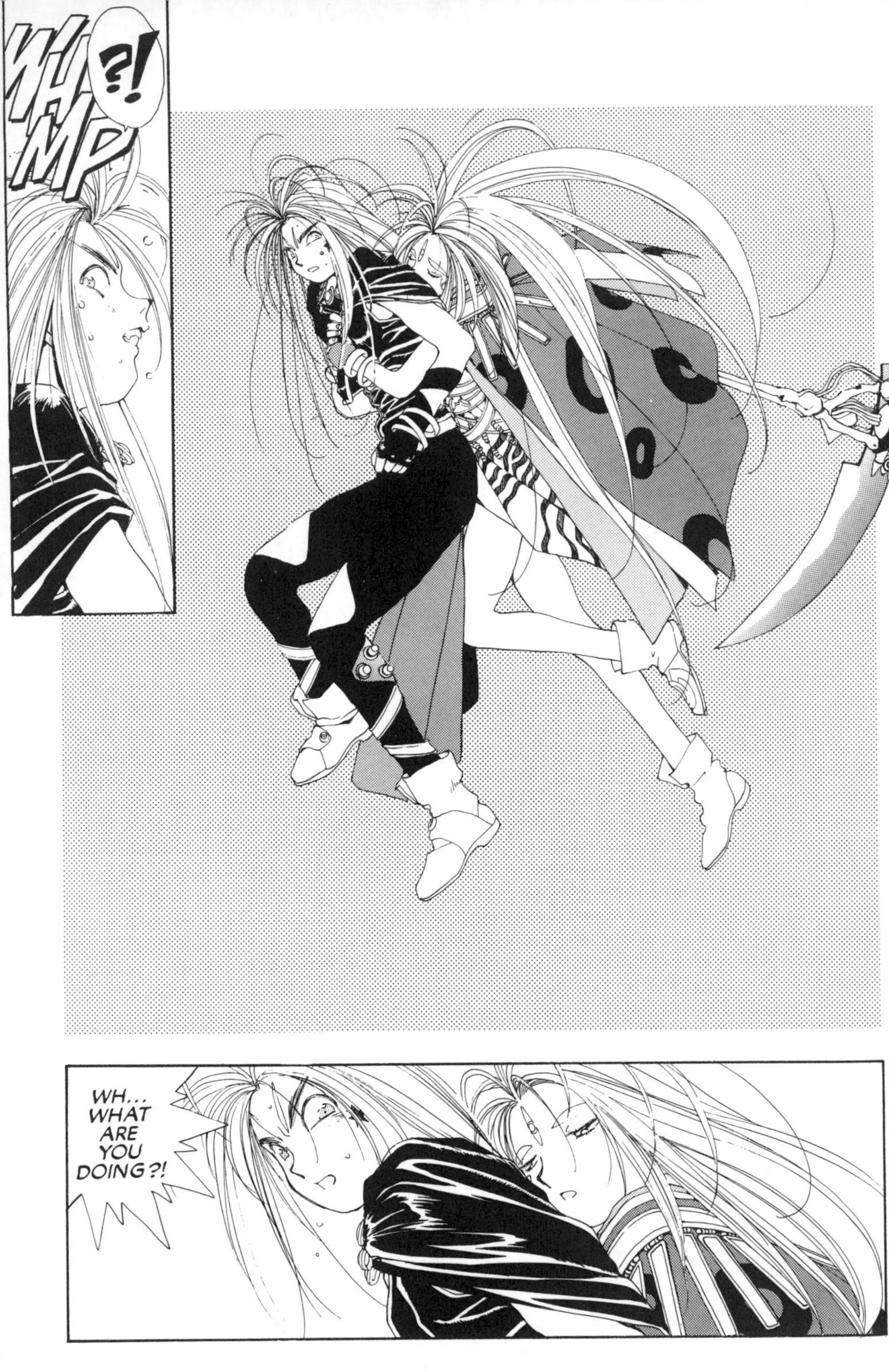
WHUMP
?!
WH... WHAT ARE YOU DOING?!

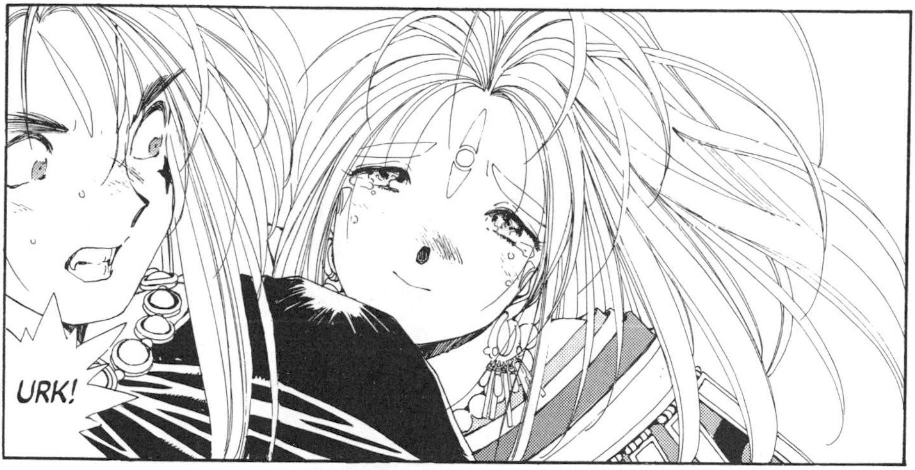
URK!

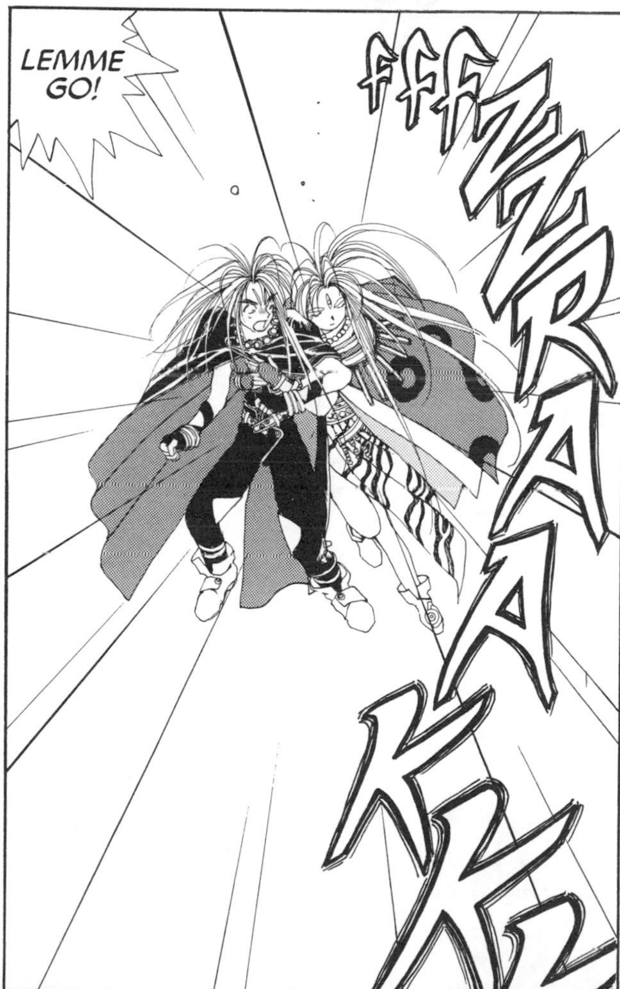
LEMME GO!

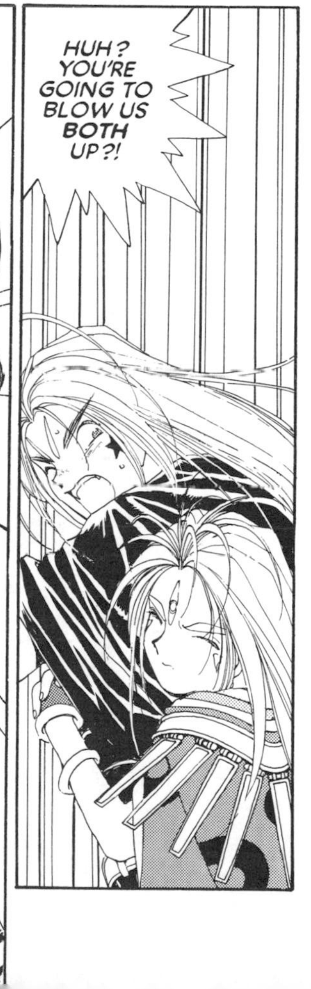
HUH? YOU'RE GOING TO BLOW US BOTH UP?!

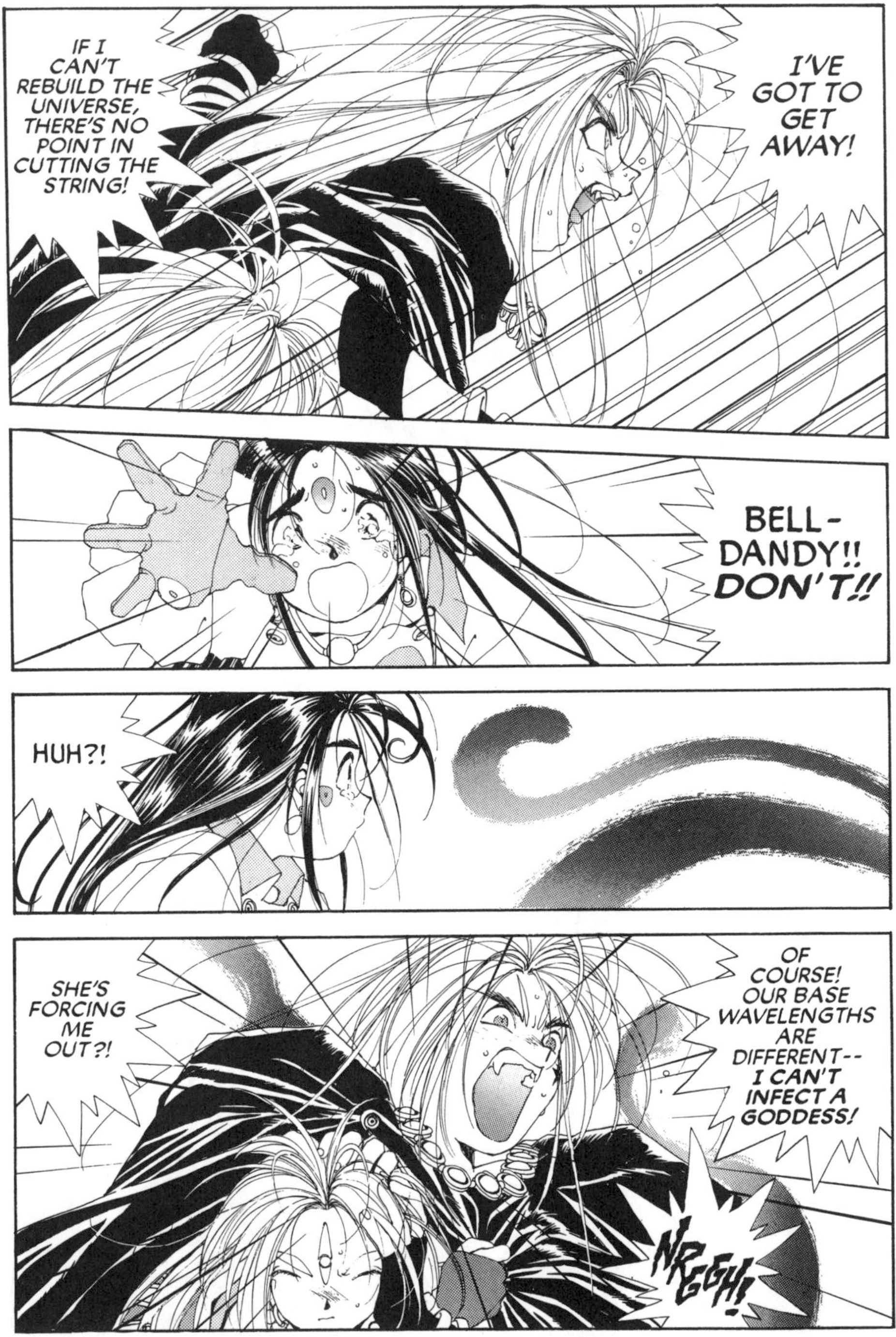
IF I CAN'T REBUILD THE UNIVERSE, THERE'S NO POINT IN CUTTING THE STRING!
I'VE GOT TO GET AWAY!
BELL-DANDY!! DON'T!!
HUH?!
SHE'S FORCING ME OUT?!
OF COURSE! OUR BASE WAVELENGTHS ARE DIFFERENT-- I CAN'T INFECT A GODDESS!
NRGGH!

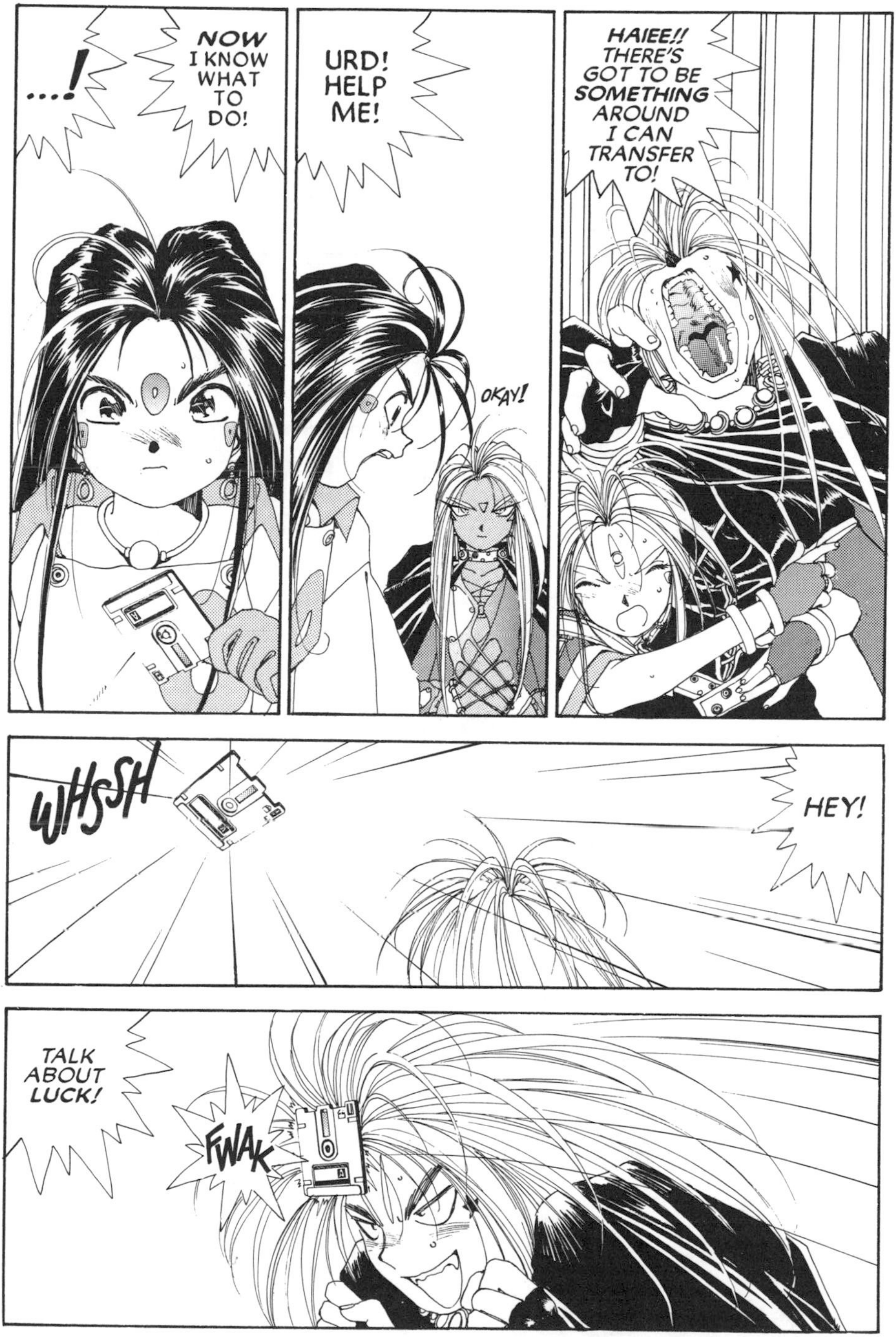
...!
NOW I KNOW WHAT TO DO!
URD! HELP ME!
OKAY!
HAIEE!! THERE'S GOT TO BE SOMETHING AROUND I CAN TRANSFER TO!
WHSSH
HEY!
TALK ABOUT LUCK!
FWAK

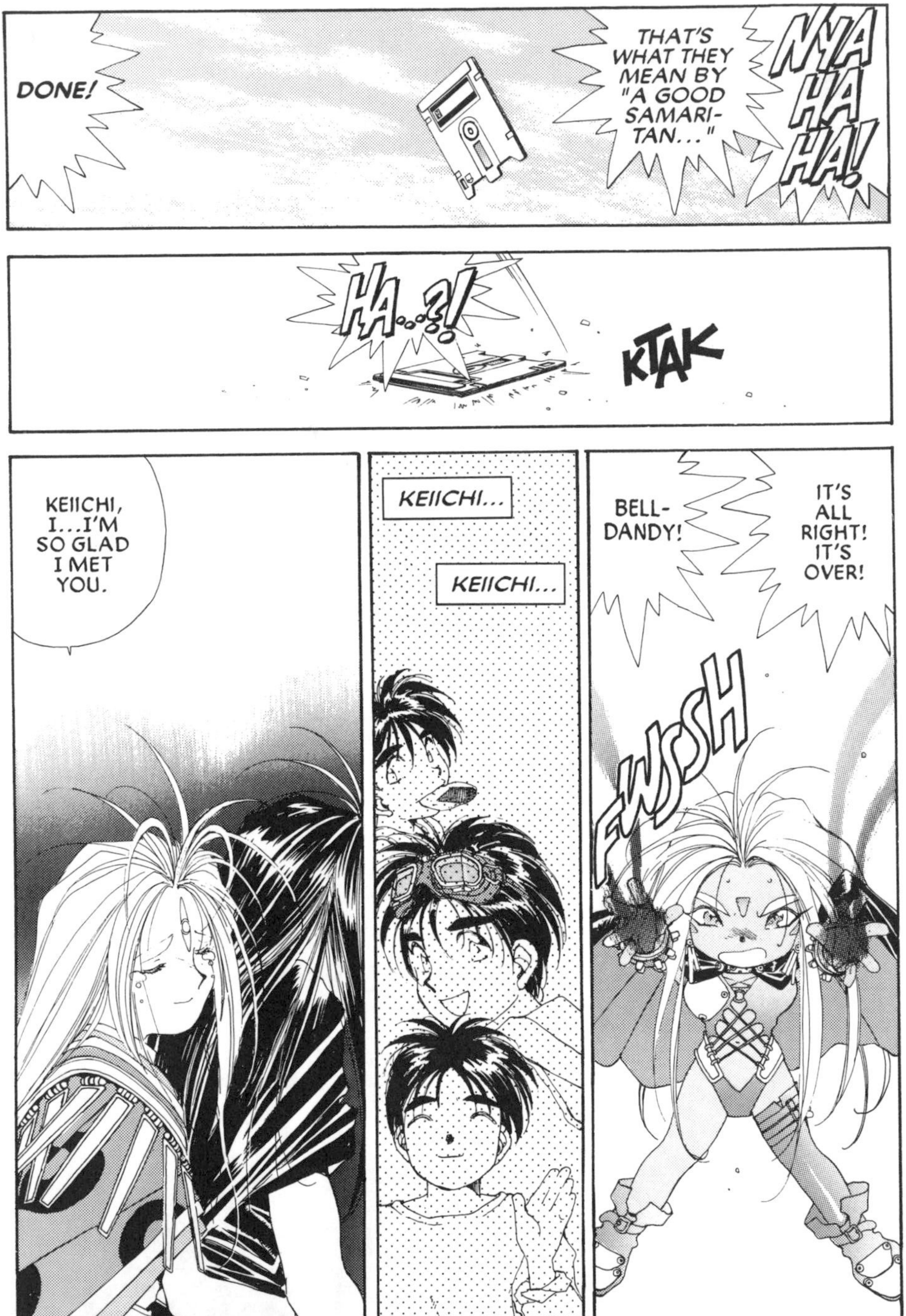
DONE!
THAT'S WHAT THEY MEAN BY "A GOOD SAMARI-TAN..."
NYA HA HA HA!
HA...?!
KTAK
KEIICHI, I...I'M SO GLAD I MET YOU.
KEIICHI...
KEIICHI...
BELL-DANDY!
IT'S ALL RIGHT! IT'S OVER!
FWSSH

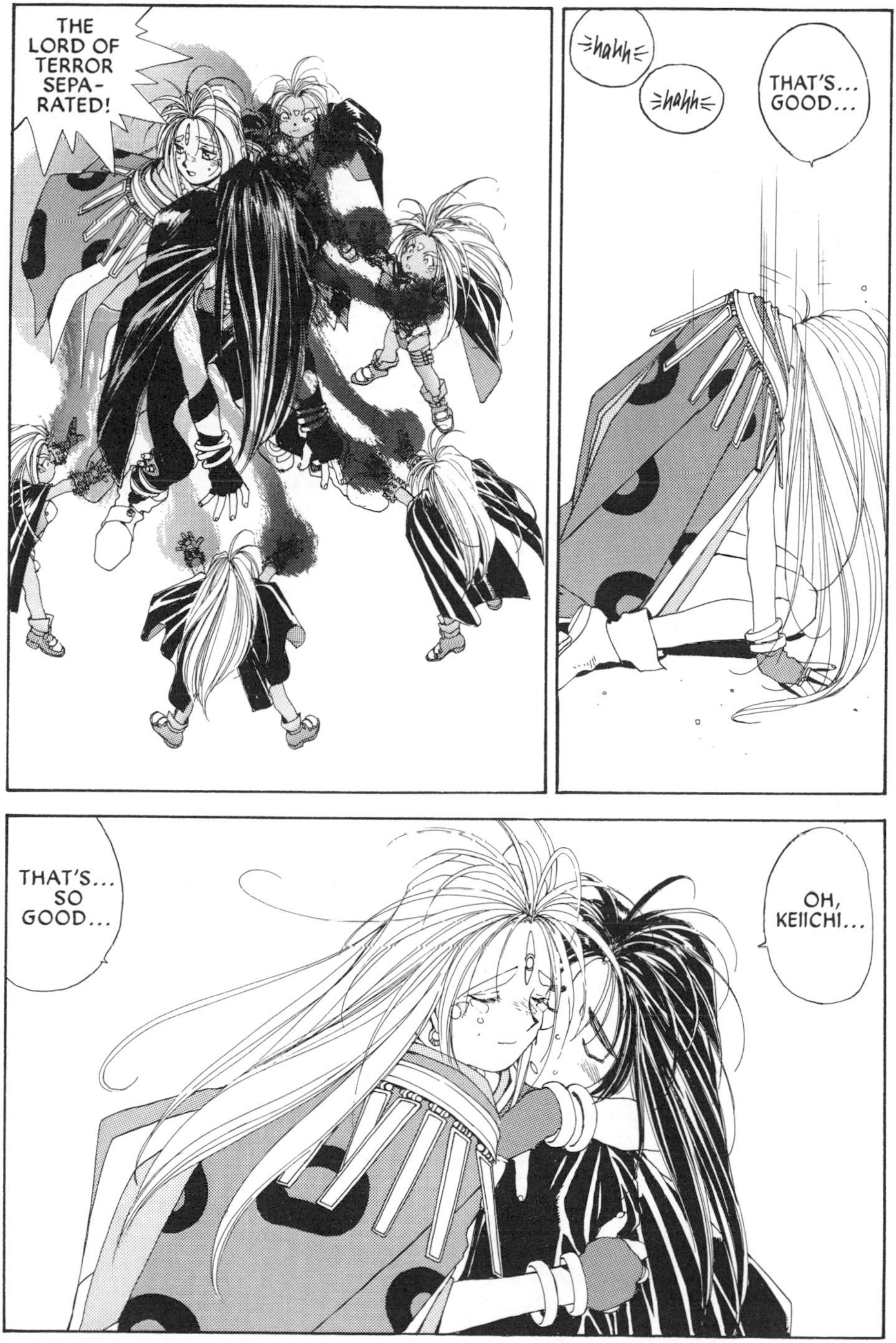
THE LORD OF TERROR SEPA-RATED!
hahh
hahh
THAT'S... GOOD...
THAT'S... SO GOOD...
OH, KEIICHI...

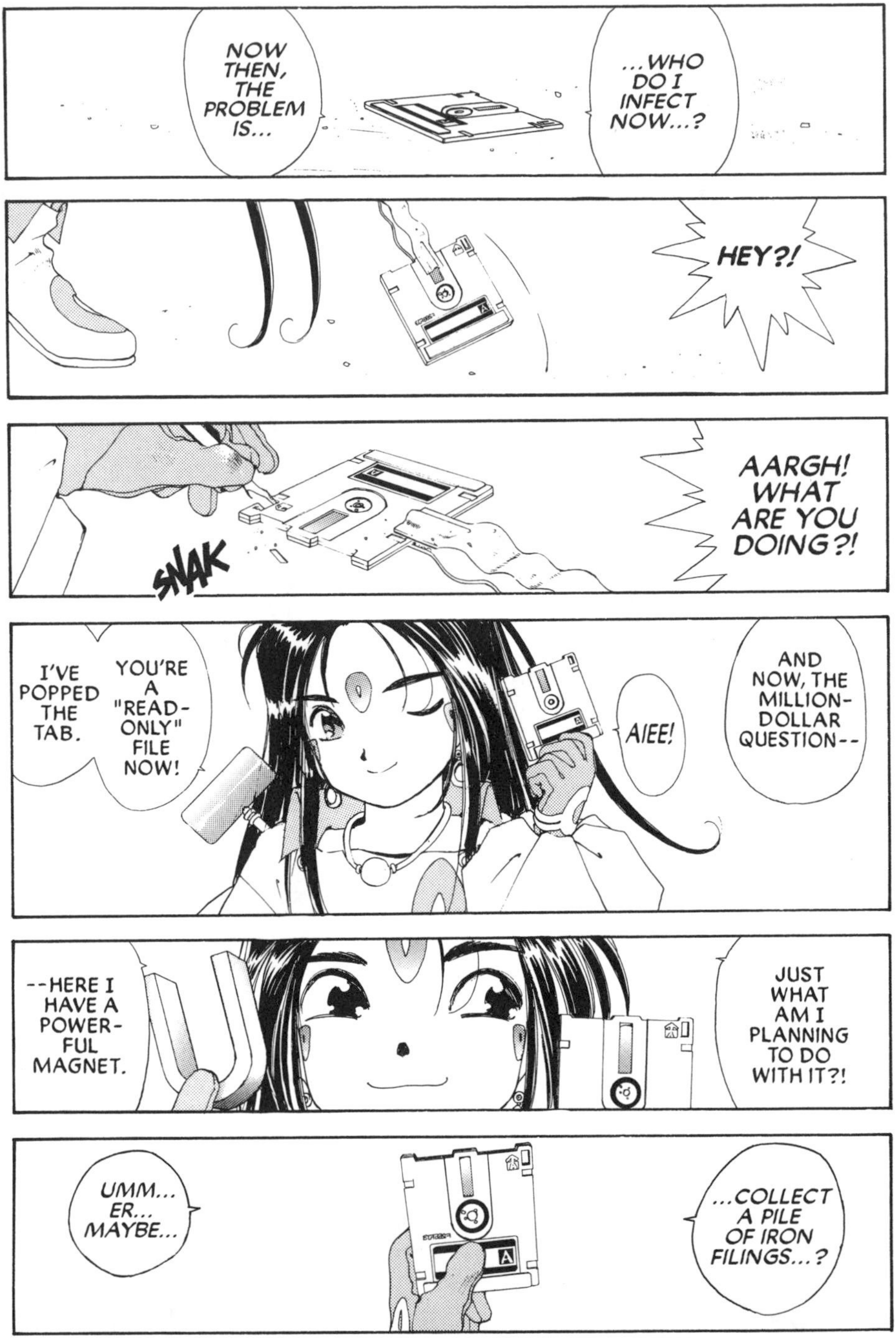
NOW THEN, THE PROBLEM IS...
...WHO DO I INFECT NOW...?
HEY?!
SNAK
AARGH! WHAT ARE YOU DOING?!
I'VE POPPED THE TAB.
YOU'RE A "READ-ONLY" FILE NOW!
AIEE!
AND NOW, THE MILLION-DOLLAR QUESTION--
--HERE I HAVE A POWER-FUL MAGNET.
JUST WHAT AM I PLANNING TO DO WITH IT?!
UMM... ER... MAYBE...
...COLLECT A PILE OF IRON FILINGS...?

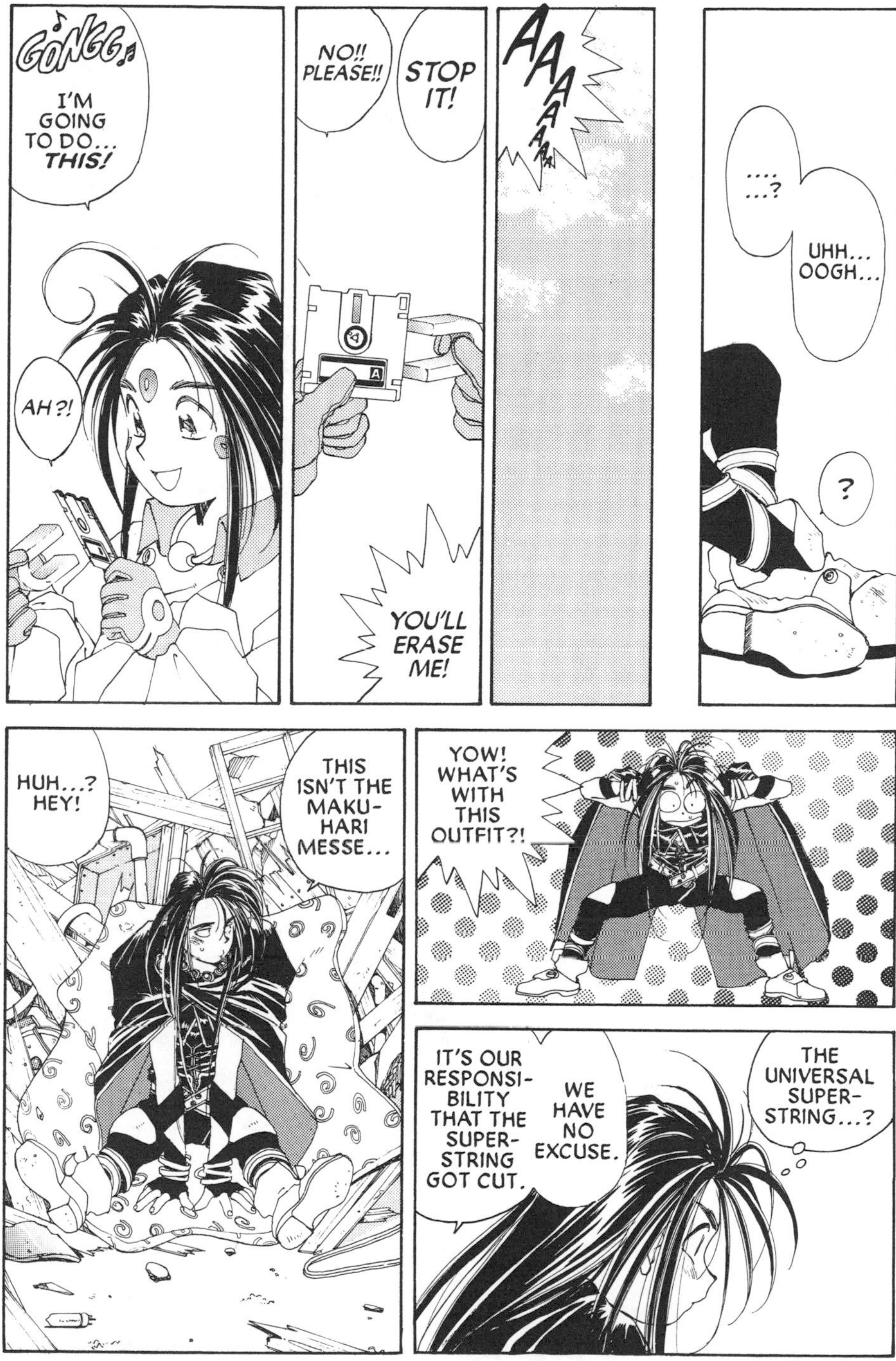
GONGG
I'M GOING TO DO... THIS!
AH?!
NO!! PLEASE!!
STOP IT!
YOU'LL ERASE ME!
AAAAAAAA
....
...?
UHH... OOGH...
?
HUH...? HEY!
THIS ISN'T THE MAKU-HARI MESSE...
YOW! WHAT'S WITH THIS OUTFIT?!
IT'S OUR RESPONSI-BILITY THAT THE SUPER-STRING GOT CUT.
WE HAVE NO EXCUSE.
THE UNIVERSAL SUPER-STRING...?

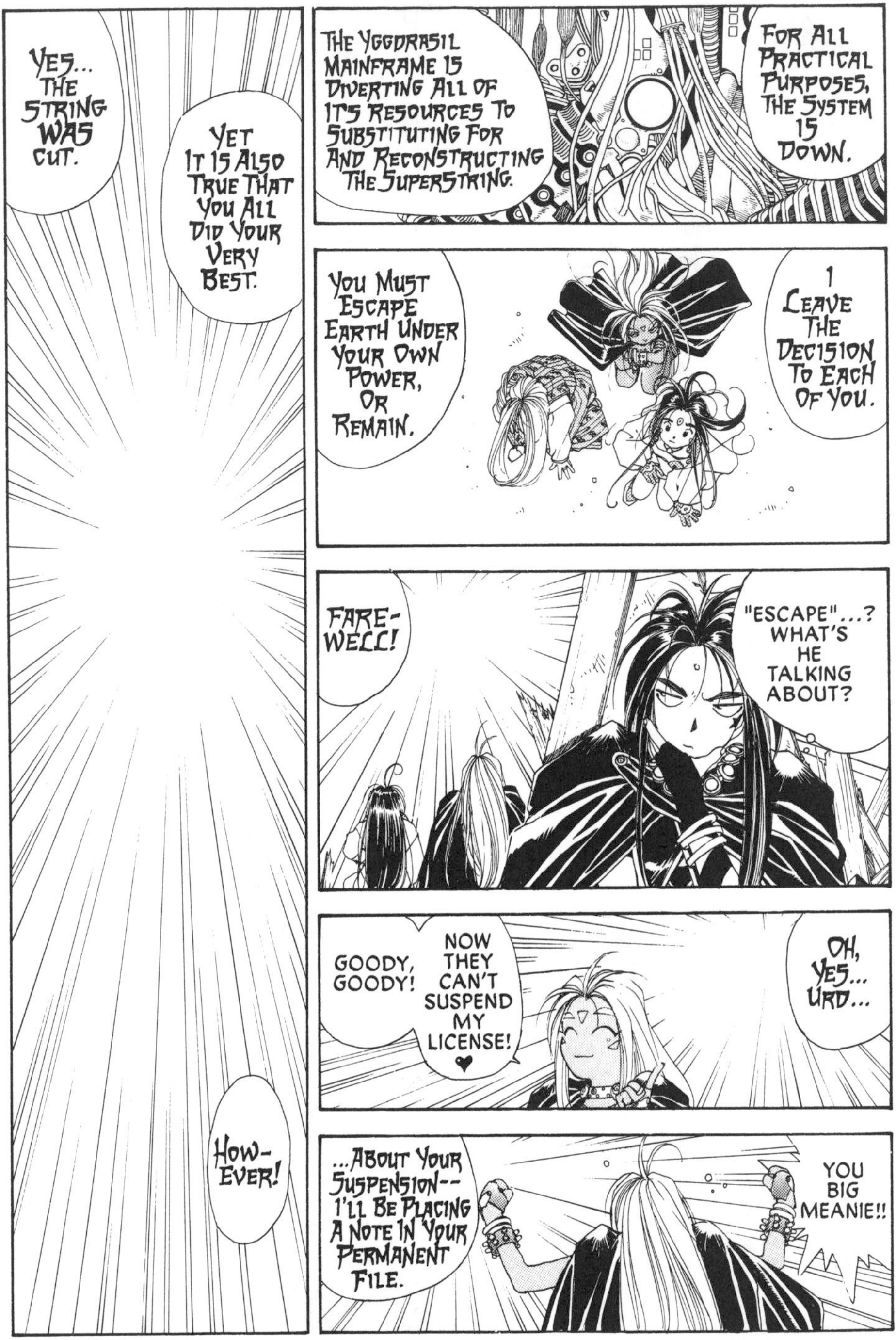
YES... THE STRING WAS CUT.
YET IT IS ALSO TRUE THAT YOU ALL DID YOUR VERY BEST.
HOW-EVER!
THE YGGDRASIL MAINFRAME IS DIVERTING ALL OF IT'S RESOURCES TO SUBSTITUTING FOR AND RECONSTRUCTING THE SUPERSTRING.
FOR ALL PRACTICAL PURPOSES, THE SYSTEM IS DOWN.
YOU MUST ESCAPE EARTH UNDER YOUR OWN POWER, OR REMAIN.
I LEAVE THE DECISION TO EACH OF YOU.
FARE-WELL!
"ESCAPE"...? WHAT'S HE TALKING ABOUT?
GOODY, GOODY!
NOW THEY CAN'T SUSPEND MY LICENSE! ♥
OH, YES... URD...
...ABOUT YOUR SUSPENSION-- I'LL BE PLACING A NOTE IN YOUR PERMANENT FILE.
YOU BIG MEANIE!!

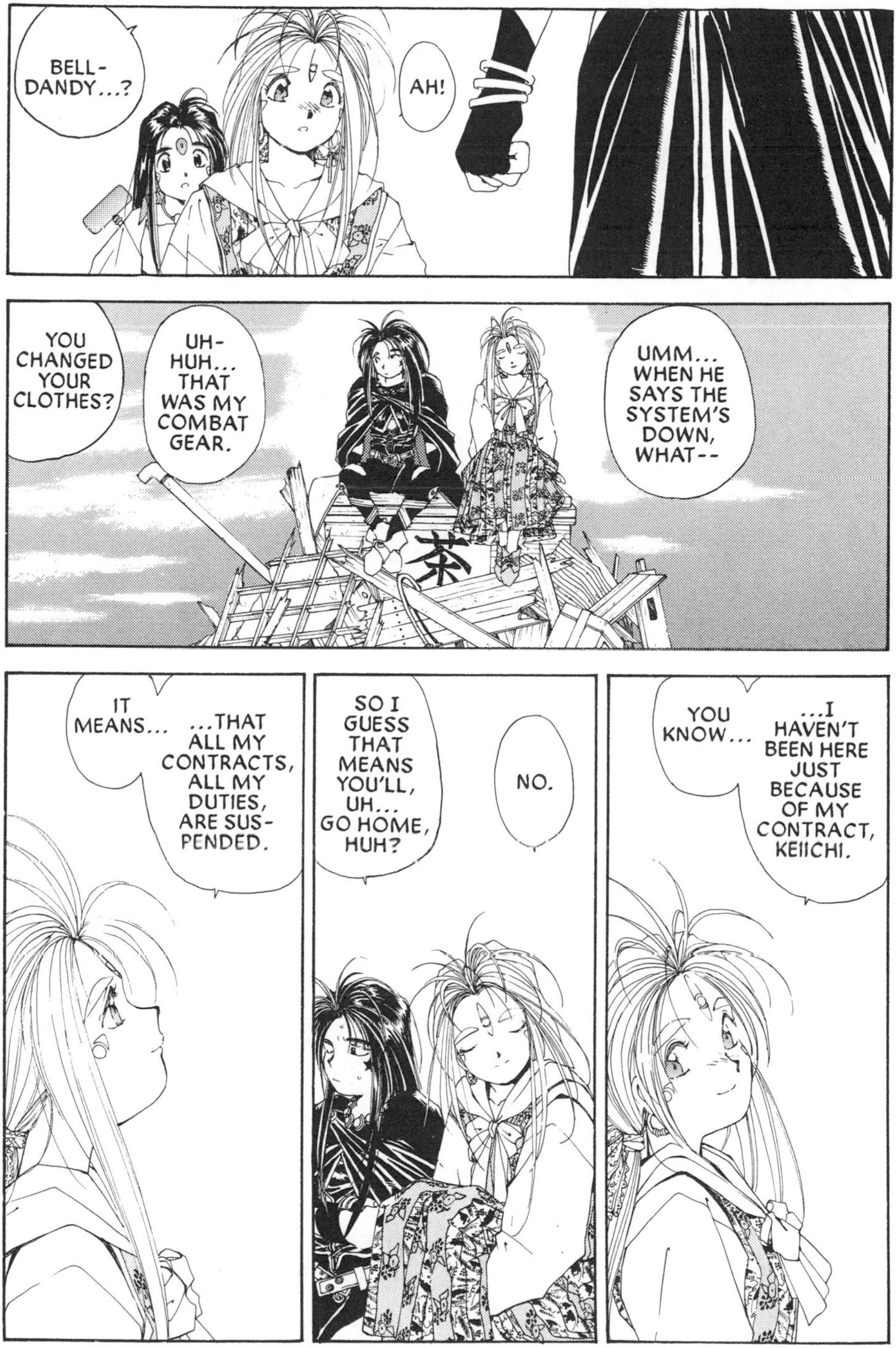
BELL-DANDY...?
AH!
YOU CHANGED YOUR CLOTHES?
UH-HUH... THAT WAS MY COMBAT GEAR.
UMM... WHEN HE SAYS THE SYSTEM'S DOWN, WHAT--
IT MEANS...
...THAT ALL MY CONTRACTS, ALL MY DUTIES, ARE SUS-PENDED.
SO I GUESS THAT MEANS YOU'LL, UH... GO HOME, HUH?
NO.
YOU KNOW...
...I HAVEN'T BEEN HERE JUST BECAUSE OF MY CONTRACT, KEIICHI.

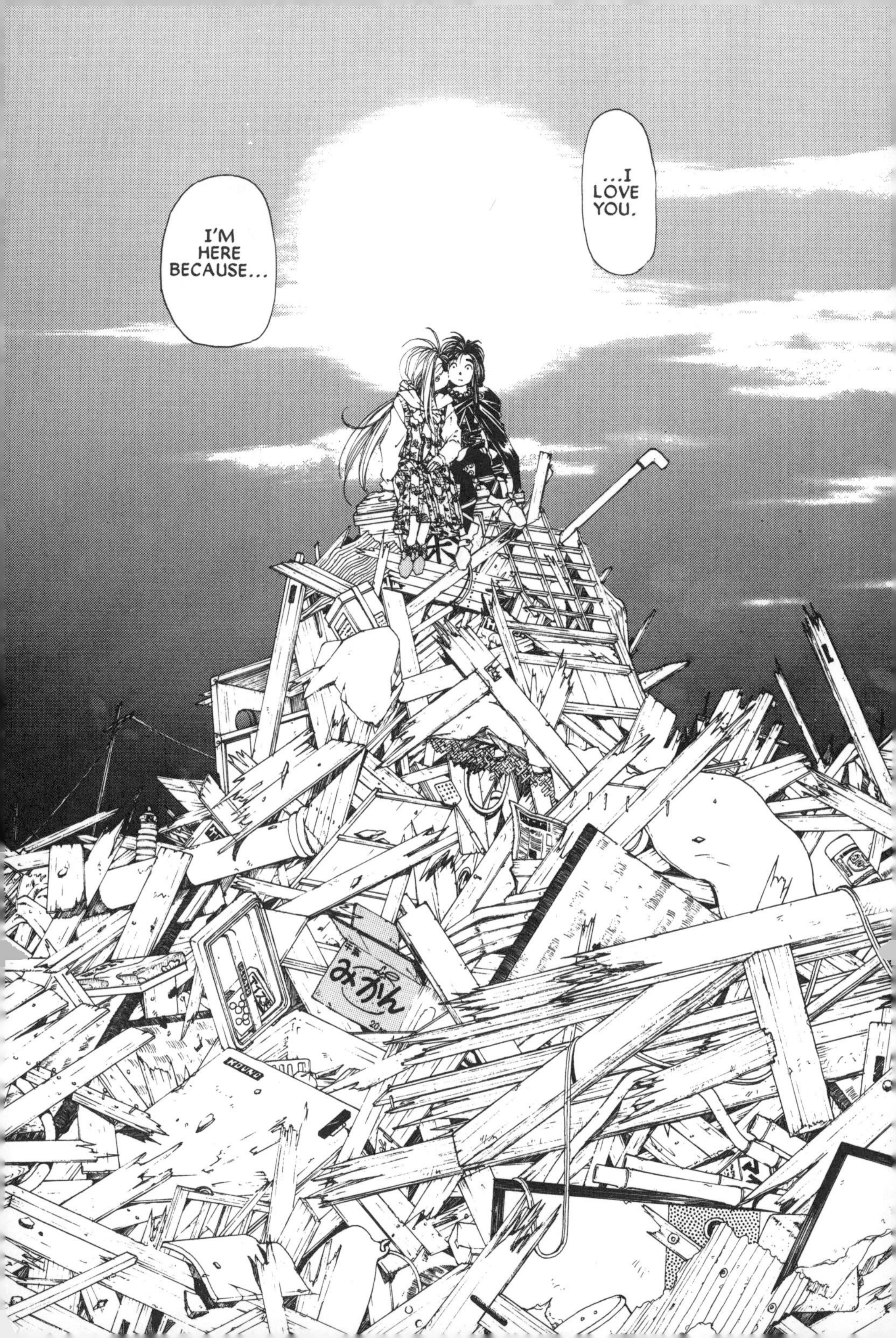
I'M HERE BECAUSE...
...I LOVE YOU.
みかん

Oh My Goddess!

ああ女神さま TERRIBLE MASTER URD

Cover Gallery

Oh My Goddess! Part III issue 6

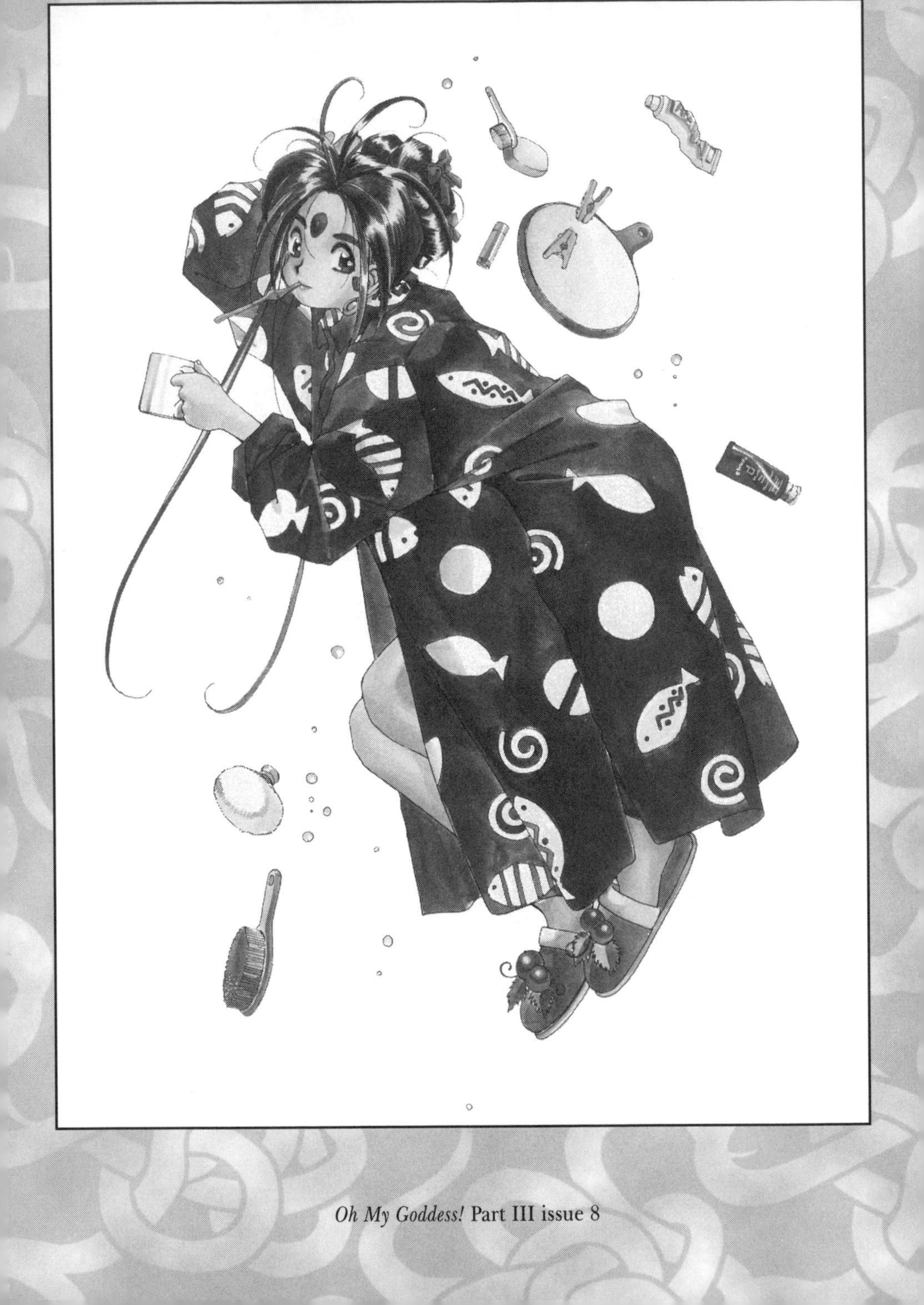

Oh My Goddess! Part III issue 8

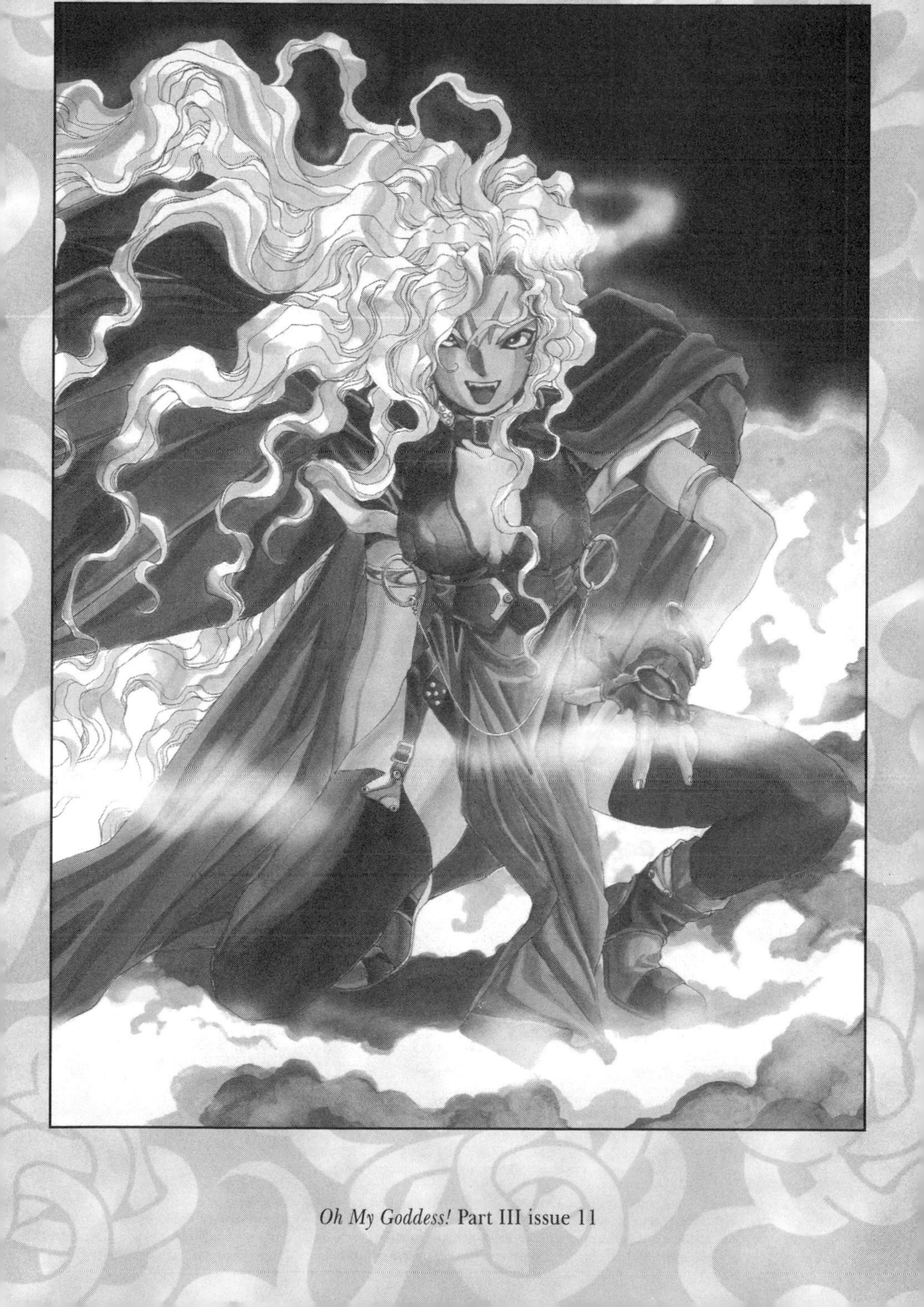

Oh My Goddess! Part III issue 11